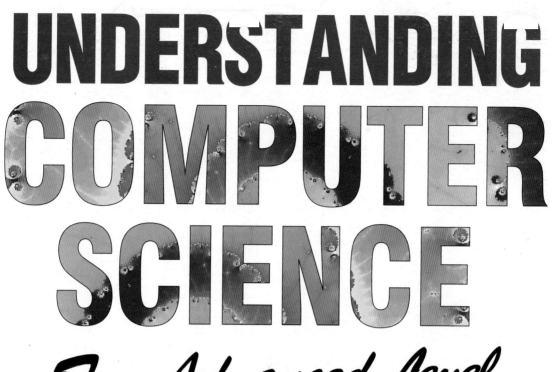

UNDERSTANDING COMPUTER SCIENCE

For Advanced Level

The Study Guide

Ray Bradley

Published in 2001 by:
Nelson Thornes Ltd
Delta Place
27 Bath Road
CHELTENHAM
GL53 7TH
United Kingdom

01 02 03 04 05 / 10 9 8 7 6 5 4 3 2 1

A catalogue record for this book is available from the British Library

ISBN 0 7487 6147 0

Page make-up by Mathematical Composition Setters Ltd, Salisbury, Wiltshire

Printed and bound in Italy by Canale

Acknowledgements

The authors and publishers are grateful to the following for permission to reproduce
photographs:

CDT Limited (Figures 14.1 and 14.2); Ericsson (Figures 56.4 and 56.5);
Nortel Networks (Figure 60.1).

Picture research by johnbailey@axonimages.com

We are grateful to the following awarding bodies for permission to reproduce
questions from their past examinations:
        Assessment and Qualifications Alliance (AQA)
        Edexcel
        Oxford Cambridge and RSA (OCR)
All answers provided for examination questions are the sole responsibility of the
author.

Contents

How to use this guide

Introduction and special resources

This revision guide is for **AS and A2 computing examinations** using the **2001/2002 subject specifications**. *It is also very useful for other courses of a similar standard.*

There are over **100 completely worked examples** in this text, and over **400 self-test questions** *with answers* to check what you know. There are **examination questions** at both AS and A2 level, and fully-worked **model answers** can be found on our **web site**. On the web site you will also find **exemplar project material** for *both* **AS** and **A2 projects**. There are references throughout the study guide to our web site, wherever you see this icon in the margin. There are units in this book dedicated to **AS** and **A2 project work**, which will help tremendously with these two important modules representing about 35% of the total marks for advanced level computing.

Material is split up into **easy to digest four-page units**, *many of which can be studied independently of each other*. At the beginning of each unit you will be **told what you are revising**, and throughout the unit **key terms** will be **highlighted** to help you revise. There are **many hints and tips** in the margins, and lots of **links to relevant web sites** too. At the end of each unit you will be **reminded about what you have just covered**.

The **first 34 units are predominantly AS level work**, but some boards are different regarding what material is contained in the AS and A2 subject specifications. To help with this there is a **detailed board-by-board mapping** beginning on page (x) of this book. This can be used as a guide, but it is **imperative you check specifications** for *your board* to determine the units which best apply to you. Use the **index** at the back of the book, and use the **electronic glossary** on our **web site** if you are not sure. *Using this glossary you can list and print out key terms for your particular board.*

AS project material

Units 28 to 33 cover a **fully worked AS exercise project**, and together with units 25 to 27 cover systems development. You should note that **this work is also relevant to the theory papers**, covering important concepts that *will* be examined.

A2 project work

Units 66, 67 and 68 cover the important **A2 project work**, and are essential reading for **starting**, **undertaking** and **writing up** this second-year project.

The theory modules

The majority of text in this book refers to the **theory modules**, as these represent about **65% of the final A-level marks**. The material is presented in a *very* concise format, which makes it ideal for **rapid revision** of important concepts. The **answers** to the self-test questions at the end of the book are also kept *very brief*, and cover **key points only**. This is in keeping with many of the **mark schemes** issued at this level. The student response might be in the form of a small essay, but **key points in the mark scheme show how marks are awarded** for parts of the prose.

New Understanding Computer Science for Advanced Level

This **revision guide** can easily be used independently. However, a **700-page A-level textbook**, now in its fourth edition, covers all of this work in more detail. To help readers who may want to enquire more deeply, references to chapters in **New Understanding Computer Science for Advanced Level** are given at several points throughout this guide wherever you see this icon in the margin.

Our web site portal is at www.revise computing.com

Visit our portal for links to all examining boards and the QCA web sites.

New Understanding Computer Science for Advanced Level (NUCSAL) ISBN 0-7487-4046-5

Set up an effective revision schedule

Using **your specification**, and the **board-by-board map**, work out **which units apply to you**. As an example, the first 33 units apply to the AQA AS-level specification very closely. Therefore, if you are with the AQA board, you have 33 four-page-spread units to revise. **A four-page spread can be read in about 15 minutes**, but *learning the material and doing the self-test questions* will take longer.

Start *weeks* before the modules are due, and decide which of the four-page spreads are to be undertaken each week. If you estimate that it will take you half an hour to cover each unit, then about **16 hours of revision** is needed to get through each of the AS or A2 material. With **one month** to go you would **need 4 hours/week**. *It is suggested that you do not leave less time than this, and preferably use the book over a much longer period*, because you may find some of the work difficult.

Find a pattern which works for you

Decide which is your best **quality time** for **revision** and stick to it. Some students get up at the **crack of dawn**, and others prefer to work **late into the night**. *Make sure that the work you are doing is productive*. If you get stuck for long periods or find yourself doing nothing, then **stop and do something completely different**.

Keep up to date

It is not possible for any book to keep right up to date, and you must, therefore, **read computer magazines, newspapers**, watch the **news** and look at **specialist programmes** which cover computer-related material. This will help considerably with the **moral, ethical, social, cultural** and **other issues** about which you are expected to be able to comment in a knowledgeable fashion.

Examination hints and tips

Examination technique

Good grades in examinations are usually the result of **good examination technique**. Knowing the theory very well may *not* get you a good grade unless you know **the rules**.

Examination jargon

It is important to know what the examiners expect, and the list of **key words** produced by **AQA** is *essential reading*. The **key terms**, referring to key words in AQA computing examinations are as follows.

Name (**What is the name of?**) Usually requires a technical term or its equivalent. Answers to this type of question normally involve no more that one or two words.

List A number of features or points, each often no more than a single word, with no further elaboration or detail required.

Define (**What is meant by?**) 'Define' requires a statement giving the meaning of a particular term. 'What is meant by ... ?' is used more frequently as it emphasises that a formal definition as such is not required.

Outline A brief summary of the main points is required. The best guide to the amount of detail required lies in the mark allocations; approximately one to one and a half minutes should be allowed per mark. This generally works out at around two or three lines in a standard answer booklet for each mark:

Describe Means no more than it says, that is, 'Give a description of ... ' So, 'Describe one feature of a graphical user interface (GUI) which is likely to be helpful to a non-technically minded user' requires a description of a feature such as a pictorial icon in terms of making the selection and execution of a program easier. 'Describe one relationship that can be inferred from the data requirements' means supplying its name and degree.

Explain This creates major difficulties for many candidates. A reason or interpretation must be given, not a description. The term '**Describe**' answers the question '**What**'; the term '**Explain**' answers the question '**Why?**'.

Suggest 'Suggest' is used when it is not possible to give the answer directly from the facts that form part of the subject material detailed in the specification. The answer should be based on the general understanding rather than on recall of learnt material. It also indicates that there may be a number of correct alternatives.

Give evidence for (**Using examples from ...**) Answers to questions involving these phrases must follow the instructions. Marks are always awarded for appropriate references to the information provided. General answers, however comprehensive, will not gain maximum credit.

Calculate This term is used where the only requirement is a numerical answer expressed in appropriate units.

State 'State' falls short of 'Describing' and amounts to no more than making bullet points. For example, for 'State one advantage of writing a program as a collection of modules' the answer might be, 'Teams of programmers are able to work on producing individual modules at the same time.'

Computing content

Some computing questions are difficult to answer for the following reasons:

- Innovations happen so quickly that old criteria may no longer apply.

Get hold of as many past papers as you can. Similar papers for other boards are useful too, especially if you get your teacher to point out relevant questions.

Learn the list of examination words shown here. This is invaluable, as it tunes your way of thinking into the examiner's way of thinking.

Visit our portal to see answers to the examination questions in units 34 and 69.

- The number of ways of doing the same thing is so vast that it is difficult to mark some material.

Examination boards have their work cut out to make sure that all questions are still relevant. Not many subjects have to check on the relevance of material so close to printing the papers.

Use the obvious answers

Don't try to be *too* clever when you answer questions, and go for obvious answers if you have a choice. Consider, for example, the following question:

State *three differences* between a **hard disk** and a **floppy disk**.

Three 'correct' answers could be as follows:

- A hard disk might use a FAT; a floppy disk never does.
- The heads on a floppy disk move in and out in a straight line, on a hard disk they move in and out on a rotating arm.
- A hard disk is sealed; a floppy disk is open to the elements.

'Better' answers, containing **more obvious differences**, would be as follows:

- A hard disk is able to store a huge amount of information compared to a floppy.
- You are able to read data from a hard disk at a much faster rate compared to a floppy.
- A hard disk is usually fixed; a floppy disk is portable, thus allowing easy data transfer between computers.

All bulleted points above are 'correct', but *the ones below would probably be in the mark scheme*, along with others like the a hard disk is much more reliable than a floppy.

Why is this so?

Students at 'A' level, especially those who have done well at GCSE, think that the 'obvious answers' are *so obvious and simple* that they do not seem much different to those required for the GCSE examination. They argue that 'A' level answers must be looking for something a lot more technical. Some of the topics, like the disk example above, are not! It is important to bear in mind that the **intricacies of the hardware** are *not required in the subject specifications*. Only the **characteristics of the devices** in terms of **speed**, **common usage** and **data transfer rates** are needed, and that is what the examiners are looking for.

Check what *you* actually need in *your subject specification*. It seems unfair, but *'right answers' often gain no marks because they are not in the specification, and hence not in the mark scheme*. Perhaps some examination questions should be more specific, but many sensible alternatives are usually catered for.

Remember, carefully following the guidance given **could gain you a grade or even two!**

Examination practice

There is no substitute for undertaking actual examination questions in the intended time. Sit down in a quiet environment, then spend $1\frac{1}{2}$ hours doing a **real examination paper** for your board. *You must then mark it according to the mark scheme; marking the 'right answers' wrong if they are not specifically allowed in the mark scheme.* **This is the only way that you will get a good indication of how you will do in the real examination.**

A bank of past examination questions can be found in chapter 34 of NUCSAL.

Visit our portal to link to the examination board sites to download specimen-computing questions.

Board Mapping for 'AS' and 'A2' Modular Courses

Study Guide Unit Title and subheadings	Page	AQA	Edexcel	OCR	WJEC	NICCEA
Unit 1 – Data information and coding	2					
Data, information and binary encoding		1	1	1	2	1
Basic binary		1	1, 2	1	2	1
Simple binary arithmetic		1	1	1	2	1
Octal and hexadecimal		1	1	1	2	1
Conversion between hex and binary		1	1	1	2	1
Binary coded decimal		1	1	1	2	1
Fractional binary numbers		4	2	1	2	1
Floating point binary numbers		4	2	1	2	1
Negative binary numbers		4	2	1	2	1
Unit 2 – Images, sound and analogue data	6					
Other encoding methods		1	1	1	3	1
Graphical methods		1	1	1	3	1
Bit mapped graphics		1	1	1	3	1
Vector graphics		1	1	1	3	1
Other forms of encoding binary data		1	1	1	3	1
Recording sounds		1	1	1	3	1
Analogue and digital signals		1	1	1	3	1
A to D converters		1	1	1	3	1
Sound synthesis		1	1	1	3	1
Unit 3 – Microprocessor fundamentals	10					
The internal components of a processor		1	1	1	1	1
Main and secondary storage systems		1	1	1	1	1
Microprocessor and internal components		1	1	1	1	1
Machine code and the stored-program concept		1	1	1	1	1
Mainframe computers and parallel processing		1	1	1	1	1
Unit 4 – Fundamental ideas about software	14					
Hardware and software		1	1	1	1	1
Different types of software		1	1	1	1	1
System software		1	1	1	1	1
Utility programs		1	1	1	1	1
Library programs		1	1	1	1	1
High and low-level languages		1	1	1	1	1
Other system software		1	1	1	1	1
Unit 5 – Programming fundamentals 1	18					
Generations of languages		1	5	1	2	2
Assembly language		1	5	1	2	2
High-level languages		1	5	1	2	2
Translating the high level language into machine code		1	5	1	2	2
Other generations of high level languages		1	5	1	2	2
Imperative high level languages		1	5	1	2	2
Data types		1	5	1	2	2
Programming concepts		1	5	1	2	2
Variable declarations and constant definitions		1	5	1	2	2
Assignment		1	5	1	2	2
Unit 6 – Programming fundamentals 2	22					
Iteration		1	5	4	2, 4	2
Selection		1	5	4	2, 4	2
Functions		1	5	4	2, 4	2
Procedures		1	5	4	2, 4	2
Parameter passing by value and reference		1	5	4	2, 4	2
Unit 7 – Programming fundamentals 3	26					
String functions		1	5	1	2	2
Binary tree structures		1	5	1	2	2
A linear queue		1	5	1	2	2
Array data structures		1	5	1	2	2
Simple algorithms		1	5	1	2	2

Study Guide Unit Title
and subheadings

Module numbers

1, 2 and 3 are predominantly AS level

4, 5 and 6 are predominantly A2 level

	Page	AQA	Edexcel	OCR	WJEC	NICCEA
Unit 8 – Communication basics	30					
Simple methods of communication		1	1	1	3	1
Classification of simple transmission systems		1	1	1	3	1
Serial and parallel communication		1	1	1	3	1
Synchronous and asynchronous data communications		1	1	1	3	1
Start and stop bits		1	1	1	3	1
Baud rates and bit rates		1	1	1	3	1
How to get more bits per baud!		1	1	1	3	1
Simple methods of error detection		1	1	1	3	1
Communication protocols		1	1	1	3	1
Unit 9 – Networking basics	34					
Local area networks (LANs)		1	1	1	3	1
Wide area networks (WANs)		1	1	1	3	1
Packet switched networks		1	1	1	3	1
Mobile phones		1	1	1	3	1
The virtual private networks (VPN)		1	1	1	3	1
Some advantages and disadvantages of networking		1	1	1	3	1
Internet resources		1	1	1	3	1
Unit 10 – A first look at operating systems	38					
The role of an operating system		2, 4	1	1	1	1
Job control		2, 4	1	1	1	1
Operating system classification		2, 4	1	1	1	1
Resource management		2, 4	1	1	1	1
Multi-user operating systems		2, 4	1	1	1	1
Unit 11 – Operating system security and management	42					
File security		2, 4	1	1	1	1
Time management		2, 4	1	1	1	1
Resource management		2, 4	1	1	1	1
Access to resources management		2, 4	1	1	1	1
Access to disk space		2, 4	1	1	1	1
Auditing the use of files		2, 4	1	1	1	1
Process control operating systems		2, 4	1	1	1	1
Unit 12 – Input techniques and data collection 1	46					
Input devices		2	1	1, 3	1, 3	1
The keyboard		2	1	1, 3	1, 3	1
Mice, trackballs and touch pads		2	1	1, 3	1, 3	1
Touch screens, pen-based input and PDAs		2	1	1, 3	1, 3	1
Graphics tablets		2	1	1, 3	1, 3	1
Joysticks and consoles		2	1	1, 3	1, 3	1
Bar codes		2	1	1, 3	1, 3	1
OCR systems and scanners		2	1	1, 3	1, 3	1
Other OCR systems		2	1	1, 3	1, 3	1
MICR systems		2	1	1, 3	1, 3	1
OMR systems		2	1	1, 3	1, 3	1
Key-to-disk systems		2	1	1, 3	1, 3	1
Unit 13 – Input techniques and data collection 2	50					
Video input of data		2	1	1, 3	1, 3	1
Speech input		2	1	1, 3	1, 3	1
MIDI		2	1	1, 3	1, 3	1
Other forms of computer input		2	1	1, 3	1, 3	1
Capturing scientific and engineering data		2	1	1, 3	1, 3	1
Capturing data from the web		2	1	1, 3	1, 3	1
Manual data collection methods		2	1	1, 3	**1, 3**	**1**
Unit 14 – Output devices and data presentation	54					
Output devices		2	1	1, 3	1, 3	1
Printers		2	1	1, 3	1, 3	1
Other printing technologies		2	1	1, 3	1, 3	1
Photographic printing technologies		2	1	1, 3	1, 3	1
Display technologies		2	1	1, 3	1, 3	1
Other display technologies		2	1	1, 3	1, 3	1
Graphics cards		2	1	1, 3	1, 3	1
Computer sound		2	1	1, 3	1, 3	1
Other forms of computer output		2	1	1, 3	**1, 3**	**1**

Study Guide Unit Title and subheadings	Page	AQA	Edexcel	OCR	WJEC	NICCEA
Module numbers — 1, 2 and 3 are predominantly AS level; 4, 5 and 6 are predominantly A2 level						
Unit 52 – Systems implementation and maintenance	204					
System implementation		5	2, 5	5	4	3
Conversion		5	2, 5	5	4	3
Parallel systems		5	2, 5	5	4	3
Phased systems		5	2, 5	5	4	3
Direct implementation		5	2, 5	5	4	3
Pilot schemes		5	2, 5	5	4	3
Systems implementation in practice		5	2, 5	5	4	3
Different phases of implementation		5	2, 5	5	4	3
Acceptance testing		5	2, 5	5	4	3
Staff training		5	2, 5	5	4	3
Simple system documentation		5	2, 5	5	4	3
Basic technical documentation		5	2, 5	5	4	3
Unit 53 – Further systems implementation and maintenance	208					
User documentation		5	5	5	4	3
Installation manual		5	5	5	4	3
User manual		5	5	5	4	3
The operations manual		5	5	5	4	3
Training manual		5	5	5	4	3
Other training methods		5	5	5	4	3
Evaluation		5	5	5	4	3
System maintenance		5	5	5	4	3
Applying these methods to your projects		5	5	5	4	3
Unit 54 – Basic internet structures	212					
The internet		5	4	6	3	4
IP addresses		5	4	6	3	4
Domain names		5	4	6	3	4
Internet registries		5	4	6	3	4
Internet registrars		5	4	6	3	4
The client server model		5	4	6	3	4
The HTTP protocol		5	4	6	3	4
The structure of a web site		5	4	6	1	4
Web page organisation		5	4	6	1	4
Unit 55 – Further web site organisation	216					
The HTML language		5	4	6	1	4
The hyperlinks		5	4	6	1	4
Other features		5	4	6	1	4
HTML editors		5	4	6	1	4
WYSIWYG HTML editors and web site creation tools		5	4	6	1	4
Database links		5	4	6	1	4
FTP		5	4	6	1	4
Telnet		5	4	6	1	4
Unit 56 – Search engines and browsers	220					
Internet search engines		5	4	6	1	4
Search techniques		5	4	6	1	4
URLs in more detail		5	4	6	1	4
Web Browsers		5	4	6	1	4
WAP enabled browsers		5	4	6	1	4
Unit 57 – Further internet-based technologies	224					
TV-based technology		5	4	6	1	4
Java Applets		5	4	6	1	4
Java Servelets, CGI scripts and PERL		5	4	6	1	4
E-mail		2, 5	4	6	1	4
Preventing forgery		5	4	6	1	4
Usenet		5	4	6	1	4
Internet Relay Chat (IRC)		5	4	6	1	4
Unit 58 – Banking, shopping and the VPN	228					
Agents		5	4	6	1	4
Video conferencing		5	4	6	1	4
On-line banking		5	4	6	1	4
On-line shopping		5	4	6	1	4
On-line security		5	4	6	1	4
Firewalls and intranets		5	4	6	1	4
Virtual private networks (VPNs)		5	4	6	1	4

1 Data, information and coding

In this section you will learn about:

- Data, information, bits, bytes and words
- Simple binary and BCD
- Simple floating-point numbers
- Negative binary numbers

Data, information and binary encoding

Data is the *raw material* on which the computer operates. When **structure** has been applied to the data it becomes **information**.

Computers use **binary digits** or **bits**. '0's and '1's build up codes inside computers. A *group of 8 binary digits* is called a **byte**. A byte is a unit of storage in a computer system. **1 Kbyte** is actually 1024 bytes of data, and **1 Mbyte** is 1024 × 1024 or 1 048 576 bytes of data. The term **word** is a *group of bytes*, usually, 16, 32, 64 or 128 bits.

Various methods of **encoding** exist. Codes such as **ASCII** (the **American Standard Code for Information Interchange**) allow computers to transfer simple text information as everybody has agreed on this *standard*. A few ASCII codes are shown here:

Character	Decimal Place Values (Column headings)							
	128	64	32	16	8	4	2	1
A	0	1	0	0	0	0	0	1
B	0	1	0	0	0	0	1	0
%	0	0	1	0	0	1	0	1
é	1	0	0	0	0	0	1	0

With one **byte**, codes 00000000 to 11111111 are employed, giving **256 combinations**. This is enough for many languages, but others, like Arabic and Chinese require more. The more versatile **Unicode**, based on a 16-bit character representation (2 bytes) is now popular. 16-bits mean that **65 536 characters** are available.

Basic binary

The **binary system** uses the column headings shown in the previous ASCII-table example. Looking at the 'A row' reveals that the letter 'A' has a decimal value of '65', because it is made up of 1 lot of 64 (the 1 under the 64 column) and 1 unit (the 1 in the 1 column).

Example

Using the small extract from the ASCII table shown above, what is the decimal value for the character 'é'?

Solution

Place the appropriate bit pattern underneath the column headings as follows:

Character	128	64	32	16	8	4	2	1
é	1	0	0	0	0	0	1	0

By observation we see that we have (1 lot of 128) + (1 lot of 2) giving a decimal value for 'é' of '130'.

Visit our portal for more information about Unicode.

We convert from **binary** to **decimal** by adding the column headings. If the decimal value for the '%' sign is '37', we work backwards to find the binary pattern having the same value, by starting with the largest column heading we can take from the number, in this case 32.

Character	32	16	8	4	2	1
%	1	0	0	1	0	1

Take one lot of 32 away from the original number 37, and we are left with 5. This means that there are no lots of 16, no lots of 8, 1 lot of 4, no lots of 2 and 1 unit, as shown in the above table. Not forgetting to put the two leading zeros back in to make a byte, the original bit pattern for the '%' sign, which has a decimal code of '37' is 00100101.

If **ASCII** is used to **code a number** like 273, then the ASCII code for 2 is followed by the code for 7, which is then followed by the code for 3. This pattern is different from the pure binary representation for 273.

Simple binary arithmetic

Binary digits may be added together assuming that the correct digits are lined up underneath each other.

Example

Add 10010_2 and 1011_2. (Note that the subscript denotes a number in base two (binary). This is often omitted if it is assumed that we are working with binary numbers.)

Solution

```
    1   0   0   1   0
        1   0   1   1   +
  _____
    1   1   1   0   1
            1 ← This is the carry
```

When 2 is reached we carry one to the next column, as in the case of the second column from the right in the above sum.

Octal and hexadecimal

Long binary strings are tedious to deal with and mistakes are common. **Octal (base eight)** and **hexadecimal (base sixteen)** are used instead. Octal uses the set of numbers {0, 1, 2, 3, 4, 5, 6, 7} and **hex** (short for hexadecimal) uses the numbers {0, 1, 2, 3, 4, 5, 6, 7, 8, 9, A, B, C, D, E, F}. A represents '10', B represents '11' and so on up to 'F' which represents '15'. When adding hex numbers we carry lots of 16. When using octal we carry lots of 8.

Example

Add $35B2_{16}$ and $247C_{16}$

Solution

```
    3   5   B   2
    2   4   7   C   +
  _____
    5   A   2   E
            1
```

Note the following:

$2 + C$ is the same as $2 + 12$ which is 14 which gives E.

$B + 7$ is the same as $11 + 7$ which is 18, which is 1 lot of 16 (the carry) and 2 left over.

Remember the easy way to convert between binary and hex.

Conversion between hex and binary

To convert a **binary number** into a **hex number**, group the binary digits into lots of 4, starting at the right hand side. Write down the value of each group in hex, and that's the answer.

Example

Convert 101100110011111010_2 into hex.

Solution

10	1100	1100	1111	1010
2	C	C	F	A

Therefore, 101100110011111010_2 is $2CCFA_{16}$.

Make sure you can use a calculator for binary, octal and hex.

Binary coded decimal

An alternative to binary is **binary coded decimal** or **BCD**. This is *not* a number base like binary or hex, but a system of coding groups of 4 binary digits to represent decimals.

Example

What is the BCD equivalent of 345_{10}?

Solution

3	4	5
0011	0100	0101

Therefore, 0011 0100 0101 is the BCD representation of 345 in decimal.

The binary representation for 345 would be 101011001, shown as follows:

256	128	64	32	16	8	4	2	1
1	0	1	0	1	1	0	0	1

Fractional binary numbers

A **binary fraction**, like a conventional fraction, contains two parts. The integer part appears before the **binary point**, and the fractional part appears after the binary point.

Example

What is the decimal equivalent of the binary number 1010.111_2?

Solution

Place values (Column headings)							
8	4	2	1	.	$\frac{1}{2}$	$\frac{1}{4}$	$\frac{1}{8}$
1	0	1	0	.	1	1	1

Tackling the integer part we get: $8 + 2 = 10$
Tackling the fractional part we get:
$0.111_2 = \frac{1}{2} + \frac{1}{4} + \frac{1}{8} = \frac{7}{8} = 0.875$
Therefore, $1010.111_2 = 10.875_{10}$

Floating point binary numbers

Numbers may be written in scientific notation like the following: $2.3 \times 10^3 = 2300$.
In computing, we use a similar system in binary. For example: $101 \times 2^3 = 101000$

The binary point, at the end of the number 101, is shifted 3 places right, as indicated by the index. The 101 part of the number is called the **mantissa**, and the power of two (the number on the top of the two) is called the **exponent**. When combined in this way, the number is called a **floating-point number**, because the binary point floats backwards and forwards, dictated by the exponent. Floating-point numbers are usually contained in a register (an electronic place into which binary digits may be stored), split into two parts as follows:

0	●	1	1	0	1		0	1	1
Mantissa							Exponent		

To work out what value is contained in the register, we move the binary point 3 places to the right, (as indicated by the **exponent**), and then use the **mantissa** to get the final value 0.1101 becomes 0110.1 giving a decimal value of 5.5.

More detail about binary can be found in chapters 30 and 31 of NUCSAL.

Example

What is the decimal value of the following floating-point binary number?

Solution

0	●	1	1	1	0		0	1	0
Mantissa							Exponent		

The exponent has a value of 2, therefore, move the binary point two places right to get 11.10, which is 3.5 decimal.

Negative Binary Numbers

Negative binary numbers work using a system called **two's complement**. It is like a tape-recorder counter shown in the following table:

Number types	Binary (3-digits)			Decimal equivalent
Negative binary numbers	1	0	0	−4
	1	0	1	−3
	1	1	0	−2
	1	1	1	−1
Zero	0	0	0	0
Positive binary numbers	0	0	1	1
	0	1	0	2
	0	1	1	3

The **number** of digits used *must* always be specified, like the 3-digit two's complement representation shown here. Positive numbers start off with a '0' and negative numbers start off with a '1'. To find the two's complement of a number use the following rule.

Write down the binary number using the correct number of digits. Starting at <u>the right-hand side</u> of the number, move left until the first '1' is encountered. Write this down then continue moving left inverting the other bits.

Further work on floating point numbers can be found in chapter 31 of NUCSAL.

Example

How is −6 represented in binary if a 4-bit two's complement representation is used?

Solution

Write down the binary number for +6 using 4 bits as shown in the following table:

Write down number for +6	0	1	1	0
Move left until first '1'			1	0
Invert the other digits	1	0	1	0

The answer is −6 = 1010 using 4 bits.

Do not forget that you can find out the size of negative numbers by using the same method.

Self-test questions

1 What is meant by the terms ASCII and Unicode?
2 Change the decimal number 39 into   (a) binary   (b) BCD   (c) hexadecimal.
3 Convert 10000101 into decimal.   4 Express 9.125 in binary.
5 Explain how to convert between binary and hexadecimal numbers.
6 Why is BCD not a true binary code?   7 Work out $1011_2 + 1111_2$.
8 Work out $1100_2 − 110_2$.   9 What is a floating-point number?
10 What is the largest positive decimal number that can be represented using 16 bits? (No negative numbers are needed.)
11 What are the two's complement representations of −29 and −56 using 8 bits?
12 If a two's complement 8 bit representation is used, what is the decimal equivalent of the number 11110000?

In this unit you have learned about:

- The difference between data and information
- Some basic operations with binary and other bases like octal and hex
- Fractional and floating-point binary numbers and negative binary numbers

2 Images, sound and analogue data

In this section you will learn about:

- Methods of encoding graphics, sound and other information
- A to D converters
- Sound synthesis

Other encoding methods

All information on the computer must eventually be coded into binary. You have seen how numeric data is encoded, so here we look at other methods.

Graphical methods

A pattern of binary digits may be used to represent image information. 1 bit could represent switches, which control the **colour** in a simple monochrome image as follows:

1-bit colour	
Colour	Bit pattern
Black	0
White	1

We could also arrange 3-bits to be used, giving 8 different colours (or shades of grey):

Colour	Bit pattern		
	R	G	B
Black	0	0	0
Blue	0	0	1
Green	0	1	0
Cyan	0	1	1
Red	1	0	0
Magenta	1	0	1
Yellow	1	1	0
White	1	1	1

3-bit colour

You can see RGB components by changing colours in applications like Microsoft Word or Adobe Illustrator

Using 4 bits would give us 2^4, which is 16 different colours or shades of grey. 8 bits would produce 256 colours or shades of grey, and the familiar 24 bits would produce 2^{24} or **16 777 216 colours**. The system used here is the **additive-colour system** (red, green, blue) used inside computer monitors. **Subtractive** colours **cyan**, **magenta**, **yellow** and **key** (**black**) would be used when driving a printer.

Bit-mapped graphics

Use the paintbrush to draw an irregular shape in a pixel-based art package like Adobe Photoshop, zoom in a long way and you will see the pixels.

Individual bits are used to represent an image on the screen in the form of **pixels**. The position is controlled by **mapping** locations in memory to adjacent parts of the picture, and the colour of each pixel is controlled by groups of binary digits in ways identical to those described in the last section. A bit-mapped image is made up of tiny squares called **Pixels**. If the image is made larger, then the quality degrades (lots of jagged edges). This is characteristic of bit-mapped graphics. If **high-resolution** is used near-photographic quality is achieved (several million pixels). Bit-mapped graphics are also called **raster graphics**, and take up large amounts of memory.

Example

How much memory would be required for a 300 dpi coloured image, the size of an A5 sheet, if 24-bit colour is used?

Solution

An A5 sheet is approximately 8.25 inches by 5.75 inches. At 300 dpi (dots per inch), we need $8.25 \times 300 = 2475$ pixels horizontally and $5.75 \times 300 = 1725$ pixels vertically, which gives us $2475 \times 1725 = 4\,269\,375$ pixels altogether.

At 300 dpi, this means there would be $4\,269\,375$ dots on the page to make up the picture. Now each pixel requires 3 bytes (24 bits) to define one of the possible $16\,777\,216$ different colours. We therefore need $4\,269\,375 \times 3 = 12\,808\,125$ bytes
Dividing by 1024 gives us $12\,808\,125 / 1024 = 12\,507$ Kbytes
Dividing by 1024 again gives us $12\,507 / 1024 = 12.2$ Mbytes

Vector graphics

Another way to derive a graphic is using vectors. Mathematical equations determine attributes of the image, made up from straight lines (called **vectors**). These straight-line segments build up into making complex **objects** like squares, rectangles and circles. The resultant graphic components are called **objects**. Vector graphics is also know as **object-oriented graphics**. Vectors are used extensively in **CAD packages**, whereas bit-mapped images are usually associated with **art packages**.

Use the paintbrush to draw an irregular shape in a vector-based art package like Adobe Illustrator, zoom in a long way and you will see the vectors.

Example

Compare and contrast the use of bit-mapped and vector graphics, giving reasons why each is suited to a particular application.

Solution

Bit-mapped graphics are made up from lots of tiny dots called pixels. They are used extensively in art packages like Adobe PhotoShop or Corel Photo Paint, for example. Vector graphics are made up from lines, which build up into objects like circles and squares etc. They are used extensively in CAD packages like AutoCAD.

Many packages like Corel PhotoPaint and CorelDraw enable us to use both vector and bit-mapped images in the same program. Bit-mapped images tend to be able to do more subtle fancy effects, and vector graphics are much sharper. Bit-mapped images take up a lot of memory and vector images are less memory hungry but can be zoomed in by vast amounts with virtually no loss of image quality.

Other forms of encoding binary data

Sound can be represented by binary data. You should recall that **MIDI**, the **Musical Instrument Digital Interface** has been used for many years to transmit binary data in the form of bytes between different electronic musical instruments, or ordinary instruments that have a MIDI interface added. Data in a typical MIDI transmission consists of bytes containing **channel information** (i.e. which of the 20 synthesisers you have connected to your computer pays attention to this data!), a program number like 15, for example, which would tell a standard MIDI keyboard to sound like tubular bells, and a **MIDI value** containing the note information. The channel and program numbers are sent less frequently.

Recording sounds

Most people are aware that sound forms an important part of a multimedia computer system. You can record your own sounds into the computer by using a standard Windows recorder like the one shown in Figure 2.1.

Figure 2.1 Recording from Windows.

Don't confuse MP3 with MPEG 3, a standard used for graphic files.

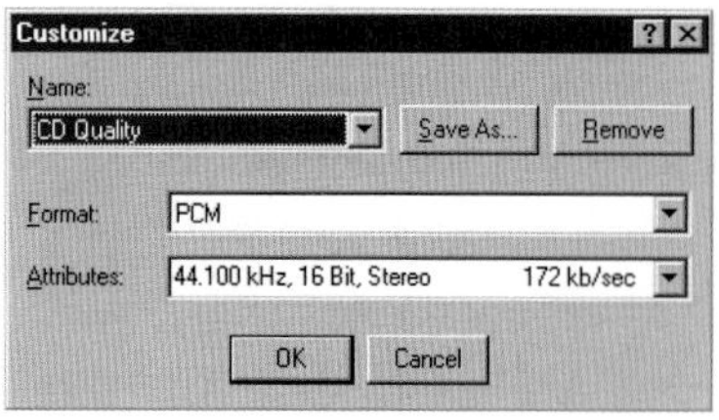

Visit our portal for examples of MP3 files.

More detail about A to D converters can be found in chapter 8 of NUCSAL.

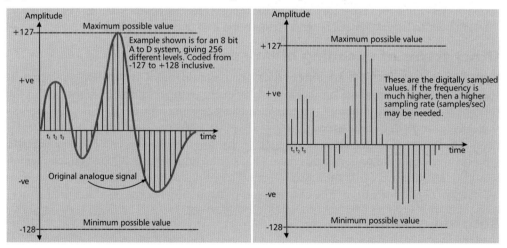

Figure 2.2 Quality settings for sound.

The quality of the recorded sound depends on the amount of binary data used to represent it. Figure 2.2 shows the Windows dialogue box, which determines the quality with which the sound is recorded. For example, we can have CD quality sound, which takes up 172 kb/sec (172 k bits/sec) of bandwidth. It is important to realise that CD quality sound takes up an enormous amount of space. A compression system like **MP3** is used, if sound is to be sent over the internet.

Example

Explain *exactly* why the CD-quality sound in Figure 2.2 takes up 172 kb for each second of sound recording.

Solution

- 16 bit stereo means (2 bytes for each sample for each channel).
- There are 44 100 samples each second (giving CD quality).

There are 44 100 samples/sec. Each sample requires $4 \times 8 = 32$ binary digits (two bytes for each channel for each sample.)

Thus $44\,100 \times 2 \times 2$ gives us 176 400 bits/sec. Not forgetting that there are actually 1024 bits in 1 k, we get $176\,400/1024 = $ **172.27 k bits/sec**. Therefore, this particular sound recording would take 172 kb/sec as shown in Figure 2.2.

Analogue and digital signals

Sound from your voice is **analogue** in nature (*continuously variable*), whereas the binary digits going into the computer, representing your voice are digital (being 'on' or 'off' only). A process called **analogue-to-digital** (A to D) **conversion** must therefore take place, to convert the voice into a binary form suitable to store inside a computer system. When the sounds are played back over your stereo system, the binary digits from the computer must be changed back again into analogue form (via a **D to A converter**), so that they can be played back via a conventional stereo amplifier and speaker system.

Figure 2.3 Analogue to digital conversion.

A to D converters

An A to D converter is an electronic circuit, usually present on most computer sound cards or data logging cards, that transforms an analogue signal, like the one shown in the left side of Figure 2.3, into digital values, like those shown in the right side of Figure 2.3.

Example

How many different levels could be sampled with a 16-bit A to D converter?

Solution

1 bit gives just 2 levels, 0 and 1 (2^1).
2 bits give 4 levels, 00, 01, 10 and 11 (2^2).
3 bits would give 8 levels (2^3).

Therefore, 16 bits would give us 2^{16} or 65,536 different possibilities of digital values.

If positive and negative values were required, as is the case in Figure 2.3, then we could go from −32 768 to +32 767 including 0, this gives us the 65,536 different possible levels. This is the **two's complement method** of representing negative numbers in binary, and is covered in unit 1.

Sound synthesis

Making electronic sounds (pure tones) is easy because any sound can be made up from groups of alternating-current signals at different frequencies. This is called **additive synthesis**. It is difficult to make the exact sound required, because more and more complexity is needed if true fidelity is to be accomplished. Other techniques used on computer sound cards include **FM synthesis** and **wave table synthesis**. FM synthesis works by altering the carrier of a wave using frequency modulation. The resulting complex wave can represent some sounds quite realistically. Many modern sound cards now have this facility.

Self-test questions

1 What is meant by 24-bit graphics?
2 What's the difference between bit-mapped and vector graphics?
3 What is MIDI?
4 How does MIDI differ from encoding sound on computer?
5 Why is MP3 important for internet music?
6 What is an A to D converter?
7 How might sound be encoded into binary?
8 What is an analogue signal?
9 What is RGB, and how does it differ from CMYK?
10 An A to D converter uses 12 bits. What is the maximum positive and negative amplitude if both are equally important?

In this unit you have learned about:

- Encoding methods for graphics and sound
- Analogue and digital signals
- A to D converters
- Methods of compression

3 Microprocessor fundamentals

In this section you will learn about:

- The internal components of a microprocessor
- The bus systems and other components like memory and the clock
- Machine code
- Parallel processing and mainframes

The internal components of a processor

At the heart of most modern computer systems is a **microprocessor chip**. One or more of these chips, housed on the motherboard inside the computer, determines the **hardware platform** on which the machine is run. For example, a PC might use an Intel Pentium Xeon, or the Apple PowerMac might use one or two Power PC G4s. An understanding of these basic principles leads to a better understanding of how a computer system operates at the most basic level.

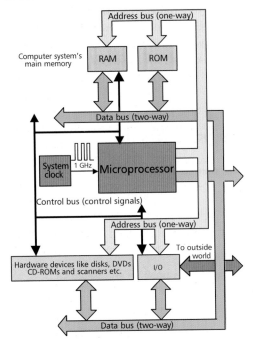

Figure 3.1 A simplified internal structure of a typical microcomputer.

A simplified system, illustrated in Figure 3.1, consists of a **microprocessor chip**, which is activated by an electronic circuit called a clock. This **clock** can generate very fast pulses, like the '1000 million tick-tock cycles per second' shown here. A **bus** is a parallel group of wires, connecting the different parts of the computer system. Binary digits, which form the data on which the computer operates, flow along the **address**, **data**, and **control buses**. Some data may go from a DVD disk to the main memory, for example.

The **address bus** is used to address memory and other devices, and the data itself travels along the **data bus**. Special control signals, like the one telling the memory chip if a 'read' or 'write' operation is taking place, go along the smaller but equally important **control bus**.

Main and secondary storage systems

You should remember that the contents of **main memory** are lost when power is switched off, therefore, **secondary storage** devices like magnetic and optical disks form an important part of most computer systems. Such devices are connected to the processor by the address, data and control buses too, and are dealt with in ways similar to the main-memory devices. In fact *any* device can be hooked up to the processor in this way, and Figure 3.1 shows a general **I/O** (Input Output) connection to the outside world. This connection might go via a sound card and an A to D converter so a microphone could be connected, or data lines might go via some electronics to control the lights in your house, for example.

Keep up to date with modern processors by reading monthly computer magazines and surfing the internet.

Visit our portal for more about microprocessors.

Example

Based on what you have just read, list *three* ways in which the speed of execution of a microcomputer system can be improved, explaining why each method is effective.

Solution

- The **speed of the clock** can be increased. This means that more cycles can be carried out each second.
- The **width of the data bus** can be increased. More data can be transferred to and from memory for each clock cycle.
- **More than one processor** could be used, thus giving a parallel-processing capability, in which more than one thing can be carried out at the same time.

Microprocessor and internal components

Considering the simplified microprocessor architecture shown in Figure 3.2, you should be able to quote the roles played by the **ALU** (the **arithmetic logic unit**), the **control unit**, and **internal memory (cache)**. Detailed work regarding registers and assembly-language programming are covered in the A2 modules.

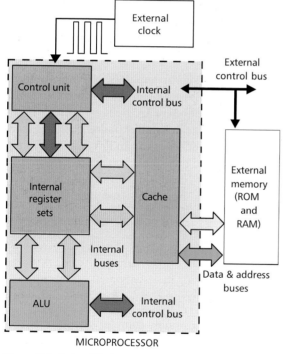

Figure 3.2 A simplified view of the internal workings of a microprocessor.

The **ALU** is the part of the processor that carries out arithmetical and logical operations. It is this unit, which would accept the binary data on which to perform these operations, and pass back the results ready for the next process. It is quite a task to make sure that all data gets routed correctly, and in our simplified system it is the job of the **control unit** to do this.

Although getting data from the main memory (RAM) is very fast indeed, the internal parts of the processor often require data even faster than this. Therefore, some memory inside the processor, usually called **cache**, is used for this purpose. It speeds things up by keeping copies of instructions that are likely to be needed soon. The instruction decoder is also considered to be part of the control unit in our simplified system.

Machine code and the stored-program concept

Groups of binary digits represent the special instructions that form the **program** on which the computer operates. These instructions are called **machine code**, and they usually reside in the computer's main memory or **RAM**. It is the job of the computer system to **fetch** a machine-code instruction from memory, decide what to do (called **decoding**), and finally carry out the required actions (called **execution**). The next instruction is then fetched from memory, so that the next part of the program may be carried out. Under the 'metronome like pulses' from the clock, complex sets of instructions can be carried out serially (i.e. one after the other). The idea of operating in this way is called the **stored program concept**, because groups of instructions called a program, stored in the main

Don't try to remember processor diagrams, work out the internal architecture from your knowledge of what they do.

memory, are being executed serially. The sort of instructions that can be carried out at this level are quite simple and may be **arithmetic operations** like 'add' or 'subtract', or **logical operations** like 'AND' and 'OR'.

Example

Briefly explain how a microprocessor, running sets of machine code instructions, can appear to exhibit intelligent behaviour like making a correct decision.

Solution

Machine code instructions consist of a variety of different forms, some of which can help make decisions, based on the results of simple arithmetical or logical operations. Therefore, using machine code, you could program the computer to take action after adding a couple of numbers together. It could, for example, carry out one action if the result was too big, or it might carry out a different action if the result was too small. In this way it is possible to make the computer take an appropriate decision and therefore appear to be intelligent.

Mainframe computers and parallel processing

So far we have looked only at single-processor microcomputer systems. Add an extra processor and you have the ability literally to do more than one thing at the same time. Network files servers, for example, commonly have two, four or even eight processors, so that the enormous workload of dealing with many users simultaneously is shared between them.

The next stages up the hierarchy are **mainframe** and **supercomputers**. Historically these were very large machines, found in University and Government-establishment research labs. However, recent **mainframes**, and even **supercomputers** are built up using a larger number of microprocessors. For example, SGI's Cray SV1 can handle hundreds of processors simultaneously! Computers such as these are awesome, and would handle complex military projects, or work out the results for weather forecasts and hurricane prediction, for example. They can handle hundreds of processors because they are designed with scalability in mind. This means that you can add another bank of processors should the need arise.

More detail on mainframe and supercomputers can be found in chapters 2 and 7 of NUCSAL.

Example

Why do we need supercomputers like those described above to predict the weather?

Solution

Running a simulation for weather forecasting is an extremely complex business, involving billions of complex interrelated calculations, even for forecasting today's weather. If much slower computers are used, the results of tomorrow's weather might be ready in about a month, assuming that the mass of data could be correlated in time. As computers get more powerful, better prediction methods are being developed.

Self-test questions

1 Explain the function of the following bus systems inside a microprocessor:
   (a) The data bus
   (b) The address bus
   (c) The control bus
2 What determines the hardware platform for a particular computer?

AS

3 What is the difference between primary and secondary storage?

4 What do the letters ALU stand for? What is the purpose of the ALU?

5 There are usually two types of primary storage associated with a microprocessor, ROM and RAM. What are these and why are both types usually used when a microprocessor is set up as a microcomputer?

6 What is machine code? Why does the machine code for one particular microprocessor not work with any other type?

7 What is cache and why is it used?

8 What is the function of the control unit inside a simplified microprocessor chip?

9 What is the fetch-decode-execute cycle?

10 What is the stored program concept?

In this unit you have learned about:

- Some of the internal components of a microprocessor like the ALU, control unit and cache
- The address, data and control buses, machine code, the fetch-decode-execute cycle, and parallel processing

4 Fundamental ideas about software

In this section you will learn about:

- The difference between hardware and software
- A further look at operating systems and some applications software
- System software, utility and library programs
- High and low level languages

Hardware and software

An important distinction is made between **hardware** and **software**. **Hardware** is *equipment* like the microprocessors, memory and disks, and the *peripheral equipment* such as printers, scanners and bar-code readers. **Software** is the *programs or instructions*, like the machine-code instructions described in this unit. Examples of software are **operating systems** and **application programs**.

Different types of software

Software can be split into two major categories – **applications software** like word processors and spreadsheets, and **systems software** like the 'Windows 2000' or 'Unix' operating systems. Applications software can be subdivided into **general-purpose applications software** like the word processors mentioned above, and **special-purpose applications software**, covering less general applications like **MIDI software** or **data-logging software**. If software is written or tailored to a unique situation, it is often referred to as **bespoke software**, which simply means 'built to order'.

The **operating system software** is the software at the heart of any computer system. This is the software that **polices**, **controls** and gives the computer **special characteristics** like a **GUI**, for example. Another important part of the system, called the **ROM BIOS** (**Basic Input Output System**) is located in a ROM chip housed on the motherboard. After this software (often called **firmware** as it is stored on a chip), has done its job, the operating system boots up so that the computer ends up in a useable state. You can think of the software inside the ROM BIOS chip as an interface between an operating system, like Windows, for example, and the hardware, like the motherboard, disks and DVDs etc.

If you have a PC, hold down the delete key just after 'switch on' to see the BIOS settings – don't alter these settings unless you know what you are doing, you could render your system inoperable.

Example

How is it possible to have operating system software like Windows interface to different types of hardware, and how do we customise this for individual users?

Solution

The ROM BIOS provides an interface for the hardware on which an operating system, like Windows, for example, may sit. Therefore, if you have different types or sizes of disk, a different motherboard or different amounts of memory, then the software inside the BIOS can interface your particular hardware to a standard operating system. Each type of motherboard needs a different BIOS. Without this facility we would need a different version of the operating system for each version of hardware available! The settings may be customised to your individual requirements by altering data in the CMOS RAM.

The **BIOS** has many special software routines embedded in it, the function of which might be checking the hardware, correctly configuring all of the settings for the disks and graphics displays etc., (via the **CMOS RAM** settings) and running the **bootstrap loader**, so

Visit our portal for modern BIOS information.

the computer is in a useable state such that the main **operating system** can be loaded from disk. After all this is done, the computer is then ready to load any **applications software**. Command-based operating systems like '**DOS**' and '**Unix**' are very much harder for novices to use than the GUI-based operating systems like Windows. This is because the user interface is less intuitive.

Example

List *two advantages* and *two disadvantages* of GUI-based operating systems like Windows compared to command-line operating systems like DOS.

Solution

A GUI, like the Windows based operating system, is easy to use by a novice; a command-based language like DOS is not. A GUI takes up a lot of computer memory, but a command-based system does not. (Note: command-based systems are still very powerful, and often the only convenient way of doing tedious administrative tasks like setting thousands of file permissions, for example.)

System Software

Apart from providing a computer system with its 'personality', it is the function of the operating system to manage all the resources. For example, the **memory allocation** for each application being run, managing the **security systems** on file servers and workstations, managing the **disk-space allocation** for different users on a network system, or **accounting** for how many colour printouts users might have made.

All other software that runs on the computer depends on the correct functioning of the operating system. If, for example, an errant application uses memory that belongs to another application which is running at the same time, one of the applications could crash, resulting in the familiar 'Page protection fault' error message, which frequent users of PCs have probably encountered at some time or other! For the purposes of AS level you need to appreciate the function of the operating system, but need few details about how it goes about these tasks.

Utility programs

Each day we take for granted many of the mundane things carried out on our computer systems. For example, backing up work onto tape, running a recovery program in case we delete something by accident, or finding a file on a disk, the position of which we may have forgotten a long time ago. Some of these utilities may be part of the operating system, and third parties may provide others.

If you have Windows Me, look in the Start/ Programs/ Accessories/ System Tools menu to see some utility programs.

Library programs

Other routines reside in the **library**. In Windows, for example, there is the **Dynamic Link Library**, in which routines are stored (**DLLs**), ready to be used by any program that can link to them. In this way applications programs and utilities can share routines that live in the library. Programming languages like C++ also have their own special library files, which programmers can call up and use when needed.

Example

What is an operating system? Outline three of the major functions, which are typically performed by the operating system.

Solution

An operating system is the software that controls the computer and, via the BIOS, interfaces it with the hardware. It gives the computer its characteristics and helps to make the system easier to use for non-specialists. Three functions, typically performed by the operating system are as follows:

- The allocation of memory to different parts of the system.
- Allocating CPU time (microprocessor time) to different operations.
- Managing the disk space on the hard disks attached to the computer.

High and low-level languages

The computer works only with pure binary codes called **machine code**, which, cleverly encoded, can represent anything from colours on the screen to sounds. Working with binary digits is a tedious and error-prone task, as can be seen from the small machine-code extract in Figure 4.1. In this example, lots of **binary digits** representing the machine code are presented as **pairs of hexadecimal digits**.

Machine code is not convenient for humans, so **assembly language**, which took a single machine-code instruction, and replaced it with 'words' representing the instruction, was invented. Assembly language, although much easier than machine code, was still useable only by computer specialists, as can be realised from looking at Figure 4.1. Machine code and assembly language are both examples of **low-level languages**, because they are close to how the computer operates at a very low level.

Machine code (low level language)	Visual Basic (high-level language)
58EC:0000 CD 20 00 A0 00 ...	Dim Number, Digits, MyString
58EC:0010 7B 27 B5 0A 7B ...	Number = 53
58EC:0020 05 FF FF FF FF ...	If Number < 10 Then
58EC:0030 CD 21 CB 00 00 ...	Digits = 1
58EC:0040 6E 70 75 74 30 ...	ElseIf Number < 100 Then

```
Assembly language (low level language)

   mov    cl,ds:[80h]
   xor    ch,cl
   mov    di,81h
   mov    al, ' '
```

```
        Digits = 2
Else
        Digits = 3
End If
```

Figure 4.1 Examples of machine code, assembly language and high-level language.

The next stage up the hierarchy was to develop languages that mirrored the way humans think, rather than the ways in which a particular computer operates. Languages like **Visual Basic**, **Delphi** and **Java** are modern examples of these **high-level languages**. High-level languages are much easier to use, as can be seen from the Visual Basic extract to the right of Figure 4.1. It is important to realise that all programs, whether they be written in a high-level language or assembly language, must still be converted into machine code to run on the actual machine.

Other system software

We need special software to **translate** any code, written in a high-level language or assembly language, into the machine code that will run on the actual computer. You must never lose sight of the fact that only machine code can run on any computer, other languages must eventually be translated into this form. An **assembler** is a piece of software that translates **assembly language** into **machine code**. It also gives much help to the assembly-language programmer in terms of error detection and organisation.

Interpreters and **compilers** are **translators** (software), which translate high-level languages into machine code. An **interpreter** does the conversion just one-line at a time, and is more interactive, whereas a **compiler** translates the whole code at once, but is less convenient to use, especially when you are debugging programs.

Lots of high-level languages are covered in chapters 13 and 15 of NUCSAL.

Example

List *two* conditions, under which it would be essential to use machine code or assembly language, instead of a high-level language?

Solution

- If speed is of the essence, as might be the case in a real-time system, then machine code or assembly language could be the only language that is fast enough.
- Sometimes a high-level language may not have the facilities to do exactly what you want. Therefore, some routine may have to be written in machine code or assembly language to carry out the desired function.

Self-test questions

1　Explain the difference between hardware and software.
2　Give some examples of general-purpose software, bespoke software and systems software.
3　What is the difference between applications software and systems software?
4　What is the ROM BIOS? Outline three different functions performed by this system.
5　List three different things that would be accomplished most easily by using a command-line operating system like DOS.
6　List three different things that would be accomplished most easily by using a GUI operating system like Windows.
7　What is the difference between a high-level language and a low-level language?
8　Give two examples of a low-level language.
9　Java is a programming language, originally designed to operate on any computer platform. It is used extensively for programming web-based applications. Name four other high-level languages giving an indication of the typical use to which each may be put.
10　Name three different utilities on a typical computer system.
11　What is the difference between a compiler and an interpreter?

In this unit you have learned about:

- The difference between hardware and software
- The ROM BIOS
- The GUI and command-based operating systems
- The concepts of high and low-level languages, utilities, library programs and other systems software
- Translation into machine code using programs like assemblers, interpreters and compilers

5 Programming fundamentals 1

In this section you will learn about:

- Generations of programming languages
- Assemblers, compilers and interpreters
- Some elementary features of high-level languages

To try your hand at assembly language you will need a program like the Microsoft Assembler.

Visit our portal to download an assembler.

Some assembly language examples are covered in chapter 21 of NUCSAL.

Generations of languages

Computers originally had to be programmed using **binary code**. Each pattern of digits corresponded to data and instructions. A typical program might look like the following:

```
0100 1110
0011 0110
1111 0010
0011 1000
```

Programming like this was tedious, time consuming and error prone. It also gives you an insight as to why **hexadecimal** (see unit 1) was invented! The same program segment, written in **hex**, is easier to read, as can be seen from the following:

```
4E
36
F2
38
```

Programming like this is called **machine code**, or **machine language**, because codes used are for a particular machine (family of microprocessor). Machine code is a **first generation** language, and is the only language a computer 'understands'. All other languages are for the convenience of humans, and *all programming instructions, in whatever language they are written, must eventually be **translated** into machine code* to run on the microprocessor controlling the computer.

Assembly language

More progress could be made if the machine code instructions were easier to interpret by humans. **Assembly language** was the next stage, and **mnemonics** (aids to the memory), representing machine-code instructions inside the micro-processor, replaced the tedious groups of binary digits. A typical assembly-language program segment is as follows:

```
MOV    AX,5B71
MOV    DS,AS
PUSH   AX
```

Mnemonics (aids to the memory) like **MOV** and **PUSH**, represent operations on **registers** inside the microprocessor. In this example, a hex number 5B71 is MOVed into the AX register. Although not user friendly, this is better than the machine code equivalent for the same operation, which is B8715B.

An extra stage has now been introduced. The computer must therefore **translate** the **assembly-language mnemonics** into the **machine code** that will actually run on the computer. To do this we use an **assembler**. This is a program, which not only translates the mnemonics into machine code, but also helps with lots of other things like being able to calculate relative jumps to labels, and detecting errors. Assembly language belongs to the class of programming languages known as **second-generation languages**.

Machine code and assembly language belong to the class of languages known as **low-level languages**. Although not routinely used, a few things, such as programs with fast response times, might still have to be done in this way.

High-level languages

Programming in a low-level language required programmers to be experts in their field. It was not an ideal environment for other professionals who wished to program computers to solve specific problems, like those found in mathematics, engineering and commerce. New ways had to be developed if computers were to become easier to use. **High-level languages** were the answer to this, as program instructions were much easier to understand. A segment from a typical high-level language is shown below.

```
If Number < 10 Then
        Digits = 1
ElseIf Number < 100 Then
        Digits = 2
Else
        Digits = 3
End If
```

Here you can see that **English-like words** have been used, and variable names, like the variables used in mathematics, help clarify this routine, which determines how many digits are in a number < 1000. **Key words** like 'IF', 'THEN' and 'ELSE' are easier to understand, and related to human logic, instead of the operations required by the machine. This is why it is called a high-level language. **Imperative** (see later) **high-level programming languages** belong to **third-generation languages**.

Translating the high-level language into machine code

Further stages of **translation** are needed to convert this human-like thought into machine code because it is further removed from binary digits to be executed by the microprocessor. High-level languages are therefore slower to process than low-level languages.

It is possible to translate high-level language in one go, by using a program called a **compiler**. This will compile all the high-level language instructions, link it with any other code that might be needed, and help to call up any library routines required. The compiler will also check for errors, and help with **debugging** the program. The end result of the compilation process is **executable machine code**, i.e. code that may be run on a computer, without the need for the high-level language compiler which originally created it.

Using a compiler is daunting for beginners, and is often frustrating. A single comma missed out from a large program, means that the whole program needs to be recompiled to run properly. Therefore, a more interactive environment has been developed, in which each line of code is **interpreted** separately. Users get instant feedback while developing and running the code. This method of **translation**, where just one line of code is translated at a time, is called an **interpreter**.

Example

Outline a typical scenario, where the following methods would be most appropriately used:
(a) Machine code
(b) Assembly language
(c) Use of a compiler
(d) Use of an interpreter.

Solution

(a) **Machine code** is rarely used for programming a computer, it is used for programming some **computer-controlled devices**, but even microwave ovens or central heating systems would be programmed in assembly language.
(b) **Assembly language** is used if a particular facility, needed by a program, is not available in a high-level language. It is also used if great speed is required, as might be needed for military equipment.
(c) Programs are **compiled** if speed of operation is important. Because the final code is compiled into machine code, this is a convenient way of selling your software, without giving your customers access to the actual high-level language code you have used to solve the problem.

Try to gain some experience using a compiled language. Get your tutor to show you the compilation process if possible.

Visit our portal to find out how to download compilers.

With Visual Basic, you can create a compiled version of your code so you do not need the VB interpreter to run it. If you have access to this, try it and see.

(d) An **interpreter** is ideal in a learning and development environment, where instant feedback regarding errors is more important than speed or efficiency of execution of the program.

Other generations of high-level languages

The **fourth** and **fifth generation** of high-level languages are covered in unit 41.

Imperative high-level languages

Imperative languages typically give *sets of instructions* (called **imperatives**) to the computer. You will also come across other language definitions such as 'Object oriented programming' or 'Declarative programming'. An understanding of these other languages requires an understanding of imperative programming too. Here we only show a few of the basic principles.

Data types

Without a rich selection of **data types**, it is difficult to express solutions to problems in elegant ways. You should be familiar with **data types** like 'String', 'Real', 'Integer' and 'Boolean' etc. These are some of the **built-in data types** available in most high-level languages. If an integer answer is required, get one by using an integer data type.

In many languages it is possible to define your own data type. These are called **user-defined data types**, and reflect using a combination of the built-in data types to solve a problem in an effective way. This might be setting up a special **data structure**, such as a 3-dimensional array of floating-point numbers.

More high-level language principles are covered in chapter 13 of NUCSAL.

Example

Using a high-level language with which you are familiar, give some examples of *simple* and *structured data types*, showing how they might typically be used.

Solution

This example uses Microsoft's Visual Basic.

A **simple data type** is a **numeric data type**. VB has 5 numeric data types, namely **Integer**, **Long**, **Single**, **Double** and **Currency**. Currency supports 4 digits after the decimal point, and fifteen digits to the left. Within this (very large) range, *the currency data type is accurate for all financial calculations*.

A **structured data type** is an **array**. Typically an array enables us to use an index to point to an individual item of data within it. This enables us to make use of loop structures to process the array. For example, you could assign a value of 10 to all 10 000 elements of an **array** (**matrix**) using the following code:

```
Dim x As Integer, y As Integer
Static MatrixA(1 To 100, 1 To 100) As Single
For x = 1 To 100
    For y = 1 To 100
        MatrixA(x, y) = 10
    Next y
Next x
```

We have to declare dimensions of the matrix (array) in line 2, which gives the computer information needed to reserve memory for all the integer variables stored in the matrix.

Programming concepts

Imperative languages, like the code given in the last example, are made up from a series of **statements**, whose **syntax** (set of rules) is defined when the language is designed.

Variable declarations and constant definitions

A **variable** is the name given to an **identifier** (storage location or label), which is allowed to vary. It is good programming practice to declare **variables** and **constants** etc. at the beginning of the program, or at the beginning of the **procedure** in which they are used. A Visual Basic example now follows:

```
Dim variablename [As type]
```

Therefore, typical examples might be:

```
DIM My_Bank_Balance As Currency
DIM Averages (30) As Double
DIM Array1 (1 to 10, 1 to 10) As Single
```

Most languages have similar ways of doing this. The principles are identical, only the **syntax** and **data types** may vary.

Constants may also be declared at the appropriate place in the program, and some typical examples might be as follows:

```
Const Pi = 3.141592654
Const Password = "PanPipes/2001"
```

Assignment

In a high-level programming language, this consists of assigning a value (which might consist of an expression to be evaluated) to a **variable**, by using an **assignment operator** like '=' or ':='. Consider the following **statement**.

```
Stock_Level = Stock_Level - 1
```

The equals sign cannot be used in the same way as in maths, because this is nonsense. This statement, in a high-level programming language is an **assignment statement**; it means that the new value of 'Stock_Level' (on the LHS) is the old value of the 'Stock_Level' (on the RHS) minus 1. We have thus reduced the stock level by 1, by decrementing the variable representing the level of the stock.

Self-test questions

1 Non-specialist students are learning to program a computer. Why is an interpreter more suitable than a complier, assuming the language has both?
2 What is a structured programming language? Give an example of a structured language with which you are familiar.
3 Why is compilation a more efficient way of generating machine code?
4 Why are all high-level languages turned into machine code?
5 Explain the terms 'assignment', 'variable declaration' and 'data type'.

In this unit you have learned about:

- Computer language generations
- The translation of languages into machine code using assemblers, compilers and interpreters
- Simple high-level language concepts like data types and assignment

6 Programming fundamentals 2

In this section you will learn about:

- Iteration or loops
- Selection structures
- Functions
- Procedures
- Passing by value and by reference
- Examples using these techniques

Iteration

Iteration means **looping**. This enables computers to do the same thing over and over again, with the minimum of code.

Example

Using a high-level language with which you are familiar, explain three different types of loop structure. Give an example, together with an explanation of how each of these iterative structures may be used.

Solution

The first example uses a FOR-TO-NEXT loop.

The **control variable**, an integer called 'counter', is set to 1. The value of the variable Name(1), is printed out. The counter is then incremented by

```
For counter = 1 To 100
      Print Name(counter)
Next counter
```

1, and the loop is executed again, printing out the variable Name(2). This process continues until Name(100) has been printed, and counter has a value of 101.

A second example is the DO WHILE loop.

If the value of the variable called counter is < 50, then the statements within the loop are executed, i.e. the counter is incremented by 1, and its value printed. When the value of the counter is 50, the loop is not executed, and control passes to the statements after the loop.

```
Do While Counter < 50
    Counter = Counter + 1
    Print Counter
Loop
```

The third example is a REPEAT UNTIL structure.

The value of the variable 'Counter' is not tested until the end of the routine. The counter is incremented and printed once, even if its value is > 50.

```
REPEAT
    Counter = Counter + 1
    Print Counter
UNTIL Counter > 50
```

Selection

These are typical of **IF-THEN-ELSE** type statements, which are called **conditional branch statements**. A condition is tested, and based on the results of the test (usually **true** or **false**), other statements may be executed or not. An IF-THEN-ELSE structure is shown here:

```
IF result > 50 THEN
    Print "You have passed"
ELSE
    Print "You have failed"
END IF
```

A selection is made, based on the value of the variable called result. If the value of result is more than 50 'You have passed' is printed, else 'You have failed' is printed instead. These statements may be **nested**, so that new IF-THEN-ELSE statements may appear inside other loops. Elegant code can be written, and selections made on sophisticated criteria.

Functions

Most high-level languages have a rich selection of built-in **functions**, plus the ability to define and call your own. Examples of **intrinsic** (built in) **functions** might be 'sine' and 'cosine', 'square roots' or 'end of file', for example. There are usually hundreds of built-in functions in a typical high-level language.

Functions may be called by name, and **parameters** (values) may be passed over to them. The result is then returned to the calling routine. If we wish to find the square root of 96.7, then we might use the following statement:

```
My_Number = SQR(96.7)
```

The intrinsic function called **SQR** (square root) is **called**, and the **parameter** 96.7 is *passed over to it*, by placing this number in the brackets. The **result** is then **assigned** to the variable called **My_Number**, which would end up with a value 9.83361581 ... depending on the precision with which it is worked out. This would, of course depend on the data type used.

Functions may be **intrinsic** to the language or may be **user-defined functions**. User defined functions are called by a name defined by the user. If you want more than one value returned, then **procedures** and **subroutines** are used.

Procedures

Procedures enable us to modularise programs. This is essential if we are to follow modern **structured programming** techniques, and in particular the technique of **modularisation**. **Procedures** or **subroutines** make programs easier to understand, and enable different programmers to undertake parts of a larger project by writing separate modules. Modules may be tested individually, and joined with other modules to form larger systems.

```
Private Sub Command1_Click()
    Picture1.Visible = False
    Label1.Caption = Int(Rnd * 10)
    Label2.Caption = Int(Rnd * 10)
    Label3.Caption = Int(Rnd * 10)
    If (Label1.Caption = 7) Or (Label2.Caption = 7) Or
(Label3.Caption = 7) Then
                Picture1.Visible = True
                Beep
    End If
End Sub
```

A variety of languages like Delphi (Visual Pascal) and C++ demonstrate the principles outlined here. You don't have to work using Visual Basic.

Above is an example of a sub **procedure** in **Visual Basic**, which responds to a mouse click over a command button, in which case the code inside the procedure is executed.

Parameter passing by value and reference

If parameters are to be passed over to a procedure, two methods exist for this, called **passing by value** and **passing by reference**.

The following is an example of **passing by value**:

```
Sub My_Procedure(ByVal My_Variable as Integer)
        .
        .  'Other code goes here'
        .
End Sub
```

A *copy* of the variable called 'My_Variable' is *passed over to the procedure* called 'My_Procedure'. As a copy of the original variable has been used, if this gets altered in the procedure, then *the original variable won't be altered*. Inside the procedure the variable is treated as **local**, which means that the other variable with the same name outside of this procedure won't get changed. This is a good idea if different programmers are working on different modules. They can use the same variable names used by others, so long as it is local to their procedure.

It is also possible to **pass by reference**, as shown in the following example:

```
Sub My_Procedure(My_Variable as Integer)
          . 'Other code goes here'
End Sub
```

The word 'ByRef' is not used. This is the default way VB passes variables to procedures. The original variable is **referenced**, and is thus irrevocably altered by this procedure. In this case the variable is **global**, as all instances of the use of this variable throughout the entire program will be altered. You declare global variables at the start of a program. This makes it unlikely that you will use the same name again for something entirely different.

Example

Using a high-level language with which you are familiar, explain how you make a pattern similar to that shown in Figure 6.1.

Solution

VB is used here. The graphic is made up from four similar graphics shown in Figure 6.2.

When working out complex programming problems, always use a paper and pencil to make sure you can do it. It is then easier to tell the computer what to do.

Visit our portal for the VB code for the solution to the curve stitching problem.

If you have time, code these examples on a computer in a language of your choice. It will help you to understand the principles.

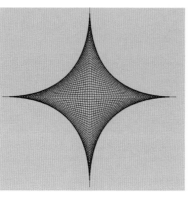

Figure 6.1 A curve-stitching pattern.

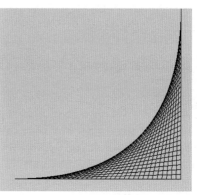

Figure 6.2 4 similar curves are used.

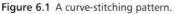

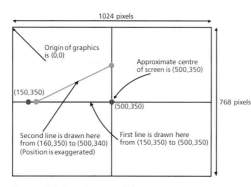

Figure 6.3 Starting conditions.

We thus solve 4 similar problems.

Figure 6.2 is made up from a series of straight lines, drawn from different starting and stopping points on the *x*-*y* axis. Our routine must draw a single line of given length, then alter the start and stop points, and draw the line again. This is continued until the desired number of lines has been drawn. We will assume a screen resolution of 1024 by 768 pixels. Positive values of *x* go horizontally right, and positive values of *y* go vertically down. Therefore, a line drawn to the position (1000, 500) would go along 1000 and down 500 graphics units.

A typical start to the solution to the problem is shown in Figure 6.3.

To generate a line in Visual Basic is simple, and the following syntax is used.

```
Line (x1, y1) - (x2, y2)
```

(x1, y1) are the starting co-ordinates, and (x2, y2) are the end co-ordinates. Let's assume, for the sake of argument, that the co-ordinate pairs, shown in the following table, will be used as the start and end points for the lines generated in this quadrant:

Typical co-ordinates for the first quadrant	
Start	Stop
(150, 350)	(500, 350)
(160, 350)	(500, 340)
(170, 350)	(500, 330)
Etc.	Etc.
(490, 350)	(500, 10)
(500, 350)	(500, 0)

From this table you should be able to appreciate that the following loop structure mirrors the patterns:

```
For x = 0 To 350 Step 10
    Line (150 + x, 350)-(500, 350 - x)
Next x
```

Using the same principles we end up with the following code:

```
Private Sub Form_Load()
    ScaleMode = vbPixels
    For x = 0 To 350 Step 10
        Line (150 + x, 350)-(500, 350 - x)
    Next x
    For y = 0 To 350 Step 10
        Line (500, y)-(500 + y, 350)
    Next y
    For x = 0 To 350 Step 10
        Line (150 + x, 350)-(500, 350 + x)
    Next x
    For y = 0 To 350 Step 10
        Line (500, 350 + y)-(850 - y, 350)
    Next y
End Sub
```

The above code has been embedded inside a procedure, and the scale mode has been set to pixels, so the co-ordinates mirror the problem.

Similar examples, making use of Pascal, can be found in chapter 13 of NUCSAL.

Self-test questions

1 Explain the difference between a function and a procedure.
2 By using pseudocode, or a language of your choice, write two functions to work out the area and circumference of a circle.
3 The IF-THEN structure is a common selection structure. Using a language of your choice, or otherwise, suggest one other type of selection structure.
4 Explain the difference between passing by value and passing by reference when a procedure is called. Give an example of each using a language of your choice.

In this unit you have learned about:

- Programming concepts like iteration (loops), selection (IF, THEN, ELSE) functions and Procedures
- Parameter passing by reference and value,
- How some of these techniques may be put into practice

7 Programming fundamentals 3

In this section you will learn about:

- String functions
- Data structures including binary trees and queues

String functions

A **string** is a set of **alphanumeric characters**. Processing strings is a common operation.

Example

Using a high-level language with which you are familiar, explain how to input a string of words, and output the words in reverse order, e.g. input any string like:
`"hey diddle diddle the cat had a fiddle"`
Then reverse the order of the string as follows:
`"fiddle a had cat the diddle diddle hey"`

Solution

Revision of this material is difficult if you have not done much programming on a computer. If you have time, try out these examples using the language which you have available.

Program flowcharts sometimes help to code problems like these; you can find extra examples in chapter 7 of NUCSAL.

The code for the solution to the reverse-string problem can be found on our web site.

The analysis concentrates on finding words in the string. Words are separated by spaces. We start at the end of the string, and count back until a space is found. This is a word boundary. We feed this word into the final string at the beginning. We carry on in this way, adding the next-to-last word from the input string as the second word to the output string etc. Let us call the input string Target$. We move 'right to left' using a for-to-next loop with a **negative step increment**. The following code does this:

```
For x = Len(Target$) to 1 step -1
(Other code to go in here)
Next x
```

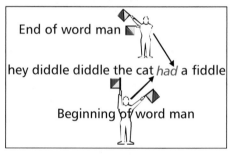

Figure 7.1 Flags for positional information.

Consider the familiar concept of using a 'flag' as shown in Figure 7.1. The man at the top has placed his flag at the end of the word. The man at the bottom has placed his flag where he has found the next space. The beginning of the word can be deduced from this by adding one to this position. The 'end of word man' can also deduce the next position to which he must go by asking the 'beginning of word' man.

If we use a loop to go from the right to the left of the string, and use 'MidString' to extract the word, then we have to maintain and modify the values of the flags as we are going along. The following code carries out the algorithm:

```
Private sub Form Load()
  Target$ = "hey diddle diddle the cat had a fiddle"
  End_of_word = Len(Target$)
  Beg_of_word = Len(Target$)
  For x = Len(Target$) To 1 Step -1
    Test$ = Mid(Target$, x, 1)
    If Test$ = " " Then
      Beg_of_word = x + 1
      Final$ = Final$ + Mid(Target$, Beg_of_word,
            End_of_word - Beg of word + 1) + " "
      End of word = Beg_of_word - 1
```

```
      End If
   Next x
   Print Final$ + Left(Target$, End_of_word)
   'Gets the first word of the string which can't be
   'extracted using the code in the main routine.
 End sub
```

You should be able to establish how the algorithm works from this code. The final part captures the first word, which is not picked up by the rest of the algorithm because there is no space for which we can search at the beginning of the Target string. However, the End-of-word flag still matches the end of the last word, and the beginning of the first word is always the beginning of the string, so the left$ function will mop up this special case rather nicely.

Binary tree structures

A **tree structure** is similar to a family tree, with parents and children, as shown in Figure 7.2.

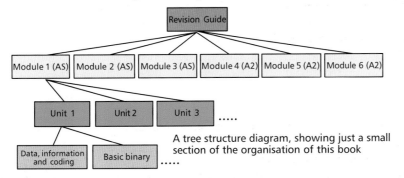

A tree structure diagram, showing just a small section of the organisation of this book

Figure 7.2 A tree structure.

This tree diagram represents part of this revision guide. The guide is one of the **parents**, and the six AS and A2 modules are **children**. Each module has children of its own, being units in the book, and each unit also has children, being the sections within each unit. Each box in the diagram is called a **node**, with the children at the bottom of the diagram called **leaf nodes**. Branches from one node to the next are called **pointers**, because they help point to the next item. Different structures in real life can be mirrored with a tree, and many **algorithms** are developed from these.

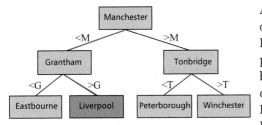

A binary tree structure showing place names inserted using alphabetical order.

Figure 7.3 A binary tree.

A binary tree is allowed to have a maximum of two children, as shown in Figure 7.3. Here Liverpool is being added. It is compared with 'Manchester', the first node, and because 'Liverpool < Manchester' alphabetically, we follow the '< M' pointer (branch). Liverpool is then compared with Grantham. Because 'Liverpool > Grantham' alphabetically, the right-hand path is followed. We finally arrive at a spare node. Liverpool is inserted as a leaf node in the appropriate place, shown by the red box.

Make sure that you understand these techniques. Without them you cannot answer questions using simple data structures like lists and trees.

Example

Explain how a binary tree might be used to search for an item of data. Why is this better than searching for data in a list?

Solution

Consider Figure 7.3. To search for Liverpool, we inspect the first node. This not being the target, we take the left-hand pointer (as L < M). Next inspect the Grantham node, and take the right-hand path (as L > G). We have then found the Liverpool node. This search took just two comparisons before finding the item of interest *because* structure has already been built up in this binary tree.

For a list, with 7 items of data, an average of 3.5 comparisons are needed. For very large lists, the binary tree search is much faster, because far fewer comparisons are made.

A linear queue

A **linear queue** is a data structure, which takes its name from the queue normally associated with a shop. If you are the first person in the queue, you would expect to be served first. Because the first in is the first out, this is also known as a **FIFO queue** or **FIFO stack**. Consider Figure 7.4(a). Seven memory locations have been set up for the purpose of a queue. At this moment in time the queue is empty. The start and stop pointers show the beginning and end of the queue. The start and stop pointers are in the same position and the queue is empty.

Consider Figure 7.4(b). We have four items (place names) after being pushed onto the stack.

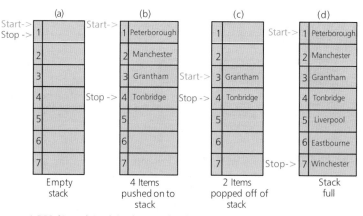

A FIFO (Queue) Stack implemented in the memory of a computer system

Figure 7.4 A queue set up in memory.

Peterborough occupies the position at the head of the queue, as indicated by the start pointer. Manchester is next, followed by Grantham, and finally Tonbridge, which occupies the end of the queue, indicated by the stop pointer.

Figure 7.4(c) shows when two items have been removed (served). Starting again, if the situation shown in Figure 7.4(d) occurs, there is no room left in memory, and the **FIFO stack**, or **queue**, is full. Start and stop pointers are managed as would be the case for a normal queue. Because of the way that the queue is organized inside the computer memory, the start and stop pointers may overlap.

Array data structures

An **array** is a one or more dimensional structure, which consists of elements referenced by subscripted variables. Consider the following list.

(12, 26, 32, 47)

We could represent each number by a variable like w, x, y and z, but we would soon run out of letters. A better way is to give the array a name, like A, for example, and refer to each element within the array as A(1), A(2), A(3) and A(4). In this way we can easily process the data making use of the familiar data structures and high-level language facilities already covered in unit 5. An array can easily be extended to two dimensions. Consider the following:

$$B = \begin{pmatrix} 12 & 26 & 32 & 47 \\ 18 & 44 & 21 & 89 \\ 43 & 97 & 0 & 36 \\ 13 & 17 & 64 & 90 \end{pmatrix}$$

This two-dimensional array called B has sixteen elements, contained in four rows and four columns. Conventionally the elements are referenced using the rows first, and the columns second, i.e. we use B(3, 2), to reference the number '97' because this is the number in the 3rd row and 2nd column.

Example

Using a high level language of your choice, explain how you might print out the contents of the array 'B' shown above. You may assume that all numbers contained in the array are integers, and that the data structure has already been set up.

Solution

A simple loop structure is all that is needed to print out the contents of the array called B. The code is as follows.

```
For x = 1 To 4
  For y = 1 To 4
    Print B(x, y)
  Next y
Next x
```

Visit our portal to get some further practice with similar algorithms.

Simple algorithms

An **algorithm** is the solution to a problem in a finite amount of time. It may be written down in many different forms, including **pseudocode** (a high-level language like structure), **flowcharts**, or may be **hand-written instructions**. You have already practised some simple algorithms in this unit, when printing out the contents of an array, printing lists in reverse order or searching for an item of data in a binary tree.

There are many standard algorithms in computing that have been developed over the years. For example, sorting names into alphabetical order, managing a circular queue, or calculating a factorial. In the early modules you would be expected to be able to **hand trace** an algorithm, by producing what is called a **dry run**. This is usually a tabular listing of the variables in the program. We then work through the code sequentially, and test to see if it works properly. As long as you are methodical in the way that you tackle the problem, these exercises are quite easy, if a little tedious.

Self-test questions

1 Write a routine that reads in a string of characters and prints the string in reverse.
2 Show how the following data types from MS Visual Basic language would be placed in a binary tree structure using the '>' or '<' rules for placing each node. The first word in the list forms the root of the tree.
   String, Currency, Decimal, Long, Variant, Integer, Double.
3 Suggest different practical examples of data that could ideally be stored in a one, two and three-dimensional array. Explain why each would be useful.
4 Suggest an algorithm for throwing two dice until a double six is rolled.
   Show your solution to this problem using two different methods.

In this unit you have learned about:

- Examples with strings
- Data structures like binary trees, linear queues and arrays
- How these programming techniques may be applied in practice

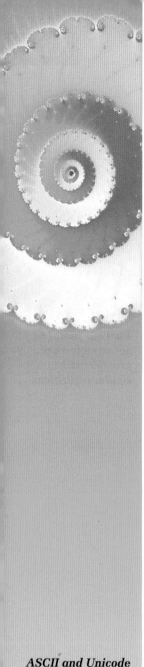

8 Communication basics

In this section you will learn about:

- Basic communications principles
- Serial and parallel transmission
- Methods of modulation
- Bit rates and baud rates
- Odd and even parity
- An introduction to communication protocols

Simple methods of communication

To transmit 'information' a change in state must occur. Changing the signal so that information can be transmitted is called **modulation**. The touch-tone phone is a good example of this, where different frequencies can be used to transmit the numbers being pressed. This is called **frequency modulation**.

Instead of altering the frequency we could alter the **amplitude** (as in AM radio stations), or alter the **phase** (the angle relative to some reference), hence the term **phase modulation**. We could code some pulses (**pulse code modulation**), determine the position of some pulses (**pulse position modulation**), or determine the width of pulses, which gives us **pulse-width modulation**.

Modern systems make full use of all of these methods, plus some others too, and *combinations of these methods* make for some very interesting modulation systems, as is witnessed by the current methods for **MODEM** communication in computers.

Classification of simple transmission systems

Simplex is the name given to a system capable of tr͟ ͟smitting in one direction only. **Duplex** is a system in which two-way communication is possible, but only one way at a time, and **full duplex** allows for simultaneous two-way communication.

Serial and parallel communications

ASCII and Unicode are covered in unit 1.

Transmitting data around the world is fundamental to the way in which society operates. You know about **ASCII** and **Unicode**, and should realise that ASCII represents a single character by using 1 byte. If we wish to send a character from point A to point B, then 8 wires would be needed, if all the bits were to arrive simultaneously. This method of transmitting data over lots of wires simultaneously is called **parallel data communication**, and is ideal for the bus systems inside a computer.

It is not easy (not to mention the expense!) to run so many individual wires across large distances, and so data has to be sent **serially**, or *one bit after the other*. This has to be reassembled at the other end, to turn it back into the bytes, which represent the actual information. Such a method of data transmission is called **serial data communication**, and is the method used for the vast majority of computer communication systems on **LANs** and the **internet**.

Synchronous and asynchronous data communications

Parallel communication of data usually happens under the direction of the **clock**, and therefore all the timing is **synchronised**. When different computers talk to each other via long distances like the Internet, there is no way for them to be able to synchronise in this way. The serial *method* of data transmission is therefore called **asynchronous data transmission**.

Example

Explain how the use of start and stop bits helps to transmit data when the data is being transmitted asynchronously.

Solution

Data from one system can arrive at any time without warning. Therefore, a method of letting the receiving device know that something's coming is essential. This is the idea of the start bit, as shown in Figure 8.1.

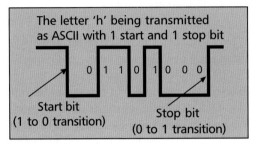

The receiving electronics is 'woken up' by the start bit going from one to zero. Assuming that the **baud rate** is set correctly, then the receiving electronics can clock in the next 8 bits (assuming ASCII, for example, as in Figure 8.1), and the stop bit will return the system to its original level, ready for another start bit to come along. In this way the asynchronous data may be received with few chances of error.

Figure 8.1 Start and stop bits are used to provide timing for the asynchronous data.

Baud rates and bit rates

Serial data (i.e. most long-distance computer communications) must be sent at exactly the right rate (bit/sec), or errors will occur in interpretation of the bit patterns. Although not strictly correct, it has been common for a long time to use **bit rate** and **baud rate** to represent the same thing. Nevertheless, clever encoding methods, using a combination of modulation techniques, mean that *more bits/sec* can be transmitted than would be indicated by the baud rate alone. Hence we also have the term **bit rate**. **Baud rate** is the number of **signal transitions(changes)/sec**, and **bit rate** is the number of **actual bits transmitted each second**. For A level specifications, remember these definitions and you will not go wrong.

Due to the inclusion of the **start** and **stop bits**, and other possible **overheads**, the actual information transmitted is slightly less than might be assumed by looking at the bit rate alone. Other ways of measuring the speed could be **characters/sec**, or **information rate/ unit time**.

Make sure you know the difference between bit rate (bits/sec) and baud rate (signal transitions/sec). Modern modems use these complex modulation methods.

How to get more bits per baud!

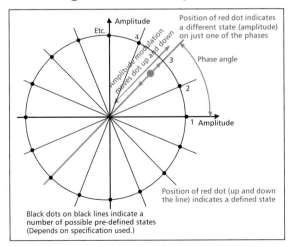

Figure 8.2 One of the clever methods of modulation giving you more bits/sec.

Using conventional modulation techniques means that **baud rate** has been synonymous with **bit rate**. However, it is possible to combine different methods of modulation, like different phases and amplitudes, for example, to create different states. Imagine a two dimensional co-ordinate system, as shown in Figure 8.2.

Each black line around the circle represents a different phase angle, and hence a different useable phase for modulation purposes in this particular system. We can also amplitude modulate each signal, and this

Much more detail on modulation techniques can be found in chapter 5 of NUCSAL.

would create a number of different amplitude positions, as indicated by the red dot on one of the phases, also shown in red. We could detect many positions of the red dot (amplitude), but here we will stick to the defined position/s shown in Figure 8.2. Using this system we now have 16 different defined states, which could correspond to the bit patterns shown in Table 8.1. This modulation technique, where both amplitude and phase are used to define a set of positions on a two-dimensional lattice is called **Quadrature Amplitude Modulation** or **QAM**.

Table 8.1 Each of the phases in Figure 8.2 may represent these bit patterns

State	Bit pattern for each state			
1	0	0	0	0
2	0	0	0	1
3	0	0	1	0
4	0	0	1	1
5	0	1	0	0
6	0	1	0	1
7	0	1	1	0
8	0	1	1	1
9	1	0	0	0
10	1	0	0	1
11	1	0	1	0
12	1	0	1	1
13	1	1	0	0
14	1	1	0	1
15	1	1	1	0
16	1	1	1	1

We have encoded 4 bits (the columns in the truth table), by using just one of the phase signals (just one signal only need be sent at any one time). The baud rate (state changes) might be only 2.4 Kbit/sec, for example, but the actual bit rate is $4 \times 2.4 = 9.6$ Kbit/sec, because we are 'transmitting' 4 bits for each phase change. This is the system used on the V series for modems, and is the reason why we have the ability to transmit data down a standard telephone signal (having a baud rate of only 3 KHz) at 56 Kbit/sec. The frequencies are cleverly arranged so they generate hardly any extra demands on the frequency spectrum.

Example

Explain the difference between baud rate and bit rate.

Solution

The baud rate is the number of signal transitions/sec, which, for simple modulation techniques, is often the same as the bit rate. However, if you use a more complex method of modulation, like QAM, for example, then it is possible to transmit more bits/sec than would be apparent by examination of the available baud rate. The bit rate is the actual bits/sec transmitted, which may be several times higher than the baud rate if these clever methods are used.

Techniques described in this unit are fundamental to communication between computers, and hence to the operation of the Internet. These are important concepts.

As the methods of modulation become increasingly complex, the possibility of errors in the data transmitted becomes ever greater.

Simple methods of error detection

You will recall that if the extended ASCII character set is *not* used, then only the least significant 7 digits are needed to represent the data being transmitted. If the top bit is not set, then this leaves us with the ability to use it for error detection purposes. There are two simple systems in operation, called **odd** and **even parity**. We can transmit the message 'hello', using ASCII, as shown in Table 8.2:

Table 8.2

The message 'hello' with no parity								
	128	64	32	16	8	4	2	1
h	–	1	1	0	1	0	0	0
e	–	1	1	0	0	1	0	1
l	–	1	1	0	1	1	0	0
l	–	1	1	0	1	1	0	0
o	–	1	0	1	1	1	1	1

If we use the top bit (128's column) as a **parity bit**, then, making sure that there are an even number of 1s in each row determines the setting of this bit. A '1' is added here if we need to make the number of 1s even.

Table 8.3

	128	64	32	16	8	4	2	1
	The message 'hello' with even parity							
h	1	1	1	0	1	0	0	0
e	0	1	1	0	0	1	0	1
l	0	1	1	0	1	1	0	0
l	0	1	1	0	1	1	0	0
o	0	1	0	1	1	1	1	1

When the message is received, a **parity check** is done on the data to see if there is still an even number of 1s in each byte received. If there are, it is assumed to be correct, if not, an error has occurred during the transmission of the data. **Odd parity** is the same idea, but an odd number of 1s is used instead.

Communication protocols

Many different **protocols** exist – these are the rules, which bodies like the **International Standard's Organisation (ISO)** agree upon. The layered ISO Open Systems Interconnection for transmission over networks is covered in unit 58. Some of the other familiar protocols, are **HTTP** (the Hyper Text Transfer Protocol), which enables web browsers to communicate with HTTP servers on the internet, or **FTP** (the File Transfer Protocol), which enables files to be copied from one computer to another over an LAN or the internet. *Without protocols you would not be able to send information from one computer to a different type of computer very easily.*

Self-test questions

1 Briefly, what is the difference between serial and parallel communication methods? Give two different situations in which each method of communication would be preferable over the other, stating why this is so.
2 Explain the difference between asynchronous and synchronous transmission methods.
3 The telephone line is capable only of transmitting signals at a few KHz. How is it possible for modern modems to achieve data transfer rates which hitherto would have been thought impossible?
4 Detecting errors in data transmission is important for data integrity. Outline how the use of parity enables the errors to be reduced. Why are more sophisticated methods needed when transmitting over the internet?
5 The trouble with standards is that there are so many of them! Why are there so many communication protocols for transmitting data between computers?

In this unit you have learned about:

- Basic communication techniques such as serial and parallel data transmission, bit rates and baud rates
- Simple error-detection methods such as odd and even parity
- Why communication protocols are needed for communication between computers

9 Networking basics

LANs and WANs are all-pervasive in modern computing. The material in this unit is of fundamental importance.

Local area networks LANs

A computer network is the connection of computers, enabling **common resources** such as **printers** and **file servers** etc. to be shared. The **topology** of the network refers to the physical connection of the wires, and common layouts are **bus**, **ring**, **star** and **tree**. A simplified layout for each **network topology** is shown in Figure 9.1.

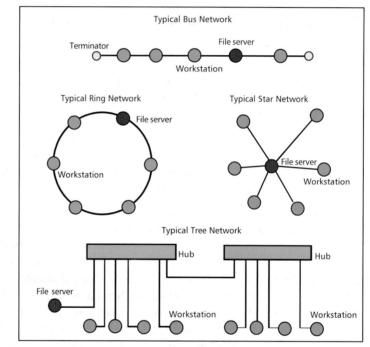

Figure 9.1 Different network topologies.

These are common examples of **local area networks** or **LANs**. They typify networks that under the control of a local organisation, spreading over a few hundred metres or just a few kilometres. Compare and contrast these with **wide area networks** or **WANs**, which use *public communication systems*.

Example

Why are bus and ring networks the least secure of the network topologies? Which is most secure? The tree network is currently the most common Ethernet network. Why is it so versatile and easy to use?

Solution

The bus and ring networks are the least secure, because information, intended for one machine must pass all the others. Hackers can gain access to the passing packets of information.

The star network is the most secure, because information from the file server goes only to the machine for which it is intended. The security of the file server is high.

The tree network is most popular as it is very versatile. More hubs may be added, and high bandwidths may be maintained between each machine and the hub. Auto sensing hubs mean that 10 Mbit/sec and 100 Mbit/sec networks may be joined, and other equipment such as routers and switches etc. adds to the versatility.

Wide area networks (WANs)

A **wide area network**, or **WAN** typifies a network that makes use of the national and global networks provided by the telecom companies. When using the internet, you are making use of a WAN. British Telecom and cable companies are now installing very high bandwidth links making use of **fibre optics**, and **satellite**. This enables faster computer communications via WANs.

Example

Explain the hardware and software that would be needed to connect a computer to the following:

(a) A local area network (LAN)   **(b) A wide area network (WAN)**

Solution

(a) To connect a computer to an LAN involves plugging in a **Network Interface Card (NIC)**. This is a piece of hardware, which enables you to connect to a typical LAN like Ethernet, for example.

You need an **operating system** that supports networking (most modern ones do), and in addition some software called a **network card driver**, which usually comes with the NIC, or can be downloaded from the internet. This software provides the interface between the card and the operating system.

Always check that you have the latest versions of software drivers. This could be one reason why recently purchased hardware may not work.

(b) To connect a computer to a WAN would need either a **MODEM**, or an **ISDN terminal adaptor**. There are other ways of doing this too, like megabit MODEMS for **ADSL** links or special cards for **satellite links**, but MODEMs and ISDN lines are typical at the time of writing. These devices change the signals into the form required for transmission over the WAN. The MODEM modulates the signal so that signals can be transmitted over an analogue phone line, and the ISDN line changes the signals so that they can be transmitted digitally. You will need specialist driver software for the particular MODEM or ISDN terminal adaptor, and this usually accompanies the hardware when purchased.

Packet switched networks

When you use the conventional telephone system, you normally have a **dedicated circuit** (line), which is in use all of the time. It does not matter if you stop talking for a few seconds; the line is still occupied, until you hang up. This is **circuit switching**, and is *not* efficient for computer communications.

It is more efficient for a computer to use the line only when needed, thus releasing the same line for other communications. A pause of a few seconds means that data from other computers can be sent down the *same* line. To stop one computer from hogging the line by sending enormous amounts of data in one go, the size of the data is limited to smaller **packets**, and this is called **packet switching**.

More information about networks can be found in chapter 3 of NUCSAL.

Appropriate **protocols** ensure that the packets are assembled correctly at one end, and disassembled correctly at the other. *Any available route may be used to send a packet, and different packets, intended for the same destination, may be routed differently.*

Mobile phones

To make the use of millions of mobile phones possible, countries have been divided up into smaller geographical areas called **cells**, hence the name **cellular network**. The idea is shown in Figure 9.2. The relatively small areas called cells are shown by the hexagons. The enlarged view shows a mobile user communicating with the base station located in one particular cell.

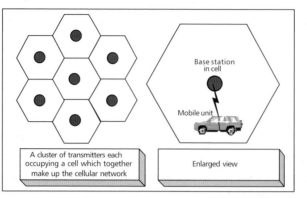

Different frequencies, used in one cell, can be used again in cells far enough away. In this way signals do not interfere with each other. When travelling between cells, the phone you are using may have to adapt to a new frequency, and all without the user noticing.

Figure 9.2 The idea of the cellular network.

The virtual private network (VPN)

You already know about **LANs** and **WANs**, and should appreciate how it is possible, via a mobile phone, to access the internet. The next extension is to be able to access a private LAN remotely via the internet i.e. to make use of the internet (or WAN) as though it were part of your own private local area network. This is obviously desirable but there are implications regarding security, and extra hardware and software are needed for this system to be effective. *If the appropriate encryption security measures are taken, then the system can be as safe as though the user were using a private line.* Such a system is called a **virtual private network** or **VPN**.

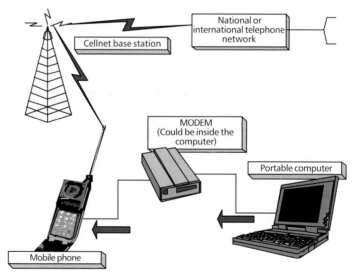

Figure 9.3 Portable connects via a mobile.

It is the security aspects of a VPN, which really make it what it is. For example, a company called V-One Corporation produces a system called SmartGate. This requires users, who are remotely logging into the LAN via the internet, to provide both a **token** and a **pass code**. The servers also verify the user, and appropriate **encryption** is used to ensure privacy. **VPNs** allow businesses to set up systems, so that employees, customers and other authorised companies may carry out effective **e-commerce** in a safe and secure manner, making use of **intranets** and the **internet**.

Visit our portal to find out about VPNs and to see a simple simulation of a VPN.

Internet resources

The ultimate use of networks at the time of writing is the **internet**. You should have made extensive use of it, and probably now take it for granted. However, for the purposes of 'AS' level, you need to know a little about the organisation of the **world wide web** (the *pages* on the **internet**).

Each **resource** on the WWW needs to have a unique address, and its **URL** or **uniform resource locator** gives this. A URL includes the protocol like **http** or **ftp** etc., and the server, on which the resource is located. For example, the Microsoft site is as follows:

http://www.microsoft.com

This is far easier than using the *actual address* of the Microsoft site, which is 1.0.187.33. It is these numbers that are key in routeing to sites on the world wide web. This is the **internet protocol (IP) address**, which uniquely identifies a computer on the internet. This is a 32-bit address, specified as 4 bytes. It is this data that helps route the packets of information mentioned earlier.

You should be able to work out that just over 4 billion unique addresses can be used. However, if washing machines and microwaves have their own addresses, as is currently being proposed for control purposes, we will begin to run out of these 4-byte numbers. Fortunately, machines on local area networks hide behind a proxy server, which connects the LAN to the internet, and therefore local addresses would not clash with those being used in the outside world.

Self-test questions

1 Outline the advantages of a star network compared to a bus or tree (hubs) network from a security point of view.
2 What is a VPN and why are they useful?
3 Why is packet switching better than circuit switching for computer communications?
4 What are the main differences between a WAN and an LAN?
5 Explain what is meant by e-commerce, and why encryption is essential for this technology.
6 What is meant by the term protocol? Name three other protocols in use on the World Wide Web apart from http.
7 What could happen if a VPN had no protection from a firewall?

In this unit you have learned about:

- LAN topologies, WANs and LANs
- The difference between **circuit** and **packet switching**
- The **cellular network**
- **VPNs**
- The advantages and disadvantages of **networking**

10 A first look at operating systems

In this section you will learn about:

- What operating systems do
- Different types of operating system
- User interfaces and utilities
- Command-based and GUI operating systems

The role of an operating system

The operating system is an extremely complex piece of software, which turns the raw hardware of the computer into a useful and easy-to-use device. Without the operating system there would be no software to interpret and process the characters typed in at the keyboard, or display the graphics on the screen; without the operating system you would not even be able to format a disk, or drive a printer attached to your computer.

Lots of help with DOS commands can be found by looking in the Windows' help files on the latest windows systems.

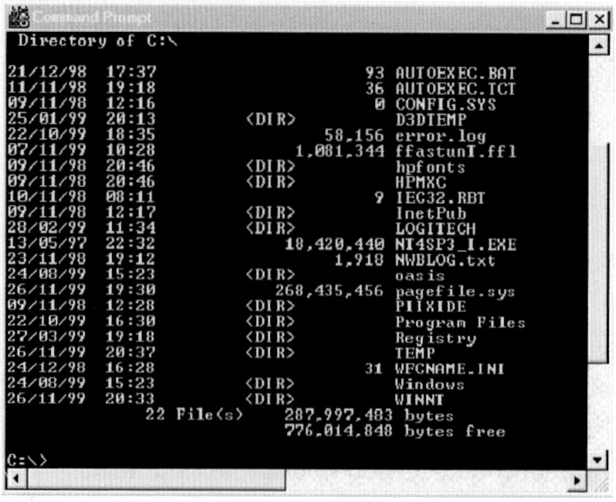

Figure 10.1 The root of a C drive, displayed by issuing a 'DIR' command from DOS.

Operating systems like the early versions of **DOS (Disk Operating System)** were quite rudimentary, and **command-line** driven. This means that the user of the system had to remember lines of code that had to be typed in, with the object of performing similar functions to those performed using the mouse and windows environments of today. A typical DOS screen, listing some files and directories, is shown in Figure 10.1.

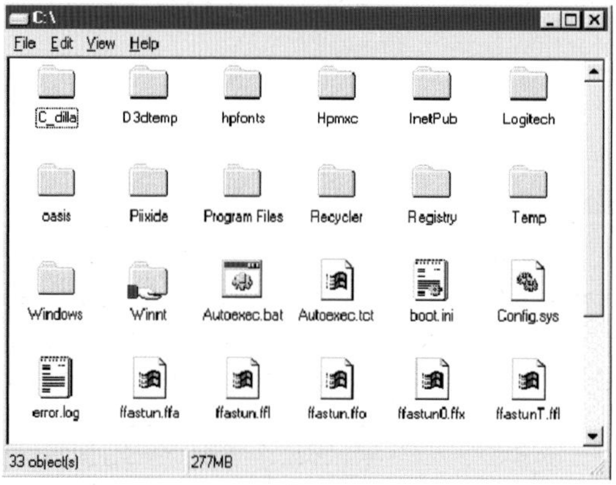

Figure 10.2 Part of the root of the same C drive catalogued via Windows.

After the command 'DIR' has been issued at the **DOS prompt** (i.e. the 'C:\>' bit), the folders and files in the root of the C drive can be seen. Contrast this with the Windows display, which can be seen in Figure 10.2.

Figure 10.2 shows the more familiar **GUI (Graphical User Interface)** based interface presented by **Windows**. **MSDOS** is an example of a **Command Language** system, and **Windows** is an example of a **GUI**. However, do not dismiss DOS or other command-line based operating systems as old fashioned and useless, *they are essential*, even in the most modern operating systems like **Windows 2000**. As you can see from the above, the operating system not only performs vital functions like listing the files on the drive, but *also gives the computer its character*. The all-important operating system is fundamental, and the concept is called a **virtual machine**.

Visit our portal to find out about current operating systems.

Example

Give an example of why it is still necessary to keep the command-driven aspects of an operating system, even when you have access to a powerful GUI-based system.

Solution

It is useful for a computer administrator to carry out similar sets of commands in a **batch**. Creating new users on a file server would be a particularly good example. Figure 10.3 shows a typical windows-based screen, into which information like 'username', 'password', and other information must be typed.

It is very easy to perform the above operations, but can you imagine doing this for 1500 different pupils in a school? It would take many days to enter the data in this way! It is far better to extract the pupils' names from the school database, and merge them with appropriate **batch commands** to perform the above operations automatically. That is the power of an operating system that supports command lines, and that's just one of the many hundreds of reasons why they are still needed.

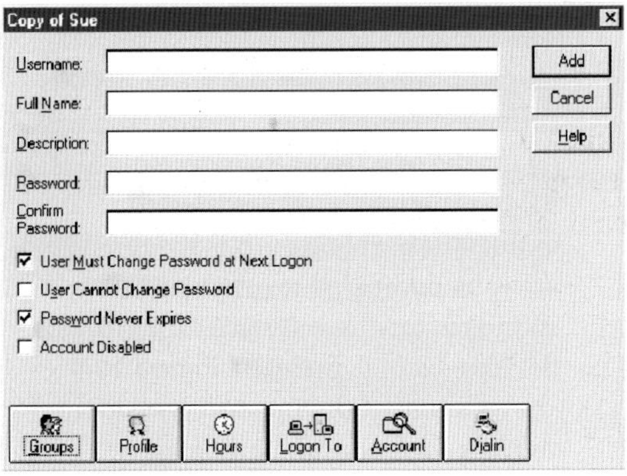

Figure 10.3 Creating users on an NT 4 server.

You can get practice with batch files by utilising the DOS prompt from windows. Some examples are shown on our web portal.

Job control

Some operating systems allow the computer operator to control **jobs** (tasks to be run) by issuing a set of **commands**. Operating systems, which allow the facility of scheduling a set of pre-determined jobs, and then providing the results at some later stage are said to be running in **batch-processing mode**. This is typical of the **BACS** system, for example.

Operating system classification

The main categories, into which operating systems may be classified, are as follows:

- Batch
- Interactive
- Network
- Real time

Batch typifies the operating system where a number of jobs may be run one after the other. Compare this to the **interactive** nature of **Windows**, where the user gets an 'instant' response. The **network operating system** supports the activities necessary to log onto file servers, share printers with colleagues over a network or get access to the internet via a proxy server. Finally, there are **real time operating systems**, which are used in mission-critical applications, where a response is essential within a specific period of time. Such a system might be employed in the control of missiles or the control of some industrial plant. **Real-time systems** are also used in situations like booking tickets, where absolute speed is not vital, but a sensible response time is.

Further information about operating systems can be found in chapters 22 and 23 of NUCSAL.

Visit our portal to find examples of real-time on-line booking systems used by the travel business.

Resource management

One of the major tasks of an operating system is to manage the available resources such as **memory**, or **processor time**. For example, if you are loading a picture into an art package, the size of which is larger than the available amount of RAM inside your computer, the operating system will cope by pretending that parts of your hard disk are available RAM (called **disk caching**).

You may be using a spreadsheet at the same time as printing out one of your word processor documents – how is the processor time allocated between these two tasks? If insufficient processing power is allocated to the WP task, you will find that you will not be able to type very fast!

Example

How does the operating system manage the computer's memory to help organise different hardware attached to the system. How might the memory be organised to run application programs like DTP systems and spreadsheets at apparently the same time?

Solution

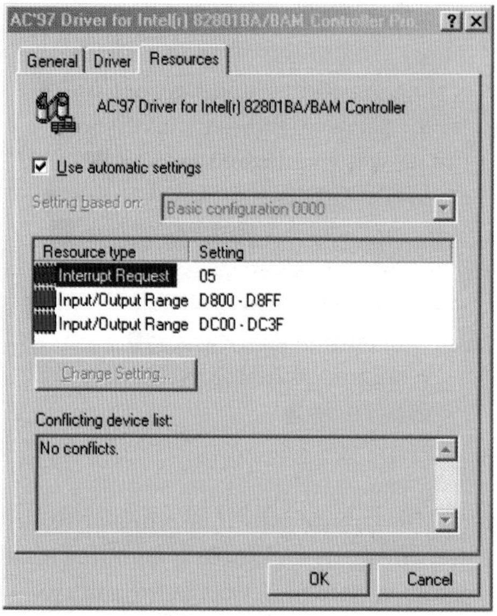

The available ROM and RAM must be mapped out into specific areas. This is called a **memory map**. Some areas will be for the storage of the operating system itself, others will be allocated to application programs. It is essential that areas be dedicated to graphics and sound, or for the interface of peripheral devices such as printers. Figure 10.4 shows some of the operating-system settings for a sound card on a PC.

These numbers act as pointers to other places in memory where parts of the operating system (code), which actually handle these devices, are located. Application programs must be allocated their own areas of memory. Failure to do this would mean that memory space in use by one application would corrupt memory space being used by another, and the computer would fail to operate correctly. It is the job of the operating system to allocate memory on the fly, so that when memory being used by one application is released, it is automatically available to be used by another.

Figure 10.4 Memory map settings.

Multi-user operating systems

Operating systems may be **single user**, like a typical PC at home, or **multi-user**, where more than one person (usually many more) can use the *same computer* at apparently the same time. Sometimes it is confusing for students to determine if an operating system is multi-user or not. If, for example, a network uses **fat-clients** (i.e. a typical PC being attached to a network), then the user of the PC has exclusive use of the operating system on his or her PC. The fact that you have a network connection means that you can share data with others, but others are not sharing your operating system inside your machine.

The term multi-user is not normally reserved for different people using the same PC in the ways described above. It is reserved for lots of people making simultaneous use of a larger system. For example, if you are running a thin-client system, where the local machines attached to the network have no local drives, and a large file server processes the requests from all of the users 'simultaneously', then this is an example of a multi-user operating system. On this sort of system, if there are 20 users, then each user will have to wait in turn until the operating system gets round to dealing with them.

Example

Explain the difference between a thin-client system and a fat-client system, indicating some relative advantages and disadvantages of each type of architecture.

Solution

A **fat client** is the name given to a standard PC attached to a network. The PC will have a network operating system like Windows, have its own local hard disks, and its own local processor etc. It is usual to load applications from the local hard disk, although the file server can be used for application delivery too, and the network is used only for sharing common resources like printers, and for storing the users' files and other information on a file server. The biggest disadvantage with this system is that it is harder to maintain, because all the local hard disks throughout the organisation have to be updated when changes are made.

The alternative is to use a **thin-client** operating system. Here there is little local processing power, other than the ability to interpret characters at the keyboard, and drive the display on the monitor. There are no local hard disks, and often there is no floppy disk either! All processing is done by sending information back to the operating system on the file server, which in turn processes it and sends it back to the client workstation to be displayed on the screen. This system is very easy indeed to maintain, as there is virtually nothing that can go wrong with the thin-client workstation. However, a large bandwidth is needed and graphics processing can often bring the system to a halt.

Vist our portal to find out about thin clients.

Self-test questions

1 Name two different types of command-language operating systems.
2 Distinguish between batch and real-time operating systems, giving an example of each.
3 Give three different examples of resources that are managed by the operating system.
4 How might an operating system manage the security of files on a file server?
5 What is meant by a multi-user system?
6 State two advantages of a fat client over a thin client.
7 State two advantages of a thin client over a fat client.
8 A user, with a single processor inside his computer, is arguing that he can do more than one thing at a time because many things are happening on screen 'at the same time'. Why is this logic flawed?
9 Why is running a batch of commands useful for network administration?

In this unit you have learned about:

- The classification of operating systems into batch, interactive, real time and network
- GUI and command-line systems
- How the operating system manages resources like memory and carries out the management of multi-user systems

11 Operating system security and management

In this section you will learn about:

- Further operating-system concepts like security
- Time and resource management
- Auditing
- Specialist operating systems like process-control

File security

Operating systems allow you to **control access** to resources and **audit** the systems in real time. In a **multi-user environment** it is essential for security reasons to control access to files, or everybody would be able to read and delete the work belonging to other people! In the Windows NT4 operating system, this can be achieved by setting certain attributes for each file on the system.

If possible, get your network administrator at school or college to demonstrate aspects of network security like file permissions and log-on hours.

Figure 11.1 shows that permissions may be set on selected items. This might be a single file, or hundreds of Mbytes of directories and sub directories within the hierarchical data structure of the file-server disks. You can specify who may **read** or **change** the files, who may **delete** the files, or who may **run executables**, for example. You can get the operating system to build up a **log** of who does what, where and when! You can also **audit events** such as printing, so that charges may be made on the number of print outs that are done, or you may charge for the time that a particular person is logged onto the system. Indeed, you can control the exact time when people may use the system, all from similar panels in the operating system.

Figure 11.1 NT4's security tag.

Such **permissions**, applied to the C drive of a workstation, can be used to make sure that users do not inadvertently (or deliberately!) delete files or programs that would render the system unusable. For this reason, *less secure* operating systems like **Windows 98** or **Windows Me**, for example, could be rendered ineffective very quickly in environments like schools, colleges and businesses.

If you have your own computer at home running Windows 2000, for example, you could set up some simple security yourself. However, don't lock yourself out of the system!

Example

Pupils in a school environment use the internet on a daily basis. What facilities provided by the operating system might prove useful in enabling the network administrator to monitor internet activity?

Solution

The network administrator could set up a log, which monitors all network activity regarding the internet. This is easy to set up if all students on the network log into the Internet via a **proxy server**. (This is now common in many schools.) If each student has to log on to use the system, then they have identified themselves to the proxy server, and the sites that they visit can be entered into a log, and saved on the proxy server by the operating system. The network administrator can then inspect the log and electronically search for any items of interest.

Time management

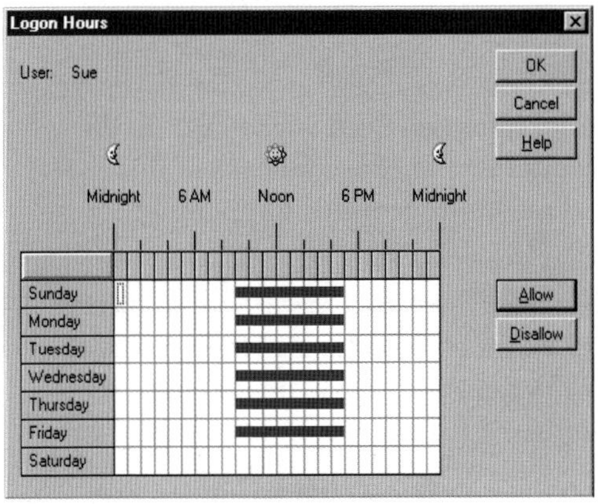

You can **account** for the use of **resources** such as **printing**, the **internet** and the **times** at which people may log onto the system. Access times can be controlled as shown in Figure 11.2.

This shows an NT4 file server being set up to allow a user called Sue, to log onto the system between 9.00 am and 5.00 pm only. If she attempted to log on outside of these hours the system would deny her access. It is also possible to disable an account completely.

Figure 11.2 Control of log-on hours.

Resource management

Other resources besides time are equally important. Printing, for example, can be audited via the help of the operating system. Each time a user uses a **network printer**, the job is **spooled** via the **file server**, and the number of pages printed is incremented in a **database**. Hundreds of users can be monitored printing to a huge variety of printers. Students could be charged for printing, and the statistics automatically exported to a database for efficient processing. In larger organisations it is more usual to charge **departments**.

Example

Suggest a way that an operating system might be able to allow some pupils access to the internet while not allowing others to use the programs from the same computer.

Solution

You could define the departments they are in, the year in the school to which they belong, or any other similar information. By inventing an internet group, it is possible to deny access to the programs or proxy servers needed to run the internet via a local area network.

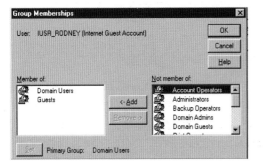

Making users members of a group, as shown in Figure 11.3, can give them access to certain resources. Defining the characteristics of a group can take a long time if the criteria are complex, but users can belong to many groups.

Figure 11.3 Assigning users to groups.

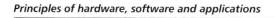
AS

Visit our portal to find out about quota management.

Access to resources management

By using a combination of **group** and **time management** outlined in the last couple of sections, it is possible to control exactly what is allowed at any particular time. This is ideal in an educational environment where you may want to deny pupils access to the internet or other software like games during a lesson.

Access to disk space

It is essential that **disk space** is **managed** effectively, and users are not allowed to save as much data as they wish. The operating system or third party software like Quota Manager, for example will manage this quite effectively. It is possible to allocate users a **fixed quota** of disk space, or allocate certain quotas to different groups within an organisation.

Example

Outline a scenario in which it is possible for an inexperienced user to fill up the hard drives on a network file server. What would be the consequences of this actually being carried out, and what can be done to prevent this happening?

Solution

A novice user might easily scan a high-quality 24-bit coloured image from a scanner, and attempt to save this huge file on the network file server. This image could be several Gbytes in size, and could fill up the entire disk on the main file server.

If this were to happen then no other person on the network would be able to save any work, and the whole system would be rendered virtually useless until the network manager or the pupil deleted the offending file.

Operating a quota for each user can prevent this happening. It is unlikely that the user would have several Gbytes of personal space on the network, and so would be prevented from saving this huge bitmap file.

Auditing the use of files

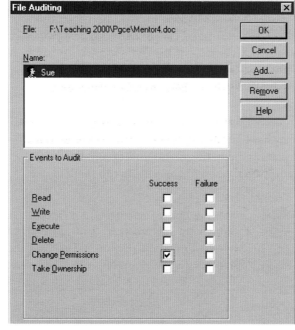

Figure 11.4 Auditing files.

Occasionally it might be necessary to track down who is making use of particular software. It is possible to put an **audit tag** onto any **file**, which means that if the file is accessed, then the user, the **time** and the **date** is noted in a **log** generated by the operating system. When the log is inspected, it is possible for the network manager to see which users have been using a particular resource.

Figure 11.4 shows a user called Sue, being monitored for applying a permission change to a particular file.

As you can see from the settings, a log entry will only be generated if she attempts to change the file permissions on this particular file.

Process-control operating systems

Some specialist operating systems are used in the **process-control** industry. These are the systems used to control processes like **manufacturing**, **power plant**, **chemical processes** and utilities such as **water treatment**. These operating systems must usually respond in **real time**, but these times need not necessarily be lightning quick. As long at the data being received by the sensors is processed in time to be useful.

Typical **real-time systems** of the sort described here are to be found in **missile control systems**, in **aircraft control** and **other time-critical computer-controlled systems**. In these systems **reliability** is of extreme importance, and this usually outweighs the consequences of cost. The term **real-time operating system** is also used in less demanding scenarios. The best definition of a real-time operating system is, therefore, *one that can respond to externally dictated inputs and provide outputs in a satisfactory amount of time.*

More information on real-time systems and process control can be found in chapter 8 of NUCSAL.

Visit our web site for examples of process control.

Self-test questions

1 Explain the need for file security in a network environment.
2 Outline three different things that you may be able to do to enhance the security of a file. Give a practical example of where each of your file-security measures may be useful.
3 When dealing with time-management aspects, it is sometimes useful for the operating system to allow log on only between set times. However, if you are already logged on, most systems will not automatically log people off. If this proved to be unsatisfactory, what else could you do to make sure that the users were safely logged off under controlled conditions?
4 A large company wants members of different departments to have different security and access rights on the network. What features of the operating system might enable a network manager to accomplish this task?
5 Even though all the security permissions have been set correctly, information from a file seems to have been accessed illegally from time to time. What features of the operating system might enable a network manager to track down who is getting illegal access to this file?
6 A legal problem has arisen regarding who made alterations to a word processor document. Assuming that auditing is carried out on all file accesses, how might this enable the company to resolve who actually carried out the alterations?
7 A process-control or real-time operating system often has to have added features and reliability. Give two examples of a real-time system where reliability would be of paramount importance.
8 A real-time operating system does not necessarily have to respond very quickly. Give three examples of real time systems where a lightning fast response is not an issue.

In this unit you have learned about:

- File security
- How the operating system manages resources like time and audits the actions of users
- Principles of process control operating systems

12 Input techniques and data collection 1

In this section you will learn about:

- Input devices
- The relationship between these devices and data collection
- Practical scenarios involving the use of this technology

Input devices

Large ranges of input devices are available. *Be aware of the characteristics of each, and be able to make an informed choice regarding the suitability of each device for any given task.*

The keyboard

A variety of **keyboards** exist, ranging from **qwerty** layouts, through **natural keyboards** which helps to prevent **RSI (repetitive strain injury)**, to specialist keyboards (**concept keyboards**) often used in controlling industrialised plant. Speeds of input depend on the operator. **Control keys** and **function keys** can call up special functions.

Example

Outline one situation in which a specialist keyboard would be essential, saying *why* it is useful in your given scenario.

Solution

Web TV, such as might be used by Sky Digital viewers, requires a specialist keyboard for surfing and e-mail. Most people will use this keyboard in front of the TV, and it would be inconvenient if a wire were trailed around. Therefore, this particular keyboard has an infrared link to the set-top box. As the keyboard has been designed with on-line shopping and e-mail in mind, it is also able to double up as the remote control.

Make sure you understand the context in which each input device may be used, and be able to apply it to new situations.

Visit our portal to check out some of the latest keyboards.

Be aware of the limitations of input devices in terms of speed of operation, suitability for purpose and cost effectiveness.

Figure 12.1 A selection of keyboard layouts – English (UK) is the default.

Other layouts exist, like the azerty keyboard in France, or the specialist keyboards for use with Far Eastern languages. Figure 12.1 shows a very small selection of different English keyboard layouts.

Mice, trackballs and touchpads

Mice and associated devices have been around for a considerable time. Do not forget the many incarnations of these devices that make them particularly applicable to some situations. It might be inconvenient to use a mouse with a portable computer or PDA; therefore, an ordinary mouse would be inappropriate for data entry here. You must always think in terms of **ergonomics** and the **GUI**. In other words, what user interface is most appropriate?

Touch screens, pen-based input and PDAs

Mice, **keyboards**, **touch pads** and **trackballs** may be dispensed with altogether if a **touch screen** is used. Menu selections may be made with either a pen or the finger, pointing at a special screen. Larger touch-screen monitors tend to have a crisscross of infrared links, whereas smaller **PDAs (personal digital assistants)** tend to have pen-based input methods. Menu selections and handwriting may be input using a pen-based system.

Example

A building firm issues its employees with a device for logging the materials used and the progress made each day. This device is to be used in a harsh environment. Suggest a suitable method of inputting data.

Solution

A specialist portable computer or PDA with a touch screen and pen would be effective, but only if it was rugged enough to be dropped. An effective membrane barrier from the corrosive effects of building materials must be provided, and it should operate in the freezing temperatures likely to be encountered. In such a harsh environment, it is unlikely that the users would want to carry out any keystrokes, especially as they might be using a gloved hand. A pen-based system making use of a touch screen would therefore be very effective here. A gloved hand could easily hold the pen, and appropriate on-screen menus could provide the necessary options.

Graphics tablets

Artists are able to use this device as a more natural form of input compared to the mouse. Strokes made with a pen on a touch-sensitive pad can be used to mirror drawing on the screen. **Graphics tablets** are available in sizes ranging from A5 to A3 and beyond.

Joysticks and consoles

Do not dismiss **joysticks** as simply a method of playing games. There are many industrial uses, like controlling industrial plant, or manipulating molecular structures in a virtual environment, for example. There are many other incarnations of the joystick, and specialist consoles vary from interfaces for games, via specialist equipment to train pilots.

Bar codes

You need to know few details other than that different systems are used in the USA and Europe, and many different bar codes exist for different purposes, including some reserved for use within individual businesses. **Bar code systems** are also internationally recognised, like the ISBN number on a book. Bar codes are important for stock control, and speed up the queues at **EFTPOS** terminals. Various methods exist for reading bar codes, including **optical wands** (like a pen), **bar code scanners** (like a gun), and **scanning mechanisms** embedded into supermarket checkouts. **Barcodes** give **error-free input** if the scan is accepted due to the extensive **error checking**.

Example

How might bar codes be used to assign books and other media like video and music CDs to students in a school library?

Solution

If books have bar codes, then these can be used, together with the database on the computer, to identify the book being borrowed or returned. A bar code could also be used on a student ID card to identify the student who is undertaking the transaction.

Visit our portal for information on specialist flight control systems.

For information on force feedback joysticks and other input peripherals.

Other media like CDs and videos will probably have bar codes too, but if any item, like a map or a fossil, does not have a bar code, then the school can use special software to invent their own bar code, for use with this system.

Figure 12.2 shows Corel's Bar-Code Wizard start up screen. Using this software, schools can easily make their own bar codes.

OCR systems and scanners

A **flatbed scanner** is normally used for **optical character recognition**, often with a paper feed, so that multiple documents can be handled easily. Some software can handle multiple column pages, and will even navigate around pictures automatically. Typical scanning software is shown in Figure 12.3.

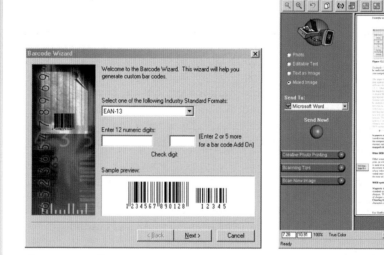

Figure 12.2 Making your own bar codes.　　**Figure 12.3** OCR scanning software.

Example

Explain the processes that have to be undertaken to turn a sheet of pre-typed text into computer-readable format.

Solution

The paper to be scanned is put into the scanner, and appropriate software is activated. (The HP software start up screen is shown in Figure 12.3.) After scanning the page it is usually in bit-mapped form, meaning that the whole page is treated like a picture. Next, select the appropriate area of the page for processing. Having selected the area, this is operated upon by pattern recognition software, which attempts to correlate the patterns in the picture with known text fonts. It is unlikely that all the text has been perfectly interpreted, and some text will need to be put though a spell-checking process. The user will be prompted to help the system if some of the text is unrecognisable. Manual intervention is normal when using OCR methods.

Scanners are the main methods for transferring **images** from the printed page into the computer. Remember that huge amounts of memory are required to store large **bit-mapped coloured images** at high resolutions.

More information about barcodes, OCR, MICR and OMR can be found in chapter 10 of NUCSAL.

Other OCR systems

Other systems like **turnaround documents** exist, in which **optical character recognition** is used in quite different ways. The turnaround document is ideal for bill payment systems, where information regarding a customer is coded onto the bill, and used for data input at the time of payment.

MICR systems

Magnetic ink character recognition (MICR) is the standard system used at the bottom of bank cheques. The clearing banks process millions of cheques each day (**Bank Automated Clearing System**). Extra magnetic ink characters are usually put onto the cheques representing the amount and other information, so the batch operation of clearing the cheques can be carried out automatically and quickly.

OMR systems

Multiple choice type answer sheets in examinations typify **optical mark reader** systems, also called **mark sense readers**. Marks, using an HB pencil or other suitable pen, are made in pre-set positions on a specially prepared sheet of paper. Do not forget that this form of input might be ideal for many forms of data capture in which answers to pre-set questions are required.

Key-to-disk systems

Some very large data-processing organisations need to enter huge amounts of data by manual methods. This technique enables many people to enter data at a computer terminal (hence the term **key**) straight onto **disk**, ready for processing at a later stage when all the data has been entered and correlated. It is possible to have the data **validated** or **verified** before being processed by the main computer system.

Self-test questions

1 Will the keyboard ever be completely replaced by voice input? Outline arguments both for and against.
2 Suggest some typical input peripherals for a PDA.
3 A WAP-enabled mobile phone is used for e-mail. What input device/s would make entry of text more convenient?
4 Outline two completely different uses of OCR techniques, suggesting where the use of each would be particularly appropriate.
5 OMR systems are used for examinations. Suggest two other uses to which these character sets can be put.
6 How is it possible for typed text to be input into a computer system so that it is in machine-readable format?
7 A joystick could play an important part in a flight simulator. Suggest three other input devices that might be useful in this context, outlining the role that would be played by each of your chosen devices.
8 Key-to-disk terminals are less used than they used to be. What is the modern equivalent?

In this unit you have learned about:

- A common range of input devices like keyboards, mice and bar codes
- OCR, OMR, and key to disk
- Typical uses of these devices in practice

13 Input techniques and data collection 2

In this section you will learn about:

- Video and speech input
- MIDI input
- Other data-collection methods
- Data capture forms and associated applications

Video input of data

Input of video images is now common. We can use a conventional **video camera**, but **digital video cameras** now mean we can download and process video images with little, if any, loss of quality. We also have an arsenal of **digital cameras**, and there are yet still more video image sources such as **DVDs**, **CD-ROMs** and the **internet**.

Powerful microcomputers are rewriting the book with regard to what users with modest amounts of money can do with **digital editing**. Whilst 'ordinary' micros are not yet up to the standard achieved by programs such as 'Walking with Dinosaurs' or films like 'Titanic' or 'The Matrix'; one day these facilities will be available on powerful home micros. The **post-production** list of software is equally impressive, varying from **non-linear editing** (i.e. assembling sequences of shots into any order), through the addition of **graphics** to the creation of **panoramic 360° shots**.

Example

A firm of estate agents have set up a database to help them sell houses. Explain how the use of 'video-capture techniques' might be helpful in maintaining information on this database.

Solution

A good-quality digital camera may be used as a mechanism for creating the pictures of the houses and inside rooms. This is ideal for an estate agent because there is no film processing involved in this exercise. Apart from static shots, video footage may be used to give a guided tour of the house, which may be replayed on a computer with a video player like Apple's QuickTime. With a suitable number of still images taken and stuck together, a '360° panoramic view' of a room or the garden, for example, may be created.

Speech input

Speech input is a perfectly usable system, provided that you have trained the software to recognise your voice, a task that usually takes a few hours. It is a bonus for disabled people, and effective for those who cannot type. Nevertheless, many people find it an unnatural form of input for many aspects of their work. For example, when writing this book, I spent much time thinking what to say, and changed my mind frequently. This methodology is more suited to the keyboard than speech input, especially when it comes to complex formatting of documents.

Speech input is an ideal form of **command-driven language**, leaving the operator with his or her hands free. In situations in which a computer must be controlled at the same time that manual tasks are being carried out, it is a vital form of data entry, and will certainly be used more extensively in the future.

Information regarding the relative speeds of modern input devices can be found in chapter 10 of NUCSAL.

MIDI

MIDI, the **Musical Instrument Digital Interface** is, of course, of use only to musicians, but if you are a musician, then this is the musical equivalent of your 'word processor'. The ability to play into a keyboard, and get the data into the computer in **real time** is a bonus. The ability to join together scores you have played yourself is fun, and the ability to **print out the music** is impressive.

Example

Explain how several session musicians in different parts of the world might compose a song together at the same time, and then make the music instantly available for distribution to members of the public.

Solution

A MIDI-equipped keyboard, connected to the computer via a suitable **MIDI interface**, could be used to play music into **specialist music software** like Cakewalk Express, for example. If the computer is connected to the internet, then the MIDI data could also be sent to the other sites, where the other musicians, using the same software, could hear what the first musician is playing, and therefore join in with the session. It would be convenient to make use of **video conferencing** so they could see each other, and hear verbal comments in **real time**. Finally, when they are happy with the digital recording that they have made, it can be saved on their internet site, ready to be streamed to the masses via suitable software, which can play MP3 files, giving almost CD quality **audio streaming** to their eager fans!

Other forms of computer input

There are many other specialist forms of computer input, with the **data glove** being just one good example. Indeed, **whole-body suits** can have sensors, which detect the position of the wearer so that they can interact with **virtual worlds** created on the computer. The data glove would enable you to control electronic systems like **robots** in a hostile environment like a nuclear reactor, or control a submarine moving along the depths of the ocean. The movements of the hand (or body in the case of the suit) are transformed into digital information by the computer, and then transmitted in the appropriate form to the computer that is controlling the action of the robot or submarine.

Example

An advanced sporting simulator is being developed in which a virtual-reality helmet is used to deliver information to the player, and data gloves and whole-body suites are computer input devices. The simulator is to be used for tennis players to improve their skills, and enable analysis of their movement during a typical game. Explain how the two input devices could be used in this way.

Solution

The player is immersed in the virtual world, by observing the 3D images that would be projected into his or her eyes via the **virtual reality helmet**. The feedback from the data glove and whole body suit would enable the computer to build up a **real-time 3D model** of the player's body position and hand movements, which could then be translated to predict what is happening to the **virtual ball** when struck by the player's **virtual bat**.

A typical scenario, like a computer-controlled player serving the ball could be programmed, and the reaction of the simulator player could be monitored by

Be aware about less usual forms of computer input, like the MIDI and data glove. You may need this knowledge to answer some examination questions.

Visit our portal for a look at virtual reality systems.

For a look at data gloves and body suits.

recording the exact positions of their body, arms and legs etc. in relation to the delivery of the virtual ball. At a later stage the player could enter the **simulator control room**, and watch a recorded version of the return of serve played back on the computer monitor. The coach may then be able to calculate a variety of statistics enabling him or her to analyse the player's movements. From this data it might be possible to predict what the player did wrong if the service was not returned, or how the return could be improved. Being a simulator, the degree of difficulty is under the control of the coach, and beginners and experts alike could use this simulator to improve their game.

Capturing scientific and engineering data

Much data in the form of **quantities** such as '**radiation**' or '**pollution levels**' needs to be captured, and this is why it is mentioned here for completeness. It is unlikely that questions regarding **data logging** would be mixed up with the general data-capture methods outlined in this unit.

Capturing data from the web

The **world wide web** has become an enormous **data-capture vehicle** for many companies. Figure 13.1 shows a typical form, filled in by users when booking a hotel.

Figure 13.1 Typical data-capture.

The user is being prompted to input data regarding the dates, number of adults, and room type (smoking or non-smoking). They are then prompted to confirm the reservation by typing in their name, address, e-mail address and any other information required. After typing in his or her credit-card number over a **secure internet link**, he or she would be given a confirmation number, and e-mail would be sent with further confirmation if an e-mail address were entered onto the **data capture form**. Much data is now collected in this way, where the information, input onto the form would be stored in the **central reservations database** for the hotel concerned. A **scripting language** like **PERL** might be used to process the data, and store it in an **SQL database** ready for further analysis by the hotel chain's computer systems.

Manual data collection methods

For the purposes of the examination you might be required to use your discretion about which input device is appropriate in a given situation. This is why so many examples have been given involving real-life scenarios. It is likely that the input devices and methods of data collection would be wrapped up in some context, probably in conjunction with output and storage devices too.

Example

An opinion poll is to be undertaken for a television company in which **10 000** people are to be sampled, gathering their political opinions prior to an election. All the data captured that day is required for the evening news bulletin. Suggest a suitable means of data capture for this project. Explain how your method would work in practice.

Solution

Assuming **preset questions**, a special **data-capture form** is designed, on which the pollsters place a tick in boxes. A very small sample of the form could be as shown in Figure 13.2. One data capture form can be used for each client interview, and marks made in the box could be used to automatically sense the answers using an **optical mark reader**.

Typically, the **OMR machine** could be set up to enter the data directly into a file, which could then be transferred into a database or spreadsheet, thus getting 10 000 forms processed in a sensible amount of time, probably within a couple of hours, which is sensible to get the statistics out the same day.

To keep the data entry on schedule, it is best if there are no questions requiring written responses for the sample. This would involve manually entering this data, and the results are unlikely to be available on time.

> Are you going to vote?
>
> Yes ☐ No ☐
>
> Which party are you likely to vote for?
>
> Labour ☐
> Liberal Democrats ☐
> Conservative ☐
> Green Party ☐

Figure 13.2 Part of the data-capture form for the opinion-poll example.

During an examination, if designing data-capture forms, remember they should be neat and tidy, well laid out and reflect the actual look of the form on the computer.

You may be expected to design your own **data capture forms**. Simple effective layouts, like the form shown in Figure 13.2 above, are all that is required in an examination.

Self-test questions

1 Suggest three different systems in which video input of data could play a vital role.
2 Speech input is replacing the keyboard in a variety of scenarios. Suggest two different applications that can make effective use of speech input, giving your reasons in each case.
3 Explain MIDI as a form of computer input. What data is easily input in this way?
4 Sophisticated robot pets are now being developed for the consumer market. Suggest three different forms of computer input that would be ideal for a robot dog or cat. Suggest how each input you describe may be put to effective use in the device.
5 Explain why data capture forms are often important ways of gathering data.
6 How might information be gathered from internet users?
7 Design a data-capture form for gathering information needed when a pupil goes to a new school. What other forms of data capture are likely to be needed in this case?
8 Design a data-capture form for use by a university regarding student applications for undergraduate courses.
9 Design an on-line form to capture data about surfers using a retail site that sells CDs, music cassettes, videotapes and DVDs.

In this unit you have learned about:

- Input techniques like video, speech and MIDI
- Alternative forms of inputs like the data glove and body suits
- Data logging, capturing data via the Internet, manual data collection methods and the data capture forms

14 Output devices and data presentation

In this section you will learn about:

- Different forms of presenting data
- A variety of output devices like printers, plotters and monitors
- Other output devices like sounds and smell

Output devices

A very large range of output devices is available. We will concentrate not on the technical characteristics of each device, but on their usefulness in different scenarios, which is typical of what to expect in AS examinations.

Printers

Colour ink jet printers are popular in the home and small business market, and the **laser printer** reigns supreme in the larger business and corporate market. There is a place for **dot matrix** printers, even though this is one of the older technologies on the market. You can also print to **film (microform)**. Any printed output in whatever form, is known as **hard copy**.

Example

(a) Why is an ink jet printer much more suitable for colour printing in the home?

(b) Why would an ink jet printer probably be unsuitable for use as a network printer?

(c) Why are dot matrix printers still used in shops and some offices?

(d) Which printer is most suitable for use by a secretary for correspondence?

(e) Which printer would be most suitable for the production of a glossy magazine? Explain why.

Solution

(a) An ink jet printer is suitable for use in the home because it is very cheap to buy, and the running costs are unlikely to be great for relatively low volume colour printing.

(b) Current ink jet printers are slow compared to laser printers. An ink jet printer is unlikely to be able to produce the volume of printouts in an acceptable time if many people are to share the printer.

(c) Dot matrix printers are useful for the production of stock reports in the retail trade. They are ideal for use with the continuous fan-fold paper, typical of that needed in this application.

(d) A laser printer is suitable for use by a secretary, as the quality of the correspondence is high. It could be a low volume laser printer connected to a local machine, or a high-volume laser printer shared between several secretaries.

(e) Conventional printers are not up to the job of magazine production. **Offset litho technology**, or expensive laser printers, used by the printing industry, would be needed to cope with exceptional quality and volumes in a sensible amount of time.

Other printing technologies

Conventional printers are not adequate for larger jobs of the sort needed by architects and engineers. Larger scale drawings are needed, and a **flatbed X-Y plotter** or **drum plotter** fits the bill. The drum plotter is most useful if floor space is at a premium. **Line printers** are also

---

You must remember the relative speed of operation and costs of modern output devices. This is so you can choose appropriately in examination questions.

Read the monthly computer magazines and pay attention to the latest specifications of LASER and ink jet printers etc. Use these to give topical answers to exam questions.

useful in the very high volume utility billing industry. This would include **batch-processing** operations such as printing names and addresses for electricity or gas bills.

Photographic printing technologies

The need to store huge volumes of printed material led to the advent of **microfilm** and **microfiche**. Rolls of film or rectangular-card systems are used to store printed material such that special machines called **COM readers** can read them. COM stands for **Computer Output on Microform**, where microform is the collective name for microfilm and microfiche.

Visit our portal for more information on COM readers, microfiche and microfilm.

Example

Give two typical places in which COM readers are common, suggesting why they are useful in one of your chosen scenarios. What new technologies are likely to replace these devices in the long term? Why?

Solution

COM readers are used in libraries and establishments like garage servicing departments. In the automobile servicing industry they are used extensively because much detailed information like pictures and text can be distributed and viewed very cheaply. The older way to view the same information was to send out thousands of manually printed pages. This is very expensive in terms of delivery to the garages, and also takes up a huge amount of space, compared to the COM readers and microforms. Finally, the users do not have to have access to a computer to view the information. It is also highly reliable. The COM readers are very much cheaper to buy than computers, although in comparison to very low cost PCs, this is no longer the case. Also, the introduction of very low cost CD and DVDs will probably mean that information, printed onto microform, will be replaced with viewing similar information from these disks.

Display technologies

Displays are categorised by considering the technologies used to implement them. A conventional video monitor uses a **CRT** display. Typically these range from about 14 in to 26 in for high-resolution colour monitors, although smaller and larger screens are available. Monitors now work in resolutions ranging from 800 by 600, to well in excess of 1280 by 1024. The larger monitors are needed to display these very high resolutions.

Liquid crystal displays (LCD) represent the thin screens, which appear on most portables. Much larger LCD displays are available, up to 48 in and beyond. Flat thin LCD displays will probably become the norm for all computers.

Recent innovations are **light emitting plastic (LEP)** or **light emitting polymer** displays, which are paper thin, and theoretically can be of any size. Some of the dreams of science fiction are coming true, as can be seen from the innovative ideas produced by the CDT company, in Figures 14.1 and 14.2.

Use the web to keep up to date with the latest technologies.

Example

Why is it likely that LCD and LEP displays will take over from conventional CRT displays?

Solution

LCD displays are much lighter than the equivalent size CRT display. Also, the LCD display uses far less energy than the equivalent CRT display, and this is why they are used in portables, where battery power is critical.

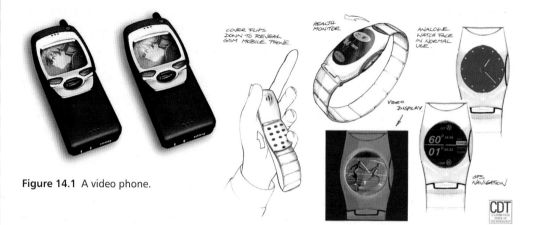

Figure 14.1 A video phone.

Figure 14.2 Some LEP display ideas.

Visit our portal for information about LEPs.

It is likely that LEP displays will be available at some time in the future, and these will be very cheap to produce compared to the equivalent size LCD display. It may also allow you to roll up the screen for greater flexibility!

Other display technologies

There is an increasing need to display information to large audiences. Currently the **projection TV** system fits the bill admirably, although the LEP displays might provide a serious challenge in permanent venues like exhibition spaces and educational lecture theatres, for example. The cost of the projection TV technology is constantly being reduced and 1024 by 768 displays are now easily affordable.

There are other very specialist displays, like the **3D holographic displays** used in the design environment to visualise manufactured artefacts. Such displays might be presented using a **head-up display** like a **virtual reality helmet**, or projected into a special area set up for the purpose. Displays that fit over conventional pairs of glasses are also being developed, and these could be useful for portable computers, or surfing the net via your third generation mobile phone.

Example

A museum of history is intending to build an interactive display for the public. They are considering a variety of display technologies. Explain how the use of a variety of computer display methods and virtual reality helmets might make for a more memorable experience.

Solution

Touch-sensitive CRT or LCD screens might present the visitor with a menu, which could be used to set up an appropriate environment. LEP displays can be wrapped to any shape. One option would be to build up a model of a human face, and cover it with LEP. This could create the illusion of movement. For example, the manikin would appear to be able to talk, smile or perform other facial expressions. When synchronised with animatronic movements of the body, and sound that appears to come out of the dummy's mouth, this could add a new dimension to an otherwise static display. For the ultimate experience the visitor could put on a virtual reality helmet. This would give the visitor the illusion of being immersed in a computerised world. Other technologies such as data gloves and whole body suits could all add to the illusion of being transported to a completely different place.

Graphics cards

You should not forget the part played by the **graphics card** inside a PC. Without a powerful graphics card, containing a suitable amount of memory (64 Mbytes is a good current standard), it is not possible to refresh the massive amount of information at a rate which is acceptable to the human eye. The higher the resolution, and the more colours that are used, the more strain is put on the graphics card. Some graphics cards are now designed to have a particularly good 3D performance, and this means that computer games and simulations, like Microsoft's Flight Simulator 2000, for example, look particularly stunning.

Computer Sound

Sound plays an increasingly important part regarding output from a computer. State of the art sound cards now have multiple channels. Many now have surround sound, based on **Dolby Pro Logic** or **THX**. Not only do you have the front left and right speakers, but a central speaker, two rear speakers, and probably a large sub-woofer to boost the base.

Such systems are useful not only to play games, but also to listen to movies on DVD systems, where sound is often encoded making use of one of the Dolby systems. These systems manage to create a sound stage, which, with effective positioning of the speakers, can make the users feel as if they are immersed in the sound stage. Not only can you have sound going from left to right, but from back to front also. The most recent systems, like **Dolby Digital**, for example, provide a completely circular sound stage.

Other forms of computer output

Computers can generate **smells**, by an injection of the appropriate chemical into the atmosphere. This is used to great effect in displays like those that can be found in the London Dungeons, for example, where mediaeval atmospheres can be created! This can further add to the realism of computer output in the entertainment and education industries. You should not forget **computer speech** as an output medium. It is relatively easy to generate computer speech, compared to the infinitely more complex task of being able to understand speech. Nevertheless, it is still quite difficult to get natural sounding speech.

Relative speeds of a huge variety of output devices are covered in chapter 11 of NUCSAL.

Self-test questions

1. Suggest a typical use for a flatbed plotter.
2. What are LCD and LEP displays?
3. Why is a graphics card needed?
4. What are the main differences in performance and use between laser printers and ink jet printers?
5. What is a COM reader?
6. What is an offset litho machine?
7. Where are dot-matrix printers still used?
8. How many pages/minute are typical for a modern laser printer?
9. Suggest a use for LEPs.
10. What name is usually given to the devices based on CRT technology?

In this unit you have learned about:

- A variety of **hard copy** devices like **printers** and **plotters**
- A range of **display** devices like **CRT, LCD** and **LEP**
- How these devices may be used in practice

15 Primary and secondary storage devices

In this section you will learn about:

- Primary storage devices like RAM and ROM
- Secondary storage devices like floppy disks and hard disks
- Practical applications making use of these technologies

Storage devices

A large range of storage devices is available. *You should be aware of the characteristics of each, and be able to make an informed choice regarding the suitability of each device for any given task.*

Primary storage devices

The most important objective of **primary storage** is speed of operation. **RAM (random access memory)** on the main motherboard is one of *the* determining factors regarding how fast your computer can operate. The current generations of semiconductor RAM are **volatile**. If power is removed from the system, the contents of memory are lost. This is why it is important to save data onto a secondary storage device. An alternative name for RAM is **IAS** or **immediate access store**.

ROM (read only memory) is non-volatile, but you obviously cannot change the contents of this primary-storage device. This is therefore useful to store programs that do not change very often, like the computer BIOS, or parts of the operating system, for example.

Both **RAM** and **ROM** are examples of **direct-access** devices. This means that it is possible to go directly to the data in memory, without having to read any previous data. You should compare this method with **serial access**, where previous data does have to be read, like reading a tape, for example.

Cache

Different technologies used to implement RAM vary in expense and speed of operation. Very fast access chips, currently having access times less than 10 nsec are used as a **buffer** between the main memory and the fast processor. If the instructions that the processor needs are stored inside this fast memory (called **cache**), then the program instructions will be executed even more quickly, leading to an overall improvement to the system.

Example

Different RAM-based technologies exist like EPROM, Flash ROM and Static RAM. They are used in different ways in a computer system. Describe these different devices, and give a typical use for each.

Solution

EPROM stands for **electrically programmable read only memory**. With a special machine called an EPROM programmer, it is possible to permanently store programs inside this chip and then use them as though they are ordinary ROM. This enables companies or individuals to program **embedded systems** with ease and is useful for development purposes. **Flash ROM** is a special ROM chip that can be programmed *in situ*. Using this chip you could do an automatic BIOS upgrade for your motherboard via the internet, for example. **Static RAM** is currently the fastest semiconductor memory available, and is used for very fast cache between the processor and the main RAM.

AS

Secondary storage devices

The primary objectives **for secondary storage devices** are **data integrity**, **reliability** and a large **mass-storage capability**. Obviously very fast data access is an objective too, but mechanical devices like hard drives or floppies cannot compete with the speed of access of electronic primary storage devices like semiconductor memory, for example.

The floppy disk

The modern double-sided high-density disks can hold *1.44 Mbyte of uncompressed data*. Although small by today's standards, floppies are still useful, especially when combined with **compression utilities** like **WinZip**, for example, which gives the option of saving a single large file on multiple floppies. The **LS-120 disk format**, which is compatible with the current 1.44 MB format mentioned above, is a magneto-optical device, capable of storing 120 MB. This is a better size capacity, but the 100 MB and 250 MB **Zip** disks are becoming very popular, as is the 1 GB **Jazz** format. **Floppies** are very slow and often unreliable. It also takes a relatively long time to find the data on these devices, because they don't usually spin when no data is being read.

Example

State the relative advantages and disadvantages when transferring data between different computers of using removable media like floppies, Zip and Jazz disks.

Solution

Virtually all computers are able to read a floppy disk. However, the file size is small, and the data transfer rate is very slow (about 500 Kbits/sec). A compression utility can be used to place larger files onto several disks. Floppies tend to be the least reliable method of transferring data. Although quite popular, not everybody will have access to a Zip drive, and therefore this method might not be available. Nevertheless larger files, typically 100 or 250 Mbytes (more if a compression utility is used) can be transferred and the system is more reliable than a floppy. The data-transfer rate is also better, giving about 1.4 Mbyte/sec.

Do not confuse a Zip disk with a compression utility like WinZip, for example. One is a physical disk and the other is a useful software utility.

Hard disk drives

Hard drives are currently the main **secondary storage** systems for all types of computer. Typically a hard drive would be 20 Gbytes or more for a typical modern microcomputer. The speed of access varies with the technology, with fast SCSII drives currently giving an access time of a few msec, with data-transfer rates currently up to about 40 Mbytes/sec. This is hundreds of times faster than the data transfer rate of the humble 3.5 inch floppy disk. Don't forget that disk drives allow **direct access** or **random access** to the data stored on them.

Hard drives are much more reliable than floppies and typically have a life span of 5 years or more. However, you can guarantee that the system will crash eventually and ruin much if not all of your precious data. A hard drive spins round all the time the system is switched on and the disk head floats above the magnetic surface of the disk. If this head inadvertently touches the surface of the disk on which data is stored, then the surface is scratched and the intricate pattern of **sectors** and **tracks**, placed there when the disk was **formatted**, are lost, together with the valuable data that the sectors contained.

Visit our portal to download a defragmentation program.

Example

Access to data on a hard drive has become very slow, compared to when the computer was new. Suggest a reason for this, and say what might be done to overcome this problem. How might we increase the amount of information that could be stored on the hard disk?

Solution

When a disk has just been formatted, information is stored on the disk, one piece after the other in an efficient way, making use of the track and sector patterns. Over time, as files are deleted, gaps appear in the middle of other files. Smaller files can then be stored in these gaps, but are unlikely to fill the available space. Files quickly get split up and this means that it is more difficult to locate all the bits of a file. Compared to when similar files used to be stored more efficiently, access times for the same information will be drastically increased.

When the above scenario happens, the disk is said to be **fragmented**, because fragments of files appear all over the disk, as shown by the red sections in Figure 15.1(a). However, run a **defragment** utility several times and the same disk, containing the same data, now looks like the picture shown in Figure 15.2(b).

It is possible to use a compression utility to compress files on the disk, and this will probably allow significantly more information to be stored on the disk compared to the original data. However, access will be slowed down because the data has to be uncompressed before it can be read.

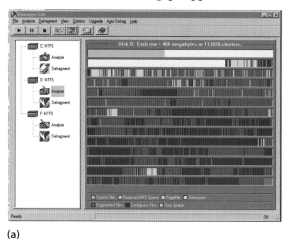

(a)

(b)

Figure 15.1 (a) Before and (b) after defragmentation.

Disk cache

A computer system might not have enough RAM to run certain programs, or to store the data for immediate use. One way to get round this is to make use of the **hard disk memory** as an extension to **RAM**. This means that data, normally held in fast RAM, would be temporarily stored on the hard disk. This is an effective way of overcoming the problem, but is obviously very slow compared to the normal speed if the data were held in RAM.

Disk arrays

Although hard disks are now able to store tens of Gbytes on a single disk, this may not be enough for the data-storage requirements of many organisations. Therefore, large cabinets of disks, called **Terabyte Disk Farms** are used to string together an array of disks.

RAID systems

A **Redundant Array of Independent Drives** used to be referred to as a Redundant Array of Inexpensive Drives. This system, usually used on network fileservers, has several advantages over using a single drive. There are **five levels** (different types) of **RAID systems**, but put simply, these disks can keep the system going in the event of a hard-disk crash (by mirroring data on a different drive), or increase the speed of access (more accesses in a given amount of time) because data, stored on different drives, can be accessed at the same time.

Example

How is it possible to increase the reliability of a network file server by the use of a RAID array? Does the system have any other advantages?

Solution

If a RAID array is used, then identical data from one hard disk may be stored on another. Under normal conditions this mirroring process may not be noticeable. However, if one of the drives were to crash, then the other could take over immediately, with no noticeable delay to the users. The manager would have to replace the errant disk drive (it would usually be swappable even though the system is still running), and the system would build up the new disk to the point where the mirroring is again functional.

If the data is spread over a couple of different drives, then both disks may be used to read the data 'twice as quickly', because we have two independent drives, each capable of mopping up the data at a specific rate. However, complex controllers and software are needed to manage this system so that no mix-ups can occur.

Self-test questions

1 RAM and ROM are both needed in computer systems. Why is this so?
2 RAM is volatile. Explain what this statement means. What can be done to prevent loss of data in the event of a power cut?
3 Explain what 'disk caching' means. How might the technique of caching enable you to have more RAM than might physically be available?
4 Explain the difference between primary and secondary storage, giving a typical use for each type of storage system.
5 Why are hard-disk drives faster and more reliable than floppy disk drives?
6 After frequent use a disk may become fragmented. Why is this a problem, and what can be done to overcome this?
7 There are various types (levels) of RAID array. Explain two problems that different types of RAID systems would help you to overcome.
8 A home computer user has just brought a computer system with 6 Gbytes of hard disk space. His old computer had only 200 Mbytes. Why is this new disk likely to get filled up sooner than he may think?
9 Explain what is meant by serial access and direct access. What type of access is supported by floppy and hard disk drives?
10 Suggest a suitable sized hard disk for use in a file server for a school that has 2000 pupils. The disk is to store data for the pupils only (i.e. no applications software). Explain exactly how you arrive at your conclusion.

In this unit you have learned about:

● Primary and secondary storage devices
● Magnetic storage devices like floppy disks and hard disks
● RAID
● How all these devices can be used in practice

16 Further secondary storage and tape systems

In this section you will learn about:

- Optical and magneto-optical storage devices
- Tape storage systems
- Practical scenarios involving the application of this technology

Optical drives

Optical technology works with LASERS instead of magnetic heads. Typical of this sort of device are the **CD-ROM (Compact Disk Read Only Memory)** drives and **DVD (Digital Versatile Disk or Digital Video Disk)** drives. A standard CD-ROM can hold about 650 Mbytes of read-only data.

The data transfer rate of a single-speed CD-ROM is 150 Kbytes/sec. Double-speed is twice this and so on. Other limits, like the software being used, will ensure that a 52-speed CD-ROM drive will not actually give you 52 times the speed of a single-speed device! You can record data onto a special type of CD-ROM called **CD-R (Compact Disk Recordable)** and may erase and write the data again on a **CD-RW (Compact Disk Rewritable)** disk.

A single-layer single-sided DVD can store about 4.7 Gbytes of data, considerably more than conventional CD-ROM drives. The current maximum capacity for a double-sided DVD is 17 Gbytes. You might also be able to re-record data by using the **DVD-E** format.

Magneto-optical drives

These **MO (magneto optical)** devices use a combination of LASER and magnetic heads to reduce the size needed to store the data on the disk. These drives are currently not quite as good as the conventional magnetic disk drive in terms of access time (time to access any item or random data) and data transfer rate. They are particularly suited as a backup storage medium.

Sometimes a magneto-optical drive is removable, in which case it is called a **floptical disk**. Some floptical disks are of the 3-inch disk format, and these drives can be read by conventional floppies too.

Example

The advent of new types of secondary-storage media such as DVD and CD-RW has caused many headaches for the music, film and software industries. What are these problems, and what might be done to combat rampant piracy? What extra problems might the internet pose?

Solution

Software is distributed on CDs, requiring special factories to make the disks. However, using recordable CD-ROMs, the consumer can make copies of CDs, and it is thus easy to pirate software or music. Recordable DVD formats mean that it is easy to pirate high-quality copies of films too but media costs are currently high.

Codes need to be typed in to activate software, but internet sites provide thousands of illegal codes that have been hacked for hundreds of software products. Illegal market stalls, often selling thousands of pounds worth of software for about £5 or £10 are also a problem. You get no manuals or technical support if you obtain software via this illegal route, and stand a chance of being arrested too. At the

You need to have an appreciation of how much these systems can store and how fast you can access data from them. This is important for examination purposes.

Read the monthly computer magazines and use the web to look at the latest storage device information.

moment there are few technical solutions to software piracy, other than the use of a **dongle** or **hardware key**. This is a device, which plugs into the computer, without which the software will not run.

The internet is posing a great threat because software, music and films can be downloaded with ease, although it might take quite a few hours to download a large software package. However, as some ISPs now give free internet access, and some even give free phone calls at certain times of the week, a long phone call would be of little consequence.

Tapes

A huge variety of tape formats exist, ranging from **DLT (Digital Linear Tape)** drives on large computer systems, to the smaller 4 mm **DAT (Digital Audio Tape)** systems used as backup devices on small and medium size file servers, for example.

The speed with which data can be accessed from the tape varies from system to system, but the **serial nature** of the storage media means that you will probably have to wind the tape a long way until you find the item of interest. Therefore, a few tens of minutes or even longer is not uncommon for data retrieval from a serially based tape. Typical 4 mm-DAT systems can store up to about 26 Gbytes. DLT tapes can store up to about 35 Gbytes, but you obviously can have many tape drives in a single system to increase the effective **backup** or **archive** storage capacity considerably.

Example

Tapes are often used as a system for backup or archive purposes. Explain the fundamental difference between these two terms. What other systems might be used instead of tapes for backing up or archiving?

Solution

A **backup** is a copy of the original files to be used in an emergency, such as accidental deletion or a system failure. Such backups would be taken at suitably frequent intervals such as the end of each day.

An **archive** is taking little-used parts of your system or data files off line so that they may be retrieved at a later data if needed. Material in the archive cannot usually be accessed quickly.

Removable storage media such as **MO disks** or **ZIP disks** are also ideal for **archive** purposes.

Large tape systems

Larger tape systems can be found in the **mainframe** and **supercomputer** environments. Some DLT tape machines can store up to 1630 DLT cartridges and have a native data transfer rate of 1.44 Tbytes/hour. Now that's some archive! One of the largest tape libraries at the time of writing is Fujitsu's F6457 tape library which holds up to 48,508 tapes, giving an enormous number of Tbytes and a native data transfer rate of 3 Mbytes/sec.

Storage-based examples

You may be required to suggest certain types of secondary storage devices and estimate their size based on a given application.

Example

An agency produces glossy brochures, and employs four people in the technical department. Most brochures are colour, and may run to 50 pages. On each page there will usually be 4 high-quality photos, each being a maximum of

Visit our portal to see some enormous tape backup systems.

Keep up to date with the latest tape systems for business.

3 inches × 2 inches in size. The rest of the material on each page is text based, although there may be a coloured logo. The company produces a maximum of 20 brochures each year, and a maximum of 6 brochures may need updating at any one time, meaning that 14 brochures may be archived.

Estimate the amount of primary and secondary storage that would be needed to store the material using the following information.

- The average size of brochure is 30 pages.
- Colour photos are stored as 24-bit bitmaps and each photo has a resolution of 300 dpi.
- The magazine material may be archived once the magazine has been produced.
- No more than 16 pages will need to be held in memory at any one time.
- You need to include some storage capacity for the applications that would typically be needed by this company.
- You also need to allow storage space for correspondence and other administrative material.
- The system must be very reliable, as brochures are produced to tight deadlines, and any delay due to technical faults is unacceptable.
- You should allow for recovery in the event of a system failure.

Your answer should include facilities for storage that is accessible by all four workstations simultaneously, and allow for backup and archiving of the material.

Solution

First estimate the size of each photo, stored at a resolution of 300 dpi, having a size of 3in by 2in. The number of bits for 24-bit colour is $3 \times 2 \times 24 \times 300 \times 300 = 12\,960\,000$ bits. Thus giving us 13 Mbit per image.

There are 4 images on each page, therefore, each page will require $13 \times 4 = 52$ Mbits. Text based storage requirements for each page would be much less demanding than this. For the purposes of estimation, we will assume 7 Mbytes are needed per page in total.

A maximum of 16 pages need to be stored in memory at any one time. Therefore, 16×7 or 112 Mbytes of RAM would be needed to store the document in memory. Not forgetting the **operating system**, **DTP** and **art package** requirements, which will probably take up a similar amount of RAM, I would suggest that a minimum of 256 Mbytes is needed for each workstation, and preferably **512 Mbytes**. On average, the brochure page extent is 30 pages. Therefore, on average, each brochure would take up $7 \times 30 = 210$ Mbytes of secondary storage.

As 6 brochures may need to be worked on at any one time, $6 \times 210 = 1.26$ Gbytes of secondary storage would be needed on the file server to store these documents. A file server is the most efficient way of storing the brochure work and other resources as the workstations can be connected to it by means of an LAN. Assuming that software like the DTP packages and art packages are stored on the file server too, then an extra 2 Gbytes would be adequate for this, as temporary files and local backups would take some considerable space. The administrative work would need considerably less storage than this, and therefore 6 G bytes would seem to be adequate for all foreseen purposes. I would suggest 10 Gbyte to act as a margin of safety.

The reliability of the system should be high, and downtime should be kept to a minimum. Therefore a RAID system with mirroring would seem necessary to

The speeds, access times and storage capacities of a large range of secondary storage devices can be found in chapter 12 of NUCSAL.

overcome a possible hard-disk crash. The mirroring would double the disk capacity to 20 Gbytes, arranged in 2 lots of 10 Gbytes.

Therefore, the disk capacity on the file server would be **20 Gbytes**. The archiving of material for each year would involve the storage of 20 brochures. This would require, on average 20 × 210 Mbytes = 4.2 Gbytes of space. Therefore, an 8 Gbyte tape streamer would seem adequate for this purpose, which could also be used for recovery of the system in the event of a system failure.

The archive system could, therefore, be an **8 Gbyte DLT tape streamer**. One tape would probably be needed for each year, and therefore several tapes capable of holding 8 Gbytes each would need to be purchased.

You should note that there are no right or wrong answers for the above, just sensible answers. For example, it would not matter if you chose a 12 Gbyte DAT machine for the archive part of the system. It is usual when estimating the size of a system to err on the generous side of things without going completely overboard. Systems designers will try to make sure that the system has some spare capacity to allow for expansion.

Self-test questions

1 A user has a 100 × speed CD-ROM drive. Why is he or she unlikely to see a 100 times increase in speed over and above a single-speed drive?

2 What other technologies are threatening the CD-ROM as the 'distribution medium of choice' for software packages like applications and games?

3 What is CD–R? Give three different legitimate uses for this technology.

4 Compare and contrast the CD–R and MO devices as a backup storage medium.

5 What is meant by an archive, and how does this differ from a backup? A company wishes to create a large (many Gbytes) archive on CD-ROM. Is this a good idea? Comment on this compared to other suitable media.

6 A company needs to backup about 50 Gbytes of data each day. State, giving reasons for your choice, whether you would put this on a single large tape or several smaller ones.

7 A company uses computers to control a critical real time process. The computer must be able to recover from a disaster like a disk crash without adversely affecting the control process. What secondary storage devices might help in this situation?

In this unit you have learned about:

- Optical devices like CD-ROM and DVD
- A variety of tape systems like DAT and DLT
- How these devices and techniques can be put into practice

17 File organisation and structure

In this section you will learn about:

- What is meant by a file
- Fixed and variable-length records
- File structure and organisation
- Serial, sequential and indexed sequential structures
- Hashing

Files and information

Always state any assumptions that you make when estimating the size of a file for examination purposes.

A **file** is a *collection of related information*. The name is derived from a file used in an office filing cabinet. Computer files come in different forms, some can be read by humans (called **text files**), and some cannot (called **binary files**). Binary files usually consist of computer data, coded such that they are easily read by a computer. A file can be a computer program itself, or it might be data in an appropriate form to be read by a computer program. **Files** form the basic units of storage on secondary media like **disks** and **tape**.

Files used for **data processing** are made up from a *collection of records*. It is easy to visualise a **record**, and one from Microsoft's demonstration database, is shown in Figure 17.1. It contains personal information like 'Address', 'City' and some general comments. Take note of the controls at the bottom of Figure 17.1, enabling the user to manually sequence through all of the records in the database. Each record is further divided into sections called **fields**. In the record-card layout shown, different boxes contain field information like 'City' and 'Phone'. A field is subdivided into **individual characters**.

![Employees record card showing Laura Callahan's Personal Info tab with Address: 4726 - 11th Ave. N.E., City: Seattle, Region: WA, Postal Code: 98105, Country: USA, Home Phone: (206) 555-1189, Title Of Courtesy: Ms., Birth Date: 09-Jan-58, Notes: Laura received a BA in psychology from the University of Washington. She has also completed a course in business French. She reads and writes French. Record 8 of 9.]

Figure 17.1 Example record card.

A **key field** identifies a record. For an employee database, employee ID is a good choice. The use of 'name' as key field is not good, as *the key field has to be unique*. This unique field is often called the **primary key field**. This is to distinguish it from other key fields, which need not necessarily be unique. These other fields are called **secondary key fields**, and may be used to identify people in different departments, for example.

A **primary key field** may be used as an **index**, so that records are quickly located. **Secondary key fields** could be used to index other information, or used to sort subsets of data.

Example

A file is to be set up containing the following information:

ID number, Surname, First name, Middle name, Six-line address, Telephone number, E-mail address, Fax number and Personal picture.

Estimate the size of the file, given a maximum of 1000 records. *Give reasons for any estimation that you make.*

Solution

Assumptions about the maximum number of characters that will accommodate each of the above criteria are shown in the table. The above are possible values only, and are a compromise between wasted space and having to truncate the data entries. If the picture is a jpeg, 1 Kb is enough for each image. For 1000 records, we need $1000 \times 1270 = 1\,270\,000$ bytes. There are **overheads** associated with files. If information were to be stored in a text file, then little extra needs to be added on. The only extra information would be the **headers** and **end-of file markers**, etc. A sensible estimate of the file size (always make it a little larger than needed) would be **1.5 Mb**.

For database projects, estimating the file size is more complex. Create the database with blank records, then measure the size of the resulting file. Next enter a record to see how much the file has grown. Multiply this growth by the maximum number of records, giving you a good idea of the likely final size. Extra processing, like **queries** and **reports** will add to the **overheads**.

Estimation of the size of each field	
Field information	Sensible size (characters)
ID number	10
Surname	20
First name	20
Middle name	20
Address 1 (Line 1)	20
Address 2 (Line 2)	20
Address 3 (Line 3)	20
Address 4 (Town)	20
Address 5 (County/State)	20
Address 6 (Post/Zip Code)	10
Telephone number	25
e-mail address	40
Fax number	25
Picture	1000
Total (Per record)	1270

Data structure of a simple employee file

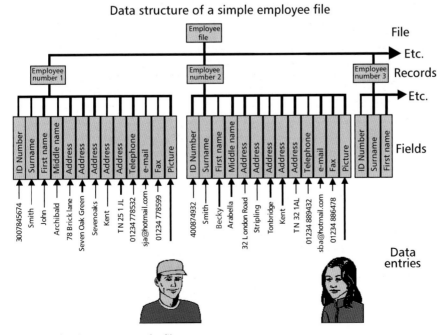

Figure 17.2 The data structure of a file.

Fixed and variable length records

The last example assumed the field length is fixed. Fixed-length fields give rise to **fixed-length records**. These are easier to process because the software routines, which access the information, may count the required number of characters. With fixed-length records, altering the contents will not alter the length.

It is also useful to have **variable-length fields**. For example, a free-flowing text field, where users want extended comments. Although efficient from a storage space point of view, variable-length records are more difficult to maintain than fixed-length ones. To save memory you might accept more complex and generally slower access methods.

File structure

The anatomy of a file includes layout, like the logical organisation of the **records** within a **file**, and organisation of the **fields** within each record. A **hierarchical data structure diagram** may be used for this purpose, as shown in Figure 17.2. The fields are subordinate to the records, which are subordinate to the file. This data structure represents the **logical structure** of the file, and not the way that the file would be stored. Each piece of data is identified by the name of the field, and the **key field** identifies each record.

File organisation

There are four main access methods, as follows: **Serial access, Sequential access, Direct access** and **Indexed sequential access.**

Serial access refers to storing records, one after the other, *with no regard to order.* Sequential access means storing information in a particular sequence. **Serial-access storage media** support these two access methods.

Direct access is the ability to go straight to a record or interest, without having to serially work though all of the previous records. The address of the record can be calculated by **hashing** (see example). Another way to find records quickly is to build up an **index** of **pointers**, which point to salient positions in the file. This is called indexed sequential access, as the index is used to access part of the file, which is then searched sequentially for the item of interest. **Direct-access storage media** like disks can support all access methods, both **serial** and **direct.**

Example

Explain the term hashing. Show how a hashing function may be used to generate addresses where a record from Figure 17.2 may be stored. What happens if the same address is generated for different records?

Solution

A **hashing function** is a **mathematical formula**, which can be used to generate an address where a record is stored. Hashing functions may generate the same address for different records! Therefore a group of records might end up in an area of memory that has to be searched **serially**.

Using Figure 17.2 as an example, we use the **key field** (**ID number**), as the number to which our hashing function is applied. For John Smith, 3 007 845 674 is used.

Let there be a maximum of 1000 employees. In this case we use a hashing function that generates numbers in the region 1 to 1000, using the 10-digit membership number as a starting point. The number generated can then be used to point to an entry in a table, where the actual data can be found.

We want to generate numbers in the region 1 to 1000. Therefore, a **hashing function**, with '**MOD 1000 + 1**' applied to the output is appropriate. Modulo 1000 generates digits in the range 0 to 999 inclusive. One of many suitable functions could be as follows.

If you have the facilities, much can be learnt from creating code to interrogate data in a file. Languages like Visual Basic and Delphi are ideal for this.

Modulo arithmetic is covered in detail in chapter 18 of NUCSAL.

Remove the middle six digits, square the number, and apply MOD 1000 + 1 to the answer. Some examples are as follows.

Membership number	Remove middle six digits	Square the number	MOD 1000 + 1
3007845674	078456	6155343936	937
4008749321	087493	7655025049	050
2014545665	145456	2000895120	121

Any account number, which generates the same address, can be stored in an **overflow table** or **bucket**. This is simply another area of memory, in addition to the table, which is used to store the overflow addresses.

If we hit on a duplicate, we apply the hashing function as described above, and the overflow table is followed until the required information can be found. It is thus usually very quick and efficient to find the required information, even though a small serial search may be required in the end.

Why use hashing?

In practice, many ID numbers are used to encode special information. The 10-digit ID number for an employee might be used to encode the department in which the employee works, and the number, encoded on an electronic key, might also give access to certain parts of the buildings. It would be very inefficient to use these 10-digit numbers for the actual addresses where the information is stored.

Self-test questions

1 A data file on a computer may be split up into records, fields and characters. Explain the terms in red type.
2 A shop keeps details of stock in a single file held on computer. They have a maximum of 10 000 items in stock. Estimate the size of the file given that the following fields are stored on each item. (State all assumptions you will make.)
   (a) Name of item
   (b) Product description number
   (c) Price
   (d) Description of item
   (e) Page number in catalogue
3 What is the difference between a serial and a sequential file?
4 Name two different types of secondary storage media that can support serial access files.
5 What does an indexed-sequential file mean? Illustrate your answer by using an example involving searching for people's names.
6 Explain why hashing is sometimes used when storing information in files.

Some code for handling files can be found in chapter 26 of NUCSAL.

In this unit you have learned about:

- How files are structured
- How to estimate file size
- Fixed and variable-length records
- File organisation
- The differences between serial, sequential, direct access and indexed sequential files

18 Security and integrity of data

In this section you will learn about:

- Security and integrity of data
- Batch totals
- Hash and control totals
- Check digits and check sums
- Cyclic redundancy checks
- Privacy of information
- Weak and strong encryption

Make sure you can explain the difference between security and integrity; it is a common examination question.

Security and data integrity

Candidates often confuse the terms **security** (keeping data safe from hackers etc.) and **integrity** (making sure that data is not corrupted inadvertently).

Maintaining the integrity of data

The most important part of a computer system is the data. It does not matter if the entire system blows up, you simply buy a new one, but the new computer will not have your precious data stored on it. Much effort goes into making sure that data is transmitted and stored safely, and backups are taken frequently. **Petabytes** (1×10^{15}) of data are transmitted between computers each day. If a single byte of this data is transmitted in error, then someone's data is corrupted.

Batch totals

A **batch total** is one method for checking the integrity of a batch of **records** in a **file**.

Example

A shop uses a batch total to check the integrity of the day's transactions. How might this be accomplished, and why is this method used?

Solution

Each record saved in the file, may have a 'total price' associated with it. We can write a routine that adds together these totals, and writes this figure as a check at the end of the file. You can use **modulo** arithmetic methods to limit the size of this number if necessary.

If the transaction file is then transmitted over the internet, the same check can be applied at the receiving end. If it is the same as the batch total calculated at the transmitting end, then the file has probably been received in good condition.

Hash totals and control totals

A **hash total** is used like a **batch total**. A **hash function** may be calculated from numeric data (unit 1). Instead of using the hash total to point to a place in a table where data is accessed, the hash total is stored at the end of the file, and transmitted, along with the data.

Many files will contain non-numeric data, in which case a hash total may be calculated by converting some **ASCII** or **Unicode** characters into their numeric equivalents. Consider transmitting a file containing three records, part of which is shown in Table 18.1.

Table 18.1

Record number	Field 1	Field 2	etc...	ASCII values of field 1
1	AA	HJK1		65 65
2	BB	DF27		66 66
3	CC	YZZQ		67 67
Hash total (Calculated below)				98

If we apply some **hashing function**, which 'adds up all the numbers, and takes the answer MOD 100', then this is achieved as follows.

$$\begin{array}{r} 6565 \\ 6666 \\ 6767\ + \\ \hline 19998 \end{array}$$

Answer **Mod 100** is **98** – as shown in the table. The **hash total** '98' is transmitted, along with the file. At the receiving end, the same hash total calculation is performed on the received data, and if it is the same; we can assume that **data integrity** has been maintained.

A **control total** could be as simple as an arithmetical count of all the records held in a file, which is then stored at the end of the file to act as a check.

Check digits and checksums

A **check digit** is similar in principle to a **hash total**, but only a *single digit* is produced. It is particularly useful when verifying a single account or stock number, where a **transcription error** (the wrong number is entered) or a **transposition error** (two digits or letters are swapped over) may have occurred.

Example

How might a check digit be calculated for account number 447546231?
What combined number is used to store or transmit this account number?

Solution

To calculate a check digit, a weighting is usually applied to each digit, based on the position of the number. The least significant bit is usually reserved for the check digit, and is assigned a weighting of 1. All the other digits in the number have a weighting of 2 to 9, repeating if necessary. The idea is shown in Table 18.2. CD is where the Check Digit is to be placed.

The method of using a weighting to provide a check digit is common. Brush up on this method and use it in your exams if necessary.

Table 18.2

	Calculation of a check digit for the number 447546231									
Number	4	4	7	5	4	6	2	3	1	CD
Weighting	2	9	8	7	6	5	4	3	2	1
Product of number & weighting	8	36	56	35	24	30	8	9	2	
Sum	8 + 36 + 56 + 35 + 24 + 30 + 8 + 9 + 2 = 208									
Mod 7 division	208/7 = 29 Remainder 5 Hence, '5' is added on at the end.									
New number	4	4	7	5	4	6	2	3	1	5

The new number, with the check digit added, is shown at the bottom of the table.

You will also come across the term **checksum**. ASCII codes of each alphanumeric character can be added together to produce a sum, which is transmitted or stored, along with the original message. Consider the message.

```
The cat sat on the mat.
```

The ASCII codes are shown as follows:

Table 18.3

Calculating a checksum	
Message	ASCII code
T	084
h	104
e	101
	032
c	099
a	097
t	116
	032
s	115
a	097
t	116
	032
o	111
n	110
	032
t	116
h	104
e	101
	032
m	109
a	097
t	116
.	046
Sum	1999

The digits 1999 are the checksum to be sent along with the message 'The cat sat on the mat.' As you can see from the above, a **check digit** is used for a single number or alphanumeric entry, and a **check sum** is used as an integrity check on a batch of data. However, it is not as effective in detecting and correcting errors, as the **CRC methods** covered in the next section.

Cyclic redundancy checks (CRCs)

The **CRC** mechanism is ideally suited to the sort of errors encountered when transmitting data over a **network**. The message to be sent is split up into predetermined lengths, like the packet-switching system described in unit 9. The binary data to be transmitted is used to generate coefficients of a polynomial. A polynomial is the name given to a mathematical function, like the one shown below. For example, if the digits **10110011** are to be sent, then this generates the following mathematical function: $1x^7 + 0x^6 + 1x^5 + 1x^4 + 0x^3 + 0x^2 + 1x^1 + 1x^0$

This is now used, together with another standard polynomial (not shown here), in a division sum, to produce an answer, with a remainder. The remainder, which is also a polynomial, is used to generate the bits in the **CRC check digits**. For example, if the remainder were as follows: $1x^3 + 0x^2 + 1x^1 + 1x^0$, the digits for the CRC check would be **1011**.

This CRC method is useful in that small numbers of digits are produced for large numbers of digits checked. The error detection rate is also one of the best that is available, but only the principles need be known. In all of the **data integrity checks**, *if an error is detected, the message is transmitted again.*

Computer viruses

A major threat to **data integrity** is a computer virus. A **computer virus** is a program which illegally enters and infects your computer system, then replicates itself, with the intention to annoy or cause damage. The worst that can happen is that you lose your data. It is essential to make backups at frequent intervals. The source of a computer virus can be an infected **floppy disk, Zip disk, CD-ROM, DVD or tape**. The **internet** is also a major source as viruses can arrive with downloaded programs, pictures or e-mail. There are **macro viruses**, which attach themselves to some of your applications, like word processors, for instance.

The only defence against a virus, aside from the unrealistic restriction that you don't share data is to install **virus-protection software**. Ensure that your software is kept up to date. If a new virus appears, the most up to date software will not protect you from it, at least not for a day or two, while the virus protection people get to work and produce an update.

Keeping the data secure

You will need to keep your data away from prying eyes. This is called **data security**. This is particularly so in industry, commerce and government, where sensitive data needs to be transmitted over secure networks. You will also need to ensure that your data is **backed up**, so that you may recover it in the event of a hardware failure, fire, or other catastrophe.

File privacy

The most common protection is a **password**. Passwords should be easy to remember, but difficult to crack. A password like 'Hello' could be subject to a **dictionary attack**, or guessed quite easily. A password like 'Sausage_Chips_Beans' is difficult to crack. The

More detail on CRCs can be found in chapter 5 of NUCSAL.

In the year 2000, a new computer virus was developed every 3 minutes! Young teenage boys are the worst offenders. You must have virus protection software.

Visit our portal to find out about computer viruses.

'word' is not in the dictionary, and other characters have been used. It is also easy to remember. The password can be used, in conjunction with operating system security to grant privileges to users, depending on their status. The only thing that protects users from logging onto a network as an administrator is the password. It is vital that passwords are kept secure, and changed at regular intervals.

Encryption

The passwords must obviously be stored on the computer system in a file, but must not be in a form that can be read, even if the system is hacked into. This is achieved by **encrypting** the passwords. Encryption is a method of keeping data safe, based on **keys**, or codes, which are needed to decrypt the encrypted data. Without the key, it would be difficult to crack the code by guesswork. The input to an encryption system is called **cleartext**, and the encrypted data is called **cyphertext**.

Visit our portal to find out about strong and weak encryption.

Example

A computer system has been protected from viruses, passwords have been used and the data is encrypted. However, a disgruntled employee, sacked a few weeks ago has got in through a back door. Explain what has happened.

Solution

People who program computer systems often need a way into the system, which bypasses any security. This is useful to fix bugs on new systems as they are being developed. If anyone leaves and this loophole is not plugged, then a disgruntled employee may easily hack into the system and cause malicious damage. Some programmers deliberately put a back door into systems unbeknown to the employer!

Public key encryption systems

Sending encrypted messages is hard because a **special key** has to be transmitted to the user, and a hacker could intercept this! A system of **public** and **private keys** has been developed, in which the public key, known to anyone, can be used to encrypt the message, but only the private key (already owned by the individual who receives the message) can decrypt it. As **e-commerce** grows, there is a growing need for stronger encryption mechanisms. A system called **key escrow** has been developed, where very strong encryption may be used. However, it must be agreed that a company or individual sends of a copy of his or her decryption key to the government, and this is obviously very controversial!

Visit our portal to find out more about Key Escrow.

Self-test questions

1 Explain the difference between the terms data integrity and data security.
2 What is a check digit. What is a check sum?
3 Explain why a cyclic redundancy check is one of the best methods to detect errors in the storage or transmission of data.
4 Outline a suitable strategy for keeping the data held in a file secure.
5 What is the difference between weak and strong encryption? Why is strong encryption controversial?

In this unit you have learned about:

- Data security and data integrity
- Batch totals, control totals, hash totals, check digits, check sums and cyclic redundancy checks
- How to keep data secure
- Privacy
- Data encryption and back doors

19 Backup strategies and file management

In this section you will learn about:

- Different backup strategies for small and large organisations
- Master files, transactions files and logs
- Grandfather, father and son files
- Hierarchical file structure and management of files
- Physical and logical drives

Backing up your data is vital. You must understand the different methods likely to be used in different scenarios for examination purposes.

Backing up strategies

As well as protecting data from hackers, we must protect data from **natural hazards** such as **fire**, **hardware failures** or **software crashes**. Large companies will have much bigger problems due to the vast quantities of data they process, and the urgency with which the data will probably be needed in the event of an emergency.

Example

A small business has just ten networked PCs and a fileserver. Suggest a sensible backup and recovery strategy.

Solution

The systems need considering in two parts:

(a) **Data** belonging to the business
(b) The **applications** and **operating systems** used by the business.

(a) The **data** regarding the business should be stored on the file server. This probably consists of many files like **databases**, **word processor documents** and **spreadsheet documents** etc. that should be allocated to specific directories.

At the end of each day, or more frequently if necessary, a **tape backup** can be made of the file server directories. One strategy would be to back up the work each day, and to label the tapes 'Monday', 'Tuesday' etc. until 'Sunday'. The next week, the tape labelled Monday is overwritten with the new data. The backups can either be **incremental** (only the files which have been updated will change), or **total**, in which case *all files* will be backed up, irrespective of whether they have been altered.

This backup strategy would not cater for people deleting work that day, *before* the actual backup is made. It would only be possible to revert to the previous day's work.

(b) The next situation to consider is a disk crash to either the file server, or to one of the workstations. It *is* possible to insert a new disk into the broken computer, install a new operating system, install the drivers and graphics cards etc., install the applications again, set up the user accounts, network settings and security settings etc. This would normally take the best part of a day. If the file server were the machine at fault, then the entire business would be out of action.

One possible solution is to have a disk image. This consists of a byte-by-byte copy of the machine in question, and can restore the entire 'operating system', applications, settings and security in one go, because the image, taken of the original disk, was set up in this way. In practice, a system like GHOST, from Symantic, does this. Indeed, if the original images are intact, a workstation or file server can be restored very quickly.

Visit our portal to find out more about GHOST.

74

Do not confuse backing up data with an archive, which is taking little used material off line.

Helping to prevent catastrophes

Data must often be available 24 hours a day, even in the event of a disk crash. Some file servers have what is called **Disk mirroring**. This is a **RAID system**, (**Redundant Array of Independent Drives**), which means that identical copies are made on two independent disks. RAID is covered in unit 15.

Other backup strategies

Lots of businesses generate a **transaction file** (transactions for a particular day). At the end of the day, this file is used to update the information on a **master file**, which then becomes the **new master file**.

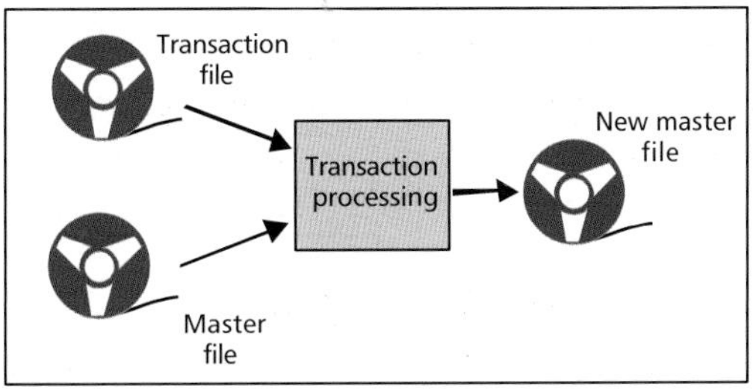

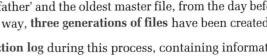

Figure 19.1 Updating a master file.

The **new master file** is called the 'son' file, because the **old master file**, shown on the left, is the 'father' file. The next day, the new master file becomes the 'son', the old master file becomes the 'father' and the oldest master file, from the day before, becomes the 'grandfather' file. In this way, **three generations of files** have been created.

The computer may generate a **transaction log** during this process, containing information about changes that have taken place. This is useful to **backtrack** to sort out errors.

Further information about generations of files can be found in chapter 26 of NUCSAL.

File management

A typical Windows-based directory structure, showing part of a Windows NT directory, can be seen in Figure 19.2. A variety of folders exist, so that the system may be managed in a hierarchical way. Each folder may contain other folders and files, allowing you to manage the system more efficiently than if all the files had to be stored in the same directory.

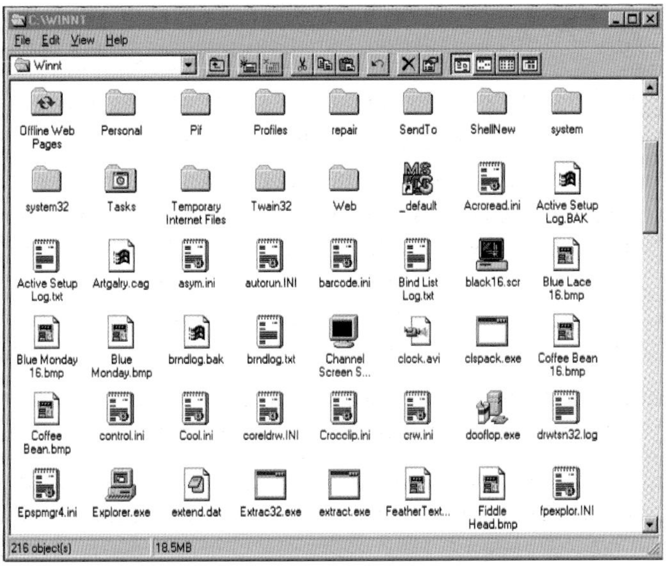

Figure 19.2 A window displaying part of the Windows NT directory structure.

The position of the **directories** (shown by the folders) and **files** (shown by the other icons) in Figure 19.2 is on the C drive, in the WINNT directory, as indicated by the directory path name on the title bar of the window. Therefore, the avi file called 'clock' is in this directory. The NTFS (similar to DOS) **file pathname** is therefore

```
'C:\WINNT\clock.avi'
```

Notice the format which is 'Drive letter' followed by '\' followed by all the directories separated by '\', and terminated by the leaf **file name**.

Figure 19.3 shows a hierarchical file structure. A **logical drive**, labelled K, is set up to store data files. The root directory on this particular disk, has directories labelled 'Art Course', 'Word Processing' and 'Finances'. The word processing directory is divided into two sub-directories, called 'Home' and 'School'. There are also other sub directories not shown. Finally, the files are put at the **leaf node** (see unit 35) position in the tree, and represent the end of a particular path structure. Therefore, the geography project, labelled 'Geog.doc' would have the following path name.

```
K:\Word Processing\School\Geog.doc
```

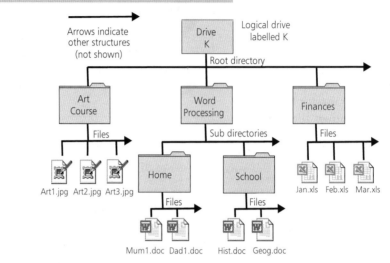

Figure 19.3 Hierarchical organisation.

When setting up a new computer it is often wise to split a large physical drive up into two or more partitions (logical drives) – one for the OS and system files, and one for the applications and data.

This hierarchical system allows use of the same file names in different directories. This knowledge enables you to understand the commands needed for **batch operations**. From Figure 19.3 you can see that drive K has been called a **logical drive**. This is to distinguish it from a physical drive, which is the drive actually present in the machine. A logical drive is, therefore, a drive simulated by software. A **physical drive** is literally the hardware device, which you can take out or put into the machine. Very large drives can usually be **partitioned** into smaller **logical drives** to make the storage of information more efficient. From the users' view a logical drive acts as though it were a physical drive in the machine.

Example

You are the network manager in a school that organises resources on several networked file servers. There are 1500 users, split up into staff, and students (Years 1 to 7). Each pupil is allowed disk space on a server. Resources like word processors are loaded from a local hard disk to cut down on the network bandwidth required. Other resources, such as clipart, web design tools and other common utilities are to be found on one of several resource servers. Suggest a file structure, including the naming of any logical and physical drives presented to the users, and the role that these drives might play in the logical organisation of the system.

Solution

We will assume an individual file server for each year, and one for the staff. To gain access to private areas on the appropriate file server, a logical drive (labelled Z for convenience here) would be mapped to that area on the file server to which the student or member of staff has read/write permissions. If, for example, the file server allocated to the upper sixth (year 7) is called Enterprise, and one of the students is called James T. Kirk, then the physical directory in which James may save his work might be:

```
:\\Enterprise\students\KirkJT
```

This indicates that the U6th student called Kirk has his work stored on the Enterprise file server in a directory called students in a subdirectory called KirkJT. This would be on one of the main disks in the file server called 'Enterprise'.

This file path name would have to be unique within the organisation. However, another student in a different year could have the same leaf directory name because the file server name will be different. The network manager would automatically map a logical drive for this student. When the student logs on, he will see 'drive Z', and any other mapped drive to which he may be entitled. The student may then attach a label (shortcut) to the Z drive like 'My Work', for example.

Other resources, like the clipart mentioned above, might be assigned a different drive letter like Y, for example, and be labelled 'Clipart'. The student would then see this drive also, and other drives showing other resources as seen fit to assign by the network manager. As far as the student is concerned, it appears identical to having the physical disk drives in their own workstation, but the files are actually loaded from any of the network file servers or other resources.

Most resources can be shared in the ways described in the previous section. For example, if you have permission to do so, you could put a CD into the drive of your local workstation, and **share** it so that all people on the network can have access to it. Indeed, on Local Area Networks you have to be very careful about sharing resources, and should not do so without your network manager's permission. It would be possible, for example, in a badly protected network, to wipe the files from somebody else's hard drive, just because they have shared it, and inadvertently set the permission to public read/write/delete!

Self-test questions

1. A chain of shops creates several transaction files, one for each branch. At the end of the day, these files are transmitted via the internet to head office, where the master file, containing up-to-date information about all the shops, is handled. Explain the batch processing that goes on each day at head office, making sure that you include the grandfather, father and son files in your explanation.
2. Both data files and programs (applications files and system files) need to be backed up to recover in the event of a system crash. Outline the different techniques that might be put in place to deal with these two very different types of files.
3. Explain the difference between a backup and an archive, outlining why each method is necessary.
4. What is the difference between a physical and a logical drive? Why are both used extensively in practice?
5. A college has many networked workstations connected to LANs and several file servers containing important data. Outline backup strategies that would be needed in the following situations:
   (a) fat clients on the networks
   (b) thin clients on the networks

Visit our portal to find out more about thin clients.

In this unit you have learned about:

- Backup strategies and how RAID systems might prevent an emergency
- Grandfather, father and son files
- The difference between physical and logical drives
- Making use of hierarchical directory structures to help manage a network

20 Simple database concepts

In this section you will learn about:

- What a simple database is
- The flat-file and relational database
- Database tables
- Implementing a simple database in practice, using Microsoft Access
- Key fields and data types

Databases

A database is one of the best applications in which to do an A2 project. Think carefully about this for the second year of your course.

A **database** is a collection of related information, possibly contained in just one file, but more usually consisting of many files, often related in special ways. These files are organised for efficient processing, like **searching** and **sorting**. If a database consists of just one file, it is called a **flat file database**. More modern databases are usually **relational** (see later) and are accompanied by sophisticated utilities to perform a variety of functions from printing out results of **queries** to managing security for many users.

Database concepts

Table 20.1 shows some information stored regarding books housed in a library. The table is not large, but already we see **duplication**, like 'publisher', shown in the highlighted

Table 20.1 Table for a library database

Small sample of library 'book' information					
ISBN	Author	Title	Publisher	Price	...
0-7487-4046-5	Bradley	Computer Science	Nelson Thornes	24.00	...
0-7833-8822-7	Farmer	NT 4 Server Secrets	Nelson Thornes	39.00	...
0-6324-2817-6	Martin	Radio Techniques	Nelson Thornes	36.00	...
0-5834-9921-7	Bradley	Quantum Computers	Nelson Thornes	57.00	...
0-3844-8463-8	Bradley	Modulation	Peter Gibbs	45.00	...
0-3523-7668-2	Prakash	Java Programming	Peter Gibbs	23.00	...
0-6543-9332-8	Burgin	CD-ROM Servers	Castle House	20.00	...
Etc.	...	...	...	...	...

If you have time, program the examples shown here using Microsoft Access – it will help considerably with your understanding.

Table 20.2 Part of the table for publishers

Small sample of publisher information				
Publisher	Address	Phone	Fax	...
Nelson Thornes	Delta Place 27 Bath Road Cheltenham Glos. GL53 7TH	01242 267100	01242 221914	...
Peter Gibbs	Gibbon Road Tunbridge Wells Kent TN 99 1JP	01732 889563	01732 994352	...
Castle House	High Street Windsor Berkshire SL 78 1TG	01753 765427	01753 895532	...
Etc.	...	...	...	...

column. In practice we may also need **attributes** (**fields** that go to make up a **record**) like 'publisher's address', 'phone and fax numbers', 'e-mail address' etc. Duplication of all this would be inefficient and so the publisher information is taken out, and put into a separate table, like the one shown in Table 20.2.

We now have less **redundancy**, which is one of the aims of good database design. With a couple of million books in a very large library, you can imagine how much storage space would be wasted. However, we now need to **link** the two tables, so that they are **related**, and hence can be updated more efficiently. This is the essence of a **relational database**, compared to the **flat-file database**, which consists of one table only, or one file only.

In a **relational database**, a **table** corresponds to a **file**, a **row** corresponds to a **record**, and a **column** contains the entries corresponding to a **field**. The highlighted columns contain **relational information**.

Example

Consider the library database described in the last section.

(a) If the tables were not related in the ways described, but were held on several independent files, **data inconsistency** may occur. Explain why this might be so.

(b) Suggest a better way of storing publisher information such that if changes were needed, like a change of name, this would have to be altered in one entry only.

Solution

(a) **Data inconsistency** means that data stored in different places may not be consistent (i.e. entries that should be identical might not be). If *independent files* are used to store information, then the likelihood of data inconsistency is high. If the name of a publisher, for example, contains an error, then this will, in effect, be regarded as a different publisher by the system. These sorts of errors can be minimised in a relational database that is well designed.

(b) It is more efficient to replace publisher names with a publisher ID. The publisher ID information can then be used to link the tables, just like the publisher name did previously. This new method is better because there is less chance of data inconsistency. Table 20.3 shows some very simple IDs for the three publishers.

More information about databases can be found in chapter 28 of NUCSAL.

Table 20.3 Publisher name replaced by ID

Small sample of library 'book' information					
ISBN	Author	Title	Publisher ID	Price	...
0-7487-4046-5	Bradley	Computer Science	1	24.00	...
0-7833-8822-7	Farmer	NT 4 Server Secrets	1	39.00	...
0-6324-2817-6	Martin	Radio Techniques	1	36.00	...
0-5834-9921-7	Bradley	Quantum Computers	1	57.00	...
0-3844-8463-8	Bradley	Modulation	2	45.00	...
0-3523-7668-2	Prakash	Java Programming	2	23.00	...
0-6543-9332-8	Burgin	CD-ROM Servers	3	20.00	...
Etc.	...	...	...	...	...

The publisher ID now becomes the primary key, shown in Table 20.4. The two highlighted columns now provide the relational information, linking the two tables. The publisher appears once only. If the name changed to 'Nelson Thornes & Sons', only one field would have to be altered, although the entire database, possibly containing thousands of references to this publisher, have been updated. The chance of **data inconsistency** has therefore been reduced.

Table 20.4 New publisher ID is primary key

Small sample of publisher information					
Publisher ID	Publisher	Address	Phone	Fax	...
1	Nelson Thornes	Delta Place 27 Bath Road Cheltenham Glos. GL53 7TH	O1242 267100	01242 221914	...
2	Peter Gibbs	Gibbon Road Tunbridge Wells Kent TN 99 1JP	01732 889563	01732 994352	...
3	Castle House	High Street Windsor Berkshire SL78 1TG	01753 765427	01753 895532	...
Etc.	...	...	...	...	...

The above illustrates the advantage that a **relational database** has over **a flat-file database**.

Library example using Microsoft Access

In an examination, never say 'use a Wizard' to help create a database or query etc. It will get you no marks. You are expected to be able to explain the main processes.

To set up the library database, load Access and, using the Wizards, create a **new database** entering the fields as shown in Figure 20.1

You are reminded about the **data types** or field types. A **text field** (i.e. alphanumeric characters) is suitable for most of the fields, but '**number**' is used for the 'publisher ID' and '**currency**' is used for the 'price'. Prudent use of data types ensures fewer errors are made.

Make ISBN the **key field**, as shown by the key next to the ISBN field name in Figure 20.1. Next use the **form wizard**, so that there is a convenient data-entry method. Add all the fields and accept the default templates. You should end up with a data entry form (record card) similar to that shown in Figure 20.2. Data can be entered directly onto the datasheet, but special forms make data entry particularly easy for novice users. In practice you would use more sophisticated methods to limit data entry errors, but these have been omitted here for the sake of clarity. The labels used on the forms do not have to correspond to the field names, but need to reflect the needs of the people who will actually enter the data. Next add the data in Table 20.3. After entering

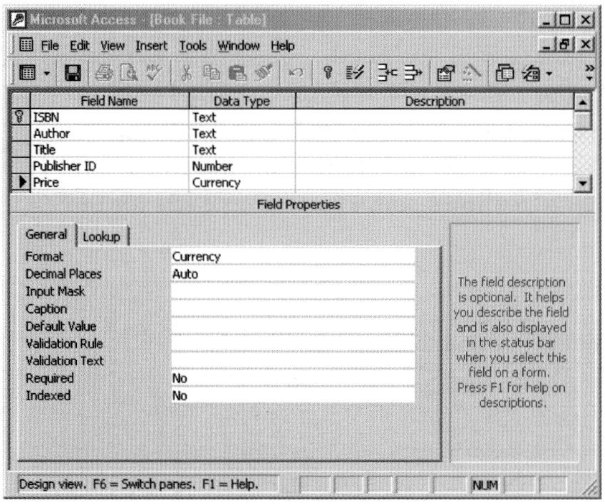

Figure 20.1 Table built up using Access.

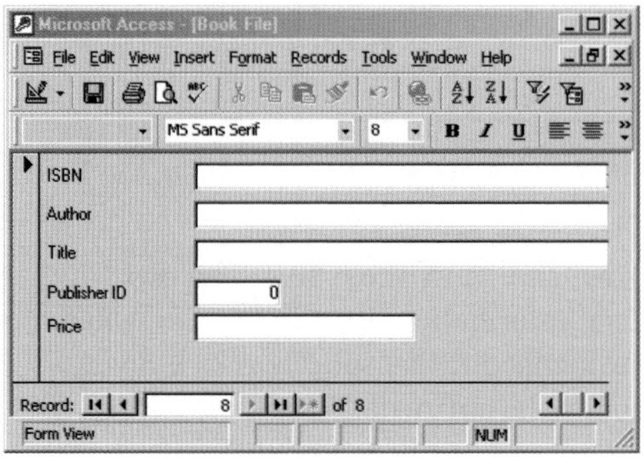

Figure 20.2 A form created in Access.

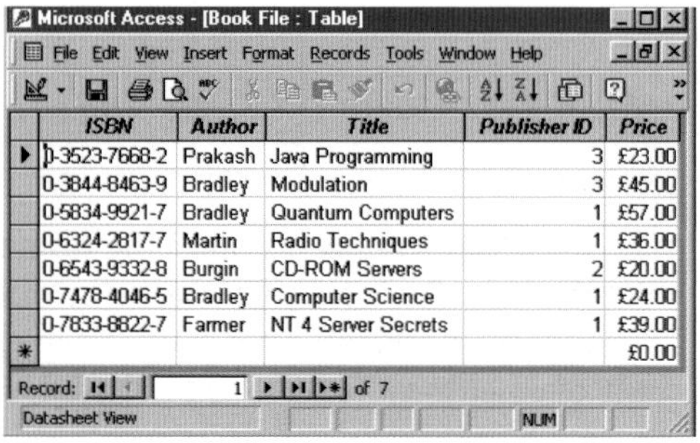

Figure 20.3 The data has now been entered into the book table.

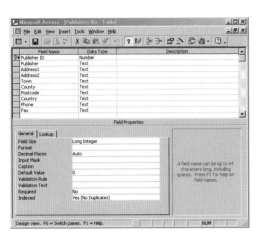

Figure 20.4 The publishers table.

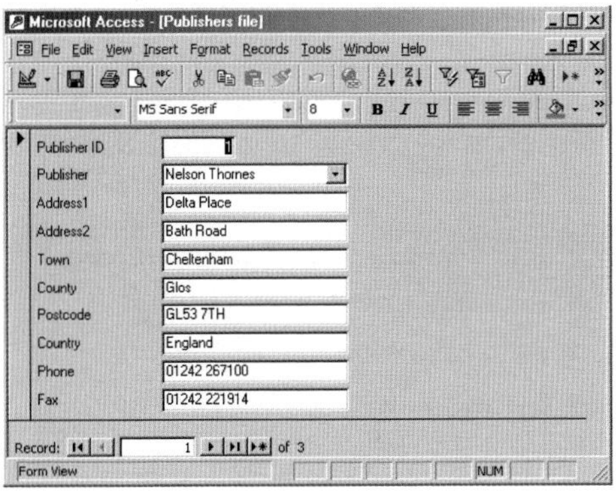

Figure 20.5 Form for the publishers file.

the data, view the **table** containing the data using the *datasheet viewing option*, as shown in Figure 20.3.

Next create the publishers table. Create a new table (*not* a new database), and set up the table, as shown in Figure 20.4.

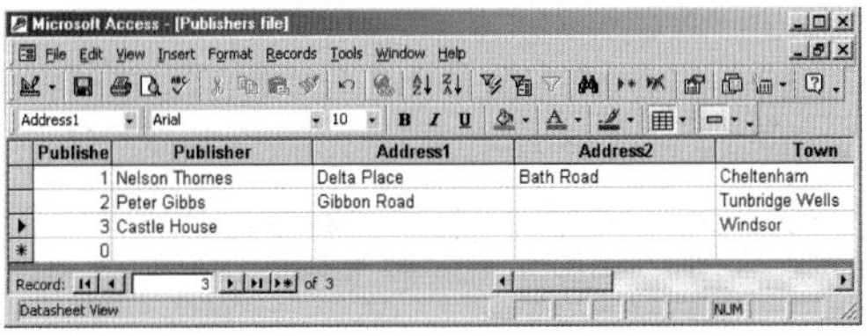

We have now allocated six different text

Figure 20.6 Records in datasheet view.

fields for the address. This is more efficient than putting the address into a single field. This enables easier searching on criteria such as 'postcode' or 'county'. As an example of this, the sixth address field contains the country of origin of the publisher. We could search for country of origin very quickly by getting a match on this particular field. We have assigned the **key field** to publisher ID. Elementary things like this need to be thought about carefully at the design stage.

Next create a form for entry of data into the publisher's table, as shown in Figure 20.5.

After all the data has been entered, confirm that all is correct by looking at the three records in datasheet view, as shown in Figure 20.6. Note that only the left-hand side of the view has been shown here because the actual view is long and thin.

Visit our web site for an A2 project making use of Access.

To find many resources for Access (examples, of reports and queries etc.).

Self-test questions

1 What it the difference between a flat-file database and a relational database?
2 How is the data in a database table related to the data stored in the file on disk?
3 What is a primary key and why is this concept important in database design?
4 Different data types may be chosen for representing the information stored in each field. Suggest a data type for each of the following, giving reasons for your choice.
   (a) Surname   (b) Age   (c) Male or Female?
   (d) A picture   (e) A telephone number

In this unit you have learned about:

- How to **create a database**
- The difference between a **flat file** and a **relational database**
- How to create a simple database using **Microsoft Access**
- **Data types** and **key fields**

21 Databse relationships and minimising errors

In this section you will learn about:

- Simple database relationships
- Primary, foreign and alternate keys
- Indexing – primary and secondary
- Data validation
- Some methods to help data entry

This unit builds on the work covered in Unit 20.

Creating a relationship using Access

In unit 20 we created two tables in Access, and now wish to create a relationship between them, based on the Publisher ID. In database design, you can create **one-to-one**, **one-to-many** or **many-to-one relationships**. Here, the relationship between the 'Book table Publisher ID' and 'Publisher table Publisher ID' is many to one, because there can be many entries in the book file or table, mapped onto just one entry in the publisher file or table.

To set up a relationship using Access, click over the relationship button on the tool bar, and make sure that both tables can be seen. Choosing the appropriate tables and clicking 'show table' in the view tool can achieve this. To create a **many-to-one relationship**, drag the Publisher ID field in the publishers file to the Publisher ID field in the Book file. You will then get the screen shown in Figure 21.1. Figure 21.1 confirms the relationship is between the Publisher IDs in both tables, but the relationship is one-to-many, not many-to-one. However, don't forget that this is with respect to the Publishers table. From the point of view of the Book file table, it is the many-to-one relationship we required, and this is confirmed by inspection of Figure 21.2. This is because the infinity sign (many) is tagged to the Book file.You should enforce **referential integrity**, as this will check that you have no references to entries that do not exist. Also, make sure that the 'cascade update related fields' box is checked, so that Access automatically updates corresponding values in the related table.

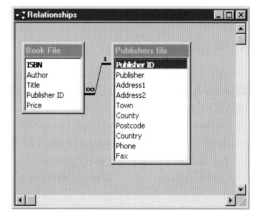

Figure 21.1 Setting up a relationship.

Figure 21.2 A many-to-one relationship.

Setting up the work covered here on a computer will aid your understanding considerably.

The relational database model is covered in chapter 29 of NUCSAL.

To confirm the appropriate relationship is set up, your tables, and the relationship between them, should be as shown in Figure 21.2.

Other relational database terminology

The **key field**, which identifies a record in a table, is called the **primary key**. **ISBN number** is the **primary key** in Table 20.1, and **Publisher** is the **primary key** in Table 20.2. Any other key not used as the primary key is called an **alternate key**.

We produce a list of books by Nelson Thornes, by matching the **primary key** to Nelson Thornes in the Publishers table. We need to decide how the results are to be sorted, as all primary-key entries are the same. We might choose 'Title', for example, so all books published by 'Nelson Thornes' are listed in ascending order of title. In this case, 'Title' is called a **secondary key**. In Figure 21.2, the **primary key field** was dragged to the **foreign key field** in another table. Taking Figure 21.2 as an example, the **primary field** 'Publisher ID' in the 'Publishers table' was dragged to the **foreign key** 'Publisher ID' in the 'Book table', creating a **one to many relationship** from 'Publishers table' to 'Book table'.

Example

(a) List *four* different data types that may typically be used when setting up a database. For each data type, suggest why it might be used. Why are data types important when designing a database?

(b) Briefly explain the following terms when applied to database design.

Flat-file database   *Relational database*
Table   *Primary key*
Foreign key

Solution

(a) Four different data types are as follows:

Text   Number   Date   Boolean

The **text** data type is suitable for entering alphanumeric characters. The **number** data type will ensure that only numbers are entered. The **date** data type will ensure that valid dates only are entered. The **Boolean** data type is a true/false or yes/no field. If suitable data types are used at the design stage, there is less need for complex validation techniques.

(b) Each term is defined as follows:

A **flat-file database** is one in which the whole database is **contained in a single file** or **table**. A **relational database** is one in which a number of linked related tables are set up to store the data. A **table** represents an individual file, whose rows represent the records and whose columns represent the fields. A **primary key** is one that identifies a table.

A **foreign key** is the target key used when identifying a relationship. The relationship is usually between the primary and foreign key.

Indexing

Indexes can be used to locate information stored in files efficiently. As a database is little different from a sophisticated collection of files, it is not surprising to find that indexes are used to good effect here too. Most database software will automatically create an index on the primary key, which is called the **primary index**, but you can set up **secondary indexes** too, based on any other keys. Not all fields can be indexed, because of their data type. The use of these

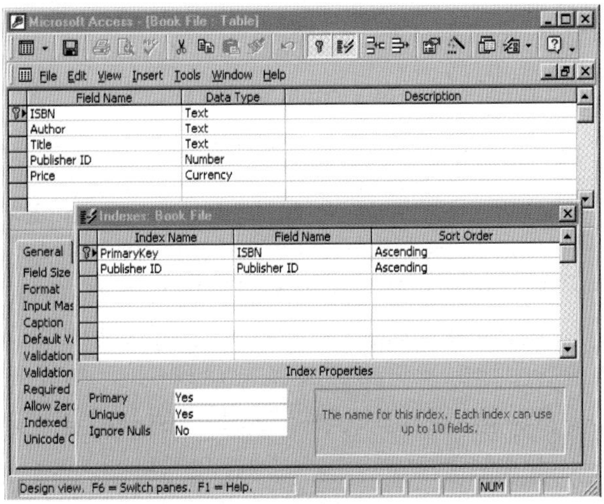

If you don't have a copy of Microsoft Access, you can use other databases to set up similar systems to those shown here.

Figure 21.3 Viewing the indexes.

indexes speeds up operations like **searching** and **sorting**. If the field is indexed, then the time taken to find an item of data will be reduced. However, you should not index everything, or the overheads and complexity will become overly great. If you frequently make a search on 'Publisher name', for example, then this field would be worth indexing.

To view an index, the table needs to be loaded and design view must be selected. Next view the indexes by making use of a submenu under the view option on the toolbar. The indexes set up for the 'Book table' in the library example (Unit 20) can be seen in Figure 21.3. Here you can see the **primary index**, created automatically for the **primary key** ISBN number, and a **secondary index**, for publisher ID. You can add extra indexes, and may alter attributes of each index.

Validation techniques

Always validate data in your AS and A2 projects; you can lose many marks if you don't.

Creating rules that must be obeyed before data is entered in to the system will **validate** the data. For example, a pupil at a secondary school may have his or her age validated to be in the range 11 < age < 19. Therefore, if a data-entry clerk were to enter 51 instead of 15 (called a **transposition** error because the two digits have been transposed), then the **validation rule** would ensure that this data did not get entered. Assuming you can think up a suitable set of rules, then validation is very easy to achieve. Using the above age example, we can set up this rule on an age field in Microsoft's Access as shown in Figure 21.4.

Here the validation rule for the age field has been set to:

```
>=11 And <=19
```

Note the syntax. We do not need the name 'age' anywhere because this is the validation rule for the age field. This method will ensure that only those values between 11 and 19 inclusive are accepted.

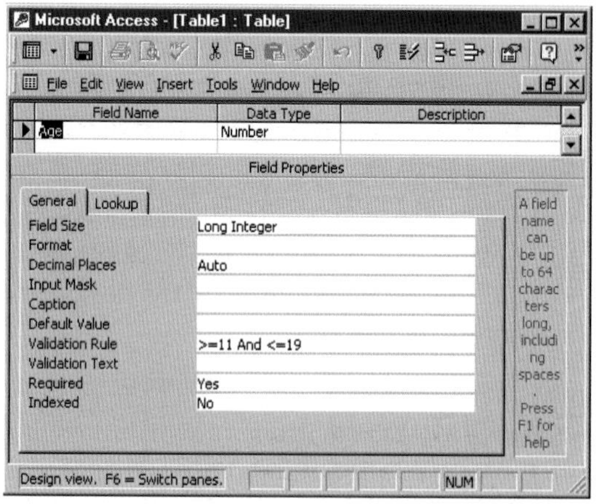

Figure 21.4 Some validation parameters.

Example

Visit our portal to see some of the validation methods in the database project.

(a) Suggest a sensible way of validating the following data using any acceptable syntax:

Date	***Weekdays only***
Two or three digit number	***Person's name***

(b) What is meant by data verification?

Solution

(a) (i) It is not necessary to design a set of complex validation rules to check if a date is entered correctly. Set the data type to a date field. Further validation may be required if dates need restricting further.

(ii) If days of the week are to be entered in full, a function like the following is required.

```
Monday OR Tuesday OR Wednesday OR Thursday OR Friday
```

(iii) Assuming that the # sign is the wildcard for a number (i.e. the sign that represents any digit 0 to 9 inclusive), then the validation rule may be something like:

```
'###' OR '####'
```

(iv) Names cannot usually be validated. There is no way of telling whether they are right or wrong (e.g. should a surname be Clark or Clarke?)

(b) Although validation cannot usually be used to determine the correctness of a person's name, it is possible to verify that the name has been entered 'correctly'. Verification can be achieved by entering the same data again. The computer then checks to see if the new data is the same as the original data. If the two data sets are in agreement, it is assumed that the data is correct. If there are differences, then this is brought to the attention of the operators, who check the data again. This reduces the likelihood of error, but cannot eliminate it completely, especially if the data on the **data capture form** is wrong, for example.

The validation rules can be of enormous complexity. If there are not enough functions within Access to perform what is required, then you may write your own **validation methods** making use of the programming language **VBA** (Visual Basic for Applications).

Look up columns

Although there are other ways to enter data, one worthy of note, if you are developing a database in the window's environment, is the **look up column**, (on the Publisher field) shown in Figure 21.5. This is useful if a **defined set of data** must be entered in a particular field.

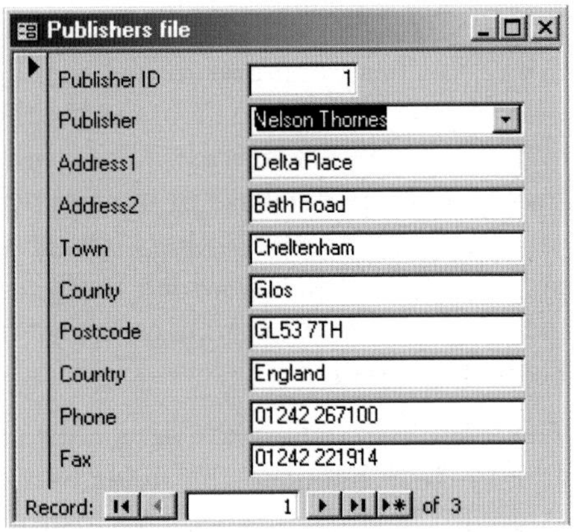

Figure 21.5 A look up column.

Self-test questions

1 Explain the terms primary and foreign keys.
2 Explain what primary and secondary indexes are, with respect to a relational database, giving an example of each.
3 What is data validation? Suggest a suitable validation rule for the following:
   (a) The age of a male old-age pensioner.
   (b) The price of an item in a shop.
4 Suggest two different ways in which facilities in a typical database may be used to help prevent tired data-entry staff making errors.

In this unit you have learned about:

● Simple database relationships
● The difference between primary, foreign and alternate keys
● A variety of data validation methods to help minimise errors during the data entry phase

22 Database queries and reports

In this section you will learn about:

- Database queries and reports
- Complex search criteria
- Designing reports
- Exporting data from a database to other applications
- The CSV format

Realise that the whole point of setting up a database is to perform queries and reports. These two utilities are this important.

Queries and reports

A **query** is a method of extracting data from a database, and presenting it to the user. A query is easy to create using the query wizard. Let us extract records from the library database in the last two units, containing the authors 'Bradley' or 'Farmer'. We specify which fields are to be included in the search, as shown in Figure 22.1.

The 'Book file' (table) has been chosen, and we have included the fields called 'Author', 'Title' and 'ISBN'. We instruct Access to run the query and find the records, if they exist, where the field 'Author' has a value of 'Bradley' or 'Farmer'. The results are shown in Figure 22.2.

The query has found four records, corresponding to the correct entries given in Figure 20.3 of Unit 20. The information in the fields 'Author', 'Title' and 'ISBN' are displayed as requested.

Queries can span multiple tables, and contain complex search criteria, with combinations of operations such as 'OR', 'AND', 'NOT', '<>' etc.

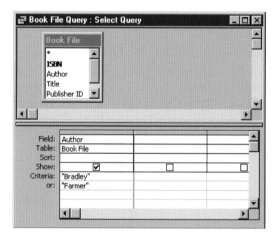

Figure 22.1 Setting up a query.

Author	Title	ISBN
Bradley	Computer Science	0-7487-4046-5
Farmer	NT4 Server Secrets	0-7833-8822-7
Bradley	Quantum Computers	0-5834-9921-7
Bradley	Modulation	0-3844-8463-8

Figure 22.2 The result of the query.

Example

Write a query to list the 'Author', 'Title' and 'Publisher' of books in the library database, which contain the word 'Computer' or 'Computers' in the title.

Solution

Run the query wizard, choose the fields 'Author' and 'Title' from the book file, and 'Publisher' from the Publisher file. Set up the Title to contain the words 'Computer' or 'Computers' as shown in Figure 22.3. From Figure 22.3 you can see that both tables have been used, because the fields requested are a combination of fields from each of the tables.

If we search for the string "Computer" in the title, we will also find "Computers". Therefore, we use the following test:

```
LIKE "*Computer*"
```

The command LIKE (placed in the title field) asks Access to Find any number of characters (*) followed by the word computer, followed by any other number of other characters (*). Running the above query confirms that the required results are obtained, as shown in Figure 22.4

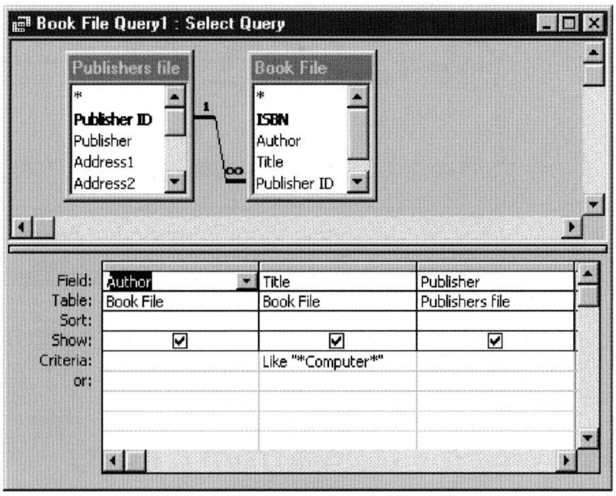

Figure 22.3 A query to find Computer in the book title.

The simple ways of expressing queries, like those shown above are often called **query by example** or **QBE**, because the novice user can tick boxes and enter data with relative ease, compared to the **SQL language** (see unit 48) which is used to implement the query.

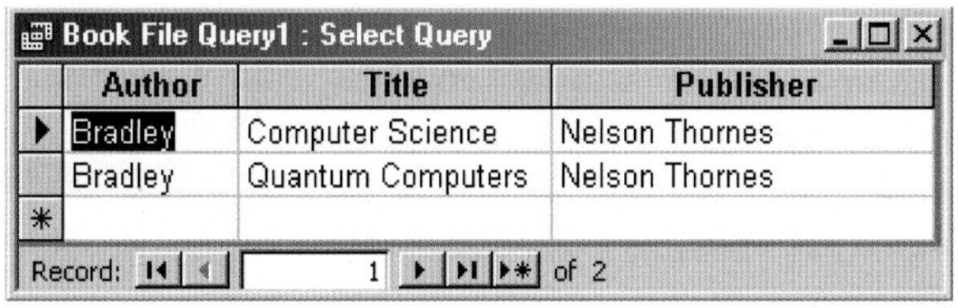

Figure 22.4 The results of the query.

Reporting

Results need to be presented in an acceptable format, with **headings**, **subheadings**, **headers** and **footers** etc. This makes the data more attractive and professional.

Microsoft's Access provides a wizard that guides you through the processes of choosing which fields will appear in the report, and how the fields will be formatted in the final layout. It allows the fields to be sorted into ascending or descending order and allows specification of headers and footers, both within sections of a report and at the top of the individual pages. It allows you to define the style of the report by the provision of set templates, and allows you to specify headings and sub-headings. You may also design reports from scratch using design view. A report is shown in Figure 22.5 and designing it is shown in Figure 22.6.

Note how the title and the 'page headers and footers' are designed. The detail of the report contains the 'Author', 'Title' and 'Publisher' fields, which list each record underneath each other in a column. The data contained in the report can be exported to other applications like word processors, spreadsheets and databases (see later in this unit).

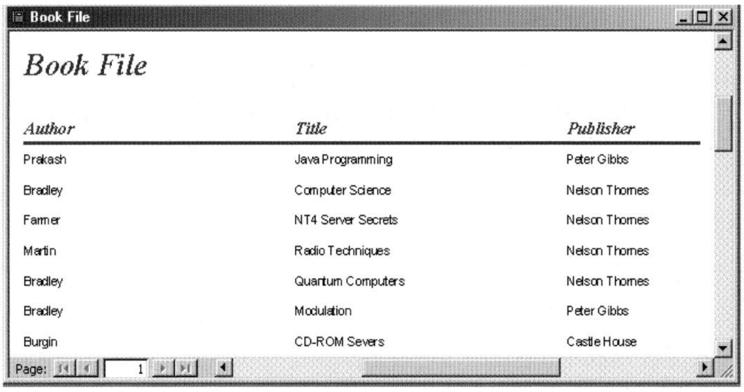

Visit our portal to see some of the queries and reports examples in the database project.

Figure 22.5 A simple report layout.

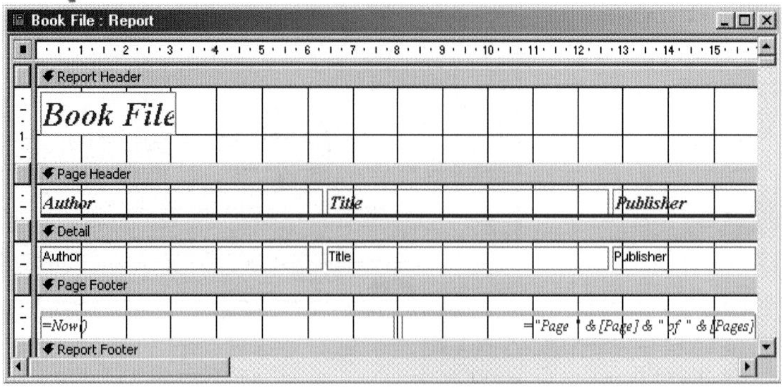

Figure 22.6 The Design View of a report.

Producing a report from a query

You can print out the entire data-base as a report, but it is more usual to specify some **query** to which the data must adhere. In the library file you may, for example, want a query which outputs to a report only those books with a value over £25. If you are using Access, for example, you can specify that the report is to operate on a query, rather than on a table. You can do this by changing the option as shown in Figure 22.7.

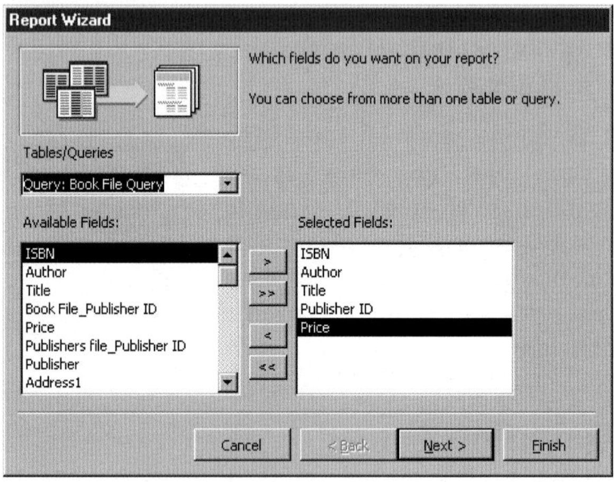

Figure 22.7 Producing a report from a query.

Accessing the data from other applications

One of the powerful features of modern databases is the fact that they can be accessed directly from other applications. For example, in Microsoft's Office 2000 suite, data from the Access database system can be accessed from **Word**, **Excel**, **PowerPoint** and **Visual Basic**, to name but a few. This gives programmers the ability to do powerful data process-ing, using facilities in an environment with which they may be more familiar (see unit 26).

Example

You will find the example given here hard to do unless you have some experience of importing and exporting data between different applications.

A medical database has been set up to store the results of experiments. It is your job to extract the experimental data from the database, analyse it making use of a spreadsheet, and then use both the original data from the database and the calculated statistics to produce a word-processed report. You need to explain how to do the following operations:

● How is the data from the database imported into the spreadsheet?

● How might the statistics be calculated and stored in the spreadsheet?
● How might the original data from the database be imported into the final report?

● How are the statistics from the spreadsheet imported into the final report?

Solution

An easy way to export data from one application to another is by using a **Comma Separated Variable** file, in which commas separate the variables, representing the data. To generate a **CSV file**, a query is defined, and the output of the query is saved in CSV format. Let us suppose we have five records, with each record containing just two fields as follows.

A,1   B,2   C,3   D,4   E,5

Importing the data into a spreadsheet, 'A' would be imported into Cell 'A1' and B would be imported into cell A2 etc. (see Figure 22.8).

For the medical database, we define a query that will extract the data and output the results of the query as a file in CSV form. Once saved, the CSV file can be imported into the spreadsheet and then changed to the native format of the spreadsheet for further analysis. If we are using Excel, for example, we might want to save the CSV data in 'xls' format. The required statistics and other analysis may now be carried out.

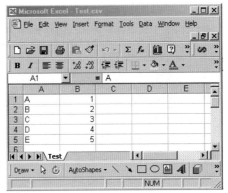

Figure 22.8 CSV data imported into a spreadsheet.

Play with the CSV import and export functions in packages like Excel and Word. They are easy to use.

The layout of the generated statistics will have to be carefully thought out, and the results of calculated formulae may have to be changed to numbers. This too can then be saved in a file in CSV format.

The final stage with the word processor depends on how the statistical data is to be processed. If, for example, data from queries is needed in the word processor, then the CSV file may be loaded directly as a table. Figure 22.9 shows the previous simple CSV data imported directly into Microsoft Word.

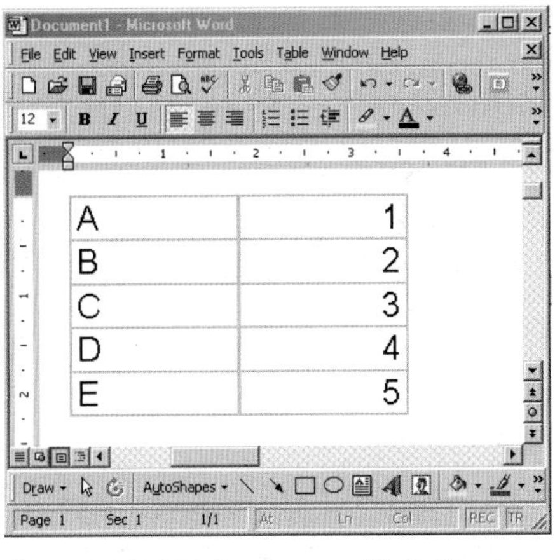

Figure 22.9 CSV data imported into Word.

It may be more appropriate to the report being created to mail merge individual records. This can also be done from the database, and the data placed in tables embedded into Word in ways similar to that shown in Figure 22.9.

Self-test questions

1 What is meant by a database query?
2 Design a suitable report layout to list the pupils in a school by house, with each house being listed by year and then form.
3 Some data contained in a database needs to be analysed using statistics, not available within the database package. However, the appropriate mathematical functions are available in a spreadsheet. Outline the principles of what has to be done to analyse the data.
4 Macro languages like VBA, for example, can be used to extend the functionality of a database like Access. Explain how this might have overcome the problem outlined in question 3.

In this unit you have learned about:

- How to produce database queries and reports
- How to produce a report using a query
- How to access data from other applications using the CSV format

23 Basic computer applications

In this section you will learn about:

- General-purpose packages
- WP and DTP
- Spreadsheets
- Databases
- The user interface
- Integration with other packages

It is possible to feel you have done well on some examination questions, only to find you are a grade down on what you expected! Read this unit carefully to find out some typical reasons why.

General-purpose packages

Students, who have used general-purpose packages like **word processors** and **spreadsheets** for years, are often unable to identify important attributes that characterise these packages. They do not understand the effects that these packages have in a business environment.

Some features contained in these packages are similar, and you should make sure that you identify critical ones. Saying that a spreadsheet could be used to check spelling is true, but would not get you a mark in a question requiring an important use of a spreadsheet! It would be far better to concentrate on the mathematical and simulation features of the package, for which the spreadsheet was originally designed.

Example

Outline four important features provided by a word processor that might be useful to a small company (about six employees) working in the legal profession.

Solution

(1) **Standard letters** and **mail merge** would allow secretaries preparing the legal documents to call up standard paragraphs from a **legal database**. This would ensure that complex language and wording is exactly right, which is crucial in legal documentation.

(2) A **specialised dictionary** containing legal terms may be added to the standard dictionary.

(3) The **data can be shared** between employees if set up to access a common area on a file server. Users would require access to different parts of the database.

(4) The **documentation** in the word processor is already in electronic form, and could thus be transferred quickly and easily to different parts of the world.

You should note from the above example that general points about the word processor have been *adapted for the legal profession*. When spell checking is considered, this example mentions *specialist legal terms*, which would be important in a firm of solicitors.

Generalisation

It is also possible that general questions may be asked. For example, you would be expected to know how computers might be used in a business to help with day-to-day procedures common to all businesses.

Example

Make a list of four uses of a computer for helping with the administration of a small business. For each of your examples state the software most likely to be used.

Solution

- The production of **promotional literature** (word processor and DTP package).
- **Financial projections** of profit, loss and cash flow (a spreadsheet).
- **Payroll** (probably a specialist package)
- **Preparation of accounts** (database, spreadsheet and word processor).

Remember that computers are used in business for very good reasons. Usually these reasons are to save time and money, and to provide the business with a competitive edge enabling appropriately calculated decisions to be made.

Word processors and desktop publishing

As word processors have become sophisticated, they have taken on the role traditionally occupied by the older DTP systems. However, even the most sophisticated **word processors**, like Microsoft's Word 2000, for example, could not hope to compete with the **DTP systems** used to typeset glossy magazines or make up books.

Word processors are used for production of text, and **DTP systems** are used for production of complex layouts. Even though it is possible to produce a good looking document in a word processor, or prepare text using a DTP system, you should never lose sight of the objectives.

Example

Outline typical software and hardware requirements enabling a small publishing company to produce high-quality coloured glossy brochures. You may assume that some customers require several hundred thousand copies of the same brochure.

Solution

Pixel-based and object-oriented drawing and art packages are needed for artwork. They need word processors to edit text, to cope with copy from correspondents and authors, and a DTP system to make up the final page layout.

The hardware is quite formidable. 21-inch colour monitors and high specification computers are needed to run software like the art and DTP packages. Several hundred Mbytes of RAM are needed in each machine, and large hard disks, together with enormous disks on a server connected to a network. This is because high-resolution coloured images could take up many Mbytes each, and hundreds of images might be stored.

Printing the brochures is a problem. The copy needs to be proofed (checked) on a colour laser, but these printers are not able to cope with printing, collating and binding large quantities of brochures. This job would have to be contracted out to a print company with offset litho technology. This is a large machine, which can deal with print runs of hundreds of thousands, and is common in the newspaper and book-publishing industry.

A common mistake that students make in answering questions like the one above is to suggest that a laser printer would be needed to produce the magazine. They normally forget it takes a long time to print thousands of pages, and don't consider the sheer volume of work!

Business applications of computers are covered in chapter 6 of NUCSAL.

Spreadsheets

No A level student should describe a spreadsheet as a package to add together columns of numbers! One of the main reasons for a business buying a spreadsheet is to run what-if scenarios, to evaluate mathematical models, or to simulate things that might be too dangerous, take too long to do manually, or be over in far too short a period of time.

Example

Researchers of economics at a major university are using spreadsheets to help with research into economic theories. Outline some the features of a spreadsheet likely to be used in this scenario.

Solution

Mathematical models of the economy could be programmed into the spreadsheet making use of the relational formulae set up between the different cells. The effect of interest rates on inflation might be typical.

Many variables need to be controlled, and used to predict outcomes if just some of the variables, like interest rates, for example, were altered. Various scenarios like 'What would be the result on inflation if we reduce the interest rates by 0.5%?' could be investigated by running the numbers.

The mathematical models usually increase in sophistication over the years, as predictions can be compared with what happens in reality. Different models would probably be used to see which is the most effective predictor.

When simulations are used, realise they are only as good as the **mathematical models**. It is like forecasting weather – you know the probability of rain tomorrow, but you cannot guarantee you are correct. If predictions are inaccurate, find out why, and modify the model in the hope of making it better.

Spreadsheets are now used in very sophisticated ways, ranging from the economic analysis outlined in the last example, to simulation of traffic conditions on the M25 motorway. Do not forget that powerful programming languages accompany most major spreadsheets, which can increase the sophistication of what you can do by many orders of magnitude. The Grungebuster's example in unit 32 is an example of this.

Databases

Databases are covered in units 21, 22 and 23. However, you should be able to list the implications that the use of these systems would have for a business or organisation. Because of computerised databases, many things that would have hitherto been impossible to do are now standard practice. Using the **queries**, **reporting** and **statistical analysis** functions (sometimes in conjunction with a spreadsheet) enables a snapshot of the state of a business to be provided quickly. These statistics provide management with cutting-edge information, which makes a large difference in the decision-making processes at the highest levels of the company.

Databases can also be used to help manage **stock control systems**, **ordering systems**, **invoicing** and other business-related tasks. Together with a **spreadsheet** and a **word processor**, the **database** completes the trio of basic software packages available in most business office systems. Organisational help with **managing schedules** and **e-mails** etc. and **presentation packages** for the production of travelling demonstrations also play a major role in most businesses too.

The user interface

It is possible for different users to have different views of the same data inside the database. The design of the user interface to cater for these differing needs is important. Some people who work in the travel agent's shop outlined above would be denied access to queries and reports providing statistical information like profit and loss. This information is appropriate for senior management, and is a good example of different user needs and interfaces.

Integration with other packages

You should note that packages such as word processors, spreadsheets and databases are not usually used in isolation. It is likely that data from a database might be exported to a spreadsheet if complex statistical analysis is required. Word processors can extract data from a spreadsheet or database to produce standard letters, and databases can extract data from a spreadsheet to provide statistics for inclusion in a database record. Also, data from most applications can be extracted by routines written in computer programming languages such as Visual Basic or C++, for example. In addition to this it is common for data to be integrated into web sites via application servers running SQL or other databases.

When studying common applications there are few, if any, areas where data could not be extracted and used in some other form. The designers of these systems usually ensure that this is so, and the all-pervasive nature of the internet and world wide web will ensure that the integration of these application areas continues with ever greater degrees of sophistication.

Self-test questions

1 Outline ten different important features in a word processor.
2 Outline ten different important features in a spreadsheet.
3 Outline ten different important features in a database.
4 Explain how data might be exported from a database to a word processor.
5 What is meant when a graph in a word processor is hot-linked to the data in a spreadsheet?
6 What is the functional difference between a word processor and a DTP package?
7 How might the data processing that can be carried out by a spreadsheet be improved?
8 Explain a typical use for a macro in a word processor and a spreadsheet.
9 Explain what is meant by mail merge.
10 What is a 'what if' scenario?

In this unit you have learned about:

- General-purpose packages
- Word processing
- Spreadsheets
- Databases
- The user interface
- Integration of these packages with other systems

Do not be put off by questions asked in application areas with which you may not be familiar. Hospitals, schools, doctor's surgeries, advertising agencies and many other areas all have many things in common regarding general computing requirements.

Make sure that you learn the salient features of common applications like databases, spreadsheets, word processors, art packages and CAD packages.

24 Further application areas

In this section you will learn about:

- Macros
- CAD packages
- Design and manufacture
- Machines to help with CAM

Customisation of common applications

Word processors, **spreadsheets** and **databases** are general in nature. It is possible to provide a high degree of customisation by the use of **macros** or a **third party** 'add on'.

Macros

Macros automate complex or repetitive operations. They are sets of instructions, which can be run under the direction of the user. Microsoft's word processor allows you to **record a macro** as shown in Figure 24.1

When recording commences the computer 'makes a note' of what you are doing, and the commands to carry out the appropriate actions are recorded in the macro language. Although cracking a nut with a sledgehammer, a typical example might be to add a table containing 8 columns and 3 rows as shown in Table 24.1.

We set up the recording, go through the manual operations to achieve the desired result, and then stop the recording. Loading the command-language editor (Visual Basic in this case), we can see the code as follows.

Figure 24.1 Recording a macro.

Table 24.1 Three rows and eight columns


```
Sub Macro1()
' Macro1 Macro
' Macro recorded 09/08/00 by Ray Bradley
ActiveDocument.Tables.Add
Range := Selection.Range, NumRows := 3,
NumColumns := 8,
DefaultTableBehavior := wdWord9TableBehavior,
AutoFitBehavior := wdAutoFitFixed
End Sub
```

Comments show the name (Macro1), date and the author. Commands then follow (shown in red). Commands for a 3 by 8 table to be inserted in the active document are shown. The advantage of tackling jobs in this way is that long and tedious manual processes can be executed by a single keystroke assigned to this macro.

During your course you should have covered a few application areas in depth. There is not time to cover many different computer applications.

In addition to creating or writing your own macros, it is possible to purchase a **third-party add on**. You should be familiar with the use of **templates** to define the style of a document in terms of layout, headers and footers etc. A typical third-party add on for a word processor could be a huge range of appropriate templates to help develop documentation like customised invoices, business cards, flyers or advertising literature. Another example could be extensions to a web-site design package giving access to a range of pre-defined styles, colour schemes and other features for designing the site. The range of third party 'add ons' is almost limitless, and their use can save considerable time and effort in a busy business environment.

Other application areas

Different computer applications cover a vast array of possibilities. You should make sure that you have experience of a range of application areas including **scientific**, **industrial manufacture**, **education**, **data processing**, **publishing**, **leisure**, **design**, **communication**, **embedded systems**, **information systems**, the **internet**, **artificial intelligence** and **expert systems**. You should also be able to comment on the **social**, **economic** and **legal consequences** of the use of computers in all of these areas.

Design

The range of design activities is huge and can vary from the design of clothes to motorcars. The thing that all specialist software has in common in this area is that it enables the designer to create and visualise his or her designs more easily. **CAD** or **computer aided design** packages play a major role in the field of design.

It is the object of a CAD package to create an image of the artefact to be designed in either two or three dimensions, in **wire frame** or rendered form, and to generate data from the image which helps with calculations such as **costing**, **engineering analysis** or aesthetics. Figure 24.2 shows a car that has been **rendered**, i.e. surfaces and textures etc. have been applied to the wire frame image shown in Figure 24.3.

It is possible for the designer to change the **colour**, **texture** (e.g. metallic, glass, wood, marble etc.), the **view** (by using **yaw**, **pitch** and **roll**) and the **components**, which may be viewed. It is also possible to change the shape of the design, and the components that make up the design. You could put different wheels, headlights, door mirrors or bumpers on the car. It is possible for a designer to try out different scenarios to see the effects of the changes before the artefact is manufactured. This can save an enormous amount of time and money and only the final model needs to be physically made up and tested.

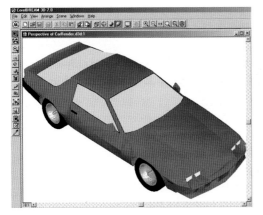

Figure 24.2 A rendered image of a car.

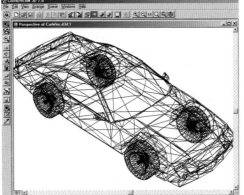

Figure 24.3 Wire frame image of same car.

Example

A CAD package is being used to help design a new museum building. Outline some of the likely features of the package that might help with the following functions.

(1) The design of the building

(2) The planning application (i.e. permission from the authorities to go ahead with the scheme)

(3) Demonstrations to the public

Solution

(1) Different designs of buildings are tested to see if they are technically feasible. Is the structure strong enough to support the roof? Different interiors in terms of materials, textures and colours may be tried out without having to physically construct the building.

(2) Planning applications may be aided by having views of the building to make sure that it fits in with the environment from each angle (e.g. the building might be too tall or obscure the view of some important other feature).

(3) Walk-through galleries may be constructed in virtual reality environments so designers and the public can give opinions about the building and exhibitions. Valuable feedback may be obtained in this way.

Other specialist CAD packages are also used. Different materials and patterns for fashion and industrial clothing may be input and tried on different computerised models. It is possible to have a **virtual tailor** to manufacture clothes to fit your body, because your body can be scanned via a special interface in which lasers create a wire-frame image.

The molecular structure of designer drugs and chemicals may be simulated and manipulated inside a CAD package. The chemist may gain a better understanding of the processes involved because they can manipulate the molecules in a virtual environment. **Data gloves** and **virtual reality helmets** (see unit 13) add to the realism of this interface.

Don't forget that collections of educational videos exist for showing a huge variety of computer applications. You need to make notes rather than just watch them.

Manufacture

Once the design data is entered into a computer there is a link between the CAD packages and the actual manufacturing process. This is prevalent in the semiconductor chip industry, but industrial manufacture such as automobiles make extensive use of these techniques too. When combined the techniques are known as **CAD/CAM**, or **computer aided design** and **computer aided manufacture**.

Example

A CAD package holds the data required to build a new microprocessor chip. Explain how computers are used to help in the actual manufacture of the chip.

Solution

The chip designer's ideas are in the form of schematics, describing how the microprocessor works in terms of internal registers, memory (cache) and the connections between these and similar devices. The first job of a computer is translation of these designs into the track layouts needed inside the chip. The computer can be used to route the tracks, turn devices like registers into standard components and provide for the inputs and outputs to be routed to the pins on the final chip.

Once designed, the layout can be tested for functionality by simulation. CAD/CAM software would be able to simulate inputs and test appropriate outputs to see if the specification is correct. Simulations can save costly errors, which would otherwise be discovered subsequent to manufacture.

The CAM software can control machines that manufacture the chip. Masks for each layer can be produced; robots can solder the leads from the inside of the chip onto the legs, and seal the chip by putting on the lid. Getting computers to automatically test each chip as it rolls off the production line continues the CAM process.

Data from the CAD packages is used extensively in the automobile and aircraft industries, where designer's drawings can be used to generate the parts required, to help control robots on the production line, to cost the product, order materials, help schedule the work and provide management with likely estimates of time for construction etc. It is almost possible to have a completely automated factory in which raw materials go in one end and manufactured goods come out at the other.

Special CAM machines

Much **mechanical modelling** is carried out when artefacts like pottery, cars and aircraft are produced. A clay model is usually made of the artefact so that designers can visualise the final product more effectively and carry out ergonomic tests or tests in a wind tunnel, for example. It is now possible to connect a machine to a CAD package in which special materials are scanned by laser beams in a 3D environment. The material is effectively etched away and the result is a 'clay like' model, which has been produced entirely by the computer. This cuts down on the enormous time, effort and skill required by artists and other technicians involved in the construction of these clay models. It is not yet possible to manufacture everything like this, but one day we might be able to do so.

Business applications of computers are covered in chapter 6 of NUCSAL.

Self-test questions

1 List ten features of a CAD package.
2 Outline why it may be useful to link the data from a CAD package to a database.
3 What is the difference between a rendered image and a wire-frame image? Under what conditions would each be useful?
4 What is CAM?
5 How has CAM revolutionised the automotive industry?
6 What is the difference between an object-oriented CAD package and a pixel-base art package?
7 Some packages can handle both object-oriented and pixel-based parts of the same drawing or picture. Why is this an advantage?
8 List 10 important features of an art package that might be used to undertake photo retouching.
9 How might CAD be used in the semi-conductor industry to help design a new microprocessor chip?
10 How might CAD/CAM and databases help with just-in-time production techniques?

In this unit you have learned about

● What is meant by a macro
● CAD packages
● Computers in design and manufacture
● How machines can help with special CAM techniques

25 Practical systems development

In this section you will learn about:

- Part 1 of the system life cycle
- Design methods using data flow and Entity Relationship diagrams
- Top down design methodology

Systems development

The following is typical of the stages undertaken for effective project development.

The classical system life cycle:

- Definition of the problem
- Feasibility study
- Information collection
- Analysis
- Design
- Implementation
- Evaluation
- Maintenance

The material outlined in this chapter not only helps with the examination, but is useful for writing up your AS projects.

Definition of the problem

The following lists activities, which should be undertaken by a systems analyst when helping to define the problem.

- **Interviews** with potential clients.
- If the system replaces a **manual** or older computer system – you need a detailed look at how the older system operates.
- Look at other **similar systems**.
- A **detailed written specification** needs to be drawn up.

The feasibility study

The problem has to be looked at in detail *before* work is commissioned. It may not be technically feasible, parts may not be improved by a computer-based solution, or it may be too expensive. Major proposals will impact on staff, possibly in the form of training and hiring, or even firing staff. Systems analysts will be aware of the financial cost of similar systems, but these are ballpark figures and many projects do go over time and budget. The **feasibility study** is crucial, as much money is wasted if conclusions are wrong.

Collecting information

If the report produced by the systems analyst is favourable and if the company decides that they wish to go ahead, then the **information-gathering phase** is triggered. The following is typical of activities that are carried out.

- **Devise questionnaires** and give to people who will use the system.
- **Interview clients** and other interested parties like customers, if applicable.
- Take a detailed look at the existing system, if applicable. *Existing methods need a very critical analysis.*

It is likely that ideas not considered before may come to light and this could mean going back and redefining certain parts of the problem. The users of the system often have the best ideas for potential improvement and wise managers will take note of sensible suggestions.

You are reminded that the development of systems is **dynamic** and modifications at this stage are the norm. The further the project is towards completion, the more difficult it is to implement even minor changes. Even if good ideas are thought up at a later stage, it may not be possible to implement them because of time delays or other financial considerations.

Analysis of the problem

A common language needs to be developed between the designers of the system and the people who will implement it. Common methods like **systems flowcharts**, **data-flow diagrams** or **entity-relationship diagrams** might typically be employed here. You would be wise to use these methods in your projects.

Data-flow diagrams are useful for describing the movement of data. They are ideal for tracing the route of paperwork through an office or factory etc. but could also be used to trace the sequences and the physical forms of data from one application to the next.

Example

A mail-merge document that uses a spreadsheet as the source of records is to generate student reports. Draw a data-flow diagram, showing a scenario for the flow of data from entering it into the spreadsheet to production of the reports.

Solution

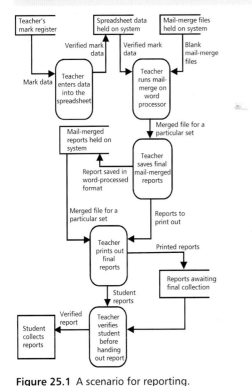

Figure 25.1 A scenario for reporting.

A data flow diagram is shown in Figure 25.1. You would not be given a report belonging to someone else and thus the teacher verifies the report before handing it back to you. This diagram allows you to analyse the flow of data, in detail, and to highlight possible problems. If you are using Microsoft Office, some of the files will need to be in Excel format, some of the files in Word format and the transition between these two forms will therefore have to be managed. This type of diagram makes it possible to identify problems, and to analyse whether the flow of data through an organisation is efficient.

Students are surprisingly reluctant to use diagrams like those shown in this unit to help with the solution to problems. They are effective ways to organise your thoughts.

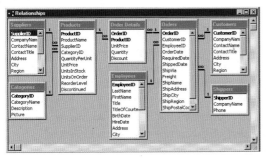

Figure 25.2 The relationship between tables.

Entity-relationship diagrams (ER diagrams) help with the design of a database. An Access representation of an ER diagram is shown in Figure 25.2, which uses Microsoft's NorthWind Database example.

Relational database design is considered in chapter 29 of NUCSAL.

Diagrams like those shown here are ideal when designing a relational database.

Can you spilt up your project by using a hierarchical diagram? If you can, then you should do so.

You are reminded about the following types of **relationship**.

- **One to many**
- **Many to one**
- **One to one**

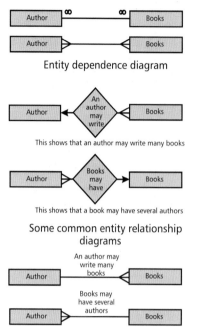

Entity dependence diagram

This shows that an author may write many books

This shows that a book may have several authors

Some common entity relationship diagrams

Figure 25.3 An entity dependence diagram and alternative forms ER diagrams.

An **entity** can be thought of as an *object* in a system. If you are designing a library, then **entities** might include 'books', 'authors' and 'publishers'. **Entity relationship diagrams** and **entity dependence diagrams** help to clarify the links between entities and the types of relationships that join them. Figure 25.3 is typical of the symbols used for this purpose. Here we show an entity-dependence diagram and two alternative forms of the same entity-relationship diagram. Sometimes the Entity Relationship diagrams are called **Entity Attribute Relationship** diagrams or **EAR** diagrams. Here the **attributes** represent the information stored about each entity. For example, a 'book' entity might have some attributes like 'title', 'author' and 'ISBN' etc.

The **entity** 'books', outlined in Figure 25.3, for example, might refer to a **table** in an Access database, like those shown in Figure 25.2. The attributes like 'title', 'author' and 'ISBN' would be listed in the boxes that represent the tables shown in Figure 25.2. Here each **entity** corresponds to a **table** and each **attribute** corresponds to a **field** within a table.

Using diagrams like those shown in Figure 25.3 at the design stage of your project, you can work out what mappings would be needed when you implement your database using software like Microsoft Access, for example.

Design methods

There are many different methods to help explain how to solve problems. The **top-down design method** is common for giving the overall solution in terms of the sub-problems that have to be solved. This should be contrasted to **bottom-up design**, which is particularly suited to programming, for example, where small modules of code are developed and tested before being joined onto other modules for making up larger systems. If this latter method were used then it would be referred to as **bottom-up programming**.

Example

You are to write a user guide regarding how to draw a grandfather clock using a typical computer art package. Show how it is possible to split up construction of the clock using a top-down design method.

Solution

The clock needs to be split up into suitable components – **case**, **face** and **mechanism** (pendulum etc.) is a good start. The face might consist of a **circular back plate**, some **Roman numerals**, some **hands** and the **holes** into which we put the key. The ideas, expanded a little further, are shown in Figure 25.4. Here you can see that the design of the little hand, for example, consists of three subsections, namely the tip, stem and centre attachment. The little hand is a part of the hands section, which itself belongs to the face, a major subsection of the clock project.

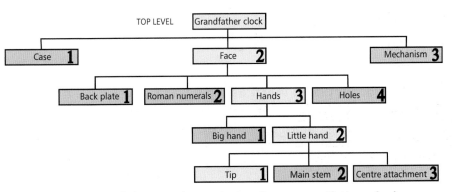

Part of the top-down design for a grandfather clock

Figure 25.4 The top-down method.

Using this method you can see that the user manual could be divided up into three major chapters. Chapter 2, on the face, could then be split up into 4 sections. The hands, being section 3, are split up into the little and big hand sections. In this way you could refer to an individual part of the project by a number and once arranged like this, you can work on the project from the bottom up, by explaining how each section of the little hand, for example, might be constructed using the package. The tip, for example, might consist of a circle and a triangle of a certain size, block filled in black.

Self-test questions

1 Explain what is meant by a feasibility study.
2 During the design of a data processing system it is usual to collect information by using a variety of methods. Outline three different methods, suggesting a typical scenario in which each would be particularly appropriate.
3 What is a data flow diagram? In what situations is a data flow diagram useful?
4 When setting up a relational database, relationships between different attributes in the database can be modelled by using an ER diagram. Show how an ER diagram may be used to model one-to-one and many-to-one relationships. You may choose any suitable example.

In this unit you have learned about:

- Some techniques that could be used in your own projects
- The feasibility study, collecting information, and analysis phases of the system life cycle
- A variety of diagrams including ER, data flow, hierarchical and top-down methods

26 Further systems development

In this section you will learn about:

- Part 2 of the system life cycle
- The user interface and prototyping
- An initial look at some testing strategies

The user interface

Never underestimate the need for a good **user interface**. If the user interface is wrong, it might be difficult or unintuitive to use. You can learn a lot from looking at programs like Microsoft Office. The **tools** on the **tool bars** have similar functions and the way that the **drop-down menus** work is the same in all cases. In short, Microsoft has tried to ensure **consistency** across the range of applications.

The following may be applied when designing a user interface:

- Has the user been consulted about what they want?
- Is it to be graphical or text based?
- Is it clear how to enter the data?
- Can the data be edited easily before being saved?
- Do you need to provide any help?
- Is the feedback to the user adequate if something goes wrong?
- Is there a security issue?
- Should a prototype be built to test the new user interface?
- Is the interface going to be used in a life or death situation like an intensive-care ward?
- Is the user experienced or a novice?
- Will any special hardware be useful?

Don't be surprised by the number of unusual scenarios that might be dreamt up for user-interface design and projects. Don't be thrown by this, use common sense and apply all the principles you have studied.

You should strive, if possible, to make sure that the user could only undertake valid events at appropriate times. If a button can be clicked to transmit information, make sure that inadvertent or deliberate clicking of the button does nothing if the information has not been entered correctly, or some of the information is missing.

Be aware of appropriate **input** and **output devices**. Use these devices as and when necessary, but do not be afraid to develop custom solutions to unusual problems. For example, how might you ensure that a parcel collection and delivery service keeps track of parcels during their journey? Your solutions might include the deliveryman running software from a portable computer connected to a mobile phone in his delivery van, which could be coupled with GPS readouts to identify position. This could be used to keep a customer database updated.

Example

Outline techniques that might be used when designing a good user interface for a tired telephone operator entering data regarding credit-card enquiries. You may assume that the following information needs to be input or retrieved from the system:

- **Customer card ID**
- **Customer name**
- **Address**

- **Details of transactions for any month, which may include the following:**
  - Date
  - Reference number
  - Description
  - Price
- **Balance**
- **Special notes**

You are not required to design the complete input screen, but should make suggestions.

Solution

It is essential that information is **verified** on entry. For example, an illegal account number cannot be entered. This could be accomplished by means of a **check digit** (see unit 18). If a valid account number is entered, the customer's name and address and all relevant details should be to hand. If the customer does not know the account number, then other information, like address, postcode and some extra security data like 'special place' or mother's maiden name, could help.

If a specific transaction is required, this should be searchable by number, or by name of the shop, if possible. If not, the price of the transaction could be used to locate it if necessary. The system should rely as little as possible on the operator manually searching for information, although this option too must still be available. Any standard enquiry such as current balance, credit limit and special requests should be available via **look up columns** (see unit 21).

Dealing with credit card information the system must obviously be secure and therefore the operators must log on using individual passwords. The workstations must be lockable if the operator wishes to take a break and transactions should be logged, both for the protection of the operator and the peace of mind of the customers. The interface should be tested extensively, using valid and invalid data.

Pseudocode

It is convenient to express ideas in a form that can easily be changed into a high-level language. If we were to validate the credit card number used in the last example, then we might apply a **check-digit** routine, like the one outlined in unit 18. The pseudocode could be as follows:

```
REM Account number checking routine
Input Account_number
Procedure Check_digit(Account_number)
If Result = FALSE
  THEN
    Display error message
   IF try_again = TRUE
     THEN Procedure
           Check_digit(Account_number)
     ELSE
        Display "Apologies message"
        Exit Procedure
  ELSE
    Load the account information
End Procedure
NEXT PART OF PROGRAM
```

Get used to writing pseudocode, you will need it for most examinations, and can use it where necessary, even if not asked specifically to do so.

The account number is entered, and the check digit routine called. If the result is false, the operator is prompted to try again, else the system can be exited without successfully entering the account. If check_digit passed back a valid result, then Result = TRUE, and the account information is therefore loaded. **Pseudocode** is *not* in any particular language, but uses good **program structure**, and can be coded into a high-level language easily. *Use pseudocode like this to make the **technical documentation** of your project clearer.*

You need to plan a project before using pseudocode. A hierarchical diagram like that shown in Figure 25.4, for example, shows how modules fit together. *It is very bad practice if the moderator of your project has to wade through a series of code (even pseudocode) to try and understand the overall project.* There must be an abstract view of the system first and this is why a diagram is essential.

Prototyping

You should **prototype** any new user interface or code that you develop. Check it out with the user to see if it is fit for the purpose, is easy to use and works. Note the constructive criticism you receive, but inform them that they are using a prototype for the purpose of testing.

One purpose of **prototyping** is to see if ideas are **technically feasible**. You could simulate part of your project interacting with another. This might help you to see if it is technically possible to get the real interaction working?

Use information obtained from developing the prototype to help write the final **specifications**. The process of achieving a final interface may involve going back to the users to refine what you have done.

The human computer interface

The way that people interact with machines is called the **human computer interface (HCI)** or human machine interface. You should be able to look at the HCI in a wider context. People must be comfortable with the use of the interface you provide, this could include considering some ergonomic and psychological factors, for example, the appropriate use of colour.

Simple testing strategies

It is rare for a system of great complexity to be delivered bug free. Testing of individual modules is a good place to start.

Dry run testing

This refers to simulating the execution of a program on paper, or running the program on the computer making use of appropriate test data. This is useful if you have found an error in the code. By inserting appropriate **break points**, you can examine variables to see if they happen to have the right values at any particular moment in time. As a simple example, consider debugging a small module, which converts temperatures from Celsius to Fahrenheit or vice versa. The formulae to do the conversions are as follows.

$$C = \frac{5(F - 32)}{9} \qquad F = \frac{9 \times C}{5} + 32$$

Table 26.1 Some salient test data

Test data for F to C and C to F conversion			
Test Data		Data obtained after run	
C	F	C	F
0	32	0	23 ✗
−40	−40	−40	−49 ✗
100	212	100	

After making up some **test data**, as shown in Table 26.1, the first test fails, because 32 Fahrenheit does not get produced as an answer when 0 Celsius has been entered. The second test also fails, as −49 is produced when −40 is expected. As we are converting from C to F, then the part of the program that deals with the second formula needs to be investigated. The Visual Basic code for this simple program is being debugged in Figure 26.1.

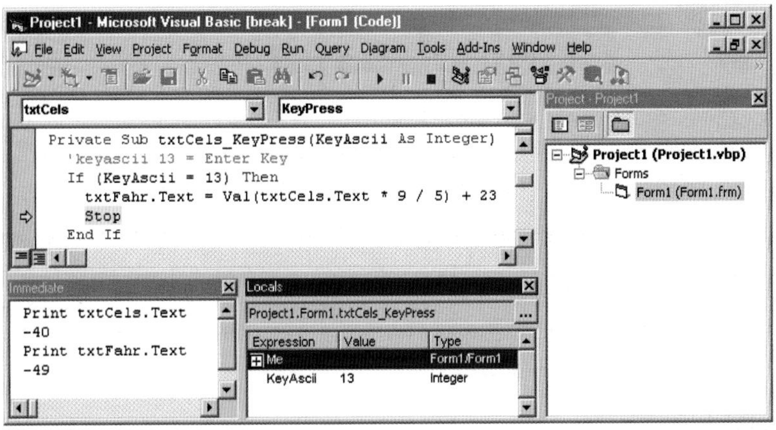

Figure 26.1 A breakpoint is set.

The input variable representing C is correct, but the variable representing F is wrong. Inspection of the formula reveals a logical programming error, as '23' has been typed in instead of '32' at the end of the line above the **break point** (shown by the **Stop**).

Environments like **Visual Basic**, **C++**, **Delphi** and **Visual Java** provide a rich variety of tools for debugging your programs. Make use of them in your projects, to show that you have tested various scenarios. You will often have to put in extra lines of code if the errors you are trying to track down are proving illusive. Such code might print out the values of important variables at various stages during execution.

The test data used for the temperature conversion program was chosen because they represent common values. However, what about −273 C? This is absolute zero, the lowest temperature, beyond which you cannot go. Therefore, if you type in −300 for a Celsius temperature, do you want your program to produce the number −508, or generate an error? This is a very simple example of possible bad specification, depending on the use to which the data may be put.

Self-test questions

1 You are designing the front end to a database. Outline some of the features that you might include when the users are entering data.
2 Outline what factors could influence the design of the human computer interface when undertaking computer-based projects.
3 What is dry run testing? Why is this particularly important when testing program segments? Give an example of a dry run on a routine of your choice.
4 Explain why prototyping is often an important part of systems development. Outline a typical scenario in which prototyping might be useful.
5 Why is it that extensive testing of a system may not find all the bugs contained within it? Is there anything that can be done about this?

In this unit you have learned about:

- Systems development
- The user interface
- Developing pseudo code
- Prototyping
- Testing strategies

27 Systems development – final phases

In this section you will learn about:

- Part 3 of the system life cycle
- Further testing
- Developing suitable test data
- Module and integration testing
- Testing the solution
- Evaluation
- Maintenance issues
- Lessons to be learned for your own project development

This unit completes the systems development necessary to be able to answer the AS questions on systems development in the theory papers.

The final phases

This unit concludes our **practical systems development**. We have already considered testing individual code by **dry running** and **debugging**. We start by looking at black box testing methodology more specific to testing on a macroscopic scale, and show how the post-testing phases of the project are implemented. The way in which this is carried out is also suitable for your own project work.

Module (unit) testing

Table 27.1 Black box test data

Conditions devised for testing unit	
Input	**Result**
Integers < 100	Error
100 ≤ Integers ≤ 1000	OK
Integers > 1000	Error
Negative whole numbers	Error
Fractions	Error
All other characters	Error

Each **module** should be tested individually. You can use the '**black-box approach**' to do this. The module (or group of modules) can be considered as a unit with **inputs** and **outputs**. If you put certain data into the system, then you expect certain data out from the system. Any data not intended to be valid input should be rejected. We will write a routine to create a record, which accepts only positive integers between 100 and 1000 inclusive. In this case, fractions, negative numbers, letters and other special characters input should all be rejected.

Important numbers to use as test data in the above case might be:

Table 27.2 Black box test data

Test data for testing unit	
Input	**Reason**
99	Integers < 100
100, 500, 1000	Valid numbers in range
−150	Negative integer
1001, 5000	Integers > 1000
0.75, −0.75	+ve and −ve fractions
A, %, +	Other characters

Keep a log of the tests you have carried out, and use this for future reference.

Although the above is not exhaustive, if the system passed these tests it would indicate a high degree of confidence in the system. *When writing software, more effort goes into validating the data than goes into writing the code to solve some of the problems!*

If the above module accepted all positive integers, then you need to specify the largest positive number that the system can handle. This can usually be found in the manual for the language you are using, or in the manual for the database you are setting up etc.

AS

Example

Devise test data to check that a routine written to validate dates in the form dd/mm/yyyy works satisfactorily.

Solution

Table 27.3 Black box test data

Some possible data for checking the date in the form dd/mm/yy	
Test	Invalid data for tests
All numeric?	23/Jan/1999 24th/12/1998
Numeric < digits for the year	23/2/99
1≤ month≤12	12/13/2000
1≤ day≤31	32/2/1999
Month is Sept, Apr, Jun or Nov – therefore day not > 30	30/9/1999 30/4/1999 30/6/1999 30/11/2000
Leap year?	29/2/1997 29/2/1998 29/2/1999

The data in the above table should reveal obvious errors in the validation routines. Testing just outside the limits of the range will usually reveal much more than testing lots of valid data within the range. Do not forget to check that the system works for valid data too!

In industry more effort is put into testing and debugging software than is put into the development of it in the first place. This shows the importance of testing.

Integration testing

Once individual modules have been tested, sub modules need to be joined together and the system tested again. It is essential to carry out this test so that no inadvertent effects between the modules are produced.

Testing the solution

When the programmers are satisfied that the entire system is working to the best of their ability, or at least the last few known bugs are being worked on, then the system undergoes what is called **beta testing**. This means that trusted customers and other similar people will test the new system under real conditions and report any problems encountered back to the programming team. When the project has undergone rigorous **beta testing**, then version 1.0 of the final product is released. Again, on large projects, the real customers will also find errors that have not been detected, and newer versions of the software (like 1.01, 1.02 etc.) are released.

The material covered in this unit is necessary for the AS theory papers, but it contains much which is useful for your A2 project work.

Construction and implementation

This phase of your practical system's exercise will depend on your method, e.g. spreadsheet, database, programming or a combination of these. Whichever method is chosen, explain why you have implemented the project like this, and why your chosen method is better than other alternatives. Limitations of your system will influence your chosen design. Do plenty of screen shots and place these in your report with explanations of the methods used, which should refer back to parts of diagrams you have in your design section.

Maintenance

After completion of a project, a vital part of customer service in the real world is to maintain the system in peak performance. This will involve providing **bug fixes** outlined in the last section, but also to make modifications to the system in the light of requests from customers after using the system in the field for some considerable time.

All software will become obsolete if not maintained properly, or not brought up to date periodically. As computer systems change and as customer requirements become ever more demanding, maintenance has become a vital part of any project activity. In industry there are more programmers engaged on maintaining systems than are developing new ones. This is a salutary lesson regarding the importance of documentation.

The **technical documentation**, which should accompany any well-developed product, is key to this maintenance function. Without good documentation, people who need to modify the system may not be able to understand it.

Technical documentation usually consists of **analysis** and **specifications** making use of diagrams such as **system** and **program flowcharts** or **hierarchical charts**. The project would be split up into major sections, **pseudocode** might be used to provide broad outlines, and actual code listings, together with suitable comments would be provided using the high-level language in which the system is implemented.

The same sort of argument applies when applications like databases and spreadsheets are used to provide the solutions to major problems. Do not forget also that macrocode like VBA, for example, would often accompany complex solutions to problems making use of such applications.

User guide

Unless your project is trivial there should be a **user guide**. This is a relatively simple document explaining how to use your system. It should contain general background information, the **hardware** and **software** needed to run your system, the **minimum specification** of the computer (operating system and processor etc.) and instructions on how to set up the system from scratch. It should preferably have screen shots of the system to help explain how it operates. It is also usual to put the author and **version number** of the software into this document.

Evaluation

How well does your project work? Don't say it is wonderful, even if it is! Instead say that it works to specification, as is demonstrated by the extensive testing that has been carried out and the **user feedback** that you have received. There may be some parts of your project that do not work well. Mention this, and you will get more marks if you supply constructive criticism.

Unless you are very clever and very lucky, it is unlikely that you will be able to solve all problems within the time frame that you have been given by the examination board. Even if you do manage to solve all problems, you will inevitably want to tweak parts of your solution to make it even better!

The benefit of hindsight is a wonderful thing. You should always be able to think up better ways of doing your project, and this should be mentioned in your evaluation section. You will get many more marks for being honest, stating what works well and what does not, compared to a bland statement saying that all is well. As a rough guide you should spend about a page or two of A4 evaluating your project.

Self-test questions

1 You are helping to test the interface on a new **WAP** enabled third generation mobile phone. The phone interface is to be simulated on the computer.
   (a) Suggest three different tasks that the phone might have to perform.
   (b) For one of your tasks, suggest some suitable testing method.

2 Outline the difference between module testing and integration testing. Why are both important parts of testing a modern system?

3 Design a suitable interface to enable a person who has impaired vision to operate a simple 4-function calculator on the computer.
   (a) What method will you use to enable the user to enter numbers?
   (b) What type of display have you chosen?
   (c) Are then any special features that you have used to enhance the interface?

4 You are going to test the calculator designed in question 3 for integer arithmetic addition. Suggest some suitable test data and describe how you arrived at the numbers and methods you will use. You must state any assumptions that you make.

5 You have to evaluate one of your colleague's projects. Outline what strategies you would set up to undertake a fair evaluation.

6 The maintenance phase of the system life cycle is just as important as the development stages. What is meant by system maintenance, why is it needed and how is it usually carried out?

7 Outline two different situations that may lead to system maintenance being carried out on a software system that has been successfully in operation for some time. What resources should the software engineers have at their disposal to undertake effective system maintenance?

In this unit you have learned about:

- The final parts of the system life cycle
- Further testing techniques
- Development of suitable test data
- Module testing
- Integration testing
- System testing
- Evaluation techniques
- System maintenance
- How these techniques could be applied to your own projects

28 Example of an exam-board exercise

In this section you will learn about:
- The design phase for tackling your set exercise project.

This chapter is useful reading before starting on your project.

The development of computer-based systems

Some boards will set an **exercise**, consisting of one or more questions similar to the ones set in this module. If your board does not set an exercise, the material in this six part module is key for project development and design. You are expected to use your knowledge of **system's development**, together with your practical experience in learning applications like **databases** and **spreadsheets**. Finally, mix this with your *knowledge of other parts of the AS syllabus*, then add a sprinkle of your **programming skills**. Armed with this experience you should be able to provide suitable solutions to a range of different problems ranging from 'payroll', though 'stock-market simulations', to 'video-rental shop databases'. All systems analysis problems require similar techniques, and many suitable skills are outlined in the next six units.

The project outlined below is of the same standard as would be expected in a board set exercise module. Projects are usually very practical in nature – they are nonetheless still **very** challenging, and *you would be well advised to start early. Two or three months are usually spent doing projects of this nature.*

Definition of the problem

You are to implement a **payroll system** for **Grunge Busters**, a cleaning company, based in Gransylvania, where the locals are paid in Gransylvanian Groats, or GGs. Your task is to produce a computer-based payroll application for just five Grunge-Buster employees, which works out their wages from the information given on their timesheets. You must make sure that the strict Gransylvanian working hours and rules are observed, and must work out the taxes owed to the Gransylvanian Government. In addition to the government sick pay and pension schemes, the company runs an additional insurance scheme for those employees who wish to contribute.

The specification

The above puts the problem in context, but does not give enough information to enable you to go ahead and solve it. For this you need a **detailed specification** of the problem.

A Gransylvanian work period is called a **term**, and runs for **8 weeks**. Each **week** is split up into **5 working days**. At the start of the next 8-week term, all data from the last 8-week term is irrelevant, and therefore statistics relating to the next term start from scratch. **For each term, the conditions of employment are as follows**.

1. No Gransylvanian should work more than 47 hours in a week. Any hours above this amount get penalised at a special 75% tax rate!

2. The complete range of Gransylvanian tax rates are shown in Table 28.1.

   These are called the **tax bands**. A salary of 200GGs, for example, would be taxed at 10% on the first 100GGs, (band 1) and the remainder would be taxed at 20% (band 2).

Table 28.1 The tax rates

Gransylvanian tax rate bands	
Tax band	Rate
1 Salary ⩽ 100 GGs	10%
2 100 GGs < Salary ⩽ 1000 GGs	20%
3 Salary >1000 GGs	45%
4 Hours in excess of 47	75%

3 Each Gransylvanian must contribute 5% of their **gross** income to the pension scheme.

4 Gransylvanians are allowed a maximum of 5 days holiday in any 8-week period. During this period they get 120% of normal salary based on a 35-hour week (or a proportion thereof if less than 5 days are actually taken). If they do not take all of this holiday, the money is added onto the 8th-week salary as a bonus, but is subject to all appropriate deductions.

5 If a Gransylvanian is sick, then he or she gets just 50% of normal salary, for a 35-hour week (or a proportion thereof for each day). They still have to pay tax and pension contributions on their sick pay.

6 If Gransylvanians are absent from work for less than 3 days, they automatically get sick pay. However, after this they get nothing, unless they have a doctor's certificate, which allows them sickness absence for up to 10 days. After 10 or more days sick in any 8-week period, they do not get paid.

7 If a Gransylvanian pays contributions into an insurance scheme, which costs them 2% of their gross salary, they get 75% normal pay if they are sick, up to a maximum of 20 days, but only if they produce a doctor's certificate.

Your system should produce the weekly wage slips, containing the following information:

- Employee number
- Employee name
- Hours worked
- Gross payment, with details of sickness, absence or holidays.
- Date of payment

- Week number
- Tax paid to date
- Pension contributions to date
- Details of deductions
- Net pay for the week

In addition your system should be able to produce the following:

- Total tax paid by each employee
- Total pension contributions for each employee
- A list of employees who have been sick in a particular week
- The total tax owed by Grunge Busters to the Gransylvanian government.

Requirements of the practical exercise

You must design and implement an appropriate solution, and demonstrate that it works using the following test data.

Table 28.2 The test data

Grunge Buster weekly statistics – TEST DATA to be used for the Gransylvanian project								
	Hours worked							
Week	1	2	3	4	5	6	7	8
NAME								
Boris	35	0 H5	48	39	20 S3 D	0 S5 D	35	42
Doris	0 H3	15	0 S5 D	0 S5 D	20	0 H3	20	20
Horace	23	0 A7	23	0 S5 D	0 S5 D	0 S5 D	0 S5 D	35 S2 D
Morris	10	5 A2	4 A3	20	50	13 S3 D	34	0 H5
Norris	17 A1	35	47 S2	43	46 A2	0 S5 D	0 S5	49

Note 1 S – Sick, followed by the number of days absent in the week due to sickness – S4 means sick for 4 days.

Note 2 D – a doctor's certificate was provided.

Note 3 A – means absent without a doctor's certificate – A2 means absent for 2 days.

Note 4 H means a holiday has been taken. H5 means on holiday for 5 days.

The members of staff are on the following hourly rates of pay.

Table 28.3 Rates of pay and other data

Name	Employee number	Rates of pay (GGs/hour)	Member of insurance scheme?
Boris	83341	100.00	No
Doris	69282	105.75	Yes
Horace	78444	150.80	Yes
Morris	83342	100.50	No
Norris	69283	120.75	No

Some sound advice on how to proceed

Most students need guidance on how to proceed at this stage. You should familiarise yourself with the problem several times at least, but *do not* start coding anything on the computer. You need to think about which application might be most suitable, and about which systems analysis methods could be used? If you decide that a spreadsheet might enable you to solve the problem in an ideal way, do you know enough about spreadsheets? If not, you will need to learn these new techniques at the same time as solving the actual problem. You may be amazed at how packages like Microsoft Excel, for example, provide the exact features to help you solve the problems posed by the examination boards. This is not really surprising, as software such as Excel could be what is used in the real world.

We will now carry out a possible solution to the Grunge-Buster problem, by tackling it in the ways just suggested – i.e. by a student who may not know enough about a particular package, and has to learn new techniques as he or she is going along.

Of course, after the written report has been produced, it will look like the student is an expert in their chosen field, and has done a superb systems-analysis job!

The analysis phase

On much larger projects, during this **data-gathering phase**, one or more **systems analysts** would interview prospective customers, and then gather the information required to determine the exact nature of the problems that need to be solved. The analysts would probably visit the company for several weeks or months, and only then produce a report, outlining possible ways forward before the system is designed in detail. *This information-gathering phase is not really needed as you have been given all the information in the exercise question.*

The design phase

A typical student is now expected be able to solve the Grunge Buster problem! Using the QCA approved AQA 2001/2002 guidelines as an example, some, or all of the following must be considered, as appropriate.

- Definition of **data requirements**
- **User interface** design including output, forms and reports
- Method of **data entry**, including validation
- **Record structure**, **file organisation** and **processing**
- **Security** and **integrity** of data
- **System design**

Notice that you may not need to consider all of these sections, but you *ignore them at your peril*. If you think a section does not apply, discuss it with your project supervisor!

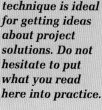

AS

Some initial brainstorming thoughts

The three main scenarios able to provide a solution to this problem are **spreadsheets**, **data-bases** and **programming**. *It is up to the student to justify the methods used*, choosing **the most appropriate tools** (like using **VBA**, for example) and *demonstrating that the implementation is efficient*. Unless a particular student is good at, and more importantly enjoys programming, then this method of solution is usually the most difficult. If a student wished to pursue this course of action, then customisation would be the key to his or her argument. Languages like **Visual Basic** and **Delphi** are particularly good, being able to provide the customised interface easily. However, it will take considerably longer to undertake some parts of the project, like the production of excellent pay slips or tax returns, which are trivial in packages like databases and spreadsheets. Most students would probably tackle the Grunge-Buster problem by using a **spreadsheet** or a **database**. Nevertheless, you will still have to be *very* competent at using either software package to implement the solution.

The brainstorming technique is ideal for getting ideas about project solutions. Do not hesitate to put what you read here into practice.

The data requirements of the system

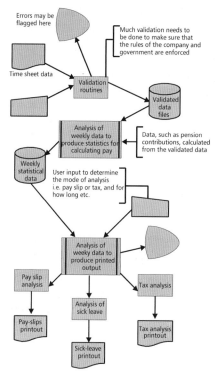

Figure 28.1 A possible system diagram.

This particular part of the design requirement is expecting you to understand the exact nature of **data** that is required for **input**, what needs to be done to the data for it to be processed, and finally, what data is to be **output** from the system. In your written report you must make it appear that you have done this detailed analysis *before* deciding on which method (i.e. spreadsheet or database etc.) you will use to implement the solution.

In the real world systems analysts would now write reports and draw diagrams similar to that shown in Figure 28.1. They would then give their ideas and specifications to programmers to actually code the system. However, *most students do not usually have the ability to go through these processes efficiently, because they are not experts in analysing a particular problem. We will shortly show you how to undertake projects in practice, by going through what I have called a **discovery route**!* Experts *will* probably know what packages are best for the solution, even before they have designed the solution to the problem. However, this is an informed choice based on years of experience!

Visit our portal to see similar AS Level projects.

In this unit you have learned about:

- An introduction to some typical AS coursework
- How to start the project
- Deciding on an appropriate application
- Carrying out some brainstorming
- A brief introduction to the 'discovery method' of carrying out this work

In this section you will learn about:

● Continuing the design phase for your AS projects

This second unit is also useful reading before starting on your project.

The data-entry phase

To understand what **data** needs to be entered, you will have to think about what the wages clerk has to do each week. He or she will enter some statistics, similar to those shown in Table 28.2 (unit 28). In a real system, this is accomplished by entering data from a timesheet, which is filled in by the employee.

There are a variety of diagrams and techniques suitable for this purpose, with **systems flowcharts** and **data-flow diagrams** being just two. A typical **system flowchart**, showing, in very general terms, how data is entered into the system and processed, is shown in Figure 28.1 (unit 28). You can also augment any system's diagrams by drawing a picture showing what data needs to be entered into the system.

By carefully reading the **specifications**, in this particular example, *after* the database has been set up, all that needs to be entered for each 8-week term is the hours worked/week for each employee, or the fact that they were sick or absent for a set number of days in each weekly period. This does not show the actual database, and the structure designed to accept the data. *A separate diagram(s) would be needed for this too, showing the processes involved in setting up appropriate structures.*

Data capture forms

Although it is *not* required in this particular case, you could well have been asked to design a **timesheet**, on which data regarding dates and hours worked/day etc. can be filled in manually by each employee. If we decided to implement this here, you would have to enter five times the quantity of data for this exercise, and this would take too long in this brief example.

Table 29.1 A possible timesheet

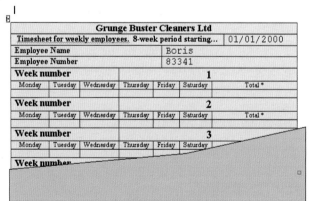

Grunge Buster Cleaners Ltd							
Timesheet for weekly employees. 8-week period starting...						01/01/2000	
Employee Name				Boris			
Employee Number				83341			
Week number					1		
Monday	Tuesday	Wednesday	Thursday	Friday	Saturday	Total *	
Week number					2		
Monday	Tuesday	Wednesday	Thursday	Friday	Saturday	Total *	
Week number					3		
Monday	Tuesday	Wednesday	Thursday	Friday	Saturday		
Week number							

This column is for your convenience; the computer will check the actual total.

The **data-capture form** can be used to help the data-entry clerk enter data into the system, which would then be correlated automatically, and presented to the other parts of the system in the form similar to that shown in the test data in Table 28.2 (unit 28). Just to give you an example of typical data-entry form design, one is shown here in Table 29.1.

This is the second of a six-part module that solves a typical AS project. Any one of these units will not make sense in isolation.

You must start your project work without delay. If you leave it until later you will probably have great difficulty completing the work on schedule.

The 'name' and 'employee number' have been entered automatically onto the system by the computer, as has the starting date for the 8-week term. This particular timesheet has been produced on Microsoft Word, and thus the information mentioned above can be held in a simple database, and the timesheets generated by using the **mail-merge** facility.

The above timesheet could be used to enter the data, some of which must obviously be validated as it is entered into the computer system. For the purposes of this examination-board exercise, we will enter the data for each week, and assume that the daily totals have already been checked to arrive at these figures.

Deciding on a suitable software package

From Figure 28.1, we can see that **validated data**, regarding the hours worked each week, are saved onto disk for each employee. Some analysis must then be done, to work out the statistics such as tax deducted, sick pay and other possibilities such as insurance premiums etc. This will generate a set of figures derived by the application, and used, along with the validated data, to produce the outputs like 'pay-slip data', 'tax data' and 'pension data' etc. We therefore need a package that can validate data on input, store the data in a database, be able to generate a large set of other data by using numerical analysis, and finally to print out documents containing the appropriate statistics.

The Grunge-Buster project can be done using a **database** or **spreadsheet**. Do not forget that it can also be done using a **programming language** too. Here we assume that a student knows little about visual-programming languages like Delphi or VB to be able to compete with the quality of implementation achievable using a standard package.

Validation would be easier if a database is used, but Microsoft Excel can provide a good degree of validation too. Microsoft Excel can also produce coloured reports of the sort needed to produce pay slips and tax returns etc. We will, therefore, use **Microsoft Excel**. Indeed, this is why the author chose a payroll program example, because he knew, from experience, that a spreadsheet would be a good solution, and **relational database** solutions using **Microsoft Access** have already been covered in units 20, 21 and 22!

Design – a discovery-based approach!

Students have limited experience of **systems analysis**, and less-than-optimum knowledge of the software. *It is inevitable, and indeed desirable, to try out small parts of the system on the computer before you commit yourself to the final design stages*. This **discovery-based approach** is really sorting out potential sub-problems, and developing strategies for solving the main problem. It will usually lead to a good system design if you implement the best strategic information found out during your discovery phases.

We start off by exploring a typical scenario, which many, if not most students will probably follow when given a problem of this nature. *Trial and error, mixed with trying things out is essential to get a feel for solving these problems – it is just that you don't tell the examiners that it was done in this way!* They will probably guess that it has been developed like this, and they too would work in similar ways if they were exploring unfamiliar methods to solve their own problems! Nevertheless, when your project report is read, it must look as if you have designed the solution, and then implemented it using your chosen package. You will obviously get marks for overcoming problems, and so **prototyping**, and **keeping a diary** is good practice too. *Also, start writing up your project as and when you are happy with each section*. You can modify things later, because your write up has obviously been done on a word processor. Now see how some typical development might proceed using the **discovery-based approach**.

Prototyping

Let's see if Excel can provide any suitable techniques for **data validation**. You might think that Access, the Microsoft database, is better because advanced validation is available.

There are usually big differences between how projects are actually carried out and the way students appear to have carried them out from reading the final report. Read these units to make sure you capitalise on this experience.

Systems analysis and design work is covered in chapter 16 of NUCSAL.

Do research similar to that shown in this unit on your own project, it will help tremendously when you come to do the write up.

A quick look at the help pages from Excel will reveal that you can restrict the entry of numbers into a cell based on **range** and **data type**, and can even present messages to the user who is entering the data. This is adequate for the Grunge-Buster project, and is demonstrated in Figure 29.1.

In this example we have limited the values to whole numbers between 0 and 8 inclusive. Thus, if the data-entry clerk inputs a number that does not conform to these criteria, an alert message is displayed, as shown in Figure 29.2.

Figure 29.1 Setting up validation.

IF-THEN scenarios

The Grunge-Buster project needs to check for multiple conditions at many points, and working out the tax is an example of this. The syntax of the IF-THEN condition in Excel is:

```
=IF(logical_test,value_if_true,value_if_false)
```

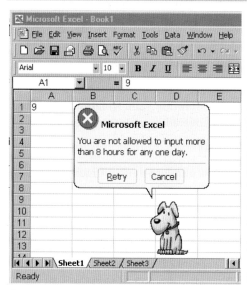

Hence, if a logical test were to be carried out on cell A1 (e.g. salary for the week), we could calculate the tax, by applying the rate to be used for this calculation, which is then placed in the cell containing this **IF function**.

Assume, for the sake of argument, that the gross salary is located in cell A1. (Have a prototype sheet in front of you to try this out.)

```
=IF(A1>=100,A1*0.1,IF(A1<100,10,))
```

The logical test condition, (A1<=100) is used, and if true, 10% tax is calculated on the value of A1, (A1*0.1), and placed in this cell.

Finally, if the salary is more than the 100 GG 10% tax limit, then the 10% tax owed in this band is obviously 10 GGs, and is taken care of by the last condition in the above logical expression.

Figure 29.2 Invalid data has been detected.

Next we calculate the 20% band as follows:

```
=IF(A1<=1000,180,IF(A1<100,(A1-100)*0.2,0))
```

If the gross salary held in A1 is >=1000 GG, the 20% band tax is 180 GG. This being made up of 20% of 900 GGs – do not forget that this is because the first 100 GGs have already been taxed at 10%. If the salary is greater than 100, but still less than 1000, the 20% tax is set to be (A1-100)*0.2. If A1<100 GG, then this band must be set to zero, and this is catered for in the last entry in the above equation.

For the 45% tax band, use the following logical condition:

```
=IF(A1<1000,(A1-1000)*0.45,0)
```

Visit our portal to see similar AS Level projects.

If the salary is in excess of 1000 GGs, then the amount above 1000 GGs must be taxed at 45%. If the gross salary is <= 1000 GGs, then this band of tax will be zero, as indicated by the last condition. Finally, the 75% punitive tax rate is triggered not by salary, but by working in excess of 47 hours. Therefore, all hours in excess of 47 will be charged at this punitive rate, irrespective of any other calculations. We must ensure that no hours in excess of 47 get put into the gross-salary cell dealt with above, and hours in excess of this amount get put in a different salary cell, which is taxed at 75%.

Testing this part of the potential solution

Once the banding has been accomplished, you should use test data, based on Table 28.1, to see if the results are correct. Figure 29.3 shows a mock up, using a separate Excel test sheet, to simulate the test. You can see from the above that a salary of 10,000 GGs has been split up into 100 GGs at 10%, 180 GGs at 20% and 4050 GGs at 45%. You must run the numbers as often as necessary to check each of the bands. (See testing in units 27 and 51.)

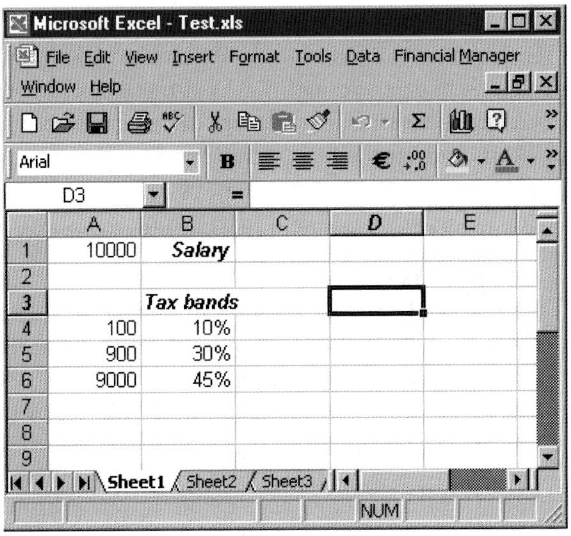

Figure 29.3 A mock-up for tax-banding.

Stop and take note!

Some students would now attempt to code the entire project in their head, working from problem to problem, and modifying the solutions to cope with things that spring to mind on an *ad hoc* basis. *However, you are meant to be designing the solution to a problem and a structured approach is needed.* We are dealing with a programming problem here, and a **program flowchart** would thus be an ideal way to express the solution. We have used Excel as an example here, but you are expected to specify the problem more generally at this stage. You can easily code all the previous statements using **pseudocode**.

In this unit you have learned about:

- How to tackle some of the initial design work
- Investigating various approaches and deciding which is the best method to use
- The discovery-based approach
- How to get many parts of the project under way

30 Finalising the design

In this section you will learn about:

- The formal design phase for your set exercise project
- Integrating your project with the theory you have learnt in the lessons.

This chapter is useful reading before starting on your project.

Design – the right approach

Although most students will inevitably think in the ways described in the last two units, the project report must *not* be written up using this *ad hoc* discovery-based approach.

Indeed, as the complexity of the problem increases (the Grunge Buster problem has appropriate complexity to demonstrate this), students will have to plan out a structured strategy to solve the problem, or be prepared to get in a total mess, and therefore waste a lot of valuable time. Try working out the sick pay, absence pay, insurance and holiday pay interrelationships in your head, and you will soon see exactly what is meant. This is why a structured approach is essential.

A good start would be to plan out a diagram of the complex interrelationships, and this is exactly what is needed to get your head around the problem.

Take sick pay, holiday and absence pay as a typical example. The specification shown in unit 28 is written down in an unstructured way. Some parts, like the tax-band example shown in unit 28 do not depend on other criteria. However, other parts, like sick pay, for example, depend on many criteria. It would depend on the number of days already sick, whether a doctor's certificate has been handed in, whether the sick leave has exceeded the maximum and whether the employee is in an insurance scheme. If not tackled in the right order, students may find it difficult, if not impossible to come up with a solution that passes all the tests that are posed by running the numbers contained in the test data of Table 28.2 (unit 28).

This is the third of a six-part module that solves a typical AS project. Any one of these units will not make sense in isolation.

Always use diagrams to help explain your designs. A picture is worth a thousand words and you will get marks more easily if you do this.

Surprisingly, you can use Excel 2000 to construct excellent flowcharts. Use the AutoShapes on the Drawing toolbar and connectors to do this.

Program flowcharts and many other diagrams to help with your projects can be found in chapter 14 of NUCSAL.

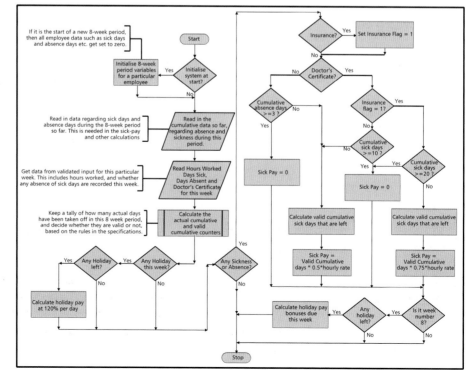

Figure 30.1 A program flowchart solution for working out the sick pay and absence pay.

The **program flowchart** shown in Figure 30.1 gives an overall impression of how the sick and absence pay and related variables like insurance and sick pay may be calculated and stored. It also deals with holiday pay, but this is relatively trivial compared to sickness and absence. These are the data needed to be able to calculate the deductions and gross pay, and therefore to print out the tax due and pay slips etc. This chart does not actually calculate an employee's gross or net pay, but provides the statistics to enable this to be done.

At this point you should take stock

The project has, so far, been approached in a discovery-based manner and modularising parts of the system has not yet been considered – the professionals would have done this before going into the above detail. For example, the tax-band problem, the sick-pay problem and the pay-slip problem are examples of **possible sub-sections**, with the sick pay part being particularly tricky to work out, as can be seen from the flowchart. Therefore, something like a **hierarchical diagram** is needed to sort out the overall system, and this must be put near to the beginning of the design section. *It will then look as if you have designed the whole system like this in the first place, and you will get high marks for this component of the course.*

Few students would be able to design complex systems in exactly the right order, but *if someone else has to mark or modify their system, then it must be written down in this professional way, or nobody would be able to follow exactly what he or she has done*, and the system would be inoperable. Indeed, finding mistakes in badly documented systems is a nightmare. If you carefully read the specifications, you should be able to produce an idea, similar in principle, to the flowchart shown in Figure 30.1. You must then **dry run** the flowchart to ensure that the logic is correct.

From observation of the flowchart, we can see that virtually all the processing will be based on a range of **IF-THEN structures**, exactly like those considered earlier. The flowchart will help to make sure that you structure the problem in the correct way. Do not forget also that **Excel** supports **VBA**, or **Visual Basic for Applications**. This is a very powerful subsection of the Visual Basic programming language, and macro routines may be called up which can tackle problems of the above complexity with relative ease.

The hierarchical diagrams

After working through the above **discovery-based approach**, and having convinced youself that **Excel** is able to handle this sort of work, you really do need to bolt yourself down and sort out your **system design**. This is what the examiners need, and it is what you need to organise your thoughts.

You should now understand Grunge Busters quite well, and this is the whole point of leaving these diagrams to a little later. You now know about each subsection, and about the relationships between them. Your knowledge can now be likened to an experienced systems analyst working on the Grunge Buster problem, and you should now be able to produce some of the diagrams with relative ease.

For example, a **data structure** has to be set up in which to place the data like employee names, hours worked, sick and absence statistics etc. If we were using a **database**, then this would be equivalent to setting up a **table**, and designing a **record-card structure**. Similarly, nicely designed wage slips, tax return forms and other tables are needed to present the Grunge Buster data in a pleasing way. If you are not used to using a spreadsheet, then this might seem a particularly difficult part. Nevertheless, take note regarding some of the Excel Spreadsheet Solution examples, like the 'Purchase Order' system shown in Figure 30.2. Excel is easily capable of producing high-quality reports of the sort needed, from the data we have stored in a range of cells.

Do not be afraid to use standard solutions to parts of your project like the invoice shown here, for example. Always put an acknowledgement in your report.

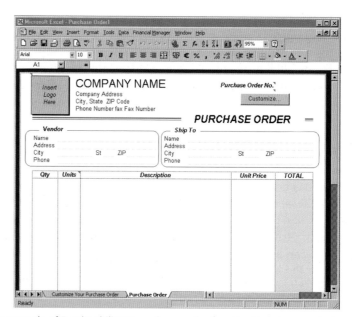

Figure 30.2 An example of Excel's ability to produce professional-looking documents.

Indeed, the purchase order shown in Figure 30.2 is so professional, that if printed out, it will not look as though it is been produced on a spreadsheet at all! A spreadsheet like Excel is a truly amazing package, and the production of sophisticated solutions, like this typical board-set exercise, enables you to explore some major parts of this package in depth.

The wage slip production sequence

A typical example of a **hierarchical diagram** is shown in Figure 30.3.

Here you can see the design of one of the subsystems of the project, which produces the actual wage slips at the end of each weekly period. From this diagram you can see that statistics regarding an employee's working week are analysed, and then validated according to the Grunge Buster rules. The data needed for the production of the wage slips, like gross pay and all deductions and details of pensions etc. are stored for future reference. Next the statistical results are imported into the pay-slip production part of the system, and the pay slips are printed out.

Visit our portal to see similar AS Level projects.

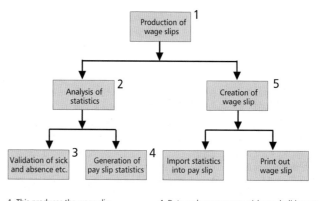

1. This produces the wage slip for a single employee.

2. The statistics, generated from the time sheet data must be validated.

3. Each attribute like sick days, absence days, holidays and insurance need to be checked to conform to the rule. (See flowchart in Figure *30.1.*)

4. Data such as gross pay, sick pay, holiday pay, pension contributions, tax deducted etc. need to be calculated from the validated statistics and stored.

5. The wage slip production part of the system is activated.

6. Validated statistical data (from 5) needed for the production of the wage slip are imported into the pay-slip printing part of the system.

7. The wage slip is printed out.

Figure 30.3 A HIPO chart is just part of the typical documentation for Grunge Busters.

Take stock again

You have been on a **voyage of discovery**, which consisted of the following stages:

- Carefully looking at the problem to be solved over a period of a few days.
- Creating an outline solution to the problem, finding out more about particular processes if necessary.
- Manually working through the problem to see if your computer solution is likely to be on the right track.
- Deciding on a particular software package that might be useful.
- Trying out some of the things that you intend to do using your chosen package.
- Learning new techniques about your package as you go along. The useful techniques may be unknown to you at this stage.
- Knocking up some prototypes to make sure you are still on the right track.
- Testing your prototypes to make sure that they will work.
- Keeping the test data that you have used to test the prototypes; this will be very useful later, when you come to write up the test sections of the report.
- Working out the details, about which you may be unsure, to make sure that you understand the overall problem completely.
- Starting to structure your solutions using systems flowcharts, program flowcharts, hierarchical diagrams or any other methodology, including pseudocode, which you have learned.

Writing up the design section of your report

You are now ready to write most of the **design section** of your report. You can impress the examiners with your overall strategy, expressed in a very general way. You can impress them even further by outlining all the subsections and having a **hierarchical diagram** for each. In some of these diagrams, you might have references, for example, to **program flowcharts**, which put meat onto your arguments.

Most importantly, you are now relatively confident that your chosen method of solution will be able to produce the goods, and you are well into learning more about a package like a spreadsheet, for example, which is needed during the implementation phase.

Other areas to note

You also need to concentrate on the **user interface**, the **record structure** for storing your data, the **security** and **data integrity** aspects, and then you will be ready to start!

In this unit you have learned about:

- How to formalise the design process, and make it look as though you have designed the project in an organised and constructive way
- How diagrams from other parts of the course help to explain your thoughts and ideas
- How to organise your final project write up

31 Successful project implementation

In this section you will learn about:

- The implementation and testing phases of a set exercise project
This chapter is useful reading before starting on your project

The Grunge Buster payroll system

In the last few units you have covered **system specifications, system flowcharts, hierarchical diagrams, and program flowcharts**. You also have a written **design stage** to the problem, which will need little modification in the final report write up. The project should now be taken through the **implementation** and **testing** phases.

Project implementation

This is the part of the project which students like best – that of sitting down in front of the computer and getting their ideas to work. *You should, however, realise the enormity of the effort that has gone into getting this far.* This is the stage, during which you look at the design section, and justify why you are going to use a spreadsheet to solve the problem. You have already seen why it is going to work, and you have already familiarised yourself with many of the techniques that will be needed.

The user interface

Keep the project **simple** and **functional**. *If you choose to have a fancy interface, it could take up too much time, and get you few marks over and above those given to a student who has chosen a simpler but equally effective one.* A good user interface will enable the systems to be used easily by the wages clerk. The window need not reflect the complexities underlying how data might actually be stored and processed. There are several user interfaces, and these are listed as follows: inputting the weekly statistics, generating the wage slips for the week, production of other statistics like the tax returns and other company data.

There are only five employees at Grunge Busters, and a simple screen is all that is needed. A suitable one is shown in Figure 31.1.

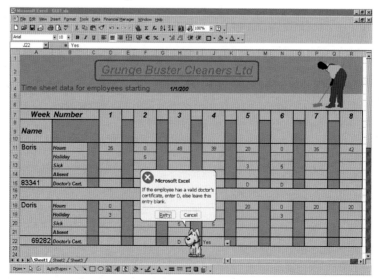

Figure 31.1 A GUI for the weekly statistics.

This is the fourth of a six-part module that solves a typical AS project. Any one of these units will not make sense in isolation.

Successful project implementation can only occur if you have done your homework at the analysis and design stages covered in the last few units.

Recall that this project has not asked you to design a system that inputs the *daily* records, only the weekly ones. Therefore, the system shown in Figure 31.1 is adequate and effective. Note also that **validation** is important on this part of your system. The diagram also shows that the operator has attempted to enter 'Yes' when entering data into the Doctor's Certificate box. The system is reminding him or her that only 'D' is acceptable if a valid Doctor's certificate has been handed in, else this field in the database is left blank. If 'yes' were allowed to be input, the statistics may be wrong.

There are several options needed – entering the data, printing the payroll or sending off the tax return form to the government. We could present the user with a menu which, if they click over the appropriate button, automatically sends them to another sheet or part of the same sheet that deals with the particular problem in an easy-to-use way. The part of the sheet being displayed in Figure 31.1 would be typical for entering the weekly data.

Validation

It is *vital* that you convey to the moderators of your project that you have validated all possible inputs to the system. Although it is not possible to validate each piece of data in its entirety, you can put sensible restrictions on the data for each employee. For example, the hours, holiday, sick days, absence days and Doctors' Certificate fields can be validated to some extent. It is a good idea to have a table, similar to that shown in Table 31.1, for each of the inputs in your project.

Table 31.1 The validation rules, used for the input system shown in Figure 31.1

Input validation rules for weekly time sheets			
Data	Type	Range	Comment
Hours	Numeric	$0 \leqslant$ hours	Positive integers only – no fractions
Holiday	Numeric	$0 \leqslant$ holiday $\leqslant 5$	No half-day holidays
Sick	Numeric	$0 \leqslant$ Sick $\leqslant 5$	No half-day sickness
Doctors	List	D only or blank	D means a valid Doctor's certificate

Assumptions have been made here. Nobody can be sick for anything other than an integer number of days up to a maximum of 5 days in any single week. In a real system you would query this – the specification does not mention fractions of a day, so why make life difficult? It has also been assumed that you cannot work for fractions of an hour for the same reasons.

The main statistical analysis section

Table 31.2 Part of the structure for Boris

Part of cell-reference pattern for Boris				
A11	A15			
Boris	Number			
Week1	Week2	Week3	Week4	Etc.
D11	F11	H11	J11	Etc.
Hours	Hours	Hours	Hours	Etc.
D12	F12	H12	J12	Etc.
Holiday	Holiday	Holiday	Holiday	Etc.
D13	F13	H13	J13	Etc.
Sick	Sick	Sick	Sick	Etc.
D14	F14	H14	J14	Etc.
Absent	Absent	Absent	Absent	Etc.
D15	F15	H15	J15	Etc
Doctor	Doctor	Doctor	Doctor	Etc.

Having entered the data into the system, the statistics now need to be calculated. The validated data is currently sitting inside defined cells on part of the spreadsheet as shown in Figure 31.1. Because of symmetry inherent in the layout, it is easy to move from one set of data to the next, based on a suitable reference and a few simple calculations. The following table shows the cell references for important data for the first user, called Boris.

Boris's name can be obtained from cell A11, and his number from A15. The statistics regarding week 1 for Boris can be obtained from cells D11, D12, D13, D14 and D15. We can use these references, placed there and validated by the data-entry clerk, to generate other statistics.

We now define the **record structure**, as required by the AQA guidelines outlined in unit 28. It is relatively easy to store information in a spreadsheet, in a similar way to storing information in a database; it is just that we refer to the compartments in a slightly different way.

We also need to understand the IF-THEN scenarios, covered in unit 29, and the program flowchart of Figure 30.1 (unit 30). We work though this program flowchart, adding logical conditions to the spreadsheet, and testing these as we go. We are assuming that this flowchart is correct, as a **dry run** has already been carried out on this structure – state this in your report, and show *evidence* of the dry run.

Assume that we have saved a blank version of Figure 31.1. For each 8-week period, we need to load a new blank, and save it with an appropriate name. We have, therefore, already carried out the instructions in the first couple of boxes of the program flowchart! Indeed, we have also read in the data, and validated it, so we have worked our way through the first six boxes already.

Working out and storing the pay slip data

We need a place for the extra statistics, shown in the program flowchart of Figure 30.1 (unit 30), and just to the right of the input data would seem to be a good choice. Therefore, the statistics for Boris would be stored to the right of his input-data form, and statistics for Doris would be stored to the right of her input form, for example. From Figure 31.2 you can see that we have a layout that reflects the convenience of the user, rather than efficiency in terms of the number of cells used. The cumulative statistics are stored in each of the white boxes, and kept for each week, in case we need to go back and find out specific data for a specific employee for a specific week.

You could verify that the cumulative figures, shown in Figure 31.3 are correct. Simply add up the columns in Figure 31.1 to see if this is so.

The figures shown here are the actual cumulative statistics, referred to in Figure 30.1.

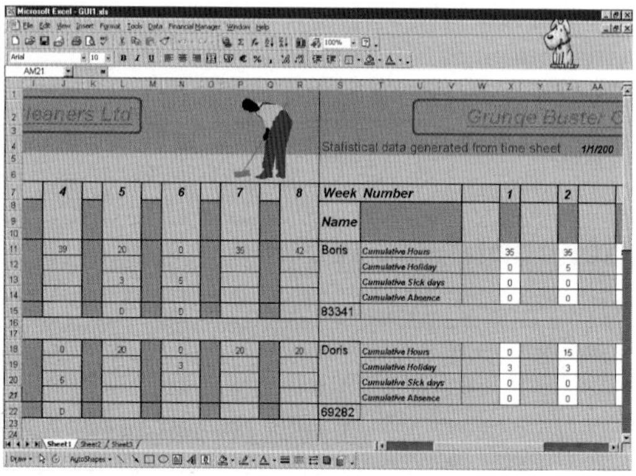

Learn how to use Excel's format painter. It helps considerably to produce screens like those shown in this unit very quickly.

Figure 31.2 Two separate data structures.

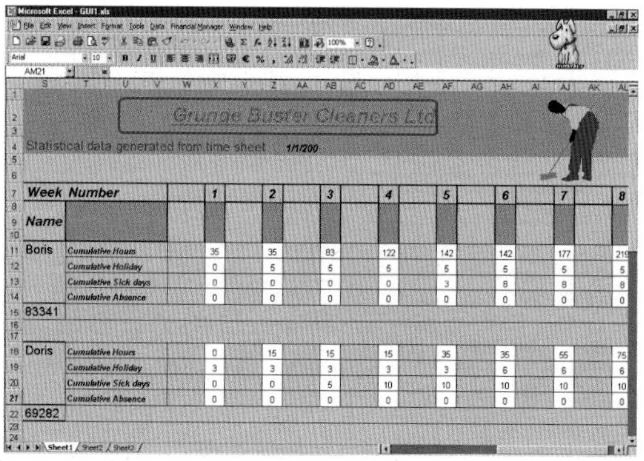

Figure 31.3 The cumulative statistics.

The user interface and design

We have already covered the part of the AQA specifications which requires that we design a good user interface, including the method of data entry and validation. We have also got some output forms, because the wage clerk can use the screens as is – we are making good progress in ticking off each item outlined at the beginning of the design phase in unit 28.

A clear and consistent user interface is an important part of any project. You will lose a lot of marks if you fail to appreciate this.

Working out the rules for validation

We now implement the rules, which will be programmed via the logical statements in Excel, to generate the validated statistics, from which the pay check data can be worked out. At the moment the cumulative statistics, calculated from the validated input data, may *not* reflect the appropriate conditions imposed by the rules. For example, an employee may have 5 cumulative sick days, but this does not necessarily translate into 5 pay days, unless they have a doctor's certificate. The rate at which they are paid will also depend on whether they are in the insurance scheme.

Holiday pay statistics

The holiday pay analysis is quite trivial, and we are now on box 7 of the program flowchart of Figure 30.1 (unit 30). We need to check if any holiday has been taken in this particular week. The cells, which hold this information have already been validated on (max days/week), and we therefore need to inspect this cell to see if it is > 0. It cannot be more than 5, because of the validation on data entry, and we can use this fact to our advantage. If the contents of this cell > 0, then the cumulative holiday total for the previous weeks needs examining, to see if any valid holiday is left. An example will make this a little clearer.

Constantly check against the original specification. Failure to do so could cost you many marks. Do not be careless in this area.

Table 31.3 Some test data.

Some holiday pay test data		
Previous week	Current week	Validated holiday days
Typical cell references		
C1	D1	E1
5	3	0
5	5	0
0	5	5
1	4	4
1	2	2
3	2	2
0	0	0
3	2	2
2	5	3
4	3	1
5	5	0
4	4	1
3	5	2

From Table 31.3 we establish that the data splits naturally into three different conditions, which are analysed in a formula to allocate the valid number of days. The conditions are as follows:

1 Either $C1 >= 5$, in which case, no holiday days are due, irrespective of the number in D1.

2 Assuming that condition 1 is met, if $C1 + D1 <= 5$ this means that we allocate the holiday days held in cell D1.

3 If condition 2 is not met, then we allocate 5-C1 holiday days.

This is summarised, for typical references in the table, using the following formula:

```
=IF(C1>=5,0,IF(C1+D1<=5,D1,5-C1))
```

This formula can be used as a basis, from which to calculate the actual holiday pay due, by producing a valid number of holiday days for any week. Note that a separate bonus calculation is needed to add any unused holiday to any week 8 pay, as shown at the end of the program flowchart.

In this unit you have learned about:

- That successful implementation comes only after a successful design phase
- The user interface
- Data validation
- Checking your project implementation against the original specification

32 Further development and debugging

In this section you will learn about:

● Phase two of the implementation and testing phases of a project

This chapter is useful reading before starting on your project

Cumulative absence and sick pay statistics

We now need to process the absence and sick pay in ways similar to that suggested in the holiday-pay section in the last unit. The determining factor is the doctor's certificate, unless an employee is sick for 3 days or less during a period of 8 weeks. A table, similar to Table 32.1, can be used, with suitable test data, spread across the range. (Do not forget that this test data is useful for the testing section later on – it is not a waste of time.) Recall the available data for each week. This is in two parts as follows:

1 'Hours', 'Holiday', 'Sick', 'Doctor's Certificate' and 'Absence' from the time sheet in Table 28.2.

2 'Cumulative Hours', 'Cumulative Holiday', 'Cumulative Sick Days' and 'Cumulative Absence' from the statistical data generated in Table 28.2.

This is the fifth of a six-part module that solves a typical AS project. Any one of these units will not make sense in isolation.

Table 32.1 Some test data to for holiday pay

Some sickness and absence pay data for development purposes					
Typical cell references					
Test Person		Week 1	Week 2	Week 1	Week 2
	C	D	F	X	Z
Insurance flag	Yes				
11 Hours		33	0		
12 Holiday		0	4		
13 Sick		1	1		
14 Absence		0	0		
15 Doctor's Certificate		D	D		
11 Cumulative Hours				33	33
12 Cumulative Holiday				0	4
13 Cumulative Sick Days				1	1
14 Cumulative Absence				0	0

These data are placed in Table 32.1, this time working with a different layout. The top half of the table refers to data for part 1 above, and the bottom half points to the data for part 2. You can see the insurance flag, which will be set up in the part of the sheet being developed now. We are now on the 'Any Sickness or Absence?' box in the flow-chart of Figure 30.1. We check to see if the employee has had any sickness or absence during this week, which is done as follows:

```
If(d13<0,"Yes","No")
If(d14<0,"Yes","No")
```

These are the sickness and absence flags. If the flags are stored in with the pay slip data, they could be used, along with the logic outlined in the program flowchart of Figure 30.1 to deduce the data needed for the other boxes, shown in the test screen of Figure 32.1.

With so few employees, and an 8-week term to consider, the replication of data like that shown in Figure 32.1 is acceptable. Do not forget that the system shown here would score a large number of marks, because it meets the examination criteria. *Problems of this sort can become very open ended, and you must not end up wasting an unnecessary amount of time on a really professional interface.*

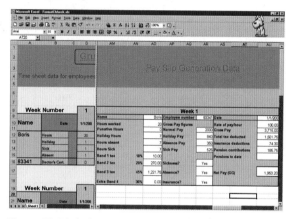

Figure 32.1 A test screen developed for the algorithm to validate holiday pay.

Further development and debugging

The method chosen was to get a pay-slip interface up and running, and then use the cumulative statistics generated earlier, to see if the appropriate answers are generated. At first, no checking for doctors certificates or other conditions like 'have they exceeded their holiday quota' etc. was implemented. If you develop too much at the same time, you may get in a mess. The split-screen facility in Excel is useful for **debugging**, as shown in Figure 32.2. On the left you can enter data for week one, and on the right you can see how the data input produces outputs like deductions etc.

Figure 32.2 Excel's split-screen facility.

You must test different scenarios, and make sure it works. For example, you might have zero work days, sick days, absence days and holiday. Assuming there is no absence pay, have you checked that results, like tax and net pay get put to zero? If you have some mistakes in your system you may find that you owe negative tax or have to pay tax on zero pay! Next increase the pay by small increments making sure that only the 10% band is affected initially. When the 20% band kicks in, make sure that the 10% tax stays the same.

Silly mistakes could mean that the lower bands keep rising. Gradually rise up through the bands, by increasing hours until all bands are active. Did the 20% tax band stay at the maximum tax possible, and did the 45% tax band cut in etc.

Make sure that if an employee is a member of the insurance group, they get sick pay at 0.75 instead of 0.5 etc. Indeed, I would suggest that you make up a table, which proves that you have carried out appropriate tests. Part of the table could be as shown in Table 32.2.

Table 32.2 Some test data to develop the algorithm for valid holiday pay

Test data for debugging the tax-band and other calculations				
Pay 100 GG/hour	Gross pay	10% tax	30% tax	45% tax
0 hours	0	0	0	0
1 hour	100	10	0	0
2 hours	200	10	20	0
10 hours	1000	10	180	0
20 hours	2000	10	180	480
40 hours	4000	10	180	1350
100 hours (●)	10 000	10	180	4050
● 75% rate to kick in as hours >47				

Other statistics, like pension contributions, insurance premiums, net pay etc. should be included too. *Do not discard data combinations that bring to light errors corrected during the development stages. If you do not keep evidence of the sort shown in Table 32.2, then you have lost valuable testing strategies, which you can use later on.* It is difficult to think up data to test the project when it is working well.

The final part of the program flowchart

Having got a suitable mechanism for generating the wage-slip data from the cumulative results, we now need to make sure that the final set of rules, shown in the right-hand side of the program flowchart of Figure 30.1 (unit 30) are implemented. We already have the structure, it's a matter of adding extra conditions into the cells, regarding whether a doctor's certificate has been obtained or whether someone has run out of the total amount of sick pay for the 8-week period etc.

Absence pay

Table 32.3 Table to establish formulae

Pattern for award of absence in weeks 2 to 8			
Previous total	Requested total	Awarded total	Request awarded?
0	1	1	Yes
1	1	1	Yes
2	1	1	Yes
>=3	1	0	No
0	2	2	Yes
1	2	2	Yes
2	2	1	No
>=3	2	0	No
0	3	3	No
1	3	2	No
2	3	1	No
>=3	3	0	No
0	>3	3	No
1	>3	2	No
2	>3	1	No
>=3	>3	0	No

If an employee is absent, they get a maximum of 3 days pay, after which they have nothing, unless they have a certificate, in which case they are covered by the rules developed later. We give them no more than 3 days absence pay in any 8 week period. In week 1, they cannot have absence pay already, so they can be awarded 1, 2 or 3 days. If they request 4 or 5, they will still only get 3, because they have used up their allocation. For week 1, the formulae, working out the absence hours will be:

```
=IF(W15>=3,W15*7,3*7)
```

where W15 is the cumulative total of absence days for week 1. For week 2 and all other subsequent wage slips, the formulae will have to be modified, because all the days may have been used up already, as shown in the program flowchart for cumulative absence days >=3. The formulae will have to examine the cell before also, and check *if* all three days have been used up. A small table will help.

From the analysis in Table 32.3, you can see that if the requested total is >3, then we treat the requested total as if it were 3. If we now analyse the top two-thirds of the table we can see that if the (previous total + requested total) < = 3, we award the requested total, as indicated by the yes/no. However, if the (previous total + requested total) is >3, we award the (requested total – previous total). If we assume the following storage locations for week 2, then we can develop the Excel formula shown on the right, which calculates the awarded absence hours, by multiplying the days by 7:

```
Previous Total (PT) = W15
Requested Total (RT) = F15
Awarded (AW) = AX14
```

Forgetting the need to multiply the answer by 7 for a moment, changing the above code into Excel's formulae is carried out as shown:

```
If(PT < = 3, 0,)
If(AND(PT>3,(PT+RT)>=3),RT,)
If(AND(PT>3,(PT+RT)<3,3-PT,)
If(AND(RT<3,PT>3,3-PT)
```

Oh dear – what next?

It is difficult to use Excel's formulae for more complex conditions. To get over these limitations Excel provides access to sophisticated features via **VBA (Visual Basic for**

Visit our portal to see similar AS Level projects.

Applications). The VBA Editor can be called up from Excel by clicking on the Editor button on the Visual Basic toolbar. Next run the editor, view the code, and

```
Cells(1,1) would refer to A1
Cells(3,4) would refer to D3
Cells(3,27) would refer to AA3
```

select the 'Worksheet' and 'Selection Change' options, as shown in Figure 32.3. Row and column references link the cell references on the Excel worksheet into VBA as above.

It is almost inevitable that you will need to learn a macro language like VBA to do the harder parts of some of the board-set exercises.

Although it is awkward to refer to the cells like this, it is ideal for counters in loop structures used in VBA. The use of modules now makes the code much easier to use, and the end user will be unaware that complex coding is checking his or her data entries.

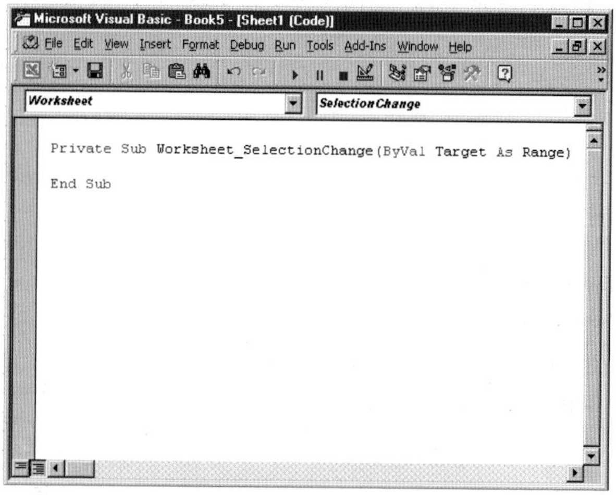

Figure 32.3 The VBA interface.

The final code for the absence pay

This final code, including the days-to-hours conversion, can be coded more conveniently using VBA as follows:

```
Private Sub Worksheet_SelectionChange(ByVal Target As Range)

PT = Cells(15, 23)
RT = Cells(15, 6)
If PT < 3 Then AW = 0
If PT > 3 And (RT + PT) >= 3 Then AW = RT
If PT > 3 And (PT + RT) < 3 Then AW = 3 - PT
If RT < 3 And PT > 3 Then AW = 3 - PT
Cells(12, 50) = AW * 7

End Sub
```

We have now increased the power of the validation system by orders of magnitude. Instead of struggling with Excel formulae, we have the power of VBA behind us. It will run in the background without user intervention, and enables us to implement the rest of the flowchart of Figure 30.1 (unit 30) with ease.

Sick pay and bonuses etc.

It is left up to the reader to implement the few other conditions in this way. The principles are literally identical.

It will usually take a lot of extra effort to complete a project in its entirety. More difficult things towards the end might only get you a few marks for a lot of work.

In this unit you have learned about:

- How a typical project can be developed and debugged
- How extra ingenuity is needed as you go deeper into the solution of a problem
- Using macro languages like VBA, for example, when tackling projects at this level

33 The final implementation and testing

In this section you will learn about:

- The final part of your exercise project presentation

This chapter is useful reading before starting on your project

This is the final part of a six-part module that solves a typical AS project. Any one of these units will not make sense in isolation.

Units 25, 26 and 27 contain information that is important for your project write up. Read them and incorporate the ideas into your own AS projects.

The wage slip print outs

We now develop the wage slip and tax return mechanisms, and give advice on testing. We need an attractively designed slip, which will take the final data like 'Gross Pay', 'Tax Deducted', 'Net Pay' and 'Sick Pay' etc. and place them on a pay slip along with the date, name and employment number etc.

It would be useful if the user could click on a button to print out a wage slip or set of wage slips. We could utilise the existing pay slip design, which has now been developed into that shown in Figure 33.1.

Print Slip		*Week 1*			
Name	Boris	*Employee number*	83341	*Date*	1/1/200
Hours worked	35	*Gross Pay figures*		*Rate of pay/hour*	100.00
Punative Hours	0	*Normal Pay*	3500	*Gross Pay*	6,370.00
Holiday Hours	21	*Holiday Pay*	2520	*Total tax deducted*	2,696.50
Hours Sick	7	*Sick Pay*	350	*Insurance deductions*	127.40
Hours absent	7	*Absence Pay*	0	*Pension contributions*	318.50
Band 1 tax 10%	10.00			*Pensions to date*	
Band 2 tax 20%	270.00	*Sickness?*	Yes		
Band 3 tax 45%	2,416.50	*Absence?*	Yes	*Net Pay (GG)*	3,227.60
Punative Hours Tax + 30%	0.00	*Insurance?*	Yes		

Figure 33.1 The addition of a macro button.

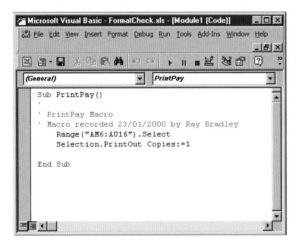

Figure 33.2 The macro code after recording.

We can use a macro to print out a wage slip. We call up the Visual Basic toolbar, click over the record-macro button, give the macro a name like 'PrintPay', and then manually go through the motions of printing a typical slip for week 1. After selecting the appropriate area to print on the sheet, and after instructing the printing routine to print only the selected area, you can then stop recording the macro. The resulting macrocode is shown in Figure 33.2.

A button can be assigned to a macro so that it is run when a user clicks over it. A suitable button for the pay slip is shown in Figure 33.1. When the user clicks over this button, because it has been assigned to the macro, the macro is called, and the actions, which were carried out manually during the recording of the macro, are executed. In the top left-hand side of the pay slip you can see the Print Slip button. The pay slip is printed out if the user clicks this.

130

The option menu

It would be possible to record many different macros, one for each wage slip. However, all that changes is the range of cells that are selected, and the horizontal position can easily be related to the week number by simple numeric patterns. For example, 'week 2' would be 9 cells along, 'week 3' 18 cells, 'week 4' 27 cells and so on. We represent this shift with a variable, which is related to the week number typed in. Also, the name of the employee relates to the vertical position of the cell range, with each new name generating a cell range 11 cells down from the previous one. If this method is used, then we need a method for getting the user to type in the name and week number, and this can be done by utilising a drop-down box from Excel. A possible modified user interface is shown in Figure 33.3.

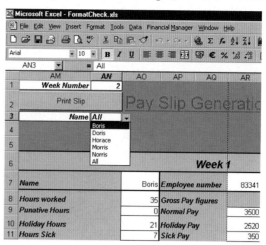

Figure 33.3 A more convenient way of printing batches of wage slips.

The button for printing the slips has been moved to the top of the sheet. We have added a cell for entering the week number (or all weeks), and have also added a drop-down menu for name (or all). For the scenarios shown in Figure 33.3, the user would be requesting all week 2 wage slips to be printed.

The macrocode now needs modification. We need to examine the contents of the cells AN1 and AN3. AN1 will contain the numbers '1 to 8' or 'All', and AN3 will contain a valid name or 'All'. From these numbers we can generate the patterns necessary to pass data to the printing macro, and loops will control execution of the selection and print parts of this macro if more than one slip needs to be printed.

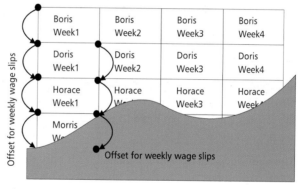

Figure 33.4 Generating different range values for each wage slip.

The range to be printed is selected using the following syntax:

```
Range("AM6:AU16").Select
```

Now the sheet of pay slips is set out as a matrix of rows and columns, where the top left and bottom right of each column can be determined by the addition of a simple number. Unfortunately, you cannot add the number onto the above string, but you can build up the string "AM6:AU16" or variations of it from the code, and this is what we will do. Consider the diagram, shown in Figure 33.4.

Starting at the top left hand side (AM6 in this case), we need to generate offsets of 11 in the vertical direction. We therefore need to generate. AM6, AM17 and AM28 etc. The other offsets will also be 11, and start at AU16. We can use the Str function, which returns a number to a string. For example, Str(99) would put "99" into a string.

The following test code would therefore print out the first week's wage slips:

```
Sub PrintPay()
'
' PrintPay Macro
' Macro recorded 23/01/2001 by Ray Bradley

    Top_Left = "AM"
    Bottom_Right = "AU"

    For slips = 0 To 55 Step 11
        Left_number = 6 + slips
        Right_number = 16 + slips
        Left_numberstring = Str(Left_number)
        'Strip out leading space reserved for sign
        Left_string = Right$(Left_numberstring,
Len(Left_numberstring - 1))
        Left_string = Top_Left + Left_string
        Right_numberstring = Str(Right_number)
        'Strip out leading space reserved for sign
        Right_string = Right$(Right_numberstring,
Len(Right_numberstring - 1))
        Right_string = Bottom_Right + Right_string
        Final_string = Left_string + ":" + Right_string
        Range(Final_string).Select
        Selection.PrintOut Copies:=1
    Next slips
End Sub
```

There are always unexpected problems when developing code. For example, to generate the simple string "AN6:AU16" from the numbers 6 and 16 from the loops above required that the 'Str' function be used. Unfortunately for this routine, this function slips in a leading zero, which is reserved for the sign of the number! This means that we must strip off the leading zeros from the string by using the 'Right$' function. Because the length of the strings can vary, we have to use the Len function to determine how many characters are present.

The above code is not quite finished, as it only prints out week 1, but the reader is now in a very strong position to finish this routine by the addition of some other loops and tests. Other routines, like the generation of the government statistics are also trivial in comparison to the above.

Data integrity and data security

Much work has already gone into ensuring **data integrity**. However, we have done nothing to address the **data security** problem. This is easy to do, as Excel provides a system of **password protection** for the sheets. In addition to this, you have the general password option when you save an Excel document. This is shown in Figure 33.5.

If anyone tried to open the file in Excel, they would be presented with a password screen. In addition to this, you can hide cells, and protect parts or all of the worksheet from inadvertent messing up. This is essential to provide an effective user interface. When applied, the wages clerk is not able to alter the appearance of the sheet, for example, unless they know the password entered by the designer of the system. This could obviously be different from the password used to open the file for editing the pay data, which would only be known to the designer of the system and the wages clerk.

Your tutor will not normally know how the marks are to be awarded on projects of this nature until (or even after) the project is due to be handed in.

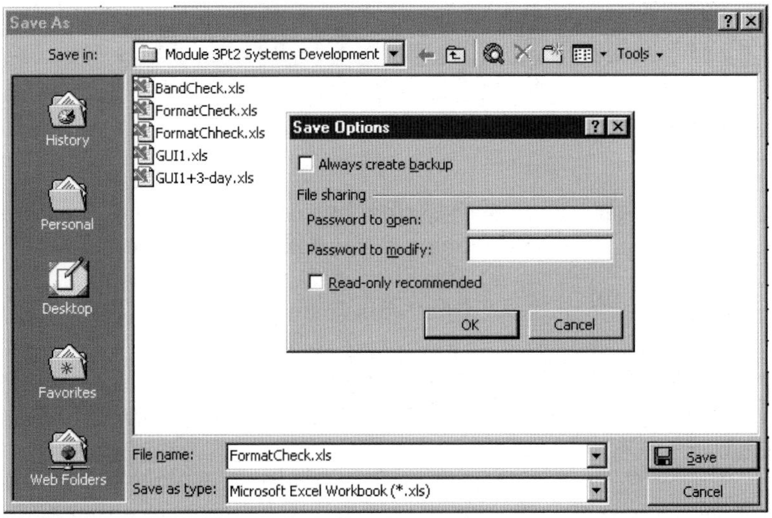

Figure 33.5 Unauthorised access?

AQA students must take their completed project into an examination to answer questions on it.

Maintenance

Most large projects will require **user** and **technical** documentation, but these are usually more appropriate to the major 'A2' level projects, and not the board set exercises, which are being considered here. **Documentation** is considered in the other project units.

Evaluation

You have to make a critical evaluation of your efforts. With the benefit of hindsight there will always be improvements that you could make. As most students will be learning the details of a particular package as they go along, it is inevitable that you will find features of the package that enable you to tackle problems in a more efficient way. However, do not forget that you are solving a particular problem in a set time scale. You must find methods that work reasonably efficiently and therefore score high marks.

The written report

It is unlikely that the examiners will ever see your masterpiece in the flesh. The written report is all that they will have to go on, and thus you *must present the evidence* that you have **designed**, **developed**, **implemented**, **tested** and **evaluated** your solution. You *must* consult your particular **mark scheme** for this module, but the following is typical of what is required in the report:

- Title page (including school name, candidate name, candidate number)
- A contents list
- A design section
- An implementation section
- A testing section
- An evaluation section
- Any extra material that might be required such as user or technical documentation
- Bibliography

A typical mark scheme for a project of this nature would normally consist of a mass of test data, testing the easy parts of your project first, then progressing through to the difficult parts. To get the final few marks is usually quite challenging.

Visit our portal to see similar AS Level projects.

In this unit you have learned:

- How to **test** the complete project, by making use of techniques, which you have covered in other parts of your course
- That certain parts of the project might need a lot of ingenuity to solve, and that this usually leads to a **law of diminishing returns** regarding the marks awarded

 **Examination questions AS**

1. Consider the following 8-bit binary integer which is in twos complement form:

0	1	1	1	1	0	1	0

   (a) State the decimal equivalent of this binary integer. (1 mark)
   (b) Show how this binary integer would be represented in hexadecimal. (1 mark)
   (c) (i) Show the result obtained when this binary integer is added to itself
       (ii) State its decimal equivalent and explain the result. (3 marks)
   OCR specimen paper for 2506 module 1

2. The following numbers are to be entered in order to be stored in a binary tree for subsequent processing:

   12, 27, 29, 23, 5, 15, 4, 7, 24

   show, with the aid of a diagram, how this data structure will store these values. (3 marks)
   AQA specimen paper 5511 module 1

3. A number of stand-alone computers are to be connected together to form a network. Identify two hardware components and two software components that are required to be added to the stand-alone computers, explaining why each is necessary.
   (a) hardware components (4 marks)
   (b) software components (4 marks)
   OCR specimen paper for 2506 module 1

4. A teacher wishes to keep records of the marks obtained by pupils throughout the year. At the end of the year each pupil is supplied with a report that contains personal details of the pupil, the percentage mark obtained by the pupil and a comment written by the teacher. Explain the role of a
   (a) Word processor
   (b) Spreadsheet
   (c) Database (6 marks)
   OCR specimen paper for 2506 module 1

5. Describe the purpose of each of the following buses. Your description must make clear the direction of the flow along the bus.
   (i) Address bus (2 marks)
   (ii) Control bus (2 marks)
   (iii) Data bus (2 marks)
   AQA specimen paper 5511 module 1

6. Sound is naturally in analogue form but it may be stored and transmitted as either analogue or digital data.
   (a) In the context of sound transmission, explain, with the aid of a diagram, what is meant by:
       (i) Analogue data
       (ii) Digital data (2 marks)
   (b) Give an example of a device which stores sound as:
       (i) analogue data
       (ii) digital data (2 marks)
   (c) Briefly explain **one** method by which an analogue signal can be converted into a digital signal when being input into a computer for processing. (2 marks)
   AQA specimen paper 5511 module 1

7. (a) Distinguish between security and integrity of data. (2 marks)
   (b) Name **two** methods by which the integrity of data may be protected, and explain in detail how each is applied. (8 marks)
   AQA specimen paper 5511 module 2

8. In the context of database management explain carefully the meaning of the following:
   (a) program – data independence (2 marks)
   (b) data consistency (2 marks)
   (c) control over redundancy (2 marks)
   AQA specimen paper 5511 module 2

9 Computer controlled greenhouses and computer controlled nuclear power stations would be run using *a real time* operating system.
  (a) Explain two important differences in the requirements of the two examples or real time systems. (2 marks each)
  (b) Gas bills would usually be produced using a batch multi-programming operating system. Justify this choice by giving two characteristics of this operating system with, for each one consequence.
    (i) Characteristic
        Consequence (2 marks)
    (ii) Characteristic
        Consequence (2 marks)
        AQA specimen paper 5511 module 2

10 One stage in the development of a computer system to develop the stock control of a warehouse is to produce a prototype.
  (a) Describe the term prototyping (7 marks)
  (b) Outline the advantages and disadvantages of prototyping for users and systems developers (10 marks)
  (c) State what aspects of development are particularly discussed with the users during prototyping (3 marks)
    Edexcel specimen paper module 2

11 (a) Briefly describe two applications in which it is appropriate to process a file serially. Explain why serial processing is appropriate in each case. (4 marks)
  (b) Briefly describe an application which requires serial access to a master file on one occasion and direct access on another. (2 marks)
    Edexcel Specimen paper module 2

12 All the offices of an insurance company are in one building. A local area network (LAN) has been set up to enable distributed computing. The managers are looking to expand the company into a second building, in another city and are exploring the possibility of creating a wide area network (WAN).
  (a) Briefly describe a LAN. (3 marks)
  (b) Describe, with diagrams, a star and ring topology. Clearly indicate where the file server and printer would be located. (6 marks)
  (c) State three benefits an office may expect from using a LAN. (3 marks)
  (c) Briefly explain the differences between a LAN and a WAN. Describe the additional hardware which a WAN would require. (6 marks)
    Edexcel Specimen paper module 1

13 Answer the following for one application you have studied.
  Identify the application, either by name or by type.
  (a) Briefly describe the main purpose of this application.
  (b) (i) Identify the most important data item(s) which is entered at the start of the process. Explain the source of this data.
        Item
        Source (2 marks)
    (ii) State the input device by which this data is entered into the system. (1 mark)
    (iii) Give one reason why this input method is the most suitable for this data. (1 mark)
  (c) Give one user-interface need and explain briefly how it has been met in your application. (2 marks)
    AQA specimen paper 5511 module 2

Brief answers to these questions can be found at the back of this book. For full answers visit www.revisecomputing.com.

35 Lists, trees and queues

Data structures

Structure is the key to organising data in a computer system. An understanding of data structures is fundamental, and forms the basis of many useful techniques.

The data structures outlined in this unit form an important basis on which many topics in the A2 specification are built. This is important foundation work.

Linear list

A **linear list** is simply an ordered set of elements. The data {dog, cat, bird, mouse, pig} forms an ordered list. This list is not in any particular order, but it *is* ordered. Such lists could easily be the product of **transactions**. This might represent the order of the animals sold in a 'pet shop' during the morning. To make a list of contents we use the following pseudocode:

```
Set pointer to beginning of list
Repeat
   Read list item
   Print list item
   Pointer = Pointer + 1
Until end-of-list
```

To **search** for data in a **linear list**, we look at every element until the item of interest is found. The algorithm below will do this.

```
Set pointer to beginning of list
Input desired_item
Repeat
   Input list_item
   If list_item = desired_item then
      Print "Item found"
   Exit procedure
   Else
      Pointer = Pointer + 1
Until end-of-list
Print "Item was not found"
```

We read all items until the desired item is found. If it is not in the **file** or **data structure**, the loop will be exited, and a message printed out. **Linear lists** may be implemented in memory by the use of **arrays**, or may be implemented via **files** stored on tape or disk.

Example

Using pseudocode, show how an **array**, consisting of ten elements, can be set up for a linear list. You may assume that the start data consists of 'dog', 'cat' and 'bird'. Show how this array may be set up and how the original list is created. Your algorithm must cope if the list is full, and allow the user to add data.

Solution

The original list may be created like this:

```
Dim A(10)
Rem create original three entries
A(1) = dog: A(2) = cat: A(3) = bird
```

We need a **pointer**, pointing to the next element of the array, used to store the next entry. If the size of this pointer exceeds the dimension of the array, then no more data can be stored. The idea is shown here. If the pointer > 10, a 'No room left' message is printed, and the procedure is exited, else the data is stored in the appropriate part of the array and the pointer is incremented.

```
Rem set up pointer to point
   to next free space
Pointer = 4
REPEAT
  INPUT "Enter data"; data
  IF Pointer > 10 then
     PRINT "No room left"
     Exit this subroutine
  Else
       A(Pointer) = data
       Pointer = Pointer + 1
  Endif
UNTIL false
```

You can visualise the data structure for the last example as shown in Figure 35.1.

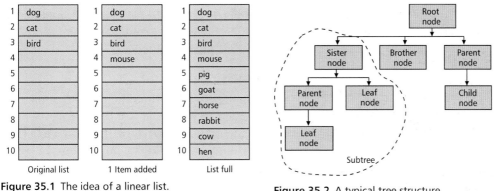

Figure 35.1 The idea of a linear list.

Figure 35.2 A typical tree structure.

Trees

A **tree structure**, is shown in Figure 35.2. Each box represents **data** *and/or* **pointers**. The boxes are **nodes**. The node at the top is called the **root node**. Names are derived from a family tree. A parent node is one that has a child. Brother and sister nodes have a common parent. Names are used according to the point of reference. Nodes may be a 'parent', 'child' and 'brother', at the same time.

The efficient implementation of tree structures depends upon the language being used to model it. Learn the methods used to implement these structures using imperative languages like **Pascal** or **Basic**. The following methods, used to model these structures, are common.

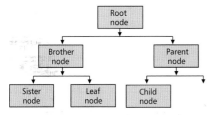

Figure 35.3 A binary tree.

Binary trees

A **binary tree** is a tree structure in which a parent is allowed to have a maximum of two children. The idea is shown in Figure 35.3.

Binary trees use '**left**' and '**right**' **pointers** to point to the child nodes, and could be built up by using relationships such as '<' or '>'.

Example

Using the following list, create a binary tree using the first element as the root. Other elements must be placed in the tree using the rule 'if name is < name in node then follow left pointer, else follow right pointer'.

```
List = {microfilm, firewall, processor, memory, heap, stack,
queue, backup}
```

Solution

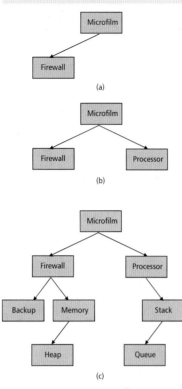

Figure 35.4 Building up a binary tree.

The first item forms the root (see Figure 35.4(a)). Next 'firewall' is read – as 'firewall < microfilm', the left pointer is followed to store the data. Next 'processor' is read, and compared with the data at the root. As 'processor > microfilm', the right hand path is taken and the data is inserted as shown. Next 'memory' is read and compared with the root data. As 'memory < microfilm', the left hand pointer is followed. Next 'memory' is compared with 'firewall', the next node in the tree. As 'memory > firewall', the right-hand path is followed, and the data placed accordingly. The final binary tree is shown in Figure 35.4(c).

Clever processing of the tree using an **in-order traversal** mechanism (see unit 37), would reproduce the list in alphabetical order.

Queues

A **queue** is like queue in a shop. The first item put in the queue is processed first. An alternative name for a queue is a **FIFO stack** (**First In First Out**). Organization is by **pointers**, pointing to the **beginning** and **end** of the queue as shown in Figure 35.5.

The **pointers** indicate the start and end of the queue as shown in Figure 35.5. These are called the **header** and **footer**. The data structure has only ten storage locations available; therefore, the programmer must manage the situation when the queue is full. Another problem arises as data is removed from the queue. The entire data set creeps down the data structure! We can set up a **circular queue**, but manage the pointers effectively to maintain the beginning and ends of the queue as shown in Figure 35.6.

From Figure 35.6 you can see that the pointers manage the positions in the queue very effectively. By crossing over, we have established a **circular queue**, but still have a ten-item limitation due to the size of the data structure (amount of memory).

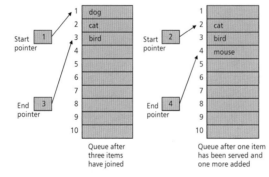

Figure 35.5 Use of pointers in a queue.

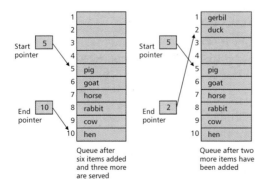

Figure 35.6 The idea of the pointers used to create a circular queue.

If you have time, try to develop your own pseudocode algorithms for carrying out tasks like those shown here. You may be required to do this in an examination.

Example

Show, using pseudocode, how a ten-element queue may have data added to it. Allow for the queue being full.

Solution

The structure of the queue is shown in Figure 35.5. We need a couple of variables called 'start_pointer' and 'end_pointer'. From Figure 35.5, we see that two conditions must be checked to see if the queue is full. These are as follows:

```
IF start_pointer = 1 AND end_pointer = 10
IF start_pointer = end_pointer + 1
```

The first condition checks when the pointers are not crossed, and the second condition checks if they are crossed. We need to string these two conditions together with an OR function in our code. If the queue is not full, we insert an item at the end of the queue, and update the end_pointer to reflect the new end of the queue. If the end_pointer gets to 10, then we put it back to 1 to start at the beginning of the array, thus forming a circular queue. At the start of the program the pointers need setting up because the queue is empty. This is achieved by putting the start and end pointers both equal to 1.

```
PROCEDURE ADD
(*Check to see if queue is full*)
If start_pointer = 1 AND end pointer =
   10 OR start_pointer = end_pointer + 1 then
   Print "Queue is already full"
   Exit Subroutine
endif
(*Check to see if queue is empty*)
if start_pointer = 0 then
   (*initialize queue*)
   start_pointer = 1
   stop_pointer = 1
else
   (* queue not empty, update pointers*)
   if end_pointer = 10 then
     end_pointer = 1
   else
     end_pointer = end_pointer + 1
   endif
endif
(*store data in the array*)
Queue(stop_pointer) = data
END
```

Detailed pseudocode algorithms for structures in this unit can be found in chapters 24 and 25 of NUCSAL.

Self-test questions

1 Explain what is meant by a pointer system, and why these systems are used extensively to implement data structures like queues and lists.
2 What is a tree data structure, and why is this particularly useful in computing?
3 Show how a two-way queue may be set up by the use of a pointer system. Draw diagrams to illustrate your answer, illustrating the use of the start and stop pointers. (header and footer of the queue).
4 Explain how a binary tree may be used to store data in alphabetical order.

In this unit you have learned about:

- Linear list, tree and queue data structures
- Binary trees
- The importance attached to pointers in the implementation of these structures
- Coding some structures using pseudocode

36 Stacks and linked lists

Stacks

The data structures outlined in this unit form an important basis on which many topics in the A2 specification are built. This is important foundation work.

You have already seen the **FIFO stack**, or **queue**, outlined in the last unit. Another type of **stack** called a **LIFO (Last In First Out)** is of paramount importance in computer science.

The LIFO stack is similar in operation to the FIFO stack, with the exception that the last element put onto the stack is the first element that is removed. Although unfair from a conventional queue point of view, this is ideal for many computer problems, such as how to handle **interrupts**, for example (see unit 45). The FIFO stack typifies trying to remember what you were doing if you get **interrupted**. For example, you might be in the middle of having a conversation and the telephone rings. You might stop what you are doing to answer the phone. After dealing with the phone, you then get back to the conversation. However, you might not remember what you were talking about, and this is the essence of the LIFO stack. When the phone rings, you pop some information regarding where you are in the conversation onto the stack. You then forget about the conversation, deal with the phone call, and then retrieve the information back from the stack when the phone call is over. The last bit of information put onto the stack (about the original conversation), is the first to be removed from the stack – hence the name LIFO stack.

If, during your phone call the doorbell interrupted you, then you could put the phone information onto the stack, and so on. Inside computers, many interrupts may be processed in this manner, by saving microprocessor register information onto an area of memory set up to be a stack, and by retrieving this information when the interrupt has been serviced.

Example

(a) **Draw a diagram to illustrate how a LIFO stack may be set up in memory. Show how pointers may be used to maintain this data structure. Illustrate your answer by pushing six items onto the stack, and then removing three.**

(b) **Write some pseudocode to manage a stack of ten elements. You must show how items may be added or removed from the stack. Your code must cope if the stack is full or empty.**

Solution

(a) The LIFO data structure is shown in Figure 36.1.
You can see that the stack pointer is pointing to 6, being the last item put onto the stack, and therefore the first item to be removed. After three further items have been removed, the stack pointer is now pointing to 3.

(b) The following code should be reasonably self-explanatory. The procedure to add an item onto the stack needs to check if it is full, and the procedure to remove an

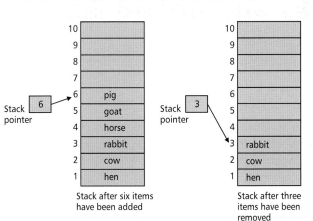

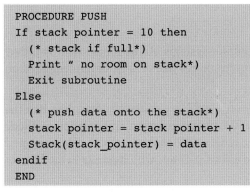
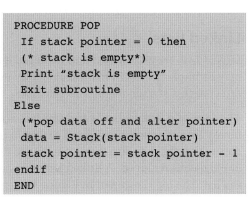

item from the stack needs to check if it is empty. The pointer will be called 'stack pointer'. The data to be put onto or removed from the stack is called 'data'. The array, set up to simulate the area of memory is an array called 'Stack'.

Stack after six items have been added

Stack after three items have been removed

Figure 36.1 An example stack.

```
PROCEDURE PUSH
If stack pointer = 10 then
   (* stack if full*)
   Print " no room on stack*)
   Exit subroutine
Else
   (* push data onto the stack*)
   stack pointer = stack pointer + 1
   Stack(stack_pointer) = data
endif
END
```

```
PROCEDURE POP
If stack pointer = 0 then
   (* stack is empty*)
   Print "stack is empty"
   Exit subroutine
Else
   (*pop data off and alter pointer)
   data = Stack(stack pointer)
   stack pointer = stack pointer - 1
endif
END
```

The principles of removing data from a FIFO stack are just as simple, and the code is shown in the second example above.

Static and dynamic data structures

It is possible to allocate a fixed area of memory to the stack, in which case this would be called a **static data structure**. It is also possible to request more memory for a stack as and when needed. In this case we would be dealing with a **dynamic data structure**.

More general areas of memory, not set up specifically for stacks, are referred to as **heaps**. A heap can therefore be regarded as a *temporary storage area*. The operating system or some of your programs will probably make use of the area of memory called the heap, and different parts of the system would need to use different parts of the heap according to what is happening at the time. The idea is very similar indeed to the organisation of memory on a disk. Bits needed by one process might be allocated to one part of memory, and other processes might not be able to fit into the available space. **Defragmentation** of the memory (heap) occurs, and it becomes less efficiently used because of the number of small spaces available. At some stage it might be necessary to clean up the heap, or you will get 'heap full' messages occurring.

Errors in programs (such as **infinite recursive calls**, for example), might cause stacks and heaps to overflow, irrespective of how much memory your system has.

Example

Give one example of a static data structure and one example of a dynamic data structure.

If you find the pseudocode work quite difficult, concentrate on the principles and the diagrams; this will allow you to score marks in these harder examination questions.

Solution

If you dimension an array in a program, then its size is fixed for the duration of running the program. For example:

```
DIM A(100) As Integer
```

might be the method used in a high-level language to reserve 100 memory locations (101 if you count location zero) into which integer numbers may be stored. This is an example of a **static data structure**, because you cannot allocate more space to the array during the execution of the program.

If you are creating a file on a direct-access media such as disk, then you can store as much data in that file as is available on your disk. Making the file bigger or smaller may be done dynamically during the execution of a program, and is therefore an example of a **dynamic data structure**.

Linked lists

Linked lists are established and managed by **pointer** systems. As with the **linear list**, they may be implemented in main memory by using structures like **arrays**, or implemented on direct-access storage media such as disks.

The idea of a **linked list** is to have fast access to data via **pointer systems**. Just like the binary tree structure mentioned earlier in unit 35, clever insertion and deletion methods ensure that the data structures don't have to be radically altered when new data is entered or old data is removed. A linked list must have a **start pointer**, which points to the head of the list. The idea is shown in Figure 36.2.

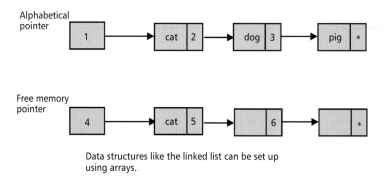

Data structures like the linked list can be set up using arrays.

Figure 36.2 A simple linked list.

The data is set up in a two-dimensional array, where data like 'cat' and 'dog', are stored along with pointer information like '2' and '3', which points to the next item in the linked list. Here, we have used alphabetical pointers to make the system very easy to understand. At the end of the list, the pointer does not contain a number used to go to the next item, but some indication that the list has ended. '*' or '−1' are quite common, shown at the right-hand side of the pig node in Figure 36.2.

If data needs to be added to the list, extra storage locations are needed, and the 'free-memory' pointer, which points to the next free space, indicates this. As the free space list is also finite, this too must have an end-of-list marker that is used to determine if the list is full.

To add a 'cow' to the list, the start pointer that points to the start of the list must be consulted. The pointers are then followed, and the 'node data' is compared to the data we wish to insert. In this case, 'cow' is compared to 'cat', and because 'cow>cat', we follow cat's pointer to dog. As 'cow<dog', we have established the position in the list at which we

Try to understand the material here rather than learn it by rote. Trivial twists in examination questions can make the pseudocode significantly different.

insert 'cow'. To insert the data, 'cow' must be put into the node represented by the free-memory pointer, and all the pointers altered accordingly. This is shown in Figure 36.3.

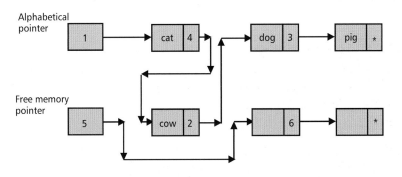

The new structure of the linked list after 'cow'
has been inserted into the list

Figure 36.3 The linked list structure after the insertion of the 'cow' node.

Note that the data 'cat', 'dog' and 'pig' etc. are stored at positions '1', '2' and '3' respectively in the data structure. After the insertion of the 'cow' node, the data at the old positions is not altered, only the pointers are. Therefore, the pointer stored along with 'cat' now has to point to node '4', the position where 'cow' has been inserted. The pointer stored along with 'cow' is altered to point to '2', the position where 'dog' is stored. The free memory pointer must also be updated to the next free location, which is now pointing to location '5'.

When data structures are large, it is not efficient to move large quantities of data, just to insert one or two new items into a list. With a **linked list**, *only the pointers are altered*, and the operation can be achieved with less processing. Nevertheless, the end result is the same as if all the data had been moved, and this is why the linked-list data structure is so useful.

Detailed pseudocode algorithms for structures in this unit can be found in chapters 24 and 25 of NUCSAL.

Self-test questions

1 Stacks are of paramount importance in computer science. Explain why this is so.
2 Draw a diagram to illustrate that you understand the term LIFO stack.
3 What is the difference between a LIFO stack and a FIFO stack? Draw diagrams to illustrate your answer.
4 Outline how an operating system might make use of a stack to queue requests for processor attention. Assume that priorities are assigned to the interrupts. What type of stack would be used for this operation?
5 Explain the concept of a linked list. Making use of some diagrams, show how data might be added to or removed from a linked list.
6 What is a two-way linked list? Suggest some data, which would benefit from being stored in this way.
7 Outline the difference between static and dynamic data structures, giving an example of each.
8 Explain the difference between a stack and a heap. For what purpose are heaps used?

In this unit you have learned about:

- FIFO and LIFO stacks
- The difference between dynamic and static data structures
- How to implement linked lists using a system of pointers

37 Further data structures

In this section you will learn about:

- Further data structures
- Algorithms for traversing binary trees
- Pre-order traversal
- In-order traversal
- Post-order traversal
- Using pseudocode to implement some of the above algorithms

Traversing binary trees

You can **traverse** a **tree** in three different ways; **Pre-order traversal, In-order traversal** and **Post-order traversal**.

These methods refer to the position in which the **node** is visited. Consider the simple tree shown in Figure 37.1.

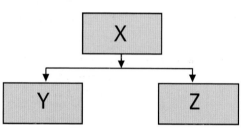

Figure 37.1 Tree for traversal methods.

By observation of Figure 37.1, we can see that the node data would be listed in the following ways, for each traversal mechanism.

(a) Pre-order traversal (visit root first, then left sub tree, then right sub tree)

X, Y, Z

(b) In-order traversal (visit left-hand sub tree first, then the root, then the right-hand sub tree)

Y, X, Z

(c) Post-order traversal (visit left-hand sub tree, then the right-hand sub tree, then visit the root)

Y, Z, X

Always do the left-hand sub tree before the right-hand sub tree.

If the tree structure is larger, then the sub trees must be treated as though you were starting the problem again, even though you are in the middle of traversing a larger tree. You will recall that the process, where you can solve a smaller identical problem, by applying the same algorithm, whilst in the middle of a more complex problem is called **recursion** (see unit 39). You can see recursion in operation in the following example.

Example

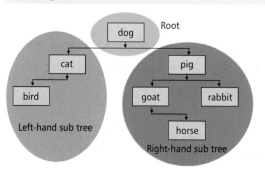

Figure 37.2 Example tree structure.

Consider the tree in Figure 37.2.

List the data in this tree by applying the following traversal mechanisms.

(a) Pre-order traversal
(b) In-order traversal
(c) Post-order traversal

Solution

(a) As pre-order traversal involves visiting the root, first, we build up the list of data as follows:

List the data at the root, shown by the green circle in Figure 37.2. Therefore, the list becomes:

> dog

Next visit the left-hand sub tree, shown by the red circle in Figure 37.2. This data itself is a tree structure, and so we apply pre-order traversal again. (This is an example of recursion.) To traverse the red tree by pre-order traversal, we visit the root node first, and extract the data 'cat'. We add this to our original list (just 'dog' at the moment), and the new list now becomes:

> dog, cat

Next we visit the left-hand sub tree, which consists only of 'bird'. As this is not a tree itself, but a leaf node, we simply list the data. The list now becomes:

> dog, cat, bird

Next we visit the right-hand sub tree. As there is no data here, we have finished the red sub tree, and have now visited the root, and left-hand sub tree in our original tree structure.

We have thus far processed the root, and left-hand sub tree in our pre-order traversal of the entire tree. Next we must process the right-hand sub tree. Again we apply a pre-order traversal, but this time operating on the blue tree. (This is another example of a recursive call.)

We must process the root, therefore 'pig' gets added to the list, and the list now becomes:

> dog, cat, bird, pig

Next we process the left-hand sub tree of the blue tree. This is yet another tree, and we apply a recursive call yet again, to traverse this by pre-order traversal.

We visit the root, which finds 'goat', and so this is added to the list:

> dog, cat, bird, pig, goat

Next we traverse the left-hand sub tree, which does not exist, therefore, we traverse the right-hand sub tree, and find 'horse'. The list now becomes:

> dog, cat, bird, pig, goat, horse

Having traversed the left-hand sub tree of the blue tree, we now traverse the right-hand sub tree. This consists only of 'rabbit', and so this data is added to the list:

> dog, cat, bird, pig, goat, horse, rabbit

We have traversed the entire right-hand sub tree, which was the final part of the original tree traversal, and have therefore produced the list of data for the original tree, using pre-order traversal. The final list is, therefore, as follows:

> {dog, cat, bird, pig, goat, horse, rabbit}

(b) The next two traversal methods are almost identical, and will therefore not be explained in much detail. The node data will simply be listed. However, make sure that you can produce the same lists.

Try inventing some new trees of your own, get your friends to traverse them, and see if you agree with the lists produced by each other.

Algorithms to maintain some of these structures are covered in unit 40 of NUCSAL.

In-order traversal will produce:

> {bird, cat, dog, goat, horse, pig, rabbit}

(c) Post-order traversal will produce the following list:

> {bird, cat, horse, goat, rabbit, pig, dog}

Using pre-order or post-order traversal mechanisms, non-binary trees may be traversed. The definitions are still just as simple, and still refer to the position in which the root is visited (also go from left to right).

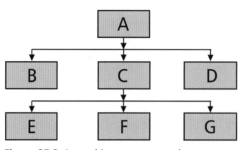

Figure 37.3 A non-binary tree example.

For **pre-order traversal**: visit the root first, then visit the child nodes.

For **post-order traversal**: visit the child nodes, then visit the root node.

Using the data in the tree shown in Figure 37.3, we get the following results:

Pre-order traversal – {A, B, C, E, F, G, D}

Post-order traversal – {B, E, F, G, C, D, A}

Data structures in practice

In unit 35 we have seen a binary tree structure in which the data elements were constructed making use of '>' or '<' based on the alphabetical position in the list. If this binary tree structure is traversed using **in-order traversal**, then the data in the list is automatically listed in alphabetical order. Other data items may be inserted in the list, without any of the existing elements being moved. Therefore, this particular arrangement is a good use of a binary tree, in combination with in-order traversal, for processing alphabetical lists. Another practical example making use of a **linked list** is as follows.

Example

A sentence needs to be stored in such a way that it may be altered by the insertion or deletion of whole words only. It is also necessary to join sentences together to form larger units. It is suggested that a linked-list data structure be used to store the words in each sentence. Explain, with the aid of diagrams, how a linked list structure may be used to store each sentence. Show also how two completed sentences may be joined together and printed out, by writing some appropriate pseudocode. State any assumptions, which you may have to make.

Solution

Let each sentence be stored as a linked list, with each word linked to the next in the sentence by a pointer, with the final word being terminated by a full stop. The idea is demonstrated in Figure 37.4.

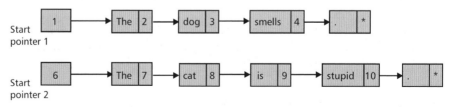

A possible data structure for the storage of sentences

Figure 37.4 Two sentences as a linked list.

Assuming that the sentences above are to be joined in the order 'sentence 1 – followed by sentence 2', then all that is necessary is to alter the end pointer of sentence 1, to point to the start pointer of sentence 2. However, spaces will have to be inserted between the words printed out, and also at the end of a sentence, unless it is the last sentence.

One possible algorithm to do this is as follows:

```
(* set max for two sentences *)
max = 2
(*set counter to number of sentences *)
For count = 1 to max
  (*Set up pointer to beginning of sentence *)
  Set Pointer = Start_pointer(count)
  (*Print out sentence, with spaces in-between each word *)
  Repeat
    Print Link(Pointer);" "
    Set pointer = Link(Pointer)
  Until Pointer = "*"
  (*don't print space after last sentence *)
  If count <> max then Print " "
Next count
```

In the above algorithm List(Pointer) is a typical element in the array called List that holds the words, and Link(Pointer) is an array, which holds the pointers in the list that point to the next word.

Detailed pseudocode for most traversal mechanisms can be found in chapter 25 of NUCSAL.

Self-test questions

1 What are the three different ways of traversing a binary tree structure?
2 Explain what is meant by a subtree, illustrating your answer with a diagram.
3 Consider the following tree structure.
   (a) List the node data using a pre-order traversal method.
   (b) List the node data using an in-order traversal method.
   (c) List the node data using a post-order traversal method.

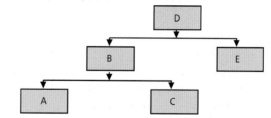

4 The following data, containing key words from the PERL programming language, is to be inserted into a binary tree, using each item in the order in which it appears. {pack, shift, closedir, chmod, getc, stat, bind}
   (a) Draw a binary tree showing the situation after the data has been inserted.
   (b) List the data contained in the leaf nodes.
   (c) List the data contained in the root node
   (d) List the data contained in the left-hand sub tree.
5 Suggest how a binary tree may be set up to store data in alphabetical order. How might the data be listed in alphabetical order?
6 Recursion is an efficient way of implementing some of the code to process data in a tree structure. Explain what is meant by the term 'recursion', and show how this technique is particularly appropriate for tree structure traversal mechanisms.

In this unit you have learned about:

- How to traverse a binary tree structure using pre-order, in-order and post-order traversal
- Some simple applications of traversing binary tree and other structures

38 Searching and sorting

Searching means finding an item of data from a list.

Linear search

Each element is examined until the desired item is found or found not to be in the list.

Example

Develop a pseudocode algorithm to perform a **linear search** on a list of 100,000 elements held in an array called List.

Work out, on average, how long it would take to search the list of 100,000 entries if it takes 0.01 seconds to search each element. Comment on the efficiency of this method, and suggest what could be done to achieve a greater efficiency.

Solution

The algorithm searches a list of any length.

```
(* Linear search procedure *)
INPUT search criteria
Count = 1
Flag = 0
Repeat
   Read List(Count)
   IF List(Count) = End of list then flag = 1
   IF List(Count) = search criteria then
      Print "Information has been found"
      Print List(Count)
      Exit procedure
   Else
      Count = Count + 1
Until Flag = 1
Print "Item has not been found in the list"
Exit procedure
```

On average, the number of attempts to find an item of data depends on how many elements are in the list. Consider the following:

(2 elements) – (1 + 2)/2 = 1.5 attempts
(3 elements) – (1 + 2 + 3)/3 = 2 attempts
(4 elements) – (1 + 2 + 3 + 4)/4 = 2.5 attempts

For 100,000 elements, we need 50,000.5 attempts, on average.

The method is not very efficient. The item may be last in the queue, in which case it is the most inefficient method possible! It is better to have a list ordered in some way, like a **binary tree**.

There are many different techniques for searching and sorting. Learn the ones shown in this unit and you should be able to tackle most examination problems.

Binary search

This method assumes that the data has already been ordered. Consider the list of numbers:

{1, 3, 6, 9, 12, 17, 31, 45, 64}

We split this into 3 parts, as shown in Table 38.1.

Table 38.1 The split list

Data for demonstration of binary search								
1	3	6	9	(12)	17	31	45	64
Left-hand list					Right-hand list			

We find the middle element, and split the list up into two other parts, a left and right-hand list. If there is no middle element, we use an element to one side. Let us find the number 45. We compare the middle number with 45. It is not the one we want, but the number is now in the right-hand list. The algorithm is as follows:

```
(* Procedure for binary search *)
IF desired number = middle number then
  Match occurs exit procedure
Else
  If number < desired number then
     Search left-hand list
  Else
     Search right-hand list
  Endif
Endif
```

When searching the left or right-hand list, call the above routine **recursively** (see unit 39). This is developed in the next example.

Example

Comment on the efficiency of the binary search compared to the linear search using the data in the previous section.

Solution

The number is found quickly after just two comparisons. This is quicker than the average 4.5 comparisons for a linear search. To see how long the binary search would take, we establish the patterns in the following table:

Table 38.2 Patterns for a binary search.

Patterns for a binary search	
Number of elements in list	Maximum number of comparisons
2	1
4	2
8	3
16	4
32	5
64	6
128	7

Figure 38.1 A maximum of 4 comparisons are needed to find a number in a list of 16.

A teaching aid for demonstrating searching and sorting algorithms makes a good A2 project if done in a visual programming environment like VB or Delphi.

As clarification, consider finding an item in a list of 16 numbers, as shown in Figure 38.1.

We see that the numbers on the right generate the numbers on the left by using '2 to the power of'. Therefore, going the opposite way we would use logs to base 2 (i.e. $\log_2 16 = 4$). Therefore, for N numbers, we would get the relationship:

$\log_2(N)$ comparisons are needed.

For 100,000 elements, this would be a maximum of:

$\log_2(100,000) = 16.6$ comparisons

Compare with 50,000.5 for the linear search!

Sorting

Sorting means putting data into order, such as **alphabetically ascending**. As 'ASCII' or 'Unicode', may used to sort textual lists, all sorting is essentially numeric.

Insertion sort

An **insertion sort** starts with the second number, and compares it with the lower elements. The number is put in the right place if necessary. Next the third number is chosen, and compared with the lower elements (now consisting of two numbers). The number is placed in the right place if necessary. Once the list is processed, the numbers are in order.

Bubble sort

Numbers processed float to the top of the list like a bubble. The algorithm is as follows:

(a) Start with the first pair in the list and compare.
(b) If a swap is necessary to put a pair in order, make a note of it by setting a flag.
(c) Go to the next pair of numbers and repeat stages (a) and (b).
(d) If one or more swaps were necessary, reset the flag and repeat the entire process.

Example

Develop a pseudocode algorithm to sort a list into ascending order using a bubble sort method. Test it with this data:

{Ford, Citroen, Jaguar, Toyota, Lexus, Ferrari}

Solution

The bubble sort algorithm, developed from the above reasoning, is as follows. We assume that the data is stored in an array called List.

```
max = 6
flag =1
REPEAT
   FOR pointer = 1 to max-1
      WHILE List(Pointer)>List(Pointer+1)
         temp=List(pointer+1)
         list(pointer+1)=List(pointer)
         list(pointer)=temp
         flag=1
      ENDWHILE
   NEXT pointer
UNTIL flag = 0
```

The list of data, sorted, using the bubble sort algorithm is shown below. Data is shown only for changes in the list. Swaps are shown <u>underlined</u>; comparisons being made are shown in red.

Other search and sort algorithms are shown in chapter 19 of NUCSAL.

First pass
{Citroen, Ford, Jaguar, Toyota, Lexus, Ferrari}
{Citroen, Ford, Jaguar, Toyota, Lexus, Ferrari}
{Citroen, Ford, Jaguar, Toyota, Lexus, Ferrari}
{Citroen, Ford, Jaguar, Lexus, Toyota, Ferrari}
{Citroen, Ford, Jaguar, Lexus, Ferrari, Toyota}

Second pass (As swaps were needed)
{Citroen, Ford, Jaguar, Lexus, Ferrari, Toyota}
{Citroen, Ford, Jaguar, Lexus, Ferrari, Toyota}
{Citroen, Ford, Jaguar, Lexus, Ferrari, Toyota}
{Citroen, Ford, Jaguar, Ferrari, Lexus, Toyota}
{Citroen, Ford, Jaguar, Ferrari, Lexus, Toyota}

etc. until

Fifth pass (As no swaps were needed)
{Citroen, Ferrari, Ford, Jaguar, Lexus, Toyota}
{Citroen, Ferrari, Ford, Jaguar, Lexus, Toyota}
{Citroen, Ferrari, Ford, Jaguar, Lexus, Toyota}
{Citroen, Ferrari, Ford, Jaguar, Lexus, Toyota}
{Citroen, Ferrari, Ford, Jaguar, Lexus, Toyota}

No swaps were needed; therefore, list is in order.

Self-test questions

1 What is meant by a linear search technique?
2 What is a binary search?
3 What special condition has to be applied before a binary search may be performed?
4 Why is a binary search usually more efficient for finding an item compared to a linear search?
5 Calculate the average number of comparisons that would be needed to find an element in a list of 100 if a binary and linear search is used.
6 What is an insertion sort?
7 What is a bubble sort?

In this unit you have learned about:

● How to do a linear and binary search
● How to sort a list using an insertion sort and a bubble sort

 **Recursion**

In this section you will learn about:

- Recursion and recursive techniques
- Binary trees and recursion
- Pseudocode to implement some of the above

Recursive techniques

A **recursive routine** is one that can call itself. Most modern high-level languages support recursion, and you should be able to compare and contrast methods written recursively with those that are not. In general, a recursive routine is more elegant, and leads to simpler coding.

Recursion provides a mechanism for writing code in one of the most efficient ways possible. Master the principles here and your programming skills will rocket.

Example

A factorial of number N is written as N! This is a number, worked out as follows:

$N! = N \times (N-1) \times (N-2) \times \ldots 3 \times 2 \times 1$. Also, $1! = 1$ and $0! = 1$

Therefore, $5! = 5 \times 4 \times 3 \times 2 \times 1 = 120$. Write two routines to work out a factorial N, one that uses recursion, and one that does not.

Solution

Consider writing the code *without* recursion. A loop structure is used, with special cases for the answer if $N = 0$ or $N = 1$.

```
(*non-recursive procedure*)
INPUT N
IF N = 1 OR N = 0 THEN
   factorial = 1
ELSE
   count = 2
   factorial = 1
   REPEAT
      factorial = factorial*count
      count = count + 1
   UNTIL count = N+1
ENDIF
```

A recursive routine (one that can call itself) is as follows:

```
PROCEDURE factorial(N)
   IF N = 1 OR N = 0 THEN
      Factorial = 1
      EXIT PROCEDURE
   ELSE
      Factorial =
N*Factorial(N-1)
   ENDIF
END PROCEDURE
```

The variable called 'factorial' returns the value.

You can see the elegance of the recursive method. A parameter, N, is passed to the procedure. If $N = 1$ or $N = 0$, then the factorial is trivial, $N = 1$ and the procedure is exited. If $N > 1$, then the procedure calls itself. The number of times depends on N. A **stack** (see unit 36) manages recursive calls.

Binary tree example

In unit 35 you saw how binary trees can be set up by inserting items into a list. (i.e. if data to be inserted is alphabetically greater than the data in the node, then the right-hand pointer of that node is followed, else the left hand pointer is followed etc.). We will now develop some pseudocode to create a binary tree, using the following list as data. Furthermore, the pseudocode will make use of a recursive routine for simplicity:

Tree structures provide a wealth of possibilities to manipulate data. You will need to understand the principles of this work to be able to cope with recursion in examinations.

```
{Maths, Geography, Physics, Computing,
Technology, History, English}
```

Let us create the binary tree. The first data item, being 'Maths', is set up as the root node. This is shown in Figure 39.1(a). The left and right pointers are set to null. Next the data item 'Geography' is to be inserted. As ('Geography' < 'Maths'), then the left pointer from 'Maths' is set up to point to Geography, and the 'Geography' data item is stored as shown in Figure 39.1b.

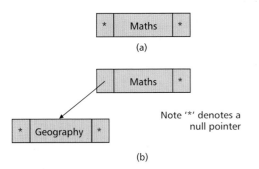

Figure 39.1 Constructing the binary tree.

Each data item in the list is compared with the data in the root node, and the appropriate pointer is followed or set up, until the place where the data needs to be stored is encountered. The tree is shown in Figure 39.2.

Next consider the data shown in Table 39.1, taking particular note of the three columns to the right, which contain the left pointer, actual data and right pointer respectively.

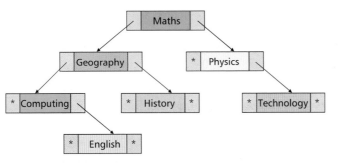

Figure 39.2 The complete binary tree.

The colours for each data item match the tree in Figure 39.2, and were inserted into the data structure in the order given by the original list. You should be able to build up a table like this yourself. As 'Geography' < 'Maths', and 'Geography' is the second data item to be inserted, 'Geography' is physically put into position number 2, and the left pointer belonging to 'Maths' gets set to 2, being 'Geography's' position in the list etc.

Table 39.1 The binary tree structure

Position	Left pointer	Data	Right pointer
	Possible data for binary tree shown in Figure 39.2		
1	2	Maths	3
2	4	Geography	6
3	*	Physics	5
4	*	Computing	7
5	*	Technology	*
6	*	History	*
7	*	English	*
8	*		*
9	*		*
10			

We can store the data and pointers in three **arrays**, called 'Left_Pointer', 'Data' and 'Right_Pointer'. Therefore, Right_Pointer(4) is Computing's right pointer, or Data(3) is the actual data 'Physics', for example.

We need some sort of pointer like 'Position', to determine the actual address in the array where new data may be stored.

If the binary tree structure is empty, then the first node to be inserted ('Maths' in this case) is special, as there are no left or right pointers yet set up to follow. Therefore, we set up the root node, by inserting the data, updating the position pointer to 2, and setting the left and right pointers to null (*). Having initialised the binary tree by creating the root node, we need to develop the algorithm for inserting the next items of data.

We must basically find the place in which to store the new node, and add it onto the existing tree structure, maintaining the pointers as we go.

There are two stages to the algorithm, depending on whether we follow a left or right pointer:

(a) Check to see if the data we need to insert is lexically less than the data in the node being considered. If it is, we look at the left pointer of the current node, which is either empty, in which case we insert the new node here, or else we have to follow the left pointer, and call this routine again.

(b) Check to see if the data we need to insert is lexically greater than the data in the node being considered. If it is, we look at the right pointer of the current node, which is either empty, in which case we insert the new node here, or else we have to follow the right pointer, and call this routine again.

You should check to see that you agree with the above reasoning, then apply it to constructing the tree in Figure 39.1 to make sure you understand.

The clever part comes from treating any sub-tree as though it were another binary tree; therefore, the root of the sub-tree can be treated as though it were the root of the main tree for our **recursive algorithm**. This idea of treating any new node to be the root node of a new sub-tree is essential to understanding the following algorithm. A variable called 'Root' will be set up to maintain the root of the sub-tree currently under examination.

We now need to turn the above English-like statements into pseudocode. We will call the routine INSERT NODE, and pass the parameters 'root' and 'data' over to it. Root is a variable, which acts as a pointer to the root node of the binary tree currently being considered, and 'data' is the actual data to be inserted. As an example, if we want to insert 'Geography', because the only entry so far is 'Maths', we call the insert-node routine as follows:

```
INSERT_NODE(1,Geography)
```

The pseudocode to insert the nodes is as follows:

```
(* Initialise binary tree *)
Dim Left_Pointer(10)
Dim Right_Pointer(10)
Dim Data(10)
Root = 1
Position = 1
INPUT data
(* Create root node as tree is empty *)
Left_Pointer(root) = *
Data(root) = data
Right_Pointer(Root) = *
Position = 2
(* Create the rest of the tree *)
While data <>"999" Do
   INPUT data
   CALL INSERT NODE(root,data)
END WHILE
END
(* node creation procedure based on the algorithms just developed *)
INSERT NODE(root,data)
(* left-hand sub-tree search *)
IF data<Data(root) THEN
   IF Left_Pointer(root) =* THEN
      (*Insert new terminal node here *)
      Data(position) = data
```

Recursion is a difficult but worthwhile topic to grasp. You may need to put in extra effort to master the work in this unit.

A2

```
      Left_Pointer(position) =*
      Right_Pointer(position) = *
      (* update root pointer *)
      Left_Pointer(root) = position
      Position = Position + 1
    ELSE
      CALL INSERT_NODE(Left_Pointer(root)
                                  ,data)
    ENDIF
  ELSE
    EXIT procedure
  ENDIF
  (* right-hand sub-tree search *)
  IF data>Data(root) THEN
    IF Left_Pointer(root) =* THEN
      (*Insert new terminal node here *)
      Data(position) = data
      Left_Pointer(position) =*
      Right_Pointer(position) = *
      (* update root pointer *)
      Right_Pointer(root) = position
      Position = Position + 1
    ELSE
      CALL INSERT_NODE(Right_Pointer(root)
                                  ,data)
    ENDIF
  ELSE
    EXIT procedure
  ENDIF
  END PROCEDURE
```

Recursion is covered in detail in chapter 18 of NUCSAL.

Self-test questions

1 Explain what is meant by the term recursion. Why does this lead to elegant and efficient programming compared to some other non-recursive methods?
2 What data structure do you think that the programming language would use to enable you to implement recursive techniques? Explain by using an example.
3 File permissions on a hierarchical directory structure of a computer need setting to make sure that only the administrator has full control. Explain how recursion would enable the operating system to carry out this process.
4 The following is a piece of code to produce a sequence of numbers.

```
Function fib(n)
        If (n = 0) OR (n = 1) Then
           Fib = 1
           Else Fib = Fib(n-1)+Fib(n-2)
        Endif
End Function
```

Dry run the code for a value of n = 4, outputting the results for the function call fib.

In this unit you have learned about:

- the technique of recursion
- How to *use* recursion in a variety of techniques using factorials and binary trees

40 Maintenance of tree structures

In this section you will learn about:

- More advanced examples using recursion
- Detailed processing of ordered binary tree structures
- Some advice on tackling these harder questions in an examination

Further recursive techniques

This unit develops further algorithms for **binary tree structures** using the techniques of **recursion**. It uses the same data set as unit 39.

Example

Develop an algorithm to delete a node from an ordered binary tree shown in Figure 39.2. Explain with reference to deletion of the following nodes:

```
English   Physics   Geography
```

What happens if we want to delete Maths?

Solution

There are a number of different cases here.

(1) We will need an algorithm to search the binary tree. If the node to be deleted cannot be found, an error message is displayed.

(2) If the node to be deleted is a **terminal node** (i.e. having null left and right-hand pointers), then the node may be deleted, and the pointer to this node from its parent set to null. This is shown in Figure 40.1.

(3) If the root node is to be deleted, this is a special case, and we need to create a parent for the deleted root node. A dummy node, containing no data, but still keeping the left and right-hand pointers does this.

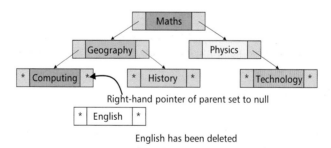

Figure 40.1 Deletion of the English node.

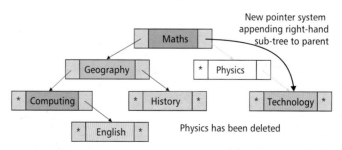

Figure 40.2 Deletion of the Physics node.

Do not attempt to carry out the work in this unit unless you have worked through unit 39. The work here also requires knowledge of unit 37.

(4) If the node to be deleted has a null left-hand pointer, then the right-hand sub-tree can be joined onto the parent, as shown in Figure 40.2.

(5) If the note to be deleted has a null right-pointer, then the right sub-tree is empty, and the left sub-tree can be joined to the parent in a similar way to (4).

The final part of the algorithm will be covered in two parts.

(1) The case where the node to be deleted is a parent of its in-order successor.

The original list of data is as follows:

{Maths, Geography, Physics, Computing, Technology, History, English}

After entry into the binary tree, (using < and >) the data is in alphabetical order:

{Computing, English, Geography, History, Maths, Physics, Technology}

Deletion of 'Geography' should result in a tree structure which, when processed by **in-order traversal**, results in the following list:

{Computing, English, History, Maths, Physics, Technology}

The important points to consider here are the **parent** of 'Geography', namely 'Maths', and the **in-order successor** to 'Geography', namely 'History'. If 'Geography' were to be deleted, the new tree will be as shown in Figure 40.3.

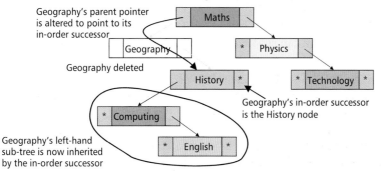

Figure 40.3 The Geography node was a parent of its in-order successor (History).

If the node 'History' had a left sub-tree already, (it did not in this case) then the 'Computing' and 'English' sub-tree would have to be added on to the extreme left of 'History's' left sub-tree.

(2) If the node to be deleted is not a parent of its in-order successor, then we need to do things in a slightly different way. We will do a couple of examples to establish how the binary trees must be altered in this case.

To demonstrate this, we need more subjects. Let's add 'Biology', 'Chemistry' and 'Drama', and the original (unordered) list now becomes:

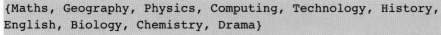

{Maths, Geography, Physics, Computing, Technology, History, English, Biology, Chemistry, Drama}

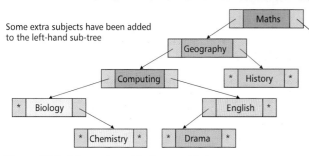

Some extra subjects have been added to the left-hand sub-tree

Figure 40.4 A few extra subjects are added.

The new tree structure, showing the left sub-tree only, is shown in Figure 40.4. Suppose we wish to delete the node 'Computing'. 'Computing' is not a parent of its in-order successor, 'Drama'. The simple algorithm developed for the deletion of 'Geography' will therefore not work in this case.

If you have to process a node in a tree, it is usually not hard to find some attribute of the node, that is unique to the process being carried out. For example, a terminal node has no left or right pointers – use facts like these to determine if you have reached a terminal node.

We must alter the binary tree to that shown in Figure 40.5. If you perform an **in-order traversal** of the tree, you will find that the data is listed properly in alphabetical order.

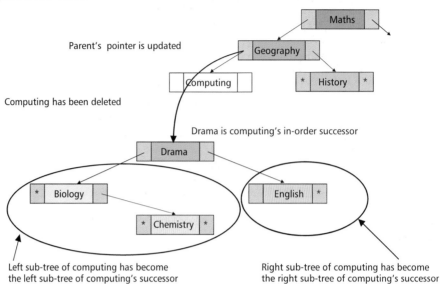

Figure 40.5 The binary tree after deletion of the Computing node.

From Figure 40.5 we can see that the right sub-tree of 'Computing' (as seen in Figure 40.4) has become the right sub-tree of 'Drama', the successor to 'Computing'. The left sub-tree of 'Computing' has become the left sub-tree of 'Drama', the successor of 'Computing'. This is easier to handle because the node 'Drama' had no sub-trees attached in Figure 40.4. However, if it did, then there would be one extra stage – that of attaching the sub-tree to the parent of the deleted node, and this is considered next.

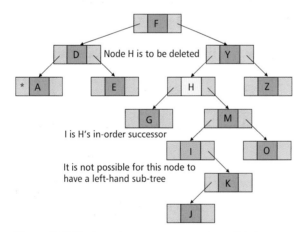

Figure 40.6 The in-order successor cannot possibly have a left-hand sub-tree!

As this is a complicated procedure, we will do one more deletion as a final example to establish the pattern of what's happening. Consider the brand new tree shown in Figure 40.6, which has been set up for purpose of this last example.

If we are to delete the H node in Figure 40.6, then H is not the parent of its in-order successor I. Also, H has left and right sub-trees, and the successor I also has a sub-tree. In this case, we must change the tree to that shown in Figure 40.7.

If you perform an in-order traversal of the binary tree in Figure 40.7, you should find an alphabetical listing, with node H missing. Note also the important point that the in-order successor node cannot possibly have a left-hand sub-tree, because the node to be deleted is the one before this one! To achieve all of this we had to carry out the processes outlined in detail in Figure 40.7.

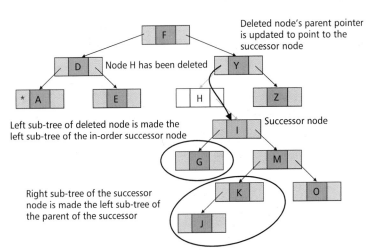

Figure 40.7 The binary tree structure after the deletion of the H node.

We may now finalise the last stage of the algorithm (following on from stage 5 on page 157) as follows:

(6) If the node to be deleted is a parent node of the successor, then we put the left hand sub-tree of the deleted node onto the extreme left-hand side of the sub-tree of the in-order successor. (See example shown in Figure 40.3.) However, if the node to be deleted is not the parent of its successor, as was the case in figure 40.6, then we perform the methods outlined in parts (7), (8) and (9).

(7) We make the right sub-tree of the in-order successor's node the left sub-tree of the in-order successor's child. (See how J and K have been moved from Figure 40.6 to Figure 40.7.)

(8) We make the left-hand sub-tree of the node to be deleted the left-hand sub-tree of the in-order successor.

(9) Finally, we must not forget to update the pointers for the parent of the deleted node to point to the in-order successor. This is the same for Figure 40.7 and Figure 40.3.

Self-test questions

1 Why are recursive techniques particularly useful to maintain data structures like stacks and binary trees?

2 Compare and contrast a binary tree with an ordered binary tree. Why is an ordered binary tree particularly useful?

3 Is the following tree structure an ordered binary tree? If not, redraw the tree so that it represents an ordered binary tree.

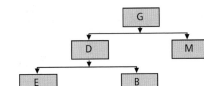

4 Explain how to insert a node into an ordered binary tree structure.

5 Explain how to delete a node from an ordered binary tree structure.

6 Explain how to list the data at each node in an ordered binary tree structure.

You are unlikely to encounter complete tree structure maintenance questions in an examination – they would take too long to answer. However, expect to be able to answer questions on maintaining parts of a tree structure, like finding and deleting a terminal node, for example.

More examples of tree structures can be found in chapter 25 of NUCSAL.

In this unit you have learned about:

● Some further ideas of **recursion**

● Applying these ideas to the maintenance of **binary tree structures**

41 Further high-level language concepts

In this section you will learn about:

- Declarative and procedural languages
- Object oriented programming including objects, classes, encapsulation, inheritance, polymorphism and containment

It is the methods in this unit, which are more important than the actual software being used. However, do try out these or similar packages if you have access to them.

Further high-level language generations

High-level languages, like early versions of **BASIC**, **COBOL** and **Fortran**, belong to **third-generation** languages. As we progress through the higher levels, the user is further removed from detail about how a problem may be implemented on a computer, and gets nearer to problem solving in the real world. A **fourth-generation language** (4GL) is designed to be nearer to human thought, and examples would be **macro languages** available in applications like word processors and spreadsheets. These languages allow non-specialists to achieve things that hitherto would have taken an expert considerable time to achieve.

Example

Explain how a non-specialist user might use a fourth-generation language to solve a problem. How might this differ from using a third-generation language?

Solution

To sort a list of names using a 3GL, users would learn a sort algorithm (see unit 38), code it, and then write routines to enter and output the results. Using a **4GL**, a user could record a macro, select the cells as shown in Figure 41.1, and using the menu selections, get Excel to carry out the process. This macro recording gives an indication of the 4GL code for this particular set of data.

```
Sub Macro1()
' Macro1 Macro
' Macro recorded 01/01/2001 by Ray
Bradley
    Range("B6:B16").Select
    Selection.Sort Key1:=Range("B6"),
Order1:=xlDescending, Header:=xlGuess,
OrderCustom:=1, MatchCase:=False,
Orientation:=xlTopToBottom
End Sub
```

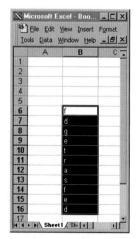

Figure 41.1 Cell selection for a sort.

The 'Selection.Sort' part of the code is typical of a fourth-generation language. Here we have not written any sort-code algorithms.

A **fifth-generation language**, like **Prolog**, belongs to languages that mimic human experts. Users have an easier time making use of them, but like the 4GLs mentioned earlier, they still require a lot of programming skill to set up. Such systems have a **knowledge base** (the database of facts etc.), and are often programmed using an **inference engine**. End-user examples include route-planning software, and knowledge-based medical expert systems. Route planning is shown in Figure 41.2, using Microsoft's Expedia, Streets and Trips 2000. We are now very far removed from the computer's way of solving a problem, and are into a human-oriented way of thinking. This example illustrates how far we are now removed from **machine code** and **assembly**

language. Do not forget that all programs, irrespective of the interface, still have to be converted into machine code to run.

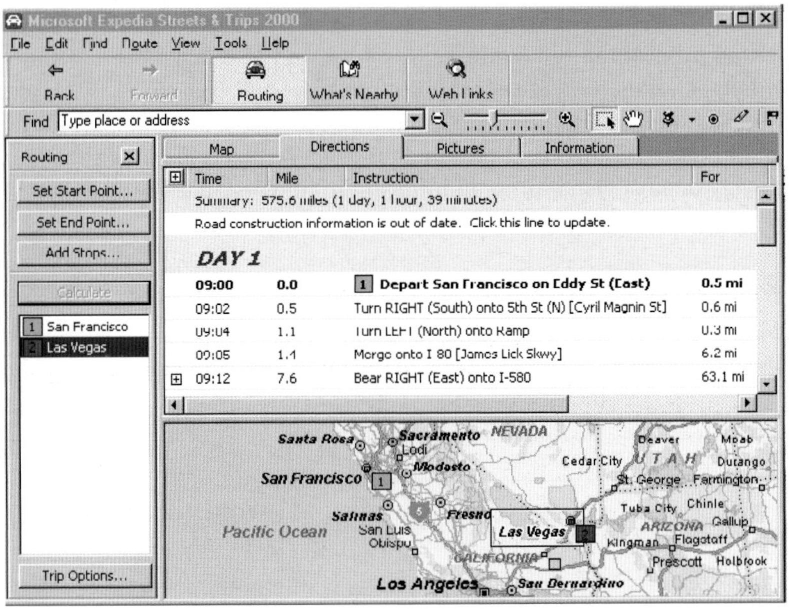

Figure 41.2 Route planning software.

High-level language paradigms

There are several high-level language **paradigms** (models). An **imperative language** typifies giving the computer sets of instructions. These are also called **procedural languages**. They are typical of earlier high-level languages, although the techniques are still used today. **Declarative languages**, like **Prolog**, typify telling the computer 'what to do' and are not concerned about the procedural processes, that is they are not too concerned about 'how to do it'. Like the mapping software earlier, or the 4GL sorting routine considered before that, we are concerned only with the data passed over to the program, and not with the way the program processed it.

Structured programming

Although not a programming paradigm, **structured programming** is as important. Structured programming involves designing the solution to the problem such that other people can understand it more clearly. It does this by **modularisation**, and by presenting the problem **hierarchically** (see unit 25).

Object oriented programming

Project development and programming is complex, time consuming and thus expensive. Conventionally, programs are divided up into smaller and **smaller procedures**, until a procedure is simple enough to be **written, tested, debugged**, and finalised in its entirety. As computer systems developed, the effort regarding software management grew unmanageable, and new programming **paradigms** had to be developed. Procedural programming concentrates on the algorithms and procedures for solving parts of the overall problem, and pays no attention to data, which accompanies a program. Because of this, there are sometimes inadvertent interactions between different parts of the system. If this occurred frequently, the procedures, already tested and passed as correct, had to be modified again, with the consequent retesting and debugging.

What is needed should model the real world. **Object-oriented programming (OOP)** does this by creating **objects** and **classes** and by giving the programmer the ability to determine which functions can have access to the data. In this way it is virtually impossible for well-written modules to mess up others. In addition, **OOP methodology** gives the programmer great convenience and flexibility through methods like **inheritance**, **polymorphism** and **containment**, for example.

Object oriented programming languages like **Java** and **C++** have been around for some time. Other languages may also support objects, like Visual Basic 5, for example, but may not be fully object oriented in their own right, because they do not support all the features necessary to be classed as an object-oriented language. **Objects** are now so useful, they are used extensively in most visual-programming environments, like **Visual Basic**, **Visual C++** and **Delphi**.

Example

The following table contains important concepts relating to object-oriented programming. Define each of the terms, using an example to clarify your ideas.

Object	Class	Encapsulation
Inheritance	Polymorphism	Containment

Solution

(a) An **object** contains both **functions** and **data**, i.e. the routines to solve a problem and the variables and data that are related to the problem. An **object** could be a 'button', (shown in Figure 41.3) placed on a form in a visual-programming environment. The designers of the language control features like the 'appearance', 'behaviour' and the 'position of the button' within sensible limits. The user can then alter attributes of the object, by changing the parameters passed over to it. *You can easily see how this particular object encapsulates both functions and data*, because the functions associated with the object (i.e. the code, written by the user, which decides what to do when it is clicked on), are buried inside the object, along with the data, which can be seen on the right-hand side of Figure 41.3. A visual environment has been chosen here because the principles are very easy to see from Figure 41.3.

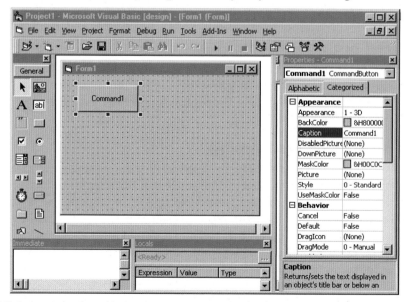

Figure 41.3 An example of an object.

(b) A **class** is a like a blueprint or plan. This **blueprint**, or class, can be used to create objects belonging to the same class. Going back to the command-button object example in part (a), we can create many different command buttons, by using the 'Command button' class. Each command button may have a different shape, position, label and colour etc. and each may have different functions depending on the code that the user assigns to it. These command buttons, belonging to a **derived class**, would all be different instances of the same **base class**.

(c) **Encapsulation** means that only the object, which controls the data, may alter the data contained within it. It does this by using the object's methods, and not by letting other modules alter them directly, in the way that is typical when using global variables in a procedural language, for example. If a language does not support encapsulation, then it is not fully object oriented.

(d) A new **object inherits** properties of the base class, from which it is derived – the new object belongs to what is called the **derived class**. You can add other properties to the derived object. This process, whereby the object just created takes on the properties associated from the base class, is called **inheritance**. You may have a base class called 'teacher', which defines all characteristics for a good teacher. Not all teachers can teach computer science, therefore an object may be created to produce a new derived object, in which you have added the **attribute** 'able to teach computer science' to the attributes that have already been inherited.

(e) **Polymorphism** means the occurrence of something in different forms. Therefore, in OOP, **polymorphism** makes it possible for the programmer to redefine a routine in a **derived class** (see inheritance in part (d)). Thus the new object, which has just been created, can be used in many different forms. Each form, after suitable modification by the programmer, can be used to perform a variety of similar operations. For example, you might have a graphics routine, which plots a shape in different sizes, colours and outlines. Now the same base-class object can be used to plot the shape, but if extra parameters are passed over to it, regarding colour and outline, for example, then the extra attributes are used along with the appropriate altered parts of the code, to redefine what the object does. You can thus have a different definition for each object, so as to cope with the extra attributes controlling the exact way in which the graphic is drawn. *Polymorphism is usually passed on through the mechanism of inheritance.*

(f) It is convenient to say that some objects may contain many other objects. For example, a garage object may contain other objects like 'cars', 'mechanics', 'workshops', 'sales staff', 'directors' and 'buildings' etc. The ability of important objects to contain lesser objects, like those described above, is called **containment**.

Self-test questions

1 What is a macro?
2 What is meant by an expert system?
3 What is object-oriented programming?
4 What is a visual programming environment?
5 Give examples of the following:
    (a) A macro language   (b) A fifth-generation language.
6 Name two OOP languages.
7 Explain what is meant by encapsulation.
8 What is polymorphism?
9 Why were object oriented programming methods developed?

In this unit you have learned about:

- **Generations of high-level languages**
- **Different language paradigms such as imperative, declarative and object-oriented programming**
- **Object-oriented programming in more detail**
- **Objects, classes, encapsulation, inheritance, polymorphism and containment**

42 Further high-level language development

In this section you will learn about:

- Further programming languages like Java
- Event-driven programming, logic programming and expert systems
- Software engineering

Java

Java is an object-oriented language. It is *the* most successful to date in obtaining **platform-independence**. Java is a fully blown **object oriented language** in its own right. It is used extensively on the web. A **Java Applet**, which is a Java **class**, running on a web browser that supports it, is shown in Figure 42.1.

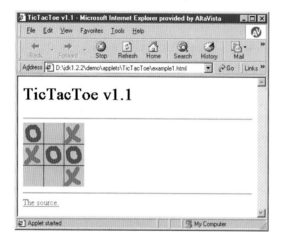

Figure 42.1 A Java Applet developed by Sun.

Java is portable, because code written in it is compiled into an **intermediate byte code** that does not rely on any platform-specific information. This code is run on the **Java Virtual Machine**, which is, in effect, a computer simulated in software. Different platforms like **Linux**, **Windows** and the **Mac OS**, for example, can all have different Java Virtual Machines, and thus code, written in Java, should work on them all. A simple example, also developed by Sun Microsystems, is shown in Figure 42.2. At the start of the source code is an import called (java.awt.Graphics). Java programs usually have imports, which are referred to in the code.

```
 * @(#)GraphApplet.java 1.3 98/03/18
 *
 * Copyright (c) 1997 Sun Microsystems, Inc. All Rights Reserved.
import java.awt.Graphics;
public class GraphApplet extends java.applet.Applet {
    double f(double x) {
            return (Math.cos(x/5) + Math.sin(x/7) + 2) *
getSize().height / 4;
    }

    public void paint(Graphics g) {
        for (int x = 0 ; x < getSize().width ; x++) {
                g.drawLine(x, (int)f(x), x + 1, (int)f(x + 1));
        }
    }
    public String getAppletInfo() {
      return "Draws a sin graph.";
    }
}
```

Try to gain some experience of using the different programming methods outlined in this unit.

Visit our portal to find out how to get a free copy of the Java Development Kit.

If you want your skills to be in demand then learning Java is a step in the right direction, it will also help to learn about object-oriented programming.

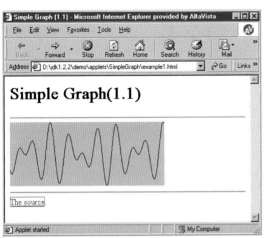

Figure 42.2 A very simple Java Applet.

The class definition comes next, contained between the {} braces at the beginning and end of the program. The privacy definition (public) is followed by the keyword 'class', followed by the class name (GraphApplet), the keyword 'extends', and the name of the parent class (java.applet.Applet). Next comes the code for drawing the graph, consisting of methods that either return something (like the string "Draws a sin graph") or returns a void (nothing), like the method that actually paints the graph.

Event-driven programming

Programs like early versions of BASIC ran as a single task. This meant they took over an entire machine, and responded to user input only under direct control of the program. Modern systems allow **event-driven code**. Programs can run in the background along with other programs, and respond to events, like a **mouse click** from the user. These **multitasking programs**, responding to input from the user were very hard to write until the advent of **visual programming environments** like Microsoft's **Visual Basic** or Borland's **Delphi**.

Logic programming

Prolog, a **declarative language**, stands for **Programming in Logic**. It is an example of a **logic-programming language**, based on the ideas borrowed from mathematical logic. Fortunately, for students at 'A' level, you don't have to know too much about mathematical logic to make effective use of **Prolog**.

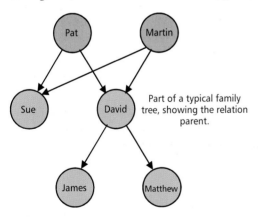

Part of a typical family tree, showing the relation parent.

Figure 42.3 A family tree.

Logic programming is a different **paradigm**. You need to know how logic programming can be used for declaring logical relationships. Consider some family relationships, like 'parent', 'child' and 'grandparent' etc. shown in Figure 42.3 and see how Prolog handles these.

In a procedurally based language like BASIC, you would have to set up these relations by implementing the tree structure with a complex set of pointers (see unit 35). A **declarative language** allows the programmer to ignore the procedural elements, and define **relations** more easily, by declaring the relations as follows:

```
parent(pat, sue)
parent(pat, david)
parent(martin, sue)
parent(martin, david)
parent(david, james)
parent(david, matthew)
```

This has effectively built up a simple database, which represents the family tree shown. We can now interrogate this simple database, by using Prolog's queries. For example, we may ask if 'david' is a parent of 'matthew', by asking the following:

```
?- parent(david, matthew)
```

Prolog should respond with 'yes', because the answer to this query is true. Prolog would respond with 'no' if the answer to a question were to be false.

Do not forget that in real life, the tree structure may be enormous, and asking individual questions like that posed above would be tedious. Prolog allows you to ask a more general question. For example, 'Who are the children of Pat?'. This can be accomplished as follows: `?- parent(pat, X)`

Prolog would respond with 'sue'. We can then ask again, and it would respond with 'david', and we can ask yet again, and it would respond with no, because 'pat' has no more children, other than 'david' and 'sue'. If we use two variables like: `?- parent(X, Y)`

Prolog would list all the pairs, satisfying the relation parent. Many extra rules can be added to further refine relations. For example, we could have 'uncle', 'auntie', 'cousin', or we could define the relation 'mother' and 'father', 'brother' and 'sister' for example.

Example

Explain, in principle, how the language Prolog might be set up to implement the core knowledge base of a program, like the routing software shown in Figure 41.2.

Solution

Consider the simplified route map shown in Figure 42.4.

Just a small part of the very simple relations shown in Figure 42.4 could be defined as follows:

```
motorway (san francisco, los angeles)
motorway (los angeles, las Vegas)
motorway (san francisco, sacramento)
motorway (sacramento, carson city)
aroad(carson city, las vegas)
etc.
```

Figure 42.4 Connecting cities by roads.

Although Prolog has much more elegant ways of defining the road network than this, you can imagine asking Prolog if there is a motorway connection between San Francisco and Carson City by using.

```
?-motorway (san francisco, carson city)
```

To which Prolog would respond with 'yes'. In this way an expert system can be built up by using the structures built into a declarative language like Prolog. The distances, alternative routes, times taken at different speeds, road numbers etc. can all be programmed into the **knowledge base**.

Although the above example is a little 'tongue in cheek', you could, if you wished, spend hours learning enough Prolog to implement a simple route-finding database. Consider Figure 42.4 again. We could, for example, implement the actual route planning by using statements such as:

To find a path between San Francisco (SF) and Carson City (CS), find either of the following:

(a) a path from SF to CS via Sacramento
(b) a path from SF to CS direct

Many other paths also exist, like a path from SF to CS via LA but this could be rejected on the grounds that the distances involved are too great, compared to the smaller distances found on the other routes. The problem would then have to be solved by determining if the shortest distance by major road is desirable, or a quicker motorway route via Sacramento, with a slightly longer mileage.

From this you should be able to start to see the power of a declarative language like Prolog. Stop to think for a moment about how you might implement the same system using a procedural language, and you will start to see why the **Prolog declarative language** reigns supreme in the world of **AI** and **expert systems**.

Which programming methodology?

The criteria, on which a programming language may be judged, are many and varied. They rely on concepts like the following:

- Modularity
- Data types
- Control structures
- Expressiveness
- Self documenting
- Parallel processing ability

In addition to this, you have to consider whether the language is **well supported**, and whether **compilers** are available on different types of computer. Finally, does the language have the power to do exactly what is needed?

Languages tend to be **general** or **specific**. Although Prolog is good for AI, it is not intended for mathematical analysis, and you would not be able to use it to forecast the weather very easily. A more conventional language like **FORTRAN** would be ideal, because of the extensive mathematical functions and the huge range of **pre-written routines**, which are available for **science** and **engineering**. Prolog would also not be able to compete with the sheer weight of experience to be found when using **COBOL** in the business sector. You must consider aspects like **experience** of the programmers, the **machines** on which the systems are to be run, and **available time** and **money**, by which the project is constrained.

Further high-level languages are covered in chapter 15 of NUCSAL.

Software engineering

As the program development environment becomes more complex, **computer aided software engineering**, or **CASE** is being developed where problems can be input into the computer, and software develops the final code, which runs on the actual computer. Programmers will never be out of a job, but much of the tedium of changing well-specified designs into actual code may eventually become completely automated.

Self-test questions

1 What is the difference between Java and a Java Applet?
2 What is event-driven programming?
3 What is a declarative language?
4 Why is Prolog suitable for programming expert systems?
5 What is a control structure?
6 List four different data types.
7 Why are some languages self-documenting?
8 Explain what is meant by CASE.
9 For what main areas are FORTRAN and COBOL suitable?

In this unit you have learned about:

- High-level languages like Java
- Concepts like event-driven programming and logic programming
- What is meant by an expert system
- What is needed to *choose* a particular language paradigm and what is meant by software engineering

43 Machine code and assembly language

In this section you will learn about:

- Simple microprocessor architecture
- The function of the clock, main memory and the bus systems
- The role played by the registers
- Interrupts and priorities
- The vectored interrupt mechanism

A simplified microprocessor system

Each family of microprocessor is different, but all share a common heritage. When learning **machine code** and **assembly language**, we can use a fictitious microprocessor, as long as it contains the conceptual elements. Figure 43.1 shows the elements of such a system.

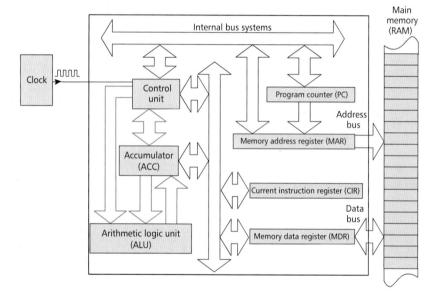

Figure 43.1 An imaginary microprocessor.

The **clock** provides the pulses needed to go through the **fetch-decode-execute cycle**. (Often just called the fetch-execute cycle.) The **programs** and **data** are stored in the computer's main memory (RAM). Inside Figure 43.1 there are some dedicated registers, each having the following functions:

- The **MDR** (memory data register) stores data taken from or put into the main memory
- The **CIR** (current instruction register) holds the current instruction being worked upon
- The **MAR** (memory address register) holds the address of the memory currently being accessed
- The **PC** (program counter) holds a number, representing the next location in memory to be accessed
- The **ACC** is the **accumulator**, which holds the results of arithmetic and logical operations
- The **ALU** is the **arithmetic logic unit**, which works out arithmetical and logical operations like 'AND' and 'OR'
- The **control unit** decodes the instructions and helps with the timing of all the operations inside the microprocessor, under the control of the clock.

The simple processor architecture considered here, together with interrupt and flag registers also covered in this unit is sufficient for A2 level examination purposes.

More detail about simple microprocessor architecture can be found in chapter 20 of NUCSAL.

A simulation of a simple microprocessor makes a stunning A2 programming project in a language like Visual Basic.

There are often more registers, even in a simple microprocessor. Those outlined above can be used to help understand what is happening when **machine code** is run.

Example

Explain a typical sequence in the fetch-execute cycle, making sure that you explain the role played by the registers shown in Figure 43.1.

Solution

The program counter (PC) is set to the memory location from which the first program instruction is to be fetched (assuming that the program to be run is already in memory).

The first program instruction is loaded into the CIR via the MDR, and the PC is incremented by 1. The control unit decodes the instruction, and appropriate action is taken. For example, this may require that a number from memory is put into the accumulator ready for an arithmetic or logical operation. The MAR would be put equal to the memory location where the number resides. The number would then be read from memory, placed into the MDR, and routed into the ACC under the instruction of the control unit. This has executed the first program instruction.

The PC is then used to alter the MAR to point to the next program instruction, and the process is carried on in this way. These processes are automatically controlled by the tick-tock action of the electronic clock.

After the execution of the last instruction contained in memory, control would be returned to the operating system.

Visit our portal to see an A2 project write-up which simulates the microprocessor shown at the beginning of this unit.

General purpose registers

Many microprocessors have **general-purpose registers**. These are assigned special significance, depending on the instruction being carried out. It is often left up to the programmer to use registers in innovative ways. For example, **sophisticated data structures**, like the **trees**, **queues** and **lists** could be set up. You are already familiar with the idea of a two-dimensional array, and pointers to data, which represent elements within an array. These could be established by making use of two different general-purpose registers. One register would effectively hold the column addresses, and the other the row addresses.

Other special purpose registers

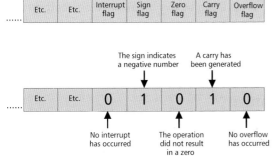

Figure 43.2 A flag register.

Two other important special-purpose registers are the **flag register** and the **interrupt register**.

The flag register is a special register containing a host of bits used to **flag** special situations like 'errors occurring with arithmetic' or to 'flag if an interrupt has occurred'.

A typical flag register can be seen in Figure 43.2. This is an example of a **dedicated register**. Here you can see that after some instruction has been carried out, the result is a negative number, which has caused a **carry** to be generated. No **overflow** has occurred, the operation did not end up with a zero result, and no interrupt occurred during this time. This is vital information, that the programmer may use to determine exactly what is happening to his or her program.

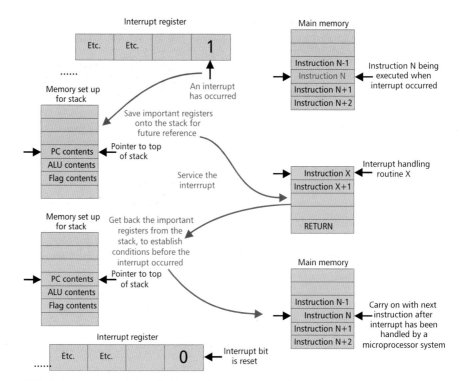

Figure 43.3 A simple interrupt, handled by a microprocessor system, occurs.

Interrupts

A microprocessor never stops executing programs, unless it is physically switched off. After a typical machine-code program has been executed, control is usually returned to the operating system, which is, of course, thousands of other machine-code programs. In fact the microprocessor is constantly switching from one task to the next, making sure that the screen display is updated, keys pressed at the keyboard are interpreted properly, or the correct response is undertaken if the printer runs out of paper, for example. It can cope with all these things, because of its ability to handle **interrupts**. *Interrupts are signals, which are used to get the attention of the processor.* They can be generated from a variety of sources, and many interrupts are happening inside a typical microprocessor each second.

The concept of an **interrupt** is simple. The microprocessor can be **interrupted** in the middle of whatever it is doing. It must make a note of what is happening, by saving all the important register settings like the **PC**, **ALU** and **Flags** etc. It must then **service the interrupt**, by setting the PC to point to the new program to be executed, and then carrying on in the ways described earlier. When the interrupt has been serviced, a **return** is made to the original program which was interrupted, the registers like the **PC**, **ALU** and **flags** etc. are put back to their original state, and the program carries on as though no interrupt has occurred. The ideas are shown in Figure 43.3.

The vectored interrupt mechanism

The Vectored interrupt mechanism is a common examination question regarding interrupts; make sure you understand it well.

The **vectored interrupt mechanism** is a way of pointing by using a **vector** (a number stored in memory) to the memory location, which contains the routine (machine code) to handle the interrupt. There will usually be hundreds of different interrupts, and we need a way of knowing where the code for each lives. In Figure 43.4, there are just two interrupt routines called X and Y.

When an interrupt occurs, shown by the **interrupt-flag register**, the processor must begin a dump of registers, usually to an area of memory called a **stack** (see unit 36).

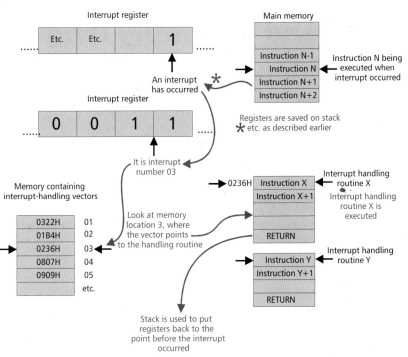

Vectors, stored in memory, help to point to the interrupt-handling routines

Figure 43.4 The vectored interrupt.

Finding out which interrupt handling routine is needed is achieved by examining a number, held inside a register, which points to a memory location where the actual address of the interrupt routine can be found. A typical example of this is the **256 interrupt vectors** used by the **BIOS** (see unit 4) in a typical PC.

Interrupts may occur during a period when some other interrupt is being handled. If the priority of the new interrupt is less than or equal to the priority of the interrupt currently being handled, then the new interrupt must wait. However, if the priority of the new interrupt is higher than the priority of the interrupt currently being executed, then the 'interrupt routine' currently being executed is itself interrupted, and the stack is used to store the important registers again.

Self-test questions

1 Describe typically what happens during the fetch-execute cycle (fetch–decode execute), explaining the role played by some registers inside the microprocessor.
2 Describe what is meant by an interrupt. How is a typical interrupt handled by a microprocessor system?
3 What does vectored-interrupt handling mean? Why is this an efficient way to handle interrupts?
4 Show how an interrupt in the process of execution may itself be interrupted.
5 How might priorities be assigned to different types of interrupt

In this unit you have learned about:

- Simple Microprocessor architecture
- The functions of a clock, main memory, and the internal and external bus systems
- The role played by the registers
- Interrupt priorities and the vectored interrupt method

44 Further machine code and assembly language ideas

In this section you will learn about:

- Assembly language, addressing modes and typical instructions
- Macros, libraries, the assembler and other architectures

Assembly language instructions

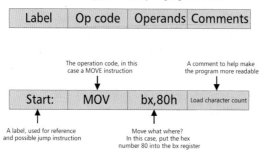

The format of a typical assembly-language instruction

| Label | Op code | Operands | Comments |

The operation code, in this case a MOVE instruction

A comment to help make the program more readable

| Start: | MOV | bx,80h | Load character count |

A label, used for reference and possible jump instruction

Move what where? In this case, put the hex number 80 into the bx register

Figure 44.1 Assembly-language format.

If you have access to an assembler then using it will bring to life many of the concepts covered in this unit.

An **assembly language instruction** is a **mnemonic**, which can be used instead of the **binary codes** representing **machine code**. The format of an assembly-language instruction is shown in Figure 44.1.

The optional **label** is used as a reference. The **operation code** contains the mnemonic, describing the operation carried out. The **operand** contains the source and destination of the data to be operated on, and the **comments** are an optional convenience.

Example

Assembly language is difficult and time consuming compared with a high level language. Explain why effort put into this type of programming is still viable.

Solution

Writing parts of an application in assembly language could give a speed advantage compared with the same application written in a high-level language. If used frequently, an application that does exactly the same job as others, but more quickly, will prevail.

Addressing modes

Addressing modes are related to physical attributes like **registers** or the **word length**. A single-byte jump instruction can jump a maximum of 255 memory locations, as this is the largest number that will fit in this register length. Double the length, and you could jump 65,536 locations, or from +32 767 to −32 768 if two's complement is used. Some common addressing modes are as follows.

Register addressing

If data is transferred from a source **register** to a destination **register**, this is an example of register addressing. For example: `mov ds, ax`

The ax register is the source of the data and the ds register is the destination. After execution of this instruction a copy of the ax register would be placed in the ds register.

Immediate addressing

The data appears **immediately** after the op code, for example: `mov ax, 20`

The decimal number 20 is placed into the ax register. This is a very convenient way of putting a number into a register by specifying the number as an operand.

Direct addressing

This refers **directly** to a specific memory location, for example: `mov ax, myData`

The memory location, specified by a **label** named **myData**, is copied into the ax register.

Indirect addressing

A number inside a register (usually an index register) is used to point to the memory location where the actual data can be found, for example: `mov ax, [bx]`

After execution of the instruction, the number in the memory location pointed to by the bx register is copied to the ax register.

Indexed addressing

This time a number contained in one register is usually used in combination with the number in another register, to point to the memory location where the actual data is stored, for example: `mov cx, [bx + di]`

The number in the bx register is combined with the number in the di register. The square brackets indicate that this points to the memory location from where the actual data to be put into the cx register can be obtained.

Base and base index register addressing

Sometimes the terms **base register addressing** and **base indexed addressing** are used. Consider these examples:

```
mov ax, bx
mov cx, [bx + di]
```

Assembly language is covered in more detail in chapter 21 of NUCSAL.

In the first example, the bx register is actually a **base register**, and is used to point to some useful data. This is an example of **base register addressing**. In the second example, the base register is used in combination with an **index register** (the di register), and is an example of **base indexed addressing**.

Example

Show, by means of an example, a typical use for an indexed addressing mode.

Solution

This is an example of indexed addressing is setting up a two-dimensional array. This would have to be mapped on to memory locations, as shown in Figure 44.2.

$$\begin{bmatrix} 10 & 11 & 12 \\ 21 & 22 & 23 \\ 31 & 32 & 33 \end{bmatrix}$$

A linear sequence of memory is mapped onto an array using two index registers. One register is used for each dimension of the array. This example shows how the fifth element in the array (i.e. 22), is accessed by putting the base index register to a value of 3, and the destination index register to a value of 1. In this case the fifth element is accessed, and the number 22 is placed in the cx register.

```
                  Memory
  Actual addresses      Indexed addressing
  Address + 0   10    Address + 0 + 0
  Address + 1   11    Address + 0 + 1
  Address + 2   12    Address + 0 + 2
  Address + 3 + 21    Address + 3 + 0
  Address + 4   22    Address + 3 + 1
  Address + 5   23    Address + 3 + 2
  Address + 6   31    Address + 6 + 0
  Address + 7   32    Address + 6 + 1
  Address + 8   33    Address + 6 + 2

[10 11 12]
[21 22 23]        Base-index register    3
[31 32 33]
                  Destination-index register   1

       Example       mov cx, [bi + di]
```

Figure 44.2 Indexed addressing.

Typical assembly language instructions

You should be aware of typical assembly language instructions, and be able to write trivial programs using them. Assembly language instructions are made up of **logical operations** like '**AND**', '**OR**' and '**NOT**', **shift left** and **shift right** instructions, **rotate instructions**, **arithmetical instructions**, **instructions to set or reset bits in the registers**, and **program-control instructions** like **jumps**, for example.

Example

Some instructions for an *imaginary* assembly language are as follows:

Instruction	Comments
LDA x	Loads the accumulator with x
STA x	Stores the contents of the accumulator in x
ADD x	Adds x to the number already in the accumulator
MLT x	Multiplies the number in the accumulator by x

You may assume that the numbers being used will not cause any problems like arithmetic overflow etc. and need not check for errors.

Write the part of an assembly-language program that could work out the value of *y* in the quadratic equation shown below. State any assumptions, which you may wish to make.

$$y = ax^2 + bx + c$$

Solution

Let's assume that labels a, b and c have been set up, which represent pointers to the memory locations in which the constants for the above equation are stored. Let there also be a location y, in which to store the answer, and three other locations, called 'temp1' ... 'temp3', in which intermediate answers may be stored. The assembly-language program, together with comments, is as follows:

```
Quad    LDA    x        ;work out x²
        MLT    x
        STA    temp1

        LDA    a        work out ax²
        MLT    temp1
        STA    temp2
        LDA    b        ;work out bx
        MLT    x
        STA    temp3
        LDA    temp1    ;Add three parts
        ADD    temp2
        ADD    temp3
        STA    y
```

Macros and library routines

It is inefficient to have to write code for standard routines. For example, reading a character from the keyboard or saving a block of data to disk. Standard routines are available called **library routines**. They may be called up as **macros** and many of the most useful routines are available as **operating system calls**. A call to a **macro** is a single command, which can be replaced by many commands that get put into the program where the macro name is encountered. This is very convenient for the low-level language programmer. There are many third party routines supplied in **assembly-language libraries** specifically for this purpose. If you need to perform some process on data, you can be relatively sure that an assembly-language routine exists to do it.

The assembler

The **assembler** is the *piece of software*, enabling you to write assembly-language programs. Not only does it help with changing the **mnemonics** into **machine code** (the assembly process), but helps to place a program in memory at the appropriate point, helps to **debug** a non-functioning program, **links** to any **library routines** and points out **syntax errors**. It also adds **macros**, and helps you with printing out both the **source code** (the **assembly-language mnemonics**) and the **object code** (the **actual machine code**, which runs on the machine).

The **debugging** part of the assembler is called the **debugger**. It enables you to *single step through programs*, and *inspect the contents of memory and registers before going onto the next instruction*. Without debugging software, assembly-language programming would not be a feasible proposition.

Visit our portal to see how to obtain an assembler.

Pipeline architectures

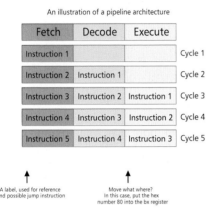

Figure 44.3 Pipeline architecture.

Much of the time machine code is being **fetched**, **decoded** and **executed** as a linear sequence of instructions. However, while one part of an instruction is being fetched from memory, another could be being decoded, and yet another could be in the process of being executed. Inside the microprocessor, a portion of memory, called a **pipe**, is used to implement these operations. You can visualise the instructions at various stages of completion, by going through a **pipeline** as shown in Figure 44.3. However, this does assume that the next instruction to be fetched is next in line. For jumps this may not be the case, and although pipelining is faster, you do not get the maximum speed because of this.

Multiple processor architectures

To do more than one thing at the same time we need more than one processor. The **operating system**, **applications software** or **programs**, which run on these **parallel-processing architectures**, must be specifically written to take advantage. Languages, like **Concurrent Pascal** and **Fortran**, enable different sub-problems to be split up in this way.

There are a variety of parallel processing architectures, including **SIMD** (**Single Instruction Multiple Data stream**), in which one processor does the fetch part of the cycle, but distributes the instructions to be executed to other processors. There is also **MIMD** (**Multiple Instruction Multiple Data stream**), in which the processors operate independently i.e. they fetch, decode and execute their own instructions.

Only professional operating systems like Windows 2000 and Windows NT support multiple processors – do not try getting two or more processors to work with an OS like Windows 98 or Windows Me.

Self-test questions

1 What is an addressing mode?
2 Give an example of indexed addressing
3 What is an assembler?
4 What is the difference between an assembler and a compiler?
5 What is a label and why is it useful?
6 What are library routines?
7 What does a pipeline architecture mean?
8 Make a list of what an assembler does.

In this unit you have learned about:

- Simple assembly-language instructions and different addressing modes
- Macros and libraries
- The assembler
- Alternative processor architectures including parallel processing

45 A final look at operating systems

In this section you will learn about:

- Multiprogramming, multitasking and interrupt priorities
- Fixed and variable partitioning and memory management
- Virtual memory and paging
- Re-entrant code and dynamic link libraries
- File management
- I/O management, handlers, drivers and interrupts
- Process and task management

Make sure you have read the material in units 4 and 43 before reading this unit.

Multiprogramming and multitasking

Multiprogramming is the ability of a system to operate on more than one program at the same time, or apparently the same time. How it does this depends on the type of operating system, and the hardware (number of processors) available. If a system gives a small amount of processor time to each task before going on to the next, this would be known as a **time-sharing system**.

It is the job of the operating system to allocate time to programs and other tasks in a time-sharing environment. Other factors, like the **priority** of the **jobs** (tasks) being undertaken are important too, and often override the requests put in by less important tasks. The ability of an operating system to handle many tasks at the 'same time' is called **multitasking**. Only operating systems with more than one processor can actually do more than one thing at the same time. Having more than one processor would be called **multiprocessing**.

It is the job of the operating system to **assign priorities** to jobs so that the maximum amount of work can be done in the shortest possible time. It is also the job of the operating system to ensure that **resources** like **printers** and **disks** are used in an optimum fashion, and to ensure that **conflicting requests** are handled sensibly.

Example

An operating system processes tasks by making use of interrupts. Explain the term interrupt, giving two typical examples, one with a high priority and the other with low priority. What sort of data structure could be used for handling these interrupts?

Solution

An interrupt is when a task needs processor attention. An example of a high-priority interrupt could be a 'disk full' situation, in which case no further data can be saved to the disk. A lower-priority interrupt could be a job that is spooling output to a device like a printer. In this case it does not matter if the print job takes an extra few seconds. The data structure, used for handling interrupt priorities, is a LIFO stack. Information regarding a process is saved onto the stack while a higher-priority interrupt is executed.

Memory management

Memory allocated to one program must not interfere with memory allocated to any other. It is the job of the operating system to actively carry out **memory-management** techniques. The concept of memory management is simple. An appropriate amount of **RAM** must be allocated to a task, and when the task is finished, RAM must be returned to the system so it can be used by other tasks. It is the job of the operating system to police the system. It does this by splitting the memory into smaller chunks called **partitions**. These **partition sizes** may be **fixed** or **variable**, depending on how the operating system is organised.

Example

Explain some advantages and disadvantages of fixed partitioning compared to variable partitioning of memory.

Solution

Fixed partitioning is easier to manage, but can be wasteful of memory space (i.e. too much memory allocated depending on the partition size). Variable partitioning is more complex to manage, but more efficient in terms of memory usage. Memory can become badly defragmented, and considerable housekeeping would have to be undertaken to sort out the variable-size 'holes' created in memory by this variable partitioning system.

Virtual memory and paging

There might not be enough physical RAM available for use by the operating system, and **virtual memory** can be used instead. This is memory, set up on disk, pretending to be RAM. With enough disk space the 'lack of RAM' problem may be completely solved, but the speed of access is very slow compared to conventional RAM-access speeds. The operating system may organise virtual memory by a system called **paging**. The virtual memory can be split up into blocks of fixed size called **pages**. Each is **mapped** onto physical disk space, so data in **virtual memory** is mapped onto **physical memory** by the operating system. A special memory management system carries out this translation (mapping) process. It is difficult to predict what data is needed in RAM and what can be **cached** to disk. Data could be constantly moving backwards and forwards, and the system can almost grind to a halt. This is known as **thrashing**.

Re-entrant code

The same code needs to be shared by different programs using the operating system. Any code, written so that several different programs may use it simultaneously is called **re-entrant code** or **code sharing**. This method ensures that the same routines do not have to reside in memory. If one program is currently using a piece of re-entrant code, another program may actually interrupt the original program and use the same code. Modern operating systems support **code sharing**. There are many software routines that reside in the operating system; indeed, the summation of thousands of these routines *is* the operating system.

Dynamic linked libraries (DLLs)

It is wasteful of memory space if all routines needed by all programs and tasks were all resident in memory simultaneously. Therefore, some routines, called **dynamic link libraries** by Microsoft, may be called up and executed when needed. These routines, stored on disk as **DLL files**, may be used as if they were part of the operating system. There are many **DLLs** provided by manufacturers, all used for specific purposes. Some DLLs, like those that help the C++ or Visual Basic programmer, for example, are more general in nature. Advanced users may use and alter DLLs provided with the idea of improving the functionality of programs.

File management

It is the job of the operating system to manage file space. For example, opened files may be too large to fit into the available RAM, or files that have just been created may be too large to fit into a contiguous disk space due to a defragmented disk. A **buffer** is often set up to solve these problems.

If possible, try to get some experience of operating systems other than the version of Windows you may have at home. Windows NT or Linux, for example, are used extensively in industry.

A **buffer** is an area of memory set up to temporarily store data until it is ready to be used. A buffer may be set up to interface the file 'as seen from an operating system perspective' to the file 'as seen from a hardware perspective'. The hardware, which interfaces the operating system to the disk, for example, will have a physical block size, which does not usually relate in any way to the record size being used by the programmer. A **physical block** of data would be read from the disk and stored in a **buffer**. The OS takes data from this buffer, in a size convenient to it, which usually relates to the **logical records** used by software. It is the job of the **file management software** in the OS to resolve these differences, and make sure that the physical limitations of disks, CD-ROMs and DVDs etc. do not encroach on the programmer's perspective, which is a logical (not physical) view of the data.

Example

Why might programs 'fill up' a disk when the sum of the bytes in each program is considerably less than the disk capacity? How is this affected by the buffer.

Solution

It is likely that the logical block sizes and physical block sizes do not match. Therefore, it is likely that a large part of the physical block is not used when small files store information in the buffer. Much empty space could be saved along with the actual information, thus accounting for the differences described in the question. The larger the buffer, the larger the holes for small amounts of data saved to disk.

I/O management

The operating system provides data in an appropriate form for I/O (**input/output**), but cannot cope with the huge variety of devices. Different printers, for example, all require data to be in different forms depending on functionality. **Printer drivers** sort out these features, which are specific to an exact type of printer and **OS**. Most **I/O devices** like sound and graphics cards etc. will need specialist **drivers** to accompany the hardware after it is installed. Without correct drivers the device probably will not work. It is the job of the driver to translate the hardware characteristics of the device into what is needed for a specific operating system. The device driver usually handles the direct interface to the device, but additional software routines, often called **handlers**, may be needed to aid the transfer of data between the device driver and the OS.

Drivers grab resources like **interrupts** to get attention from the OS. Figure 45.1 shows a PS/2 compatible mouse connected to a Windows ME OS using **IRQ** (Interrupt ReQuest) 12.

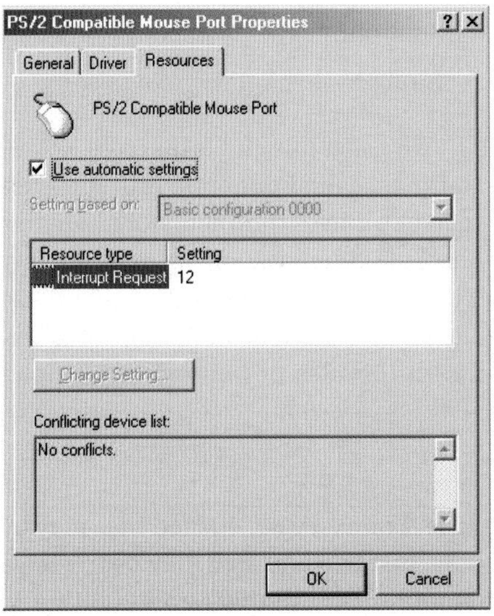

Figure 45.1 Using interrupt request 12.

If a mouse click occurs, this driver will use interrupt 12 to generate attention from the operating system. The driver will pass the data (regarding which button has been pressed etc.) to the operating system so that appropriate action, like closing a window, for example, could be taken. Devices are interfaced to the OS by the use of drivers, and these will often conflict with each other if the interrupts have not been allocated properly. This could mean that the computer fails to operate in predictable ways, or fails to operate at all. You may have to use the **BIOS** settings to resolve conflicts before restarting the computer. When set up properly, the interrupts will be handled using the priorities talked about earlier in this unit.

Scheduling

Hundreds of tasks might be going on inside the computer in a short space of time. It is the job of the operating system to **schedule** these conflicting requirements to maximise the work done in the shortest possible time whilst resolving possible conflicts. Tasks will be in many different **states**. A printer may have just run out of paper, or a program might be waiting for processor attention. All these **processes** require the attention of the operating system, which can usually do just one thing at a time. It is the job of the **scheduler** to make sure that no one process hogs all the attention, that no one process never gets attention, and that the peripherals are used in an efficient way. The operating system copes by considering each process to be in a variety of states. These could be 'waiting for attention', 'using a peripheral', or 'using the processor', for example. The operating system will usually set up a **queuing system** giving the highest priority to those tasks that need it. Sometimes it is not easy to resolve all the conflicting requirements, and occasionally processes can be **deadlocked** if the scheduling part of the operating system is not operating efficiently.

Example

Why is scheduling important in an operating system that supports both batch and interactive modes of operating.

Solution

If the batch of jobs were carried out with no regard to the priorities of other programs, then the user/s of the system would get no response until the entire batch process is finished. By efficient scheduling, the operating system can interrupt the batch process to give the interactive processes a slice of the action. If done effectively, the interactive processes should notice little degradation in performance.

Larger operating system principles are covered in chapter 23 of NUCSAL.

Self-test questions

1 What is meant by the terms multiprogramming and multitasking?
2 What is a multi-user system?
3 What is an interrupt?
4 Why are priorities assigned to interrupts?
5 How might an operating system resolve a conflict between two conflicting devices?
6 What is the difference between fixed and variable partitioning?
7 What is virtual memory?
8 What does the term 'thrashing' mean?
9 What is re-entrant code?
10 What is the advantage of a dynamic link library routine over one that permanently resides in the operating system?
11 Describe what a 'buffer' means.
12 Explain how the use of interrupts enables a computer to manage input and output.
13 What is the function of a scheduler in an operating system?

In this unit you have learned about:

- Multiprogramming, multitasking and interrupt priorities
- Ways of managing memory
- Virtual memory and paging
- Re-entrant code
- File management techniques
- I/O techniques
- Scheduling

46 Advanced database ideas

In this section you will learn about:

- Database management systems or DBMS
- Logical conceptual and physical database schema
- Data definition language and data manipulation languages
- Structured query language or SQLs
- Linking and importing data
- ODBC – Open DataBase Connectivity

Make sure you have read the material in units 20, 21 and 22 before reading this unit.

The database management system

A **DBMS (database management system)** is shown in Figure 46.1. The three main levels of architecture are the **physical database**, the **conceptual view** and the **users' view**.

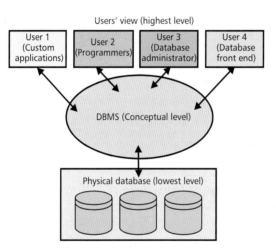

Figure 46.1 Three-level DBMS architecture.

The **physical database** is concerned with how the data is stored on disk. For example, **files** may be stored and accessed either **randomly** or **serially**. You should also be familiar with magnetic disk formats like **cylinders** and **sectors** used to store the data. The conceptual level of the database is the way in which the data has been **logically organised** to gain access to it, and manages the security of the database. You have a good idea of the conceptual view of a database from creating tables as outlined in unit 20. In this unit we will concentrate mainly on the mechanisms associated with the DBMS.

The highest level is the **users' view**. Some advanced users, such as programmers, for example, would be able to access the data in very sophisticated ways, enabling them to process the data in ways limited only by their imagination. On the other hand, non-technical users of the system would need simple front ends designed to enable them to process the data in pre-defined ways. The users' view is also known as the **external view**. A powerful **DBMS** would allow many users to have completely different views of the same data.

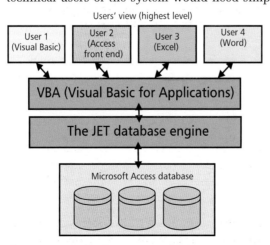

Figure 46.2 Applications access a database.

Database schema

These views of the database are often referred to as **schema**. You will see terms like the **external schema**, which is the users' view, the **logical schema**, which is the conceptual view, and the internal or **physical schema**, which is the physical database.

If you have used **Microsoft Access** then you may have used **VBA** (Visual Basic for Applications) or Excel, for example, to access information contained within an Access database. Figure 46.2 shows how it is possible to do this using the Microsoft Access database.

Here you can see how applications like Word or Excel, for example, can access the Jet database engine (the **DBMS**), and hence gain access to data held inside Microsoft Access. Jet stands for Joint Engine Technology.

Example

A DBMS will support a data definition language and a data manipulation language. Explain these terms, giving an example using a database with which you are familiar.

Solution

Any DBMS, such as Access's Jet, for example, will have a **data definition language** or **DDL**. This helps the **database administrator**, or **DBA**, the person responsible for setting up and administering the system, to define a new database, by setting up tables, fields and indexes etc.

The following is the full syntax, taken from the Access help pages, using Jet's DDL to define a table in Microsoft Access:

```
CREATE [TEMPORARY] TABLE table (field1 type
[(size)] [NOT NULL] [WITH
COMPRESSION | WITH COMP] [index1] [,
field2 type [(size)] [NOT NULL]
[index2] [, ...]] [, CONSTRAINT
multifieldindex [, ...]])
```

You can see that the table has a name, followed by the fields that are created within the table. Other attributes involve data type, like Boolean or integer, for example, and the length of the field.

A **DML**, or **data manipulation language**, is used to manipulate the data once it has been created by the DDL. Tasks such as adding new records, editing existing records or performing queries would be typical of what can be programmed using a DML.

One of the DML statements in Microsoft's Jet database is as follows:

```
SELECT [predicate] { * | table.* | [table.]field1 | [AS alias1]
                    [,[table.]field2 [AS alias2] [, ...]]}
    FROM tableexpression [, ...] [IN externaldatabase]
    [WHERE ...]
    [GROUP BY ...]
    [HAVING ...]
    [ORDER BY ...]
    [WITH OWNERACCESS OPTION]
```

Here you can see the Jet DML syntax for a SELECT statement, helping to retrieve records from tables that satisfy certain conditions. You can see the table name, field names, and how the data is grouped. You would not be expected to remember the syntax, but should be able to quote some of the things that can be accomplished by programmers using a DML.

There is some overlap between functions that can be carried out by the DML and the DDL. The DML and DDL are intimately tied up with, and indeed are often part of, the **structured**

If you have the Access database, try out some of the advanced features outlined here. It will make the principles easier to understand.

query language called SQL. This is the language that is used to structure, manipulate and manage the database. Sophisticated queries can be carried out using SQL. An example of an SQL statement, making use of Microsoft Access is as follows:

```
Sub CountX( )
Dim dbs As Database, rst As Recordset
' Modify this line to include the path to Northwind
Set dbs = OpenDatabase("Northwind.mdb")
' Calculate the number of orders shipped to the United Kingdom.
Set rst = dbs.OpenRecordset("SELECT"
          & " Count (ShipCountry)"
          & " AS [UK Orders] FROM Orders"
          & " WHERE ShipCountry = 'UK';")
'Populate the Recordset.rst.MoveLast Call EnumFields to print
the contents of the Recordset. Pass the Recordset object and
desired field width.
EnumFields rst, 25
dbs.Close
End Sub
```

This example, from Microsoft's North Wind database, uses the count function to calculate the number of orders shipped to the UK. As you can see, powerful programming features are available in the SQL language.

Example

Given that the DDL, DML and SQL mentioned in the last few sections are extremely powerful, why is it necessary to add to this functionality using a programming language like Visual Basic, COBOL, or C++?

Solution

The SQL language provides a very powerful set of features to create and manipulate data in the database, but does not have versatile programming features like 'Do While' or 'For-to-next' loops etc. Therefore, we can combine the features provided by the DBMS, and powerful object-oriented languages like C++, or Visual programming languages like VB or VBA. The interface facilities provided by the SQL, DML and DDL languages, together with all the advanced programming facilities of traditional 3GL and 4GL languages, provide an environment in which programmers are able to manage and manipulate any attribute of the data stored inside the database.

Concurrent access to data

If two or more users are using the same database then problems can arise with updates. For example, two people could be attempting to book the same theatre ticket at the same time. There are a variety of ways to get over this problem, and the DBMS allows the DBA to specify which system is currently in use.

An **exclusive lock** can be used to prevent others from locking items until the lock is cleared, usually by closing the record after editing. When different people are using a database simultaneously, excluding others from being able to update the information within a particular record is a common option.

You can open a database by locking the whole lot, as would probably be the case when using a stand-alone PC, but this is not ideal for **concurrent** or **multi-user access**. **Record locking** or exclusively locking any part of the database will not prevent others from looking at the data, but will prevent others from updating the data. Also, for **relational**

tables, parts of one table, related to data being edited, might also have to be locked, or the relational updates will not maintain their **integrity.**

Databases may be too big for local resources. Microsoft Access, at the time of writing, limits Office 2000 professional to a 2Gbyte local database (i.e. a database held on a local hard disk). Via systems like **ODBC,** it is possible to link larger databases via a network.

Open database connectivity (ODBC)

Open database connectivity is now the de-facto standard for applications, which provides a standard interface to a database, often via the Windows operating system and a network.

Databases have varying syntax for their SQL interfaces – especially those that were made before official SQL standards were developed. This makes it difficult to interrogate alternative data sources. **ODBC** overcomes this, as long as the application supports it. With ODBC you can link directly to the data in these foreign applications via Windows. You should note that this is not the same as importing data into a database via **CSV,** for example. ODBC will actually allow your database to interrogate the data in the other database, even though the SQL syntax may be different. Make sure that you understand the difference between **importing data** and **linking to data.**

Self-test questions

1 Into what three levels is a DBMS split? Explain the need for organising a large database in this way.
2 Explain the role that the DDL and DML play in the construction and interrogation of a database.
3 Who is a DBA and what does he or she do?
4 Outline two advantages of using a DML compared to standard manipulations via the easy-to-use front end of a database.
5 When creating a large database, the DDL provides facilities over and above those that would be provided by the front end to the database. Suggest two things, which could not easily be done via the standard user interface, which would be easy for a programmer to do via a DDL.
6 Explain the term importing and exporting data. Give an example of how a small amount of data may be exported from a typical database to an application like a spreadsheet, for example.
7 A database needs to be accessed simultaneously by several hundred people. Outline some of the hardware and software requirements that would be needed in this situation.
8 If many people have access to the same records, data integrity is often a problem. What can be done to overcome this?
9 Suggest two advantages of linking to a database as opposed to importing or exporting data to it.

Your teacher or lecturer may be able to demonstrate ODBC examples. Lots of schools use these facilities to transfer data between different parts of the school administrative systems.

Many advanced database ideas are covered in chapters 28 and 29 of NUCSAL.

In this unit you have learned about:

- The role of the **DBMS**
- Different conceptual views of the **database schema** such as the physical, and logical levels
- Data definition languages (DDL)
- Data manipulation languages (DML)
- Structured query languages (SQL)
- Linking and importing data
- Open database connectivity (ODBC)

In this section you will learn about:

- Relational database modelling
- Normalisation
- First normal form

Database design – the relational model

The **relational model** is the most popular method of database design. To make management of the data efficient, and to prevent undesirable errors, the database has to be designed *very carefully*.

This is the first part of a two-part unit dealing with advanced concepts of relational databases.

A **database schema** is the 'definition of the tables', and this is what we are trying to perfect when building a **relational database**. Each table should describe a single **entity**, where an entity is an **object** within your database. Entities might be 'books', 'authors' or 'publishers' in the library database shown in unit 20. Typically an entity will refer to a **record**, or **row**, in a single table.

We can define **relationships** between various objects or entities. For example, a customer may place many orders, where there is a **one-to-many relationship** between the entity customer, and the entity order. There are four possible types of mathematical relationship, but only three are used in relational database design:

- One to one
- One to many
- Many to many

Relationships are expressed in an **entity-relationship (ER) diagram**. An ER diagram for 'customer and orders' is shown in Figure 47.1, where the three alternative forms are outlined. It does not matter which form you use, as long as you are consistent. This diagram shows a **one-to-many relationship**.

Example

When using relational databases, it is not possible to model many-to-many relationships. How is this limitation overcome?

Solution

Do not attempt to read the material in this unit unless you have understood the material in unit 20.

It is easily possible to model a many-to-many relationship by breaking it down into many one-to-many relationships. Therefore, the only way that the database can be built up in practice is by using **one-to-one** or **one-to-many** relationships only.

Entity relationship diagram examples

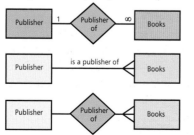

Figure 47.1 Different forms of ER diagram.

Each entity in a table is made up from several **attributes**. The 'book information' table of Table 20.3 in unit 20 has the attributes ISBN, Author, Title, Publisher ID and Price, for example. Each of these attributes usually corresponds to a **'field'** in a **record**. To save drawing out tables, a convenient way of describing them is using **shorthand notation**. Using the library example in Table 20.3 in unit 20 again, we get the following:

Books(<u>ISBN</u>, Author, Title, Publisher ID, Price)

All the attributes representing the entity 'book information' are listed separated by commas. The **key field** is <u>underlined</u> to emphasise the important role that ISBN plays in the list. (As we shall see later, this is not a particularly good table for describing the books.)

Normalisation

Normalisation is the process that may have to happen to achieve an efficient relational database design. There are three main stages to normalisation, called **first**, **second** and **third normal forms** respectively. Even if a database is in third normal form, it is still possible to have some redundancy, and so another form, called **BCNF** or **Boyce-Codd normal form** is also used. It is quite likely that data normalised to third normal form *is already in* BCNF. Designing a database to **third normal form** or **BCNF** is very common practice.

Example

It is more efficient if a relational database is normalised when being designed.

(a) Why is it necessary to do this?
(b) Under what circumstances might you decide to denormalise the data?

Solution

(a) If a database is 'designed' with little thought, you may encounter the following:

- The database might contain redundant data, and this would be wasteful of space.
- When updating the database, other data contained within it might accidentally become corrupted, or not get updated.
- Deleting data in one part of the database might inadvertently cause data to be deleted in another part of the database.
- Calculated totals may not get updated properly when inserting some extra data.
- Often it is not possible to carry out complex *ad hoc* queries if the database is stored in an inefficient way.

Normalisation will get over these and similar problems, and should prevent exhaustive and unnecessarily long searches for some items.

(b) You may get so many tables and links, that accessing large databases might become unacceptably slow. This is one instance where additional, redundant data might be inserted to speed up queries, and this is quite common.

Codd's normal forms are based on a special organisation of tables into **relations**. This should not be confused with the term relationship, which is used to define the one-to-one or one-to-many connections.

Before (and during) normalisation it is best to make sure that the following criteria apply, and that each table applies to only one particular subject (entity). Most databases, like Access, for example, will pay no attention whatsoever to the table name, but rely on the **primary key** alone for the purpose of identification. A **relation** is a table with the following properties:

- **Each table must have a unique primary key.** You may have to group several attributes (fields), or even introduce a completely new attribute to form a composite primary key. If a table had identical primary keys, then the subject of each table would not be unique.
- **Each row in the table must be unique** (i.e. no two rows of the table can be identical – it would be a *very* bad choice of key field if this were the case!).
- **A table should model only one entity.** (We should not have 'books' and 'authors' in the same table like that shown in Figure 20.3 of unit 20, for example.)

The work covered in units 47 and 48 is vital if you are undertaking an A2 database project. A flat-file database is unlikely to be an acceptable A2 project.

- **The ways in which the columns and rows are laid out is not important**. (The order of the rows in the table, or the order of the attributes in each row is irrelevant.)
- **All the attribute names (i.e. column headings) in a table must be different**. (You cannot have the same field name appearing twice within a file!)

Normalisation examples

Normalisation is best understood by means of examples, and the ones that follow contain parts of databases to illustrate methods of normalisation. **Normalisation** is confusing, not because the rules are complex, but because *a lot of experience is needed to decide how particular data should be modelled in the first place*. For example, it is best not to design a database into which you put all the subjects studied by a student at school into a single 'Subjects' field, especially if you wish to do a search on who does what subject.

It is better to put all the subjects into different fields, or to have a single subject field in a different table. The data does not alter; it is just that the tables get linked together in more efficient ways. You may add data to make management of the database efficient.

Table 47.1 An unnormalised database

Some unnormalised computer-shop data			
Order number	Customer ID	Date	Items sold
45799	20063	18/3/2001	1 keyboard, 1 mouse, 2 Zip disks
45830	20026	18/4/2001	1 scanner
45701	30087	19/4/2001	10 floppy disks, 3 reams of paper
46333	30003	23/4/2001	2 computer books, 1 magazine
48777	40023	23/4/2002	3 computer games, 1 floppy disk

Consider Table 47.1. This would benefit from a numeric code for each product. As it stands we cannot differentiate between types of computer books or games! *Always* work out how the database is to be used *before* designing the database on a computer. In Table 47.1, the primary key is shown in yellow, and a particular customer order (for customer 20063) is shown in green.

As another example, you could put an address into a single field, but this is restricting. It is better to have separate fields, because it is easier to search on 'post code', for example. *Again it is all related to the ways in which the data will be used*. This is what good database design is about. If, however, the whole address in this example *were* a single attribute, the

Table 47.2 A better arrangement of Table 47.1

One of the possible first normal form representations for the computer-shop data						
Order number	Item number	Date	Customer ID	Quantity	Item ID	Item sold
45799	1	18/3/2001	20063	1	9537	Keyboard
45799	2	18/3/2001	20063	1	7833	Mouse
45799	3	18/3/2001	20063	2	6534	Zip disk
45830	1	18/4/2001	20026	1	8878	Scanner
45701	1	19/4/2001	30087	10	9983	Floppy disk
45701	2	19/4/2001	30087	3	3326	Ream of paper
46333	1	23/4/2001	30003	2	5346	Computer book
46333	2	23/4/2001	30003	1	1122	Magazine
48777	1	23/4/2002	40023	3	1990	Computer game
48777	2	23/4/2002	40023	1	9983	Floppy disk

normalisation process would be different from considering the address as multiple-valued attributes. *There is no substitute for analysing how data is used. Normalisation will help make the database efficient, but it will not get over problems regarding lack of research into how the data is to be used in practice.*

First normal form

To put a table into first normal form, apart from the common-sense requirements listed earlier, requires the following to be carried out.

Attributes having multiple values must be removed so that the rows (records) in a table are all the same length.

In other words, you cannot have lots of things put into a single field, or a variable number of fields in a single record.

An example of a multiple-valued entry is the 'Items sold' field shown in Table 47.1. However, before putting the above data into **first normal form**, consider *why* we are doing this. Laid out in an unnormalised way, searching the database is a nightmare. It is difficult to find out how many 'floppy disks' have been sold, without doing a detailed search *within* each of the 'Items sold' attributes. This is because the 'Items sold' attribute has multiple values. Also, searching for 'floppy disks' could create an error, because this would not pick up the single 'floppy disk' sold to customer number 40023. We can put the database into first normal form by arranging the table as shown in Table 47.2.

In this new tabular relationship, the **order number** is no longer unique (it appears several times in the above table) and therefore *cannot be used* as the **primary key**. To get over this problem, we introduce a new field called **item number**. This **composite primary key**, consisting of the attributes order number and item number, *is unique*, and the **composite key** *can* be used as the **primary key** (shown in yellow in Table 47.2). Customer number 20063 now takes up 3 records and is again shown in green. Contrast this new table with Table 46.1. As Table 46.2 no longer contains attributes with repeating keys, has **unique primary keys**, and the **rows are all the same length**, it is now in **first normal form**.

You might not have approached this problem in the same way as the author, and this does not matter. The end results of further normalisation, to be carried out in the next unit, always work if you apply the rules properly.

If you are undertaking relational database work for your A2 project, you will lose marks if you have not attempted some normalisation.

Self-test questions

1. What is a relational database?
2. Why are relational databases the most popular database design method?
3. What is a database schema?
4. Why are ER diagrams used?
5. What is a relationship?
6. What is a table in a relational database?
7. Explain the shorthand notation for describing a table in a relational database.
8. Why is normalisation needed?
9. What is meant by first normal form?
10. Explain the following database terms: an entity; table; rows and columns; primary key.

In this unit you have learned about:

- The relational database model
- First normal form

48 Further normalisation

Second normal form

This is the second part of a two-part unit dealing with advanced concepts of relational databases.

Database tables must be in first normal form before putting them into second normal form.

Second normal form means making sure that all the attributes in an entity are functionally dependent (depend only) on the primary key.

Do not forget that the primary key may include several attributes, and this functional dependence must be on the composite key, not just part of it.

Tables should store information about one entity only, this means that every non-key item in our tables must now depend only upon the entire primary key. Therefore, you need to analyse each and every non-key attribute and check to see if they are uniquely dependent (i.e. depend totally) upon the primary key.

The work in this unit may be difficult to understand if you have not worked through units 20 and 47.

We now put the computer-shop database shown in unit 47 into **second normal form**. Using Table 47.2 as our starting point, and working through the non-key elements, we start with 'Date'. 'Date' is not functionally dependent on the composite primary key, but is dependent on 'Order number' only. Therefore, the date is removed to another table. Next comes 'Customer ID', this is functionally dependent on order number only, because we can determine the 'Customer ID' from 'Order number' alone. Therefore, 'Customer ID' should be removed to another table too. All the remaining attributes in Table 47.2 (unit 47) depend only on the composite primary key ('Order number', 'Item number'). Therefore, we can split up Table 47.2 into two different tables as shown in Tables 48.1 and 48.2.

Table 48.1

Order table – second normal form		
Order number	Customer ID	Date
45799	20063	18/3/2001
45830	20026	18/4/2001
45701	30087	19/4/2001
46333	30003	23/4/2001
48777	40023	23/4/2002

Table 48.2

Items table – second normal form				
Order no.	Item no.	Stock no.	Qty	Item sold
45799	1	9537	1	Keyboard
45799	2	7833	1	Mouse
45799	3	6534	2	Zip disk
45830	1	8878	1	Scanner
45701	1	9983	10	Floppy disk
45701	2	3326	3	Ream of paper
46333	1	5346	2	Computer book
46333	2	1122	1	Magazine
48777	1	1990	3	Computer game
48777	2	9983	1	Floppy disk

The attributes shown above are now **functionally dependent** only on the entire primary key, and both tables are therefore in **second normal form**. We have better ways of storing the data compared to the first normal form table in the last unit. The 'Date' and 'Customer ID' don't have to be repeated and the database is easier to update.

Third normal form

We assume that the tables are in second normal form before we apply the following rule.

There should be no functional dependencies (unique associations) existing between attributes (or groups of attributes) that could not be used as an alternative to the primary key.

In other words, there should be mutual independence between all non-key elements.

If dependencies exist between non-key elements, situations may arise during updates, where dependent information may get left behind or other information deleted. Looking at Table 48.1, no dependencies exist between 'Customer ID' and 'Date', and therefore the table is already in third normal form. However, from Table 48.2 there *is* mutual dependence between 'Stock number' and 'Item sold'. (They are the same – you cannot have a stronger dependency!) These items must be taken from the main table, and put into another one. By doing this, the database is more efficient. If you sold many keyboards in many separate orders, you would have to enter *both* the stock number (9537) and the word 'Keyboard' many times. This extra effort is eliminated by splitting Table 48.2 into two tables as follows:

ITEMS(Order no, Item no., Stock no., Qty)

This is now shown in Table 48.3

If you are undertaking a relational database project, to get maximum marks, ensure that you have normalised any relational database to third normal form or BCNF.

Table 48.3

Items table – now in third normal form			
Order no.	Item no.	Stock no.	Qty
45799	1	9537	1
45799	2	7833	1
45799	3	6534	2
45830	1	8878	1
45701	1	9983	10
45701	2	3326	3
46333	1	5346	2
46333	2	1122	1
48777	1	1990	3
48777	2	9983	1

Table 48.4

Products – now in third normal form	
Stock no.	Item sold
9537	Keyboard
7833	Mouse
6534	Zip disk
8878	Scanner
9983	Floppy disk
3326	Ream of paper
5346	Computer book
1122	Magazine
1990	Computer game

Having removed the stock number and item sold from Table 48.2, we need to put these in their own table, and this is shown in Table 48.4, i.e. **Products(Stock no. Item sold)**

All the data is now in **third normal form**. Our database consists of Tables 48.1, 48.3 and 48.4.

Example

Tables in a database are edited, and a 'referential integrity' error occurs. What does this mean? Give an example of what might be causing the problem.

Solution

When linking tables, we may have references to data in both tables. In a library database, there is a reference to 'Publisher' within a Publisher table, but there might also be a reference to 'Publisher' in a Book table. If we delete a publisher from the Publisher table, then this publisher must also be deleted from the Book table. By not doing this, we have a dangling link, which is a reference to a publisher entry in the book file to a non-existent publisher. This is called a **referential integrity error**, because the integrity of the reference here has been compromised.

BCNF

Most tables, already in third normal form, are probably in **BCNF** or **Boyce Codd normal form** too. If the data can be further normalised into BCNF, some anomalies may be avoided. The table must be in third normal form.

A relation is in BCNF if every determinant is a candidate key.

A candidate key can be used to uniquely identify a record. (It is possible for a record to have several different candidate keys, of which only one is used as the **primary key**. It is up to the database designer to choose.) Any candidate key that is not used as the primary key is called an **alternate key**. Finally, a **determinant** is an **attribute** (or possibly a combination of attributes), which is **functionally dependent** (depend only) on any other attribute or combination of attributes.

More simply, **a table is in BCNF if all the attributes in the table are just facts, nothing but facts, about the primary key.**

A BCNF example

Table 48.5 Is this table in BCNF?

Student ID number	Main course	Tutor
661739	Computing	Bradley
661739	Maths	Evans
234777	Computing	Pinkstone
233338	Computing	Bradley
393362	Maths	Lucas
653349	Physics	Longly
983335	Biology	Belbin
265533	Chemistry	Clugston

Here, an example is given to see a third normal form table put into BCNF. From Table 48.5 we see that the primary key is the pair of attributes ('Student ID number', 'Main course'). The Student ID is not unique, because student 661739 does two different courses.

Look at the **determinants**. One possibility is the pair (**'Student ID number'**, **'Main course'**). Each pair uniquely determines the tutor. Another possibility is the pair (**'Student ID number'**, **'Tutor'**), which uniquely determines the 'Main course'. Yet another possibility (assuming that the Tutor specialises in one course only) is the **'Tutor'** uniquely determines the 'Main course'. These are three possible **determinants**.

Table 48.6

Student ID number	Tutor
661739	Bradley
879933	Evans
234777	Pinkstone
233338	Bradley
393362	Lucas
653349	Longly
983335	Belbin
265533	Clugston

Table 48.7 The split list

Tutor	Main course
Bradley	Computing
Evans	Maths
Pinkstone	Computing
Lucas	Maths
Longley	Physics
Belbin	Biology
Clugston	Chemistry

To see if the table is in BCNF, we must see if each of these determinants is also a **candidate key** (i.e. a possible alternative to the primary key). Now the (**'Student ID number'**, **'Main course'**) and (**'Student ID number'**, **'Tutor'**) pairs *are* **candidate keys**, but **Tutor** (the last of the three determinants) *is not*, therefore the table is not in BCNF. To get over this, we split Table 48.5 into two further tables, which are now in BCNF.

Querying a database

A typical **SQL** or **structured query language** uses **clauses** such as 'Select', 'From', 'Where', 'In', 'GroupBy' and 'OrderBy'. Constructs can be used in conjunction with *multiple tables*, which are **related**. The **union query** allows selection of items from different tables in the same query.

```
SELECT [CompanyName],[City]
FROM [Suppliers]
WHERE [Country] = "Brazil"


UNION SELECT [CompanyName],[City]
FROM [Customers]
WHERE [Country] = "Brazil"
```

Note the use of the syntax of the clauses 'Select', 'From' and 'Where', to perform the query. In this example [CompanyName] and [City] are fields from the Suppliers' table (top) and the Customers' table (bottom).

Don't forget that databases are created with the sole aim of extracting data via reports and queries. You need a liberal sprinkling of these in any database project.

Reporting

It is necessary to produce a written report from a database query, and both the layout, ordering and grouping of the data within the report may be formatted in a variety of ways. Consider the following Microsoft Access SQL code:

```
SELECT LastName, FirstName
FROM Employees
ORDER BY LastName;
SELECT LastName, FirstName
FROM Employees
ORDER BY LastName ASC;
```

The **Orderby** clause is used to sort the output from a query, report or table into some order, like alphabetical ascending, (ASC), as shown. The **Groupby** clause combines records into a single record so that you can perform some aggregate function, like generating statistics.

Database server

A database server is a machine that holds a shared database. It is usually a file server in a network environment, giving people access to the shared database via an **LAN**, or via a **VPN** and the **Internet**, for example. The operation of a database server is similar in principle to running a local database, with the exception of security and multiple users. The security is arranged so that unauthorised personnel do not have access to inappropriate data.

Object-oriented databases

A table is an object. Microsoft's Jet database engine is partly object oriented, and allows programmers to program the Jet database directly through a programming language called **DAO** or **Data Access Objects**.

Self-test questions

1 Give an example of a typical problem that could occur if data in a database is not stored in first normal form.
2 Give an example of a typical problem that could occur if data in a database is not put into second normal form.
3 Give an example of a typical problem that could occur if data in a database is not put into third normal form.

In this unit you have learned about:

- Second and third normal forms
- Normalisation to BCNF (Boyce Codd normal form)
- Queries, reports, database servers and object-oriented databases

49 Further systems development

In this section you will learn about:

- Methods of gathering information
- Reporting techniques
- Data flow diagrams
- ER diagrams
- Data dictionaries
- Volumetrics

This unit develops material covered in unit 25 from an AS perspective. Here you are expected to use this methodology in your A2 project work.

When doing your own projects have a bank of questions ready before you interview your client.

Systems development and data modelling

The techniques of **modelling data** shown here are essential in industry and commerce. Some of the methods have already been covered in the AS modules, and will only be dealt with briefly. You should apply these, and other methods covered in the AS project modules to your A2 project work.

Methods of gathering information

Interviewing clients and **users** of the system is a major technique. Systems analysts would usually make a list of different categories of people and **interview** them. The interviewees know the existing system much better than the analyst does, and much can be learnt here.

Example

When collecting information about possible computerisation, it is desirable to conduct interviews to gather important information. Name *three* other methods, giving reasons why you might use them.

Solution

(1) If the system is operating manually, or an older system is being updated, then **observation** is a useful technique. You can make notes about how the current system operates, and think up possible improvements. Making notes about the **data flow** between individuals or departments is particularly useful, and new suggestions can often cut down on the time taken to do things.

(2) You can design a **questionnaire** to conduct a survey. It is important to frame questions carefully so that useful information is obtained, and answers are unambiguous.

(3) You could review the **existing paperwork**, to see if any of the current methods used are still useful, and see if it is possible to devise ways of improving the existing system. Useful paperwork includes **invoices, filing systems, instruction manuals** and ways of **communication** between staff. Checks should be made regarding the relevance.

It is important to **analyse** the results with the least hassle. What happens if you do not understand an answer to a questionnaire? If the respondent is anonymous, you will not be able to go back and ask the person to clarify points.

The **observation** part of the proceedings can give useful insights. If people have been using a method for years, they do not question existing ways. A stranger observing what is going on can often detect if things can be improved.

Examination of **existing paperwork**, existing manuals or other documentation is helpful. If manuals are available they will list what should be done. It is only by observation that you determine if this is what is actually done!

Reporting techniques

After gathering the information using a variety of techniques such as **questionnaires**, **interviews** and **observations**, you need to catalogue the results of your findings in a form suitable for the **systems analyst report**. A variety of methods are available to do this.

Data flow diagrams

Data flow diagrams help to get an idea of how data is moved around. By using a data flow diagram you are able to see the source of the data, what processes need to be applied to the data, and what outputs to expect. The data flow diagram may also include the people involved in these processes.

Example

Time sheets (showing hours worked) must be processed; so validated data is entered into the computer for the weekly payroll run. Show, by making use of a dataflow diagram, how these forms are likely to be processed during the data-entry phase.

Solution

One possible scenario is shown in Figure 49.1. It indicates what happens to the paperwork if errors are detected. Obvious errors, like data being omitted might be detected before the data is entered into the system, and can be corrected by passing the form back to the employee. The computer could detect less obvious errors, like an incorrect date, and the form is again passed back to the employee for rectification.

Other types of diagram and systems' development tools can be found in chapter 15 of NUCSAL.

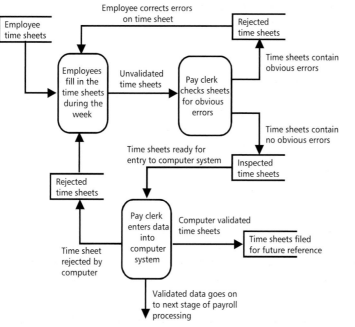

Figure 49.1 A data flow diagram.

Don't forget to question each stage of the manual process. It is no good mirroring an inefficient process. Analyse each stage to see if more efficient ways exist. It is the job of the analyst to see if the existing methods can be improved. Just because something has been done for many years does not mean it is the best way. Data flow diagrams can often highlight inefficient methods, or point to better ways of carrying out the processes.

EAR modelling

An **EAR** (often called **ER**) diagram is an **entity attribute relationship** diagram. As seen in unit 47, they are particularly useful when building up a **relational database**. An **entity** is a single thing of interest that is to be modelled, for example, a 'car', a 'person' or a 'sales order'. An entity is represented on an **ER diagram** in a rectangular box as shown in Figure 49.2.

A **relationship** can exist between different entitles like 'a customer places an order', or 'a person likes a car'. Here the relationships would be 'places' and 'likes'. A simple ER diagram, showing the relationship between the person and the car is shown in Figure 49.2(a).

An **attribute** describes some property of an entity. If we are modelling a customer who is interested in buying a car, the customer might have attributes like 'bank account number', 'address' or 'customer number'. If an attribute is shown on an ER diagram, then conventionally it is shown inside a bubble, and the customer attributes described above are shown in Figure 49.2(b). An alternative is to show the entity inside the square box as shown in Figure 49.2(c). The car will also have lots of attributes like 'engine size', 'model' and 'colour', for example, and these are shown in Figure 49.(2)d.

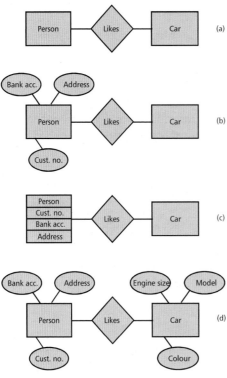

Figure 49.2 ER or EAR representations.

The relationship shown in Figure 49.2 (i.e. person likes car) is an example of a **one-to-one relationship**. Many-to-one relationships, like 'a customer may place many orders' is modelled using a slight modification of the diagram like that shown in Figure 49.3.

Figure 49.3 A many to one relationship.

In this case the **entity** usually refers to a **table**, of which the individual records are particular instances of the entity, and the **attributes** usually refer to **fields** within a record.

Example

Students study a variety of courses. Derive a simple EAR diagram showing the relationship 'Studies'. You may assume any suitable attributes for your chosen entities.

Solution

One possible data model is shown in Figure 49.4

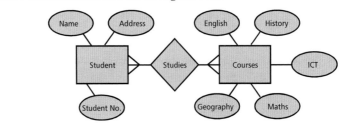

Figure 49.4 EAR diagram for students.

Data dictionary

A **data dictionary** is data about the data. It is information about managing data for a system, and detailed information can be entered into the data dictionary. Data dictionaries are often associated with relational database management systems, but are also used more generally than this. They can be applied to data about any system, computerised or not.

One of the entries in a data dictionary might be as follows:

A simple data dictionary entry	
Name	The name of the data element
Data type	e.g. integer, long integer, real, date, currency of string etc.
Size	e.g. 4 byte, 256 characters etc.
Domain	This would consist of acceptable values of the data. For example, integers only between 0 and 65,536.
Units of measurement	e.g. feet, yards or miles, etc.
Links	Possible links to other data in a database, or on a website, for example.
Comments	There may be special situations in which the data can take on some specific meaning.
Etc.	Lots of other attributes may be appropriate for different systems.

The data dictionary can be a long list of **data attributes** that defines each data element within a system. It is a good idea to produce a data dictionary for your own project.

Volumetrics

It is important to have an appreciation of how much data might have to be processed in a given amount of time. A print run of 100 copies/day would need very different design requirements compared with a print run of 1 000 000 copies/day. The software and hardware required would be different. It is unlikely that **volumetric data** would affect projects at 'A' level, but in industry it is vital to get large systems working efficiently.

Self-test questions

1   When planning to computerise a system, observation of the existing system is vital. Suggest two different reasons for this.
2   Explain how ER (EAR) diagrams can play an important role when modelling data, especially when building up the models for a database. Give an example.
3   What does a data dictionary mean? Give two different examples of entries.
4   Why is it necessary to consider volumetrics when designing a project?

In this unit you have learned about:

- Methods of **gathering information**
- Reporting
- **Data flow diagrams**
- **ER diagrams**
- **Data dictionaries**
- **Volumetrics**

You must have a data dictionary in your A2 project work, especially if you are undertaking a database project.

Visit our portal for some good practical examples of volumetrics.

In this section you will learn about:

- User characteristics, designing a system and system flowcharts
- Prototyping
- Some testing strategies

Characteristics of users

Understanding **characteristics of users** helps you design a more effective project. You are more likely to get the **user interface** correct if you understand the people who will use it.

Example

Suggest characteristics of users that help during the information-gathering phase of a project. Suggest a hierarchy of job descriptions that might exist in a company that develops computer games, and how characteristics of the users in this particular scenario might influence project development.

Solution

Who are the line managers? How do individual departments interact? What functions do individual workers within the system carry out? A **hierarchical diagram** is useful to describe the hierarchy of authority or areas of responsibility, and **dataflow diagrams** (unit 49) help with interaction regarding movement of data. A possible diagram for a games software company is shown in Figure 50.1. Three major departments, 'artistic', 'technical' and 'sales', are under the company director. Who controls **technical information** and the flow of information between the design team and programmers? How is this managed? Who makes sure the projects are on **schedule**? If a problem exists which customer support cannot handle, how is it passed over to the technical department and dealt with? It is likely that key personnel will have multiple roles, and the analysts must understand this.

Make sure that you understand the users for your A2 project work. Communicate with them frequently and develop a good user interface.

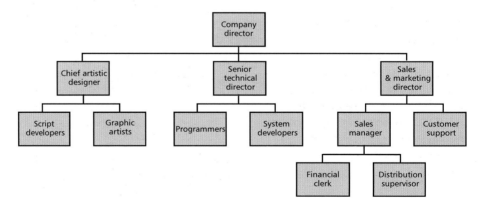

Figure 50.1 A hierarchical diagram.

Users are well defined in larger companies compared to smaller ones. In a large company it is likely that **data-entry staff** spend all day typing, and it is easy for the analyst to define this role. In a smaller company the financial clerk might also have to carry out the payroll function. The characteristics of this particular user would therefore be complex. It is possible to list job functions, and to determine if existing ways of doing things can be improved.

Designing a system

Once information regarding a system has been collected and analysed, assuming the system is **feasible**, it is time to start the design. **Systems flowcharts** are popular for doing this. Typical system-flowchart symbols are shown in Figure 50.2. These flowchart symbols are, of course, in addition to the conventional program-flowchart symbols, which include start and stop boxes, and decision symbols, for example.

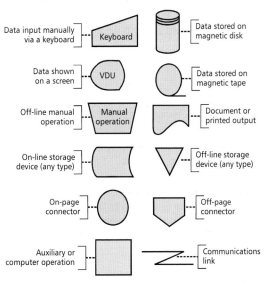

Figure 50.2 System flowchart symbols.

Look at the computerisation of Corpus Crumbly library in chapter 16 of NUCSAL for further examples of designing a system.

There are few A2 projects that would not benefit from the use of systems flowcharts.

Example

A company receives customer orders via the post. Making use of a system flowchart, show how a data-entry clerk might process these orders. Include the following:

- **Validation of customer and order items.**
- **Rejection of erroneous orders.**
- **The creation of a computerised order (transaction file) ready for use with the stock-control system.**
- **The creation of a customer invoice to be sent off in the post.**

Solution

The flowchart is shown in Figure 50.3. The data-entry clerk picks up the invoice, enters valid customer details, and creates a new transaction for this order. By referencing the stock database, the order is then processed, any entries with problems are flagged, and the invoice is passed back for correction. If the processing is successful, a customer invoice is printed out ready for sending off in the post.

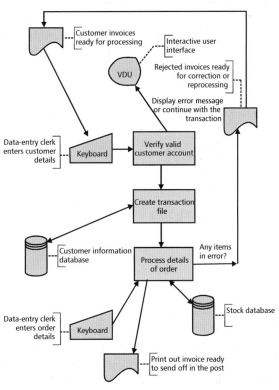

Figure 50.3 A possible systems flowchart.

Systems flowcharts are *not* detailed **program flowcharts**; they do not include all detailed processing. They are intended as a general starting point, showing major operations only. There are no unique answers, and no system flowchart is likely to be the same, except for the concepts displayed.

Prototyping

Building a **mock up** of a user interface is enormously useful. Even the best-laid plans can be put to waste if the system does not perform as expected, or if the interface is awkward to use. The users may not be able to provide any effective feedback if they have nothing concrete to work on.

Consider an interface being designed to control a piece of machinery. The **ergonomics** (the science of designing things to be used by humans in their chosen environment), must be effective, or the device might not be efficiently controlled. The ease of use, the layout of the screen, the colours used, and the information must all be thought about carefully. It is usually true that users of the system have the best ideas regarding how things should be arranged. Therefore, a **prototype** is set up to test the interface in a **simulated environment**.

Example

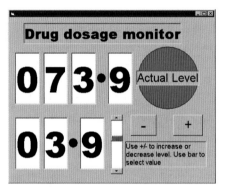

Figure 50.4 Prototype 1.

Devise two prototypes for an interface to monitor, control and activate an alarm for the level of a drug administered to a patient in an intensive care unit. The display should be easy to use, and life-threatening decisions may be taken on the basis of your analysis. Assume that the dosage of the drug is measured and adjusted in units between 0 and 100%, and must be controlled in steps of 0.1%. The nurse controls the system by instructing it to increase or decrease the drug by a set amount. Comment on the likely relative effectiveness of each interface.

Solution

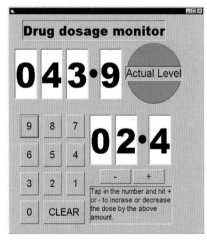

Figure 50.5 Prototype 2.

To control the dosage in 1000 steps between 0 and 1000 some digital input is essential, preferably controlled from a keyboard. Monitoring the level does not have to be controlled by the user, but we need an instant readout, and an alarm must be activated when urgent action needs to be taken. Possible prototypes are shown in Figure 50.4 and 50.5.

Aspects of the interface can be designed using alternatives, but first concentrate on the entry of dosage. In Figure 50.4, a vertical scroll bar is used to increase or decrease the dose. A touch screen could be used to activate this. The alternative in Figure 50.5, enables the user to input a figure directly via a keyboard or touch-sensitive screen. Colour is used to distinguish dangerous and safe doses. An audio alarm is needed to alert medical personnel not watching the screen. We can eliminate the '–' and '+' signs, assuming 'if the dose is too high' the number entered will reduce it, or 'if the dose is too low' the number entered will increase it.

These prototypes can be simulated quickly using an appropriate Visual Programming Language. They may represent on-screen displays, or act as simulations of a purpose-built hardware display that could be used. It is essential to get **feedback** from the users of the system, and incorporate good suggestions. An appropriate **GUI interface** is of paramount importance, and you should not ignore even small changes recommended by the users.

Specialist user interfaces

Our users might be physically disabled or visually impaired. Specialist interfaces require a lot of thought. The Windows operating system caters for people who are partially sighted, by providing very large textual and pictorial keyboards. Braile keyboards are available for people who are totally blind, and the range of input and output devices operated by various parts of the body is extensive.

Much psychology goes into the design of a user interface. An entire science has been developed with this in mind. Apple and Microsoft spend millions on perfecting the user interface. Windows, in its various incarnations, is an excellent example. We go from early examples of mice and windows at Xerox's Palo Alto research labs, via the commercial use of the GUI system by Apple, to the latest 21st century editions of Windows Me and 2000.

Top down design

This method starts at the highest level of design, and splits up a project into major parts, both for functionality and eventual coding. If a project is designed in this way it is called **top down design**, or if you design a program in this way it is called **top down programming**. A good example of the top-down approach can be seen in unit 25. Top down design is useful for large projects where teams of analysts and programmers can work on different subsections of the project. Indeed, on very large systems, many people may work on individual modules, which are also spilt up by the top down design approach.

Self-test questions

1 Suggest some characteristics of users that might influence the design of computer systems.
2 What is the purpose of a systems flowchart?
3 Why is prototyping important?
4 Suggest some considerations when prototyping a computer interface for children in a nursery school setting.
5 Suggest a specialist user interface that might be used in the following situations.
   (a) A person who is partially sighted
   (b) A person who is blind
   (c) A person who is deaf and blind
   (d) A person with poor motor control.
6 What is meant by the top-down approach to design?
7 Why are hierarchical diagrams useful when designing systems?
8 Why are GUIs particularly useful?
9 How is a VDU shown on a systems flowchart?

In this unit you have learned about:

- The characteristics of users that affect the user interface
- Designing a system
- System flowcharts
- Prototyping
- Simple testing strategies

51 Advanced testing methods

In this section you will learn about:

- Further design strategies like the bottom-up approach
- Black box testing
- White box testing
- Unit and integration testing
- Applying these methods to your A2 project work

The bottom up approach

The **bottom up approach** is useful for developing essential modules, which can then be joined together to form the larger parts of the system. The **bottom up** and **top down** approaches are variations on the same theme, and both involve much planning if the final systems are to operate smoothly.

Black box and white box testing

Black box testing is considered in unit 27. You are reminded that the system (or part thereof) is treated as a **black box**, into which salient values of variables are input and expected outputs are monitored. Extremes of data values are used to test that the system works at the limits of the design. With **black box testing** you need to know little, if anything, about the code that actually makes up the system. **White box testing** *requires an intimate knowledge of the code, and tries to ensure that all possible paths through the system have been tested*. It is possible to run complex projects for many years, and then find that a **bug** springs to light because some unusual path through the code has been taken. **White box testing** tries to trap this type of error.

It is possible to manually work through the system using white-box testing techniques, but special software can make the process easier.

White box testing is usually carried out by specialist software in industry. It is unlikely that you will have time to do this manually in your A2 project.

Look back at unit 27 for more information on black-box testing.

Example

Use white box testing to devise a test strategy for the following code:

```
if exam mark >= 40 then
  if exam mark >= 60 then
    if exam mark >=80 then
      writeln('distinction')
    else writeln('merit')
  else writeln ('pass')
else writeln ('fail')
```

Solution

First put labels on the code as follows:

```
        ENTRY POINT A
>if exam_mark >= 40 then
          B
    if exam_mark >=60 then
          C
      if exam_mark >= 80 then
          D
```

```
        writeln('distinction')
                E
      else writeln('merit')
                F
    else writeln ('pass')
                G
  else writeln ('fail')
          EXIT POINT H
```

Candidate has a distinction

Candidate does not have a distinction

Figure 51.1 Flowgraph for inner loop.

Next, construct a **flowgraph** showing possible paths through the program. Consider the flow between points D and E. There are two possibilities. Either the candidate has a distinction, in which case the middle line of code would be executed, or the candidate does not have a distinction, in which case the middle line of code is not executed. The idea is shown in Figure 51.1.

Consider the loop between points C and F. Again, this loop is either executed, or it is not. One of the possible paths contains the loop already considered in Figure 51.1, so the flowgraph between the points C and F is shown in Figure 51.2.

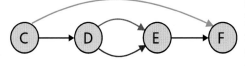

Figure 51.2 Flowgraph between C and F.

The entire program can be represented by a flowgraph using the above logic, and the final graph is shown in Figure 51.3.

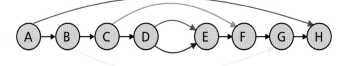

Figure 51.3 The complete flowgraph.

Arcs represent **actual code** on these diagrams. Therefore, the top most arc in Figure 51.3 will represent the path for a candidate that has failed. Next we count up the number of regions in the flowgraph, as shown in Figure 51.4.

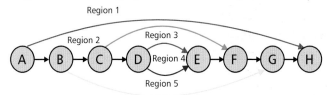

Figure 51.4 There are five different regions.

By observing Figure 51.4, we can count up five different regions, and theory shows us that there are five different possible paths through this small part of some overall larger program.

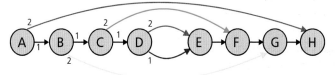

Figure 51.5 Numbers help identify the paths.

The paths through the above program, using the arc subscript numbers shown in Figure 51.5 can be identified as follows:

Path number 1 A_2-H
Path number 2 A_1-B_2-G-H
Path number 3 A_1-B_1-C_2-F-G-H
Path number 4 A_1-B_1-C_1-D_2-E-F-G-H
Path number 5 A_1-B_1-C_1-D_1-E-F-G-H

Having identified the five **unique paths** through the program, we now use **black box testing** on each individual path.

Table 51.1   Black box test data

Test data for exam loop A_2-H	
Input	Reason
0	Minimum possible number
39	Maximum integer number for this test
39.999	Non-integer valid entry
–150	Negative integer
40	No output from this loop is expected
100	No output from this loop is expected

Taking path A_2-H as an example, we must ensure that the examination mark is less than 40. Hence several examples of data < 40 should be tried. The extremes, of 39 and 0 should be included, and perhaps some erroneous data like –10. Table 51.1 shows the black-box representation for this test.

Of course, other code should be written to make sure that users could not enter non-numeric data to be processed by our system.

The other four loops need to be tested in a similar way!

NB: This example has been kept simple to illustrate some of the principles of white box testing. In practice special software would be used to test infinitely more complex systems than this.

Unit and integration testing

Most projects, whether designed by the top-down or bottom-up approaches, modularise the system into easily identifiable units. **Unit testing** is simply the exhaustive testing of each of these unit modules before being integrated into the larger system. The actual **unit testing** can be carried out by a variety of methods, including the **black box** and **white box testing** methodologies covered previously.

If **unit testing** is used, then we can join the units together one by one to form the entire system. If an error is detected in the system *after* a new unit has been added, then either the unit is at fault, or some unforeseen interaction between the rest of the system and this particular unit is occurring. Either way, it is much easier to identify the fault than would be the case with many new systems being integrated simultaneously.

When units are joined together in the ways described above, the process is referred to as **integration testing**, i.e. making sure that all the units work when being integrated into the entire system.

Applying these methods to your projects

You should use a liberal sprinkling of the methodology used in the systems development and testing sections in your own A2 project work. It would be unforgivable, for example, not to make use of **systems flowcharts** and **hierarchical modularisation** of your project into self-contained subsections. Depending on the type of project, you may also need the **EAR models** if you are designing a database, or **data-flow diagrams** if part of your project is to analyse current manual methods in some organisation.

You need to look at your mark scheme in general, and see how the marks are allocated. If, for example, quite a few marks are assigned to methods of gathering information (they

For more comprehensive white-box testing examples look at chapter 17 of NUCSAL.

probably will be), then make sure you have used standard methodology like **interviews**, **questionnaires**, and shown samples of current **data capture forms** if they are available. Do not forget also that you could design your own data capture forms specific to your project.

The whole point of the methods outlined in the **systems development** and **testing** sections is to make you aware of current methods in industry, and allow you to apply similar methods to your project work.

Do not go overboard with these methods. Although you are expected to make use of standard methods, you should use your common sense to save you a lot of work. Do not forget that marks are awarded for methods you have used. You do not usually get marks for repeatedly using the same method. Therefore, make sure you have used a variety of appropriate methods.

Take white-box testing as an example. You would not really be expected to apply these methods in your project, as they are tedious to undertake manually. In industry, more people are usually involved in testing a project than are involved with the original design. You have not got the time or the resources to test your code in this particular way. However, black box testing is relatively easy to do, and you should incorporate this at frequent intervals throughout your project testing section.

Do not forget that the examiner is trying to award you marks for testing. If you have a testing section, in which you have used many of the standard methods and applied them appropriately, then this is very easy to do. If you have a test section in which you have made no use of the standard methods, then you are unlikely to get very many marks at all, even though you might think you have tested the system.

Too many students develop systems, and then get them 'working' with little or no testing. These students can often demonstrate that their projects work well, and start to become annoyed because to them they seem to be testing something that 'obviously works'. It becomes annoying to have to go through the test procedures after they have 'finished' the system, just to get the marks for testing. However the *marks for testing constitute a large chunk of the A2 project*. It is far easier to develop a test strategy whilst you are designing the project, and then this is seen as a natural part of the development, it is more pleasant to do, and does not seem a waste of time.

Self-test questions

1 Compare and contrast the bottom up and top down design methods. Outline two typical scenarios in which each would be more appropriate than the other.
2 Describe what black box testing means, and give an example of a typical black box test.
3 White box testing provides a more comprehensive test of computer code than black box testing alone. Outline the white box testing methodology.
4 Both unit and integration testing is important. Why is this so?
5 White box testing is tedious to carry out manually, especially if the code is complex or long. What is done in industry to overcome these limitations?
6 Make a list of the key phases that should take place during systems development and testing, from the information gathering stage through to comprehensive testing of the system. What stages are to be undertaken after this?

In this unit you have learned about:

- The bottom up approach to design
- Further testing methods including **black box** and **white-box testing, unit** and **integration testing**
- How these methods may be applied in your own projects

52 System implementation and maintenance

In this section you will learn about:

- System implementation and maintenance
- Conversion using phased and parallel systems
- Pilot schemes and phases of implementation
- Acceptance testing
- Staff training
- System and technical documentation

The techniques covered in this unit are applicable to large projects.

System implementation

Once a computer system has been developed and tested (see unit 51), effort needs to be put into the **implementation phase**. This is a critical phase, as customers start to make use of the system in real-life. Techniques, borne out of experience and developed over the years, are outlined below.

The methods used depend on whether the new computer system is replacing an older system. If it is brand new, then life is easier. After testing, a **pilot scheme** could be run before going live. However, if the computerised system is replacing an old one, then problems during the changeover are likely to occur.

Conversion

This is moving from the old system to the new. It is most inadvisable to throw out the old system completely on a Friday afternoon, and start using a new system on Monday morning! It would be a brave and rather foolish analyst who implemented this particular strategy in a mission-critical system!

Each case is considered on its merits, and the implementation of a control system in a chemical factory would be very different from the implementation of a new stock control and ordering system. However, we can identify common strategies.

Parallel systems

Running the new system in **parallel** with the old system is a good option if this is possible.

Running the new system in parallel with the old system is the safest method when converting conventional business systems that have been in operation for some time. It is not without a considerable number of difficulties, not least being the fact that you operate two systems at the same time. This is frustrating for the staff, but does have the advantage that the old system kicks in if the new system goes completely wrong. A business could be destroyed if it becomes totally reliant on a new system that has not been extensively tested under live conditions.

During the **parallel running phase**, any discrepancies between the two systems must be analysed, to see whether it is the new system or the old system that is at fault. After a period of time, dictated by the volatility of the new system, the old system will be taken off line when the new system is satisfactory.

Phased systems

It might be easier if the new system is implemented in **phases**. If you are computerising a school, then reporting, examination entries, administrative tasks, etc. could all be computerised at different intervals. Each phase of the system could be checked and made good before proceeding to the next. For some projects this may not be an option, as all parts of the system might have to be operational for it to be of use.

Direct implementation

This option means going live all at once. Although risky, extensive **testing** and **prototyping** ensures that the system has few operational glitches. If the system fails, then it could be catastrophic, and patches to get the new system up and running would have to be done under conditions of extreme stress, with possible damaging consequences to the business relying on the new system.

Pilot schemes

Any system of consequence would only go live after practice runs, and this is where **pilot schemes** come in. Do not forget that this is expensive. Staff involved in the pilot scheme don't make contributions to normal business activity. Nevertheless, the considerable cost could be well spent if operational errors are encountered. Even if they are not, then the peace of mind from **dry running** the system in this way can be worthwhile.

System implementation in practice

Implementing a real system is often a combination of a number of strategies. It depends on the system being computerised, the budget available, and the time over which the system is implemented.

Never lose sight of the loss of confidence that can be generated by a system failure. A recent high profile example was the London Stock Exchange computer system, which failed on 5 April 2000. This meant that traders could not operate effectively, and there was little or no trade until 3.45 pm. This was embarrassing as it was the last day of the tax year, when investors traditionally tie up all of their investment portfolios. Although very rare indeed, a crash such as this, regarding such a high profile system, and one in which billions of pounds are at stake, goes to show how much testing is needed on mission critical systems.

Example

Whizbang.com are to launch a new web site. Whizbang products are stored using a database, and clients access stock levels and order items over the internet. Items are paid for by credit card. Suggest why direct implementation is the only available method in this case. What testing and implementation strategies are most appropriate?

Solution

After going live, the major part of the site (i.e. stock control and ordering etc.) must be operational. It must work immediately because real customers will need to use all of the facilities straight away. The project can be modularised. The order system, credit card verification, database and stock-control systems can all be tested as units, and then integrated into the whole. When the prototype site is up and running, probably via an intranet proxy server, mock customers can place fictitious orders and the whole system can be tested.

Finally, the web site can go live, but with password protection. This means that mock customers, and probably some chosen real customers too, can access the real web site on-line to check that it all works as planned. With the password-protected part of the site removed, the site is then ready to be launched.

Different phases of implementation

Once **unit** and **integration testing** (see unit 51) has been completed, it is usual to involve real customers. Most computer people are aware of **beta releases** (pre-release versions) of major software packages on the internet. Customers can download copies of software like Word 2000 or Windows 2000 etc., which are known not to be bug free. The idea is to get hundreds of thousands of people to test the software in a real environment. This pre-release phase of testing is known as **beta testing**. The initial testing is known as **alpha testing**. The software vendors hope that the users will report back any of the bugs that have come to light and the users can get their hands on the latest versions of software. The known bugs are fixed and another version of the pre-release software is then put on the internet.

Similar ideas are used where in-house software is being developed. After the software has been designed and alpha testing has taken place, in-house beta testing is used to check the system with 'real' data, making use of the personnel who will eventually use the system.

Acceptance testing

After going through all the phases of testing, it is up to the IT personnel in the users' company to **officially accept the system**. They will do this only when they are completely happy that the system is reliable, is functioning to specification, and will provide an efficient service if used by their clients. There will usually be an official hand-over date, when the programmers and analysts will no longer be involved in the day-to-day operation of the system. This is usually a little time after the system has gone live for the first time, but this is not the end of the story, and **maintenance** of the system (see later in this unit) will then take on a high priority.

Staff training

Staff need to be trained to make use of the system. From the clerk who enters the data at the terminals, to the IT personnel who will manage the system, all need to be experts in using the new system. Training must take place before the system goes live, as personnel involved in day-to-day operations will then be responsible for running the system. A **training schedule** should be set up during the development and beta-testing phases.

Example

You are to manage staff training for implementation and maintenance of a new computerised system in a large store. Over 100 users, ranging from clerical data entry to technical personnel are involved. Comment on the training options available, and salient periods in the development cycle during which this training should take place.

Solution

Staff will be split up into levels of competence. The clerical staff have different requirements to departmental managers, responsible for the day-to-day operation of the clerical side of the system. The IT managers, responsible for the technical running of the system must also be trained.

Clerical staff can usually be trained during final development. They will need to enter data, be aware of common problems like invalid data and know how to reset the system if errors occur. Training will not take more than a few days, but because of the numbers involved, it will have to be scheduled. Staff being trained will also be needed to operate the old system currently in action in the store.

The departmental managers who will look after the data-entry clerks (sales staff) in their department will need a higher level of training. They will need to be aware of the objectives of the new system, and be able to troubleshoot non-technical problems that may occur on a day-to-day basis. These departmental managers will probably have access to routines not available to the shop personnel (e.g. generation of departmental statistics and the like). These managers must be trained for a longer period of time, and would be actively involved in development and beta testing.

The technical managers who troubleshoot the system will need to be trained. These few personnel will probably have to be sent on a residential course to the software company. Training may take a few weeks or more, and these personnel would need a high standard of computer literacy. As these are key personnel, it is likely that they will be maintaining the old system too, and scheduling the entire team at the same time could prove difficult.

Simple system documentation

The documentation that accompanies a new system will vary depending on the system in question. Simple documentation like a **user manual** usually accompanies any new software release, such as that of an application package (paper-based manuals are succumbing to disk-based electronic manuals) usually in **HTML** or **Adobe Acrobat format**. These electronic manuals have a variety of advantages, namely the low cost of distribution, and the ease with which they may be searched. Windows-based help files may also accompany systems that are specifically designed for PCs.

System documentation is considered in more detail in unit 53.

Basic technical documentation

The often complex **technical documentation** should include the following items:

- The system specifications
- The design of the system
- Diagrams like hierarchical diagrams and systems flowcharts etc.
- Pseudocode
- Program listings
- Detailed file and data specifications.
- Modifications made to the system (with dates and author etc.)
- Test data with results
- Information to help maintain the system

The technical documentation here contains many of the things you need in the report for your A2 project.

Self-test questions

1. Conversion of a system to a new computerised system (even if the old system was already computerised) is a complex business. Outline some of the strategies used in practice.
2. Why is it often bad practice to completely replace an old system with a new computerised one? Under what conditions might this actually have to be done?
3. After the unit and integration testing has been carried out, it is often desirable to involve the users in the testing process. Explain the concept of beta testing, and how this usually improves the software being developed. What are the disadvantages of beta testing for the user?
4. Staff training is a vital part of the implementation of a new system. Suggest three different methods by which staff training may take place, giving the pros and cons of each method that you suggest.
5. Technical documentation usually accompanies a system. List five different parts of the technical documentation, giving reasons for their inclusion.
6. System documentation used to be supplied in huge manuals. Describe several modern methods that have replaced this. What are the advantages of these modern methods compared to the older computer manual systems? Are there any disadvantages?

In this unit you have learned about:

- Systems implementation and maintenance
- Conversion using phased and parallel implementation
- Pilot schemes
- Acceptance testing
- Staff training
- System and Technical documentation

53 Further system implementation and maintenance

In this section you will learn about:

- User documentation and installation manuals
- Operations and training manuals
- Other training methods
- Evaluation
- System maintenance
- Applying these principles to your own projects.

User documentation

User documentation varies from simple manuals, a few pages in length, to many volumes, depending on the complexity.

Installation manual

Apply some of the techniques shown here when you create the user manual for your A2 project.

If the installation of a new system is complex, an **installation manual** is needed which specifies how parts of a system may be installed. This may have to outline different **installation procedures** for different operating systems, or how to make sure that the latest versions of the drivers and other software such as a Java Virtual Machine or an Internet browser, for example, needs to be installed before the new software can be used.

If a complex system is being installed then **technical installation manuals**, used by the personnel setting up the system can be long and complex documents. These often reflect a huge degree of customisation that can be accomplished. Indeed, these manuals can run to hundreds of pages, with tick lists resembling a pre-flight check plan on a Jumbo Jet!

At the other end of the scale, a novice user might click on an installation file and the software could be automatically installed on a PC with no user interaction whatsoever. In this case the installation manual could be a single paragraph at the beginning of the user manual that explains how to click on a file. It is now common for a CD to be inserted in the drive, and the program can then **auto run** to set the system up automatically. If all goes well this is a superb method of software installation.

Essential information in the **installation manual** would usually include the following:

- Operating system
- Recommended minimum processor
- The amount of RAM required
- The amount of hard disk space needed
- The type of CD-ROM drive
- The graphics mode
- The versions of applications software with which the new software will work
- Other special hardware requirements etc.

Upgrading to new versions of software can sometimes have adverse effects on other software in the system, and these must often be upgraded too. For example, Word2000 has a single document interface, whereas Word97 has a multiple document interface. This means that Dragon Dictate (one of the speech recognition systems) does not work with Word 2000, unless you upgrade to the new version 4 or later of Dragon Dictate. Similarly, the 98 version of Encyclopaedia Britannica does not work with Internet Explorer 5, and this too has to be upgraded to a later version. You can now see why the software vendors love **beta testing**. It enables tens of thousands of people to test their software in hundreds of thousands of different computer configurations.

The installation of new software is often fraught with difficulty, and **technical help lines** are an essential part of being able to guide the user through the many things that may need altering.

The internet comes to the rescue if you need the latest versions of software drivers or need to download new versions of browsers or virtual machines. The internet also has the manufacturers' sites which answer **frequently asked questions (FAQs)**, and many other sites may also be of help, including UseNet user groups dedicated to getting operating systems or other specialist software up and running. Most technical departments dealing with software installation would not be able to function efficiently without the enormous number of resources now available on the net.

User manual

The **user manual** might also contain the installation instructions, but concentrates primarily on enabling users to make effective use of the new software after it has been successfully installed.

The user manual can be used either in a **training role**, or as a **reference** if the user needs to learn something new, or has forgotten how to do a particular process. It is usual for the manual to be extensively cross-referenced, and to take the user through virtually every conceivable operation that can be undertaken with the system. It should contain many different examples, and contain a large variety of screen captures showing the system in operation. It should be easy to use by non-technical staff, and above all it should be easy to find information contained within it.

The user manual may be split up into many different sections for ease of use. Some of the general ideas could be as follows:

- Introduction to the system
- Getting started
- Elementary operations
- Tutorials
- Advanced operations
- Reference sections
- Index

It is likely that electronic versions of the manual will be available to the operators of the system.

The operations manual

This type of manual documents **operational procedures** such as 'preparation of data' and other manual techniques. It could document which departments are responsible for different parts of the system, and who takes control of particular processes. If the procedures in the operations manual are followed, then the system should run smoothly. These procedures should have been fine-tuned during the development stages of the project, but will need to be placed under continuous review in the light of real experience.

Training manual

Specialist **training manuals** can be provided, either as a stand-alone book, or for use with a training course. They are often not the same as the **user guide**, which is intended to deal with *ad hoc* queries on a day-to-day basis.

The training manual could be split up into different sections, depending on the level of the staff being trained, or be issued as totally separate books. The role of this manual is to

The documentation, which accompanies large system installations, takes many people months to write. Do not try to emulate this level of detail in your A2 projects.

provide a comprehensive course taking the users from little or no knowledge about the system, up to and including expert level.

The training manual may be accompanied by a simulated system, which takes the users through different scenarios, including dealing with problems and other expected errors that may occur. The training manual could be issued electronically on a CD-ROM, or distributed via the internet, where it can be viewed with a conventional web browser. Distance learning techniques and use on a PC at home can easily be accomplished via these electronic methods.

Other training methods

You must not forget also that all the above documentation can go hand in hand with conventional **teacher-based training methods**. **Lectures**, **demonstrations**, discussions, computer-based presentations like Power Point, **videos** and **simulated teamwork** all play a role when training. The increased motivation when working with other people on a training course should not be underestimated, and time spent away from the job on training is usually quite productive.

Evaluation

Once a project has been successfully up and running for a few months it is essential to have an **evaluation**. This evaluation should be attempted sooner if there are pressing problems with the current system.

Feedback from users is essential here, and **constructive criticism** must be taken seriously. Designers of a new system ignore what the users think at their peril, and usually act to alter parts of the project not going well.

Example

A new project has been up and running for a few months. Outline some of the methods, that may be used to evaluate the effectiveness of the project.

Solution

A complete audit of the project is necessary to evaluate its effectiveness. Are there any errors in the systems that have not yet been corrected? Are the users happy with the efficiency of the system, or is it more difficult to operate than originally intended? Has extra stress been put on the users, or is the system running smoothly? Are people having to work harder or longer hours to operate the new system? Have there been any complaints from customers regarding the new system?

New projects are bound to have teething problems, and they should be identified at **audit** and dealt with. If this is not done then the users and customers will become disillusioned with the new system and the business will ultimately suffer. Further audits will be required at longer intervals, until the system is running as effectively as possible.

System maintenance

Even if a system is running perfectly, after a period of time, the needs of a customer may change, and the system should be able to grow accordingly. If the system has been designed properly, then this should make it easier to change at a later date.

The **documentation** that accompanies a system is the *key* to its **efficient maintenance**. If the system has been **modularised** properly then new modules may be added more easily. The object-oriented programming methodology outlined in unit 41 will also help considerably towards this goal. Any modular additions or alterations should ideally not affect any other modules in the system.

If, as is likely, mistakes are discovered some considerable time after the system has been in operation, then the technical documentation is the key to sorting out the problems quickly. It is likely that the people who programmed the original system will not be available, and even if they are, they will probably not remember exactly how things work, unless they refer to the technical documentation.

System flowcharts, **structure diagrams**, well written **code** with **comments**, and helpful programmer's notes all go a long way to making it easier to code new modules that will work well with the existing system. Any new modules must also undergo rigorous **testing** and **evaluation**, just like the procedures to which the original project was subjected.

Applying these techniques to your own projects

The principles outlined here are important. Your A2 project should, for example, contain a **user manual**. It is unlikely to be like the user manuals described here. Even so, it should have a section on the **system requirements**, a **getting started section** and a '**what to do if errors occur**' section. Your **technical documentation** (i.e. a large part of your project report) should suffice for the technical documentation and **system maintenance**. It is unlikely that you will need to write an **operations manual**, as these strategically important documents would probably not be appropriate for a project of the magnitude that you will undertake at A2 level.

You should appreciate the importance attached to the system maintenance part of the project when projects are undertaken in the real world. In your case you will probably be undertaking your degree work when any project you have written for 'A' level goes wrong. It is unlikely that you will be available to help sort out problems, unless, of course, you have written the project for a relative or friend.

Do not forget that you should not promise that any part of your A2 project is going to work perfectly forever! As you have seen in this section, even the experts cannot do this, and you are much less likely to be able to do so.

Look at the mark scheme for your project in detail, and make sure that you have all the documentation required for your board.

Self-test questions

1 A user manual should contain instructions for the installation of software. What other components will probably be present? What techniques might be useful to make the software as easy to install as possible.
2 A training manual may accompany large systems. What other techniques could be used to enhance the training of new users?
3 Evaluation of a new computer-based system is usually carried out after it has been in operation for a short period of time. Outline the feedback that is usually obtained during this period, and the likely methods of providing technical solutions to any of the problems that may be encountered.
4 A well-designed and implemented computer system has been in operation for a few years. Why is this system likely to become unsatisfactory eventually?
5 Carefully explain what happens during the maintenance phase of software implementation.

In this unit you have learned about:

- What goes into installation manuals
- The contents of user documentation
- The operations and training manuals and other training methods
- Evaluation and system maintenance and applying these methods to your projects

54 Basic internet structures

You can be 'expert' at surfing the Net without realising how it operates. You will not get away with this superficial level of knowledge at AS or A2 level.

The internet

The **internet** is a vast collection of computers communicating with each other making use of the **TCP/IP protocol**. At its heart lies the high-speed interconnections that link the **node computers**, which manage the computer data by effectively **routing** it around the world.

IP addresses

Each computer connected directly to the internet needs a **unique ID**. This is given by a set of numbers called the **Internet Protocol** or **IP address**. The current IP address format is a 32-bit number, split up into groups of four. Although routing computers make effective use of IP addresses, humans prefer a more user-friendly system of **domain names**. As an example, if you make a call to NatWest's on-line banking service, the full domain name, including the protocol, is given by '**https//:www.nwolb.co.uk**'. However, after being typed into the browser, this would be converted into the 32-bit number '**62.172.189.210**', which is the **IP address** for this particular subsection of the '**.uk**' **domain**.

Domain names

The internet is organised hierarchically by the **domain name system** or **DNS**. At the top level are the '.com' or '.org' domains etc. We have one unique name for each domain; therefore, 'www.widget.com' may be a different company from 'www.widget.co.uk'. We are rapidly running out of domain names, and so new domains like '.web', have been developed. The '.com' names are the most prestigious.

Internet registries

A registry is a **database**, held on special computers placed at strategic points on the internet, so people can use domain names easily. A **name server**, also called a **host**, is needed to perform the function of converting the **domain names** into the **IP** addresses. These are provided by ISPs (Internet Service Providers) such as CompuServe and AOL, for example. The registry itself contains only the domain names, IP numbers and server names. No personal information concerning the person or company owning the domain name is present. At the top of the hierarchy are some **root servers** that contain authoritative data for the 'com', 'net', 'fr' and 'uk' etc. domains. These are located in the USA, UK, Sweden and Japan.

Internet registrars

Internet registrars are companies that register domain names for individuals and other companies with the **primary domain name servers**, like '123 Domain Names UK' for example. Many companies can allocate unused domain names, and are examples of internet registrars.

The client server model

You are already aware of the **client server model** from an LAN point of view, i.e. many different servers providing a range of functions such as application delivery, database access and other local information. You can imagine the entire internet to operate on this strategy too, with millions of servers and hundreds of millions of clients connected to them. The **domain name servers** deal with **routing requests**, the **root servers** organise the system world wide, and millions of other servers host individual sites. The **client-server model** of the internet sums this up exactly.

The HTTP protocol

HTTP, or **hypertext transfer protocol**, is the method by which pages are transferred from Web servers to the browser on your local machine. For example, the **URL** (**uniform resource locator**) for NatWest on-line banking is as follows:

https//:www.nwolb.co.uk

The **http protocol** is being used. The '**s**' at the end stands for '**secure**', which in this case allows for the use of **128-bit encryption** through a **secure port** to NatWest Bank's computer.

The structure of a web site

Once you have entered the URL for a particular site, you are directed to the main page of the site.

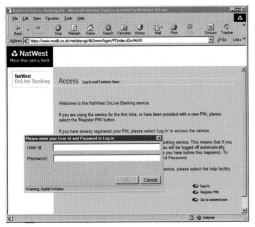

Figure 54.1 The screen for secure banking.

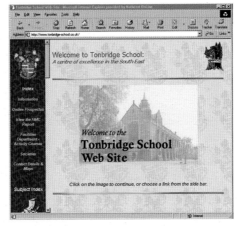

Figure 54.2 Part of a main page.

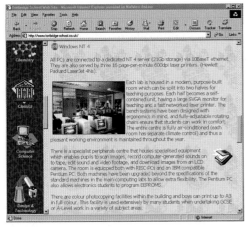

Figure 54.3 The computing page.

The main log-on screen for NatWest banking is shown in Figure 54.1. As the **https (secure)** protocol is being used, the **padlock**, displayed in the bottom right-hand side of the browser confirms that we have a **secure link**. In addition to this, after clicking over the 'log in' **hyperlink** on the secure screen shown in Figure 54.1, the user is prompted to enter his or her user ID and password. A **Java Applet** controls the box shown in Figure 54.1.

Web page organisation

At some stage in your course you should have developed a web site. If not, if you have time, make one up. It will make the principles here easier to understand.

Web sites are organised **hierarchically**. If you design a site for your school or college, you would need a main page to greet people when they first log onto the site. The opening page for Tonbridge School is shown in Figure 54.2

Users click the centre image to enter the main pages. They can also click over **hyperlinks** on the left-hand side of the page to visit areas like the 'on-line prospectus', 'societies' or get an 'on-line map' if they wish to visit the school.

Users scroll down the left-hand frame to visit departments like 'Maths', 'Physics' or 'Computing'. The computing page is shown in Figure 54.3. Organisation of the site is obvious, and Figure 54.4 shows the root directory of the site, where an **HTML (HyperText Mark up Language)** document called **index.htm** is located. On the right-hand side of Figure 54.4, the directory contains folders, which mirror the **hierarchical structure** of the site.

On the left of Figure 54.4 we have opened up the 'subjects folder', which contains other folders, in which resources are held. Figure 54.5 shows resources inside the computing folder.

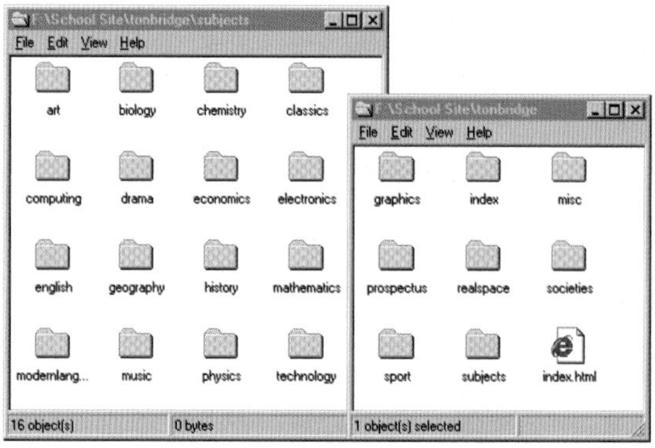

Figure 54.4 Structure for Tonbridge School.

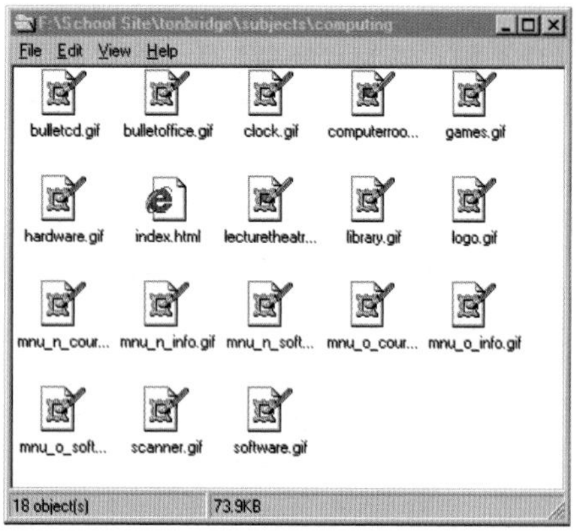

Figure 54.5 Computing resources.

Figure 54.5 shows an individual html page called index, which is the page displayed in Figure 54.3. You also have the gif files, which are the pictures displayed on the computer department page. The picture of the computer room, displayed in Figure 54.3 is called 'computerroom.gif'. The **site** is organised in a **hierarchical** way, with resources belonging to each directory contained within easily identifiable folders.

Example

Suggest a suitable web-site structure for a large shop selling electrical goods from washing machines to video recorders. You should take into account the fact that the customers can buy goods on line.

Solution

The goods customers buy can be categorised into main sections. The following is typical:

- **Household** (washing machines etc.)
- **Sound and Vision** (video recorders etc.)
- **Personal electrical** (shavers etc.)
- **Computers** (PCs, printers etc.)

In practice there may be other categories, but the above is suitable for illustrative purposes.

For extra material on the internet look at chapter 4 of NUCSAL.

Typically each of the above categories would have subsections. For example, the 'Sound and Vision' category could be split up as follows:

Video Recorders	**TVs**
Hi-fi	**DVD players** etc.

Each section could then have a picture of the devices, together with general information and price, and a hyperlink over which you could click to add the device to your order. It might, however, be preferable to split up these sections further. The TV section could be split into 'portable', 'conventional' and 'wide screen'.

The ordering system itself would be a major subsection. It could consist of the typical shopping-trolley idea, into which customers can make up their order. The customers would have to be confident with the system, and secure transactions using a credit card would need to be implemented. You would also need help, contact addresses, and store information if the chain had more than one branch. Therefore, the following are typical of the main categories that need to be added:

- **Secure ordering system**
- **Help system** (use of site, place an order)
- **Company contact** (address + telephone number + email)
- **Search engine** (a means of searching the site for specific information)
- **Other information** (e.g. special offers or new lines etc.)
- **Branch information** (locate the stores within this group)

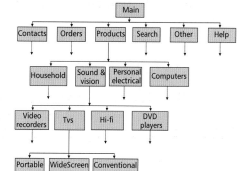

A hierarchical structure diagram, showing the salient features of the web site is shown in Figure 54.6.

Figure 54.6 A possible structure.

Self-test questions

1 What is an IP address?
2 What is the difference between an Internet registry and an Internet registrar?
3 What is a domain name? Give an example.
4 What is the difference between the internet and the WWW?
5 What is meant by the http protocol?
6 What does https stand for?
7 How are web pages usually organised?
8 Suggest a suitable web-site structure for a shop that sells recorded music.
9 What is a domain name server?
10 What is a root server?

In this unit you have learned about:

- IP addresses
- Domain names, registries
- The client server model
- The HTTP protocol
- The structure of web sites and web page organisation

55 Further web site organisation

In this section you will learn about:

- Web page construction
- Hyperlinks and other features
- HTML and WYSIWYG editors
- Database links
- FTP and Telnet

The HTML language

The language behind web-site construction is called **HTML**, or **HyperText Markup Language**. A web page is an HTML file, usually with extra graphics and maybe other resources like JavaScript. The file is made up from text-based HTML commands.

By all means use a specialist web-design package like FrontPage 2000, but you need some knowledge of HTML too.

Any web site can be constructed using a simple **text editor** like notepad. All you have to do is to type in the **HTML commands**, and you can construct a satisfactory site. The structure of a simple HTML file is as follows:

```
<HTML>
   <HEAD>
   </HEAD>
   <BODY>
      Hello
   </BODY>
</HTML>
```

The HTML commands are contained within **<tags>**, many of which come in pairs. The start of the HMTL document is given by **<HTML>** and the end is given by **</HTML>**. No heading information is used in this example, and the body consists of the single word 'Hello'. When viewed in a browser, we get the site shown in Figure 55.1. Very sophisticated sites can be constructed like this – it is quite easy as long as you learn **HTML**.

Figure 55.1 Running the HTML code.

The hyperlinks

Hypertext links can be placed anywhere on the page. For example, the index list, on the left-hand side of Figure 54.3, has many **hyperlinks**. Some of the **HTML** code, for the Computer Science and Design Technology departments is shown below and on the next page.

```
<p> 
<p>
<a
href="../subjects/computing/index.html"
target="mainframe"><img
src="indxcompsci.gif" border=0><br>
Computer Science</a>
```

```
<p> 
<p>
<a
href="../subjects/technology/index.html
" target="mainframe"><img
src="indxtech.gif" border=0><br>
Design &amp; Technology</a>
```

This code is in two near-identical parts. Note the syntax of the lines starting with **'href'**, which shows a **relative path name**. Resources are created in a **hierarchical way**, as it is easy to misplace images belonging to a particular part of the site. If the site is arranged as a suitable set of sub directories, you can transfer the whole lot, as is, when you publish the site. This is why the **relative path names**, shown above, are essential. If you use **absolute path names** such as `'C:\index\subject'`, for example, this will not work when you publish to the Web, because the C drive on your local machine is not available.

Other features

Get familiar with designing web sites. Use facilities like **animated gifs** (a set of gif files played in sequence to give the appearance of motion), **marquees** (scrolling text), **counters** and **e-mail** etc. Some of these features, like counters, only work when the web site is published, or put on a proxy server, because special server-side features are needed.

HTML editors

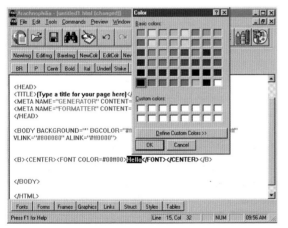

Figure 55.2 Using an HTML editor.

Instead of a **text-based editor**, you can use an **HTML editor** like Arachnophilia. This enables you to create web sites much more easily than coding HTML directly.

In Figure 55.2 the user has highlighted the word 'Hello', applied the bold and centre style, and chosen a colour from the colour menu. The user has *not* had to type any HTML code; the editor generated this automatically as shown below:

```
<B><CENTER><FONT COLOR=#00ff00><FONT
COLOR=>Hello</FONT></FONT></CENTER></B>
```

Without a specialist **HTML editor**, the user would have to work out colours from the RGB components (see unit 2). Looking at the `<FONT COLOR= #00ff00>`, Red and Blue are turned off, but Green is set to FF (Hex for 255) which is maximum. The word will be in green.

WYSIWYG HTML editors and web site creation tools

Web-site design is even easier with a **WYSIWYG HTML editor**. The operations outlined in the last section would consist of centring the word 'hello', applying the bold style, highlighting the word 'hello', and then applying green. The user would see no HTML code whatsoever. However, specialist web-site creation packages go much further than this.

As with any major project, it is the organisational structure to your web site that is crucial. Without proper organisation, it will not work properly if published.

Figure 55.3 A corporate web site.

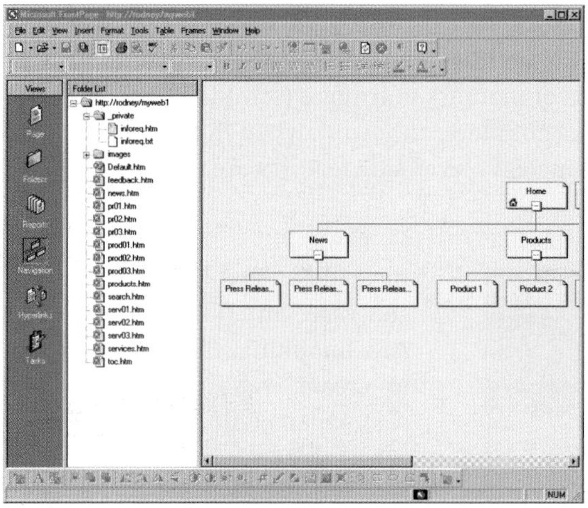

Figure 55.4 A site hierarchical diagram.

Using a package like Microsoft's FrontPage is much easier than learning to code or using a specialist HTML editor. Indeed, for the novice, you do not have to know that the HTML language is behind the design of the site. You could create a business web site with FrontPage 2000's Corporate Presence Web Wizard, where you are presented with a large number of options. You are asked if you want a company logo, if you want an e-mail contact or if you want a feedback form? Accepting the defaults, gives the results shown in Figure 55.3.

A particular **theme** (consistent style) for the site is chosen, and the user can change this style, even after the site has been designed. This is trivial, compared to manual alteration of the HTML code to achieve the same result. An entire directory structure has been set up to sort out the site into folders, and many default pages have been constructed. These are shown on the left-hand side of Figure 55.3.

A useful **hierarchical diagram** can also be generated, and this is shown in Figure 55.4.

Example

List some advantages and disadvantages of designing a web site using an HTML editor, compared to using a package like Microsoft's FrontPage, for example.

Solution

A novice can use a web-site creation tool in a similar way to a word processor without the need to understand HTML code. If everybody used these facilities then most sites on the internet would look very similar.

Often the code produced by a package such as FrontPage is not the most efficient possible, and this can be a disadvantage in terms of speed. Not all ISPs provide appropriate facilities for some specialist packages. Sites constructed using conventional HTML facilities will always work. If something goes wrong with the development of the site then knowledge of HTML code is definitely needed.

Database links

A simple web site will not be enough for an A2 project. However, add some JavaScript and/or Java, and link it is to a database on the server, then it is an ideal A2 project.

Linking a web site to a **database** is important if you wish to provide facilities like ordering goods and paying by credit card. You can create **forms**, which the user fills in to send information back to the server. The information at the server end is then processed, and interacts with a database, which probably resides on the server. In this way, information typed into boxes at the browser end will be able to be processed as though it were being entered into the records of a database at the server end.

FTP

The **FTP (file transfer protocol)** is currently the most common way to publish a site. Using the 'Cute FTP software' is one way of doing this, as shown in Figure 55.5. If you have designed your site making use of **relative path names** suggested earlier, have used a suitable **directory structure**, and have a **main html file** labelled '**index.html**' in the **root directory**, it is ready to be published.

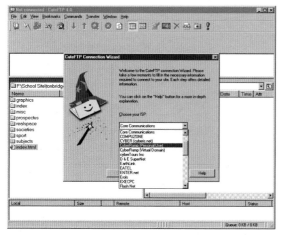

Figure 55.5 Cute FTP used to publish a site.

From Figure 55.5 you can see that the site, constructed and saved on the hard disk is identified by Cute FTP and displayed in the left-hand window. You then run a Wizard, into which you type information regarding your **ISP**, a label to identify the site, the address of the **FTP server**, a default directory from which to obtain the site, and, most importantly, a **user ID** and **password**, which will be used to help manage the site.

Once you have made the **FTP transfer** your site is up and running. Software packages like Cute FTP also enable you to manage your site effectively. You can make a change to one or just a few pages without having to upload the entire site again.

Telnet

Telnet is a **protocol** enabling users to manage a remote computer connected to the internet. A **Telnet terminal** is shown in Figure 55.6.

After logging on, assuming that you have the appropriate privileges on the remote computer, it is as though you are sitting at the keyboard of the remote computer. The **Telnet console** operates in a very similar way to a **conventional DOS-based window**.

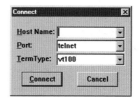

Figure 55.6 A Telnet terminal.

Self-test questions

1 What is HTML and why is it important?
2 What is a hyperlink?
3 Outline some of the features offered in an HTML editor.
4 What is a WYSIWYG HTML editor?
5 What is a feedback form on a web page?
6 How might a web page be linked to a database?
7 What is FTP and why is it used?
8 What is an FTP server?
9 What is Telnet and why is it useful?
10 Why must your site be properly organised before being published to the Web?
11 How might you publish a web site?

In this unit you have learned about:

- HTML, hyperlinks and other features
- Some HTML and WYSIWYG editors
- How to create database links
- FTP and Telnet protocols

56 Search engines and browsers

In this section you will learn about:

- Internet search engines
- Search techniques
- URLs
- Web browsers
- WAP enabled browsers

Internet search engines

To locate information on the web we make use of a **search engine** like **Yahoo**, for example. This search engine is shown in Figure 56.1.

At this level you should know more than just how to use a browser or a search engine, for instance you should know the difference between search engines and meta search engines.

Figure 56.1 Yahoo's search engine.

When adding URLs to the favourites list in your browser, don't go too deeply into the site. Individual html pages often change position with minor revisions of the site.

Figure 56.2 Searching for 'Cute FTP'.

For example, finding the Cute **FTP software** (see unit 55) to upload a web site, typing Cute+FTP or 'Cute FTP' into the engine may get the results shown in Figure 56.2.

Without using a ' + ' sign or putting the words in quotes, then the engine might find all sites with the word 'Cute' and all sites with the word 'FTP', but most search engines try to obtain an **intelligent default** if you fail to do this. The intelligent default would give the most likely combinations to start with.

At the bottom of Figure 56.2 the Cute FTP download has been found. You are directed to download the software from GlobalSCAPE's web site. Without the use of search engines like **Yahoo**, **AltaVista** and **Dogpile**, for example, finding things on the web would be virtually impossible.

When performing a search you are not actually searching the entire web, but searching a **database**, or **several databases** compiled by one or more search engines. There are basically two types of **search engine**. Ones that compile their own databases, and ones that search other search engines, called **meta search engines**. **Dogpile** is an example of this.

The search engines that compile their own databases do so by employing electronic robots called 'bots', which go trawling the web pages compiling lists of key words. It is also possible to submit the address of your own site to be added to a particular search-engine database.

Search techniques

You should refine your search techniques and use the **Boolean operators** like **AND**, **OR** and **NOT** when necessary. Also, make use of the **+ sign for inclusion** and the **– sign for exclusion**. Also, do not forget that many search engines have advanced search options, and remember to make use of the 'help' if you're not sure of the syntax for a particular engine.

Example

Using appropriate syntax for a search engine with which you are familiar, suggest a search string for each of the following search criteria. You must ensure that only the appropriate sites are listed, eliminating unwanted possibilities.
(a) Search for the computer programming language called Python
(b) Search for the Python reptile
(c) Search for Monty Python.

Solution

The following are suggested syntax for finding the above information quickly:
(a) Python -Monty -Snake
(b) Python + Snake
(c) Python + Monty

It is usually obvious if you have clashed with another use of a word, and the above search strings can easily be built up if you inadvertently hit on your search words being used in a different context.

URLs in more detail

A **URL** is a **uniform resource locator**, which is effectively an **address** on the **web**. It consists of a **protocol** like **http** or **ftp**, the name of the **server** on which the site is hosted, and perhaps the path name of the particular html document of interest. For example, at the time of writing, the html document, representing the Sunday Times front page is at the following address:

```
http://www.sunday-
times.co.uk/news/pages/times/frontpage.
html
```

http is the **hypertext transfer protocol**

The **'server'** on which the site resides is

```
//www.sunday-times.co.uk
```

The individual html page is located within the web site hierarchy at

```
/news/pages/times/frontpage.html
```

By typing in a **complete URL** for a document you can go straight to a specific page of interest on a specific site, but *individual pages do change frequently as sites are restructured.*

Web browsers

To surf the net you need an **internet browser**. The two most popular browsers are Microsoft's **Internet Explorer** and Netscape's **Navigator**. Both provide a similar degree of functionality, enabling users to surf the net, compile lists of favourites, print or save web sites, manage **secure transactions** using strong **encryption techniques** and provide a history of what you have done to name but a few.

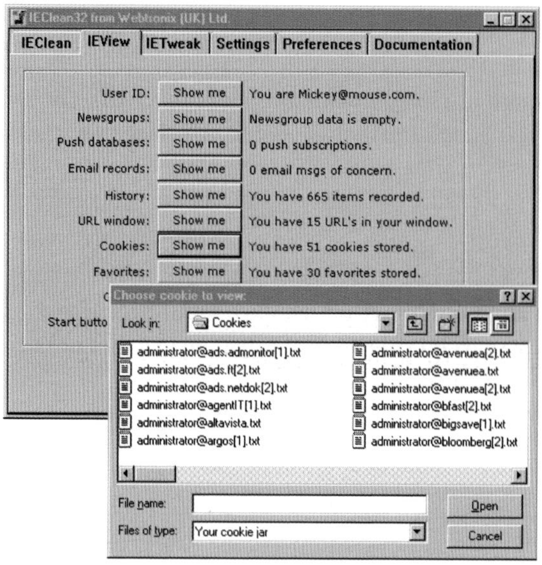

Browsers organise and store a large amount of information. Running the IE clean software from WebTronix, for example, as shown in Figure 56.3, reveals information about **User ID** (which can be set as an alias to prevent junk mail from sites you are visiting), **Newsgroups**, **push databases, e-mail records, histories, URL windows, cookies, favourites, caches** and **start documents**.

Your internet habits, sites you have visited, and what you do on a day-to-day basis leave a trail of information, which can easily be stored. Figure 56.3 also shows the **cookies directory**, containing 51 different

Figure 56.3 Information stored by browsers.

cookies stored from recently visited sites. A **cookie** is information, placed by the server, when a user surfs a particular site. The browser can use customised information, which does not then have to be entered again if the site is revisited. You can view the cookies on your system by looking at the text file in notepad, but they are usually a set of meaningless numbers to the user.

You can instruct your browser to accept or reject the cookies, or to warn if a cookie is about to be saved to your disk. However, it is annoying if you have to keep responding to these messages. As with the history database information, you can delete your cookies at frequent intervals if you do not want them. However, be prepared for some sites to ask you to type in a lot of set-up information if you do this, and this can be annoying too. If you use on-line banking, then deletion of a cookie belonging to this can mean that you have to enter quite a lot of extra data, as though you have never logged on before.

WAP enabled browsers

Figure 56.4 A WAP enabled computer.

Other browsers exist, like the **micro-browsers** for **WAP** enabled mobile telephones. **WAP** stands for **wireless access protocol**. It is a standard enabling devices to access digital services via mobile phones and other portables.

PCs use HTML, but WAP devices use **WML**, which stands for **wireless mark-up language**. This is similar in principle to HTML, but is tailored for the small screens to be found on portable electronic devices. Just like HTML, WML commands are included between tags, and some examples of WML commands are as follows:

```
<img>, <anchor>,<big>,<card> and
<input>
```

Keep up to date with the latest technology by using the Web to search out recent technical developments. For example, there is no reason why a mobile phone cannot have an infrared link to beam a WAP web page directly to a suitable printer.

Handheld computer devices like the Ericson computer, shown in Figure 56.4, are **WAP enabled**.

Many mobile phones now have a micro browser, and some phones now have a credit-card interface for on-line transactions, as shown in Figure 56.5.

Figure 56.5 A mobile credit card interface.

Example

Comment on some of the advantages and disadvantages of WAP-enabled mobile technology compared to the conventional HTML browsers operating on a PC via a land-based, radio or satellite link.

Solution

The obvious advantage for WAP enabled mobile technology is portability. However, you do have the disadvantage of a very small screen size and fewer facilities. Nevertheless, when using the internet on a WAP based mobile phone, you are unlikely to use it in the same way as on your PC. Special WML web sites present the information in ways convenient for a small screen, and this is ideal for looking up text-based information such as 'share prices', 'who's top of the pops', or for 'getting telephone numbers' for example.

Devices like **third generation mobile phones** are ideal for statistical information on the move, but conventional internet browsers and PCs are more suited to a rich internet experience, or finding out more copious amounts of information. It is currently not possible, for example, to download large computer programs, print out web pages, scan information to be transmitted over the Net or add attachments to your e-mail via your mobile phone. No doubt some of these facilities will be available in the near future.

Self-test questions

1 Explain the difference between a conventional search engine and a meta search engine.
2 Explain how the use of advanced syntax may help to instruct a search engine to search for specific data. As an example, show how you might find a 'Jaguar animal' without finding 'Jaguar cars'.
3 What is a URL?
4 Outline some of the typical security features that would be provided by a modern web browser.
5 Some people think that cookies are an invasion of their privacy. Explain why this may be so.
6 What is a WAP-enabled browser?
7 Why can't WAP systems have the full functionality of a conventional computer-based browser?

In this unit you have learned about:

- Search engines and search techniques
- Computer-based Internet browsers and WAP-enabled browsers

57 Further internet-based technologies

In this section you will learn about:

- TV-based technology
- Java Applets and Servlets, CGI scripts and PERL
- E-mail
- Prevention of forgery
- Usenet and Internet Relay Chat

TV-based technology

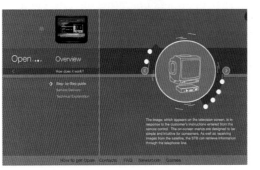

Figure 57.1 Sky Digital's Open system.

Some set-top boxes, designed to surf the internet using your TV, now have provision for attaching a printer. This adds to the functionality by several orders of magnitude.

Many people do not own a PC, and television companies like Sky enable people to use e-mail, conduct on-line banking and buy things on-line using a TV set. A screen from **Sky Digital's Open** is shown in Figure 57.1.

You need to subscribe to the service, have a **satellite dish** installed, and have extra electronics called a **set-top box**, which receives the satellite signals and is connected to the **telephone** for sending information. Satellite is a high-bandwidth link, and Sky transmits data at 64Mbits/sec. The **modem** in the **set top box**, transmits at 28.8 Kbit/sec. Reception from satellite ensures a high quality interactive experience, but users with a remote control would find e-mail frustrating. A special keyboard enables users to type in information, albeit at a relatively slow pace. Because of TVs limited resolution compared to monitors, text-based parts of the experience are limited, with 40 characters/line being typical.

Java Applets

Extra interactivity can be added to a site if it is capable of being viewed in a **Java-enabled browser**. A **Java Applet** can be referenced by the **HTML** language, then downloaded and run. The user can then interact with the site in special ways. Interactive games may be played, and the user can interact with utilities such as calculators or customised financial portfolios.

Running **Java Applets** from **untrusted sources** can be dangerous. It is for this reason that Java Applets are not allowed to be as powerful as applications written in the **Java language**. *They are not allowed to run applications on the user's machine, and are restricted to running inside set boundaries.*

To increase what an Applet may do we use a **digital signature** (see later). Applets from **trusted sources** may then perform operations, which would be unwise from an untrusted source. Examples are on-line banking, shopping or setting up accounts from well-known commercial organisations. A Java Applet running in a secure browser from a trusted source can be seen in Figure 54.1. The user is being prompted to enter the password and User ID to log into NatWest on-line banking using **128-bit encryption technology** and the **https protocol**.

Example

A web site must be designed to appeal to children. It is intended to include puzzles, games and questions. How could Java Applets enhance interactivity?

Solution

Java Applets can make the site more interactive by monitoring input from the children. Colours can change when a mouse is clicked over an area of the screen, or sounds can be made to play under similar conditions. You could reveal pictures or answers to questions, and perhaps keep a tally of how well the user is progressing in a set series of tasks. Scores for each task can be transmitted back to the server for inclusion in a database, which could be interrogated by a teacher. It is more likely that a **Java Servlet** or **GCI script** is needed at the server end to process this particular information (see below).

Thousands of pre-written Java Applets are available on the web, ranging from traffic simulations to playing a virtual instrument like a guitar via your browser.

Java Servlets, CGI script and PERL

Information must be processed at the server end, like accessing a database, processing credit-card transactions or managing a secure link. With a suitably enabled web server, information can be processed using **Java Servlets**. Think of a **Java Servlet** as a Java Applet, which runs at the server end. This is how a search engine might process a string to provide you with information. A Java Servlet is written in **Java**, and thus has extended facilities compared to limitations imposed on Java Applets. All Java **APIs (application programming interfaces)** are available, and interaction with applications is allowed.

Before the advent of **Java Servlets**, CGI (**common gateway interface**) scripts and **Perl** (**practical extraction and report language**) scripts, were major ways of processing server-side interaction. There are millions of **CGI** and **Perl scripts** in operation, and they are unlikely to be superseded by Java Servlets in the near future.

It is additional functionality like Java Servlets and PERL scripts, for example, which turn a simple web site into a fully blown A2-standard project.

E-mail

E-mail, like word processing, databases and spreadsheets, is an example of a **killer application**. This means that people will buy computers, mobile communication devices, TVs, or special telephones just because of their ability to support e-mail. E-mail is electronic text or other files, sent from one system to another, via networks such as **LANs** or **WANs**. Facilities available depend on the device you are using. A WAP-enabled mobile phone, for example, will have limited e-mail capability compared to a PC.

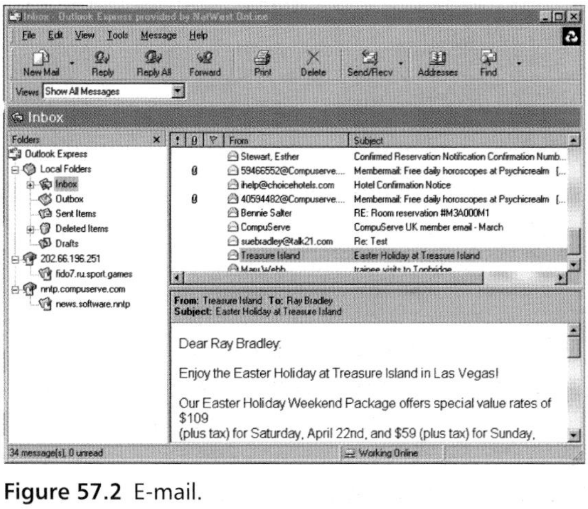

Figure 57.2 E-mail.

E-mail is compiled by the sender and sent to a **mail server**, where it is distributed to another server which hosts the recipient's e-mail account. When the recipient logs on to their system and downloads e-mail, the text or other files get transferred from their mailbox into their local computer. If on an LAN, then a local mail server will probably handle contact with the ISPs mail server. The e-mail can be viewed when a user logs on to the LAN. Typical e-mail software is shown in Figure 57.2

You can see icons representing an '**inbox**', an '**outbox**', '**sent items**', '**deleted items**' and '**drafts**'. A list of e-mails appears in the top right-hand window, and a particular e-mail is displayed in the bottom right-hand window. You can usually read and create e-mail off line. This saves paying phone bills while constructing or reading text. You can have **multiple e-mail accounts**, all being downloaded automatically by the software.

One advantage of using e-mail on a computer is that you can send an **attachment**. This is a computer file of any form. Anything stored on a computer can be sent via an **e-mail attachment** including pictures, sound, video, computer programs, web sites or viruses!

E-mail was originally designed for text-based messages, and parts of the internet still use ASCII making use of the **parity bit** (see unit 8). This messes up other types of information, often coded in more sophisticated ways making use of the parity bit for other purposes. There are several encoding methods in use to get over this problem, of which **MIME** (**Multi-purpose Internet Mail Extensions**) is a particular example. These encode information to be sent making sure the parity bit is used for its original purpose. A MIME encoded document is larger than the original.

With a typical e-mail application you can manage an **address book**, which can be generated automatically by incoming mail. You can manage **groups of users**, which is useful in schools and colleges when sending the same e-mail to people in a specific department or pupils in a particular class.

Most students at this level have an e-mail address, either at school or at home, but you must make use of e-mail to be able to understand all the features.

Preventing forgery

One problem with simple e-mail is you can never be sure that it is from the person who appears to have sent it. A way round this is to make use of a **digital ID**. Software like Outlook express works in conjunction with digital IDs allocated by the appropriate bodies.

A digital ID is similar to **public-key encryption** (see unit 18). There are three parts – a **public key**, a **private key** and a **digital signature**. If you put a digital signature with your e-mail message then the combination of the public key and digital signature is called a **digital certificate**. This can be obtained from companies such as Verisign. The recipient of e-mail uses the 'digital signature' as a verification mechanism, and your 'public key' is used to encrypt messages they send to you.

Digital IDs can be obtained from an **independent certification authority** like ID Safe. Companies like this act as trusted third parties to provide authentication via the information held by the company. Not only is this useful for e-mail, but for other aspects of 'e-commerce' where **confidentiality** and **authentication** are essential. Anyone who uses a **digital signature** or **certificate** can be easily traced, and made responsible for any of his or her actions. When you receive an e-mail that has been digitally signed, the software, like Microsoft Outlook Express, will automatically contact the company holding the digital certificate to see if it is still valid, or has been revoked.

Usenet

It is essential that you use Usenet and IRC to gain a feel for, and appreciation of, the differences in functionality of these systems.

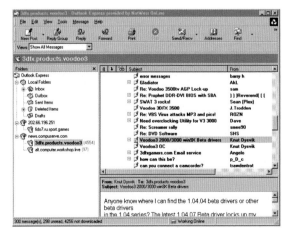

Figure 57.3 Newsgroups.

Usenet is similar to a **bulletin-board** system where users read material placed there by others. Anybody can post material to Usenet groups. The **Usenet user groups** are often unregulated, and therefore any sort of material can be found. At the time of writing there are over 50 000 newsgroups on many of the **news servers**, ranging from 'changing light bulbs', through support groups to finding technical details on a variety of subjects. A large number of these groups contain absolute rubbish, with much of the material being illegal. Fortunately, there are an even larger number of sites with essential information. To access newsgroups you need access to a **news server**. CompuServe's server can be found at 'news.compuserve.com'.

In Figure 57.3 you can see Outlook Express accessing a Voodoo3 graphics-card newsgroup. There are 4554 messages, all about topics for this graphics card! You can see just one of these messages displayed, which is a request from a user about beta versions of graphics-card software. People often use news groups to request help from other like-minded people, and this is the whole point of Usenet. If your **ISP** does not have a **news server**, many **public news servers** are available.

Internet Relay Chat (IRC)

The Usenet use groups are very passive in that you could be reading messages that have been posted months ago. Similarly, people may never read your particular posting! **Internet relay chat** provides a **real-time experience** where you can chat to people who are currently on-line and logged into an **IRC server**.

Messages can be exchanged interactively if you have appropriate software on your machine. Figure 57.4 shows the mIRC software during a session in which users are chatting about how to use the mIRC software! At any one time there will be a variety of IRC channels in session, and you can join in by selecting an appropriate one.

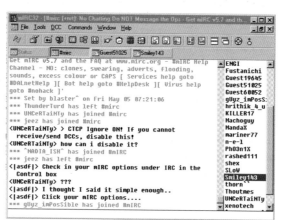

Figure 57.4 Internet relay chat.

Self-test questions

1 How can you surf the web without a computer?
2 What is a Java Applet?
3 Explain what the terms Java Servlets, CGI scripts and PERL scripts mean.
4 What is MIME encoding?
5 What is a digital certificate?
6 Discuss the pros and cons of Usenet.
7 What is internet relay chat?
8 What is a news server?

In this unit you have learned about:

- TV-based web browsing technologies
- Java Applets, Java Servlets, CGI scripts, and PERL scripts
- E-mail and the prevention of forgery
- Usenet and Internet Relay Chat

58 Banking, shopping and the VPN

In this section you will learn about:

- Agents
- Video-conferencing
- On-line banking
- On-line shopping
- Security on the internet with on-line transactions
- Virtual Private Networks.

Agents

An **agent** is a program to search for information, especially on the internet. There are many specialist and general-purpose agents, like the shopping agent called BargainDog, as shown in Figure 58.1. BargainDog is an example of a **specialist agent**, set up to enable shoppers to hunt for bargains. Although selective, a shopping agent can present the user with a good range of bargains, usually at the lower end of the price range.

A general-purpose intelligent agent is worth watching; it really does speed up the searching process, because undertaking the same tasks manually is time consuming.

Figure 58.1 A shopping agent.

Agents can also be **general purpose**. An example of a **general-purpose intelligent agent** is Copernic 2000, and this is shown in Figure 58.2. Here you may type in a request, but rather than direct it to a particular search engine, you may search many search engines. Figure 58.2 shows Copernic searching a few tens of search engines, starting with 'AltaVista', 'Direct Hit' and 'EuroSeek'. However, there is more to an **intelligent search engine** than this. An intelligent agent like Copernic 2000 will also correlate results, eliminate duplicates and give other facilities such as restricting searches to areas like Newsgroups or e-mail addresses etc.

Bots or Robots are also examples of **agents**, which search the Web for the user. Systems like **AIRbots**, short for **Autonomous Intelligent Robots**, use software agents to help management find information from health care to transportation.

Visit our portal to download an evaluation copy of the general agent Copernic.

Video conferencing

Two different people may communicate over the internet making use of **microphones**, **speakers** and **video cameras**. If each person is on line at the same time, then digitised video signals and sound may be sent over the internet, providing you have an appropriate high-bandwidth link. Very low, but acceptable quality is possible using a 56K modem, but high-quality links need a much higher bandwidth, preferably several Mbps.

More advanced **video-conferencing** systems allow several users to participate in the same conference, by displaying multiple windows on screen in which different participants can be viewed. Business meetings are often set up like this, as 'face to face' communication is possible without the hassle of travelling. Each person may be in a geographically disparate

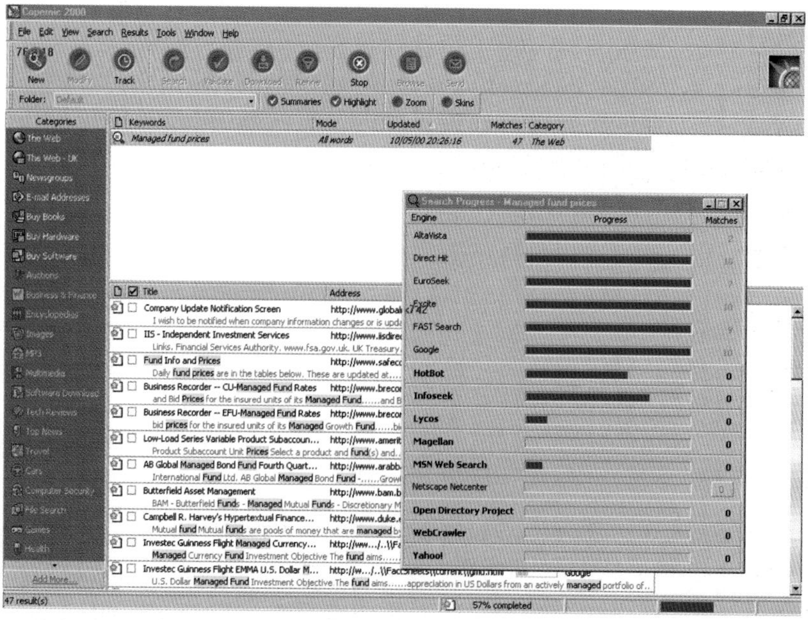

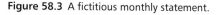

Figure 58.2 Copernic 2000.

location, but they are brought together in **conference** as if it were happening in a **board meeting**. You can show anything that is capable of being displayed on the computer screen, including graphs and drawings or doodles in real time. It is as though you are using a **common white board**.

On-line banking

On-line banking is popular for some people with computers, WAP-enabled mobile phones, and Internet-ready TVs via satellite or cable.

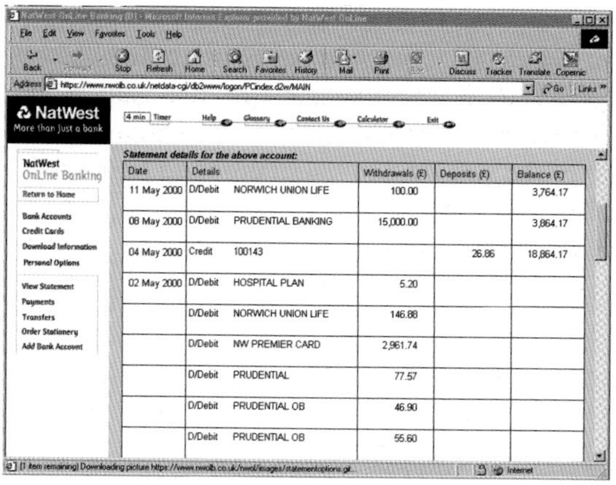

Figure 58.3 A fictitious monthly statement.

The most sophisticated service is available via a **secure web browser** and a PC. For example, you could display your monthly bank account **statement**, as shown in Figure 58.3. This statement shows **Direct Debits**, (regular monthly payments), a **transfer** of £15,000 into a *different* **Internet bank account** and a **deposit** by cheque of £26.86 etc. However, the facilities available are much more sophisticated. You can display **credit card** accounts, or download information into a spreadsheet for further analysis.

Never place a credit-card order on the net without making sure that you have a secure connection. IE5 indicates this by the use of a padlock.

Hard copy may be obtained regarding any of the information that can be viewed, and requests may be made to the bank for new chequebooks or paying-in books. About the only day-to-day thing that cannot be done via the internet is paying in cash.

On-line shopping

Virtually anything from a house to a mouse can be brought via the internet. As long as you have some valid plastic and a suitable credit limit, you can purchase goods on-line, which will normally be delivered to your door in a matter of days.

Example

A user wishes to find out information regarding DVD players in the £400 to £1000 price range. Suggest how he or she could make use of the internet from initial research, through to purchase.

Solution

A search engine can be used to find out sites with information about DVD players. The search string would have to contain the word player or many sites selling the DVD media may be selected instead. After finding a list of suitable machines and numbers, the user could log on to the manufacturer's site and download the specifications of each machine.

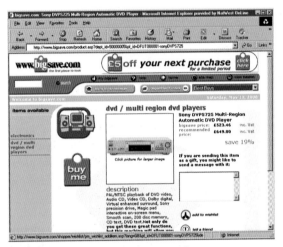

Figure 58.4 Sony Multi-Region DVD player.

Reviews of the machine may be found on other web sites, like those sponsored by the hi-fi magazines. People's opinions could also be solicited from the UseNet newsgroups.

Having decided on a machine within the appropriate price bracket, a **shopping bot (agent)** can be used to find the cheapest source of information. If, after a suitable amount of research, bigsave.com was found to be the most cost-effective source, the user could log onto the Bigsave site as shown in Figure 58.4.

If happy with the price, clicking over the 'buy me' icon would take you through to the secure credit card transaction service, assuming that you had already registered with 'bigsave.com' in this particular case. When the item is added to the shopping trolley, you may go back into other areas of the site to add other items, and then pay for them all at the checkout!

Major companies, like 'secure-bank.com' have been set up to enable on-line retailers to provide a comprehensive service to the customers. Facilities such as **secure-site checks, on-line point of sales, e-mail receipts, consumer billing, credit-card processing**, and **credit-card checking facilities** form just a part of a comprehensive on-line retailing system.

On-line security

Visit our portal to see how some of the internet security features are managed.

The security of on-line transactions is of paramount importance. We have covered using 128-bit encryption, and shopping channels may use the https protocol too. Other methods, like the **digital certificates** used with e-mail ensure the authenticity of the person at the other end of the line. However, e-commerce is open to fraud, and unscrupulous companies can set up bogus web sites to sell sub-standard goods or goods that don't exist at all!

If credit card details are to be given over the internet, then the company hosting the site will use a system making use of the **secure http** or **SSL (Secure Sockets Layer)**, one of the protocols for secure transactions.

Firewalls and intranets

Many companies, and educational institutions allow access to internal LANs (**intranets**) from the outside world, as shown in Figure 58.5. This shows a school, but these ideas apply to any organisation. Teachers, pupils, parents and hackers (unauthorised users) are trying to access the system, but the **firewall** (a machine placed in-between the internet and the school LANs) helps prevent unauthorised access.

All communication, either from the internet to the school's LANs or from the school's LANs to the internet are routed via the Firewall, which is effectively a **Proxy Server**, set up to decide if the messages coming in or going out are safe to pass. Any message deemed to be unsafe is blocked. When a user has passed through the firewall, they are allowed access to resources from inside the school site, going through the normal authentication by logging onto the school's file servers. Without the **firewall**, hackers from outside the organisation could do great damage to the company resources, or get access to information that might be commercially sensitive.

Virtual private networks (VPNs)

When set up using the advanced security measures outlined in Figure 58.5, authenticated users from the outside world are using the Internet as a virtual extension to the company's LAN. Used in this way the system is said to be a **virtual private network** or **VPN**.

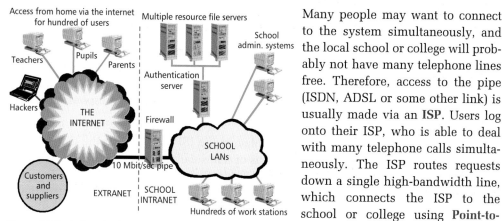

Figure 58.5 A virtual private network.

Many people may want to connect to the system simultaneously, and the local school or college will probably not have many telephone lines free. Therefore, access to the pipe (ISDN, ADSL or some other link) is usually made via an **ISP**. Users log onto their ISP, who is able to deal with many telephone calls simultaneously. The ISP routes requests down a single high-bandwidth line, which connects the ISP to the school or college using **Point-to-Point Tunnelling Protocol (PPTP)**

Self-test questions

1 What is an agent?
2 What's the difference between general-purpose and specialist agents?
3 Outline some typical features that would be available when using on-line shopping.
4 List the advantages and disadvantages of on-line banking via a PC.
5 How might a small company cope with the complexities of running a web site to provide on-line transactions?
6 Outline the concept of a VPN, suggesting what extra hardware and software is necessary to implement one for a company with many travelling salespeople.

In this unit you have learned about:

- Special purpose and general-purpose agents
- Video conferencing
- On-line banking and on-line shopping
- The companies that provide on-line services to businesses
- The importance of the virtual private network

59 Issues arising from the internet

In this section you will learn about:

- Moral, ethical, social and cultural issues
- Appropriate policies for correct use of computers and the internet at school and in the work place
- Software solutions
- International boundaries
- The use of encryption

Moral, ethical, social and cultural issues

The **internet** is powerful, and cuts across cultural and social boundaries causing problems. Conventional authorities like **Customs and Excise**, the **Inland Revenue**, and **police** have little control over what people are allowed to buy, see or do over the web. On the other hand you have **freedom of speech**, and the ability to communicate with others. Unfortunately **drug barons**, **terrorists** and **pornographers** abuse the system to distribute illegal material, or make use of **encryption** and **e-mail** for criminal activities. Legal systems in most countries lag a long way behind the current pace of technological change, and this leads to squabbles and legal battles in courtrooms to determine who is responsible for the material on the net.

A recent case involving libellous material blamed the **ISP** from which the material was obtained, but the ISPs cannot check millions of items daily. It is like prosecuting a local newsagent shop for selling libellous material! Taking the analogy further, should the computer manufacturer be prosecuted for providing the computer on which the material is viewed? Should the web browser company be held responsible for providing the software, or should the phone company be sued for providing the connection over which the libellous material was sent? In this particular case, the person most difficult to prosecute is the original person who wrote the message, because they cannot be easily traced!

The World Wide Web is also a major source of **viruses**, which can easily be spread via **e-mail**, **downloading software** and other material. A whole industry has grown around protecting innocent people from the extremes of material that can be found on the net. It would be an irresponsible parent, for example, who allowed their underage child freedom to access uncensored information from any part of the web. It would also be an irresponsible school that allowed the same thing to happen. Teachers have a legal responsibility for supervising children who use the net from their school.

Policy documentation

Educational and other organisations have taken a serious look at how their pupils and employees make use of e-mail and the web during working hours. Issues here range from **illegal activities** to the less sinister but equally inappropriate use of computers for **playing games**, **stealing software** or other **personal use**. At school, using computers for personal reasons is often appropriate, but at work it could be a sackable offence.

Example

Make a list of topics for a computer use policy document at school. It should cover the internet, and appropriate use of computers not belonging to the individual who is using them.

By reading the computer-use documentation covered in this unit, you can appreciate the huge range of issues that surround the use of computers in the workplace and at school.

Solution

The following is typical, and is what is used at the author's school:

Personal safety

(1) You should not post contact information about yourself or others to public forums. Contact information includes school and home addresses, telephone and pager numbers.

(2) You should tell your teacher promptly about any message you receive that contains inappropriate language or enclosures or makes you feel uncomfortable in any way.

Illegal activities

(1) You should not attempt to go beyond your authorised access. This includes attempting to log in through another person's account, sending e-mail while masquerading as another person, or accessing another person's files.

(2) You should not make deliberate attempts to disrupt the computer system or destroy data by, for example, spreading computer viruses or altering the configuration of the system.

System security

You are responsible for your individual account and should take all reasonable precautions to prevent others from being able to use your account. Under no circumstances should you provide passwords to another person, and if you suspect that someone knows your password, change it immediately. In any circumstances, you should change your password at least once a term.

Inappropriate language

(1) Restrictions against inappropriate language apply equally to e-mail messages, newsgroup messages, and material posted onto and downloaded from Web pages.

(2) You should not use indecent, obscene, offensive, or threatening language.

(3) You should not post information that could cause damage or a danger of disruption.

(4) You should not engage in personal, prejudicial, or discriminatory attacks.

(5) You should not harass another person. Harassment is persistently acting in a manner that distresses or annoys another person. If you are told by a person to stop sending messages to them, you must immediately stop.

(6) You should not knowingly or recklessly send or post false or defamatory information about a person.

Respect for privacy

(1) You should not re-post a message that was sent to you privately without the permission of the person who sent you the message.

(2) You should not post private information about another person.

Respecting resource limits

(1) You should not download large files unless absolutely necessary. If necessary, you should download the file at a time when the system is not being heavily used.

(2) You should not send annoying or unnecessary messages to a large number of people. This is called spamming, and consists of pages of jokes or virus warnings, which are widely circulated. Dealing with these messages wastes time and system resources.

(3) You should check your e-mail frequently and delete unwanted messages promptly.

Plagiarism and copyright

(1) You should not plagiarise works that you find on the internet. Plagiarism is taking the ideas or writings of others and presenting them as if they were your own.

If your school or college has its own computer-use document you should be aware of what is contained in it. Use it to help you revise some of the issues in this chapter.

(2) You should respect copyright. Copyright infringement occurs when you inappropriately reproduce a work that is protected by a copyright. If you are unsure whether or not you can use a work, you should request permission from the copyright owner.

Access to inappropriate material

(1) You should not use school computers to access material that is profane or obscene, that advocates illegal acts, violence, or discrimination towards other people.

(2) If you mistakenly access inappropriate information, you should immediately tell your teacher. This will protect you against the accusation that you have intentionally accessed this material.

(3) Your parents or guardians should instruct you if there is other material that they think it would be inappropriate for you to access. The school fully expects that you will follow your parents' or guardians' instructions.

Privacy

(1) You should expect only limited privacy in the contents of your personal files on the school system. The system administrators, your Headteacher, and your parents or guardians have the right at any time to request access to your school directory. As a general rule, keep nothing on the system you would feel uncomfortable justifying in front of your parents, or the Headteacher.

(2) Routine monitoring of the school's system, or a search of your files conducted on reasonable suspicion may lead to the discovery that you have infringed this Policy, the school rules, or the law. In such cases appropriate action will be taken.

Personal responsibility

(1) When you are using the school's system, you may think that it is easy to break these rules without the risk of detection. You should realise that whenever you use a network you leave an electronic trace that can subsequently be followed.

Software piracy

(1) The School has a responsibility under the terms of its software contracts to make sure that no unlicensed software is used on the school machines. Such software can contain damaging viruses: and software companies, aware that pupils in schools steal millions of pounds' worth of applications and games every year, have been prepared to prosecute.

Software solutions

Software like NetNanny provides filtering to prevent access to a range of sites containing pornographic, racist, violent or other material deemed to be unsuitable. However, the internet is a very dynamic entity, and hundreds of new sites are set up each day. It is unlikely that anything (short of not letting a person use the net) will deter a person with enough time from finding material that others would deem to be unsuitable, and this is why policies like those just covered are put into action. It is easy for people to become **addicted** to material on the net, be it illegal, or more innocent **games**. They may also get addicted to **Internet Relay Chat** or spend so much time surfing they become obsessed to the detriment of other activities. On the plus side, people have struck up long-lasting friendships over the net, and some have even ended up with marriage. It is not all bad, and this is what makes the regulation virtually impossible.

International boundaries

There is a significant amount of religious or government influence in some countries, and the force of the internet can be an unwelcome catalyst for change. Even material innocent in the eyes of a Westerner might be totally unacceptable to some cultures in the Middle East, for example, where alcohol is banned. Some books and publications would also be banned, and reading Western newspapers is frowned upon in some societies.

Laws in different countries define differently what is or is not decent, inflammatory, illegal or tolerated. Because servers may be accessed from all countries, the situation becomes muddled, and material, that is viewed in one house, might be totally illegal to be viewed in another house just a few hundred yards down the road across an international border. It is not possible for countries to try and impose their standards on others, and thus there will be international arguments over how to control the system.

Encryption

Encryption is a method of **scrambling** the data into a form that cannot be read by anyone without knowledge of the **algorithm** and **key** used to encrypt the data. Encryption is vital when sensitive data is transmitted over the internet, as otherwise anybody would be able to decipher information such as credit card details, and sensitive personal or other details. There are **weak** and **strong encryption algorithms**, with stronger ones being impossible to decipher by guessing alone in a sensible amount of time. Even governments with access to supercomputers are unable to decode strong encryption (128 bit, for example.) It is only recently that the USA allowed the legal export of strong encryption, mainly to boost confidence in e-commerce. Criminals using the same techniques have impenetrable systems, and interception of messages between hackers and criminals is virtually impossible.

Methods of encryption are covered in more detail in chapter 9 of NUCSAL.

Public and private keys

The invention of **public/private key** encryption makes it possible to exchange information easily, as the key to decrypt the message never needs to be transmitted. You send your public key to anybody who needs to send messages to you, but you decrypt the message with your own private key, to which only you have access. One proposed solution to the government's problem of being unable to decipher strong encryption is **Key Escrow**. This system has been developed in which organisations may use strong encryption, but give a copy of their private key to a government organisation. However, drug barons and other criminals are obviously not going to give the government a key, and other companies, even if they have nothing to hide, are also reluctant.

Visit our portal to find out about weak and strong encryption algorithms.

Self-test questions

1 The internet is a positive force for empowering individuals. Make a list of five positive things that the World Wide Web provides for an individual person.
2 Make a list of five negative effects that making use of the web can have on an individual.
3 Suggest several areas that should be considered by the management of a company when deciding how their employees should make use of computers during the firm's time.
4 It is possible to police every action that an individual carries out on a computer used in a school or college. Suggest how this might be done, but outline any disadvantages of actually doing so.
5 What does Key Escrow mean?
6 Explain how public and private key encryption systems operate.
7 Outline some of the methods by which software prevents people from seeing banned material on the net.
8 Why are the software methods outlined in question 7 not always effective?

In this unit you have learned about:

● The moral, social and cultural issues surrounding computers and the net
● Some typical guidelines
● Software solutions to some of these issues
● The need for and disadvantages of encryption techniques

60 Communications and networking basics

In this section you will learn about:

- Baseband and broadband networks
- Multiplexing
- Circuit and packet switching
- Layering communication systems
- The ISO OSI model
- Management of networks using bridges

Baseband and broadband communications

Baseband technology transmits only one signal at any moment. When transmitting, no other machine on the network may do so. If an attempt is made, a clash would occur and the signals would be retransmitted. This is how the **Ethernet** network operates. Signals are transmitted if the line is free, or if a clash occurs, then the system waits a small random moment in time and tries again. The number of clashes gets worse if the network is in heavy use. Slower networks (10 Mbit/Sec) can grind to a halt if many clashes occur. 100 Mbit/sec is better for the same number of users, because information gets sent more quickly, reducing the time available to clash.

Broadband networks can send different signals at the same time along the same wire, optical fibre or radio link. This is because they use different **carrier frequencies** that do not interfere with each other. An example of a **broadband system** is Nortel Networks' OPTera Metro 500

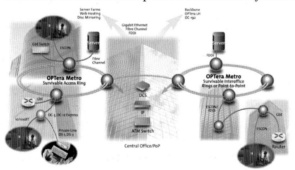

Figure 60.1 Nortel's broadband network.

Series optical metropolitan network, shown in Figure 60.1. This is a Dense Wavelength Division Multiplexing optical transport platform. The protocol and bit rate carried on a given wavelength can be changed easily without altering the transport infrastructure. The system scales to support 32 protected of 64 unprotected connections across either a point-to-point or ring network (shown).

Multiplexing

Multiplexing is sending different signals over the same link. If different times are used it is called **time-division multiplexing**, or for different frequencies, it is called **frequency division multiplexing**. You should be familiar with **time-division multiplexing**, because it is identical to **time sharing** when considering operating systems in unit 45. Each signal is given a tiny **slice** of time, usually very brief so other users, who receive information during their time slices, do not realise that others are using the same link too.

Frequency division multiplexing transmits signals at exactly the same moment in time, but on different carrier frequencies, as described earlier. It is identical to **fm radio**. Many different stations are sending out signals over the airwaves. You decide which one to listen to by 'tuning in' to the appropriate frequency. The **broadband network** idea shown in Figure 60.1 is similar.

Example

Distinguish between baseband and broadband networks, giving examples of where each system might be used. Give typical examples of baseband and broadband systems.

Solution

A **baseband** network allows transmission of information using a single frequency over a system operating time-division multiplexing. Only one signal can be transmitted at any one moment in time. The other signals have to wait until there is a free moment during which a packet of data may be transmitted.

A **broadband** network can transmit more than one signal simultaneously, often by modulating the signal onto a different carrier frequency, which is then transmitted over the same cable or radio link. The signals have to be demodulated at the other end to extract the information signal.

Ethernet, used in LANs, is a good example of a **baseband network**; a **wireless access network** like **Blue Tooth** is an example of **broadband** linking computers via radio.

Circuit and packet switching

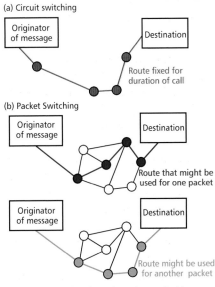

(a) Circuit switching

(b) Packet Switching

Figure 60.2 Circuit and packet switching.

Figure 60.2(a) shows a line which is dedicated to a 'conversation' between two people or computers. It could be a direct link, or routed via a telephone exchange. This line is dedicated to this 'conversation' for the duration of the call, irrespective of whether any information is actually being transmitted or not. This is an example of **circuit switching**.

Circuit switching is inefficient for computers, as the line is tied up when no useful information is sent. Data could also go via different routes, as indicated in Figure 60.2(b). This is called message switching. To prevent large messages hogging the line for long periods, the messages are split up into smaller defined-size parts called **packets**. A message sent in this way is called **packet switching**. With packet switching you do not 'own' the same line for the duration of the call, and are therefore said to have a **virtual circuit**.

Layering communication systems

Communication between machines is often arranged in **layers**. Hardware or software can interface to its own layer without affecting all the others. Before the **International Standards Organisation (ISO)** established the layered approach, communication between computer systems was virtually impossible. One model is the ISO Open Systems Interconnection or **ISO OSI model** shown in Figure 60.3. The model consists of **7 layers**. Starting with the data to be transmitted at the **application layer** (the top layer), we add data (in the form of headers) to the packet to be transferred, until enough information to transmit the message using the appropriate **protocol** is assembled (see Figure 60.4). The **data link layer** adds a final footer. The **physical layer**, unlike other layers, deals only with the 'nuts and bolts' of the hardware.

The principles of layering are more important than trying to remember what each particular layer does in the ISO/OSI model example.

The anatomy of a packet

A **packet** contains the data to be transmitted, but also contain information like **ID**, **source** and **destination** of the packet, and some **error checking** too. It corresponds to **layer 3** of the **ISO OSI model**. The exact form of the data depends on the systems being used, and proprietary systems have their own names for the different protocols corresponding to the different layers of the ISO OSI model.

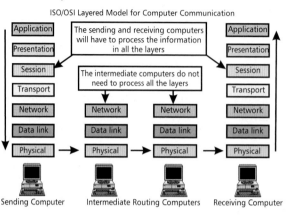

Further work on the ISO/ISO model is covered in chapter 5 of NUCSAL.

At the **application layer** we have the original data to be transmitted. This would usually be part of an entire message. In a simple **Ethernet** system, the next layer to add information is the transport layer (**layer 4**), which puts a header onto the data to be sent, as shown in Figure 60.4. The **network layer** (**layer 3**) adds a header, and the **data-link layer** (**layer 2**) adds a header and footer too. An Ethernet packet, assembled for transmission, is shown in Figure 60.4.

Figure 60.3 The ISO OSI layered model for computer communication.

Managing a complex network of networks

The distance along a network that a signal may travel before degrading is limited. The higher the transmission rate, the less distance can be travelled. Devices help manage these problems, and help with the routing too.

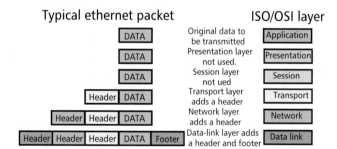

Figure 60.4 Building up the layers.

Ask your network manager at school or college to show you around the network, making sure, if possible, to look at repeaters, bridges, hubs and switches.

Repeaters are simple devices to boost signals so they can travel over longer distances. **Bridges** may also be used to boost the signal so that you end up with a longer physical network. **Intelligent bridges** are used to *pass packets* from one network to the next, or to *filter packets* so preventing them from using up valuable bandwidth on parts of the networks that do not need to be affected.

Example

LANs are being set up in a science department. Chemistry, Biology and Physics wish to run their own, so traffic does not interfere with each other, or with the main school network. They sometimes need to connect to each another, via the school backbone, and the Physics Department is also a long distance from Chemistry and Biology.
Show how this network may be implemented using bridges and repeaters only.

Solution

Figure 60.5 shows a possible configuration making use of bridges as a filter. If Physics had a spare bridge available, but no repeater, then a bridge (which is set up to let all the traffic through) could have been used instead of the repeater.

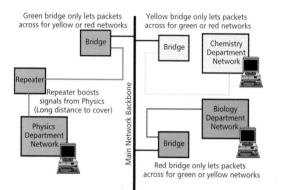

Figure 60.5 Bridges as a filtering mechanism.

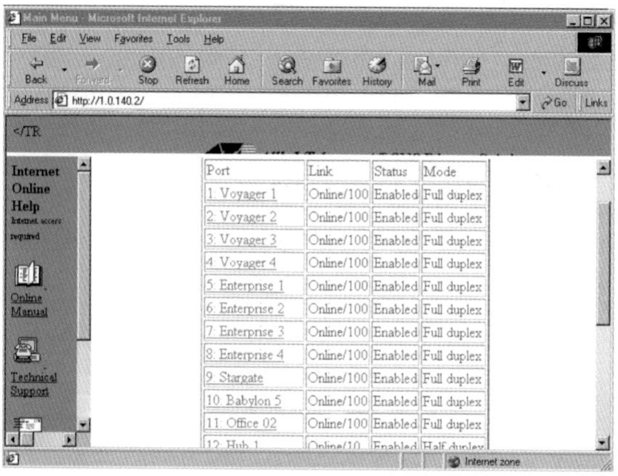

Figure 60.6 Programming a switch.

In more sophisticated systems, intelligent **switches** could be used instead of bridges. As switches become cost effective, they are becoming popular. A **switch** performs a similar function to a bridge, in that it can either block or let through traffic. However, unlike a bridge, a **switch** can route a single input to a single output, can route a single input to multiple outputs, or can concentrate multiple inputs into a single output. The switch boxes may also be programmed from a remote computer via the network, and a typical switch interface, running in an internet browser at the author's school is shown in Figure 60.6.

It is called a switch because it performs the switching operations described above. It is the job of this switch to alter the connections, similar in principle to operations carried out in a telephone exchange. It is possible to maximise the bandwidth between computers if this method is used.

Self-test questions

1 Explain the difference between baseband and broadband communications.
2 What is multiplexing?
3 Explain the difference between circuit and packet switching.
4 Why do computer communication systems need to be organised in a layered fashion?
5 Large networks need to be managed so that unnecessary network traffic from one section does not swamp another section. How is this accomplished in practice?
6 Explain how a packet of data might be built up ready for transmission over an **LAN** or **WAN**.
7 What is the difference between a bridge and a switch on an **LAN**?

In this unit you have learned about:

- The difference between broadband and baseband networks
- Circuit and packet switching
- The need for layering of communication protocols
- The ISO OSI layer model
- The management of networks using bridges and switches

61 Networking devices and media

In this section you will learn about:

- Routers and gateways
- ATM
- TCP/IP protocol stack
- Different LAN configurations and types of connection media

Routers and gateways

We continue our tour of network devices started in the last unit. **Routers** provide much functionality, and can be implemented, either by **hardware** (special boxes) or **software** (e.g. a proxy server).

Routers are often used to connect **LANs** to **WANs**, i.e. they can route Internet requests from multiple users on an LAN, via a proxy server to a WAN, for example.

The **TCP/IP** protocol, (**Transmission Control Protocol/Internet Protocol**) is a good example of sending information via a router. Routers have to communicate with each other to establish how many hops would be needed to get from one part of the WAN to another. If you are in London, and type one of the Las Vegas Hotel www addresses, then you may be routed via New York, Chicago, Denver and Las Vegas. The routers decide the best available route at the time, based on geographical location, availability and current traffic.

The internet itself is formed as a vast interconnection of networks, and **gateways** are the names of the computers that help to join these interconnected networks together. They often perform protocol conversion so that information may go over many different network links.

Table 61.1 A summary of network devices

A summary of the typical uses of networking devices		
Gateway	The name often used for computers on the internet which connect the different parts of the network. These form the glue by which the Internet is constructed. They can also carry out protocol conversion.	This device is usually a computer.
Router	Used to connect the same or different networks. Used on the web to route traffic, or for the connection of an LAN to a WAN. Some routers can handle interconnecting LANs of differing architectures, whether or not they use the same or a different protocol.	This device operates at the *network layer* (**layer 3** of the ISO OSI model).
Switch	Can perform the same function as a bridge, but the box has much more sophistication, and can deal with many segments (see Figure 61.1).	This device operates at the *data-link layer* (**layer 2** of the ISO OSI model).
Bridge	Used to block or let through signals. Can be used as an expensive repeater. Depending on type, some bridges are only able to handle the same protocol but others can handle different protocols. For example, Ethernet and Token Ring. (See example in Unit 62 Figure 62.5.)	This device operates at the data-link layer (**layer 2** of the ISO OSI model).
Repeater	Used to boost signals over longer distances. (See example in Unit 60 Figure 60.5.)	This device is related to the *physical layer* (**layer 1** of the ISO OSI model).

Talk to your network manager and ask about the topology and network management strategy used in your school. For example, how is the network segmented?

The difference between networking devices

Students are often confused about the terms **repeaters**, **bridges**, **routers**, **switches** and **hubs**. This is not surprising, as the definitions of these devices have changed over the years. You have only to look at the arguments in the networking **newsgroups** to appreciate this! With the introduction of new technology, the functionality of these components becomes ever more impressive. A summary of current usage of the technology is shown in Table 61.1. The only device missing from the table is a **hub**, which is simply a device allowing many computers to share the same bandwidth. The idea of a hub is shown in Figure 62.2. All devices prevent networks from being clogged up, by routing, switching and blocking data.

Example

Show how a switch might be used to manage communication between four different computer rooms and a file server.

Solution

Figure 61.1 shows how the switch manages the connection via a 4-port network card. The bandwidth is shared out efficiently according to the traffic in each room.

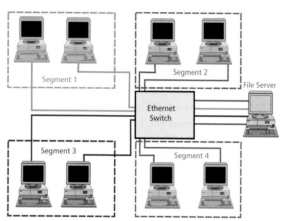

Figure 61.1 A switch connecting the rooms.

ATM

ATM is **asynchronous transmission mode**. Unlike most other networks, this is designed with simultaneous transmission of **computer data**, **audio** and **video data** in mind. It is thus ideal for multimedia communications and video-conferencing.

Example

A university is upgrading its existing 10 Mbit/sec Ethernet networks to ATM. Explain why this is not as easy as upgrading to a faster Ethernet technology. Comment on the arguments in favour of upgrading to a faster Ethernet system.

Solution

ATM is a radically different technology to Ethernet, and there is no easy upgrade path. Both systems are incompatible with each other. It may be more cost effective for the university to upgrade to a faster Ethernet system because of compatibility with the old system, which could work in parallel with the faster Ethernet.

The **physical layer** of the **ISO/OSI architecture** defines the **ATM system**. A standard-size 53-byte packet is used to simultaneously transmit audio, computer data, and real-time video over the same cable. Current implementations of ATM range in speed from 155 Mbit/sec to about 660 Mbit/sec.

Example

You covered the physical layer, the data-link layer and the network layer in unit 60. What do you do in practice to implement these? Use Ethernet as an example.

Relating the ISO/OSI layers to practical examples as shown here makes the layered system easier to understand.

Solution

Layer one is the **physical layer**. It consists of the connections and network hardware. You install an Ethernet card (**NIC**) to enable it to be connected to an Ethernet network.

Layer two is the **data-link layer**. This is the software driver for a particular Ethernet card. This driver interfaces the card to the operating system, and implements the data-link protocol.

Layer three is the **network layer**. Software, which supports IP is installed (or activated from the operating system). Higher-layer protocols (TCP representing layer 4) may be installed at this stage on the client machine. TCP/IP would be installed at the same time.

The TCP/IP protocol stack

The TCP/IP stack incorporates many protocols with which you are familiar, like **FTP (file transfer protocol)**, **telnet (terminal emulation)** and **SMTP (simple mail transfer protocol)**. Over 100 different protocols are supported in the TCP/IP suites.

The **TCP/IP stack** is a set of **protocols** (layered as a stack), which work together to help machines communicate over a typical network like an LAN and the internet. The operation is all down to **port numbers** on the client machine, which are set up to deal with each different protocol like telnet or FTP. **65535 port numbers** can be assigned to different functions, with **port 80**, being the popular **http protocol**. A port number ensures that the computer sends information to the right software inside the machine so that it can be dealt with without getting mixed up with other information using other protocols.

Different LAN configurations

A local area network can be set up in a variety of ways, according to the type of technology being implemented. The most popular LAN is **Ethernet**, which can be split up into several types depending on the speed of communication required.

Types of cable – twisted pair

If possible, ask your network manager to show you different types of cable and fibre optic connections.

Figure 61.2 A shielded twisted pair cable.

Twisted pair is where two insulated wires are twisted together, as shown in Figure 61.2.

Twisting helps prevent electromagnetic interference, and **shielding** gives further protection. Many cables do not use extra shielding as twisting is effective for preventing noise corrupting the signals. Twisted pair cable is common in **100 Mbit/sec** Ethernet.

Types of cable – coaxial

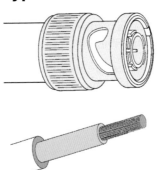

Figure 61.3 A coaxial connector and cable.

A **coaxial cable** and connector is shown in Figure 61.3. This cable has two conductors (one in the middle and one around the outside), which *share the same axis*. Coaxial cable is common in **10 Mbit/sec** Ethernet systems.

There are different types of coaxial cable for different purposes, such as **baseband Ethernet**, **cable TV** or **broadband radio signals**, for example. As different types of coaxial cable are used for each of these applications, it is not as versatile as the other media, and is not used in new installations.

Fibre Optics

Twisted pair and **coax** are examples of **copper-wire connections**. **Fibre optic** connections are made out of **glass** or **plastic**, and transmit **optically** instead of electrically.

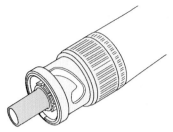

Figure 61.4 A fibre-optic connection.

Fibre optic suffers less from interference, and is easily capable of transmitting at **1 Gbit/sec** or more. It is used for **backbone connections**, but as speeds increase, will probably connect workstations too. A fibre optic connection is shown in Figure 61.4. Fibre optic cable is much more difficult to install than twisted pair or coaxial cable. The ends of the cable have to be finely polished, and the connections must be of an exceptional standard for it to work properly.

Self-test questions

1 What is the difference between routers, hubs, bridges, repeaters, switches and gateways?
2 Ethernet is a popular network for many companies and schools. Outline the different types of Ethernet network that are available, indicating the speed and typical use of the connections.
3 Explain why ATM has some advantages over other network technologies.
4 What extra facilities are likely to be possible with Gbit Ethernet compared to the conventional 100 Mbit Ethernet.
5 Outline some of the advantages of a fibre-optic cable compared to copper-based technologies like co-axial and twisted pair cables.
6 What Ethernet technology would you use to connect the following computers, which are standalone with no file servers, but need to share a printer
   (a) Two computers
   (b) Three computers?

In this unit you have learned about:

- Routers and gateways
- The ATM protocol
- The TCP/IP protocol stack
- The differences between and typical uses of repeaters, bridges, switches routers and gateways
- A variety of network connection media including twisted pair, coax and fibre

62 Network topologies and the internet

In this section you will learn about:

- Different network topologies
- Peer-to-peer and server-based networking
- Value-added networks
- EDI
- On-line service providers and ISPs

Network topologies

Physically changing one type of network topology to another is a headache because of the re-wiring involved. Organisations do not undertake these upgrades lightly.

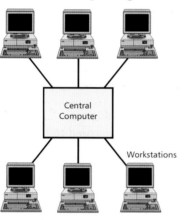

Figure 62.1 A star network.

Topology refers to the way in which the cables connect the machines together. A **star-network topology** is shown in Figure 62.1.

Each workstation has a unique connection to the node computer, ensuring **maximum security** and **no shared bandwidth**. A similar system can be implemented by using a **hub**, *but the bandwidth advantage is lost* because the connection on the other side of the hub is shared, as can be seen in Figure 62.2. This is called a **tree network** because it is like a tree, especially if other hubs are used too. As the hubs contain a bus network inside, it is also sometimes called a **star bus network**.

A bus network is **terminated** at each end to prevent unwanted reflections of signals. Large bus networks are uncommon, as the bandwidth of the network is not used efficiently. It is better to split it up into smaller segments by the use of **bridges** (see unit 61.) or some other means. Traffic for one part of the network does not have to interfere with traffic from another. If arranged like this it is called **segmentation**.

Without proper segmentation and planning, the performance of bus networks would be unsatisfactory for all but the smallest of networks.

A **bus network** is shown in Figure 62.3. Messages for one machine have to pass by other machines, and so the security of this system is lower than that of a star network.

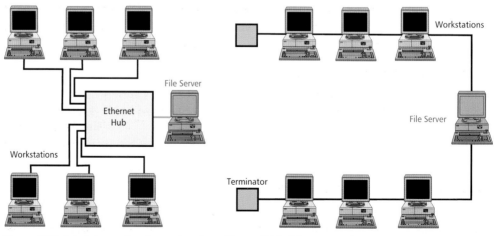

Figure 62.2 A hub to create a tree network.　**Figure 62.3** A bus network.

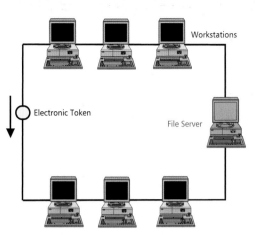

Workstations

Electronic Token

File Server

Figure 62.4 A ring-network topology.

Another network topology is the **ring network**, as shown in Figure 62.4.

The system shown in Figure 62.4 is a **token-ring network**. An **electronic token** is passed around the network and grabbed by a machine for a limited period of time. During this time no other machine can transmit information, and thus there is *no possibility* of **collisions**, as with the **Ethernet system**.

Example

You set up a simple network for three computer users. There is one machine with a printer, which needs to be used by all three people. What is the simplest and cheapest way to do this? You may assume that there are three PCs running a recent version of Windows.

Solution

The simplest way is to use **peer-to-peer networking**. This involves putting an Ethernet card in each machine, and connecting them via a hub, in ways identical to that shown in Figure 62.2. Next you would install the drivers for each of the cards, and set up shared resources. The printer would need to be shared, so that the other people who do not have a printer attached can print to the shared one. Some folders on each of the disks may need to be shared so users may transfer data using the network.

Peer-to-peer vs. server-based networking

A minimal network was shown in the last example. On larger networks it is not efficient to organise the management in an *ad hoc* way. If a **file server** is used instead, it is a **server-based network**. It is sophisticated because dedicated server software gives managers access to facilities in terms of **security** and **accounting**, for example (see unit 11).

A **file server** with **ultra-fast disk drives**, operating in **RAID** configuration, is suitable for server-based networking. In larger LANs there could be entire **server farms**. Nothing (other than the security imposed by the system managers) stops clients on **server-based systems** setting up **peer-to-peer networks**. Managers do not like this, as a consequence of doing this might be that important data on the client machines gets lost.

Wide area networks (WANs)

The topologies and methods considered so far typify hardware for an **LAN**. A **WAN**, or **wide area network** makes use of the *public communications system*. If you are using the **phone system** to connect to the **internet**, then you are using a **WAN**. Using WANs opens up new possibilities, of which the resources available on the **world wide web** are an example.

Value-added networks (VANs)

A **VAN** is a network in which additional functionality (over and above just carrying your data or voice) is provided. Facilities to route messages, or to connect computers transmitting at different speeds over the network is typical A **value-added network** provides

More network information can be found in chapter 3 of NUCSAL.

Peer-to-peer networks are now frequently set up in the home, especially if two or more computers are used in the same house. Reasons vary from sharing the home printer to playing multi-user games like Quake III.

facilities like checking formats for storing and forwarding messages, which is often necessary when **EDI** (see below) takes place. Additional security features may also be provided. You should contrast the **VAN** aspects of the **WWW** with the more limited range of facilities available on an LAN.

Virtual private networks (VPNs)

A **virtual private network** or **VPN** is one in which clients log onto an intranet via the internet as if logging on locally. A VPN is shown in Figure 58.5.

EDI

EDI is **electronic data interchange**. EDI uses formats for exchange of information electronically. This could be in the form of invoices or other special documents. An example is the system used by exam boards. Instead of using **OMR** forms (see unit 12), we enter exam marks via the computer. This is convenient as data is in computer-readable format when it arrives at the board.

On-line service providers

Companies such as **AOL** and **CompuServe** are examples of large **on-line service providers**. In addition to providing internet access, these companies have huge databases, which their users can access for a variety of services. Typically, services provided by CompuServe are Education, Business, Money, Travel and Sport etc.

Internet service providers

An **ISP**, also called an **internet access provider** or **IAP** provides a connection to the internet. These companies do not have to provide a whole host of other facilities like the added value databases given by the on-line service providers, but the distinction between these two is blurred to say the least.

Example

You connect to your ISP via a dial-up connection and modem. Draw a diagram showing a typical route between your PC and the ISP network file servers, that provides the eventual internet connection. Make sure that you include a mail server and news server in your diagram, and explain why the ISP might sometimes be busy.

Solution

Study the diagram that shows connections to a typical ISP. It really does bring together the idea of networks and how facilities can be provided via a WAN and the net.

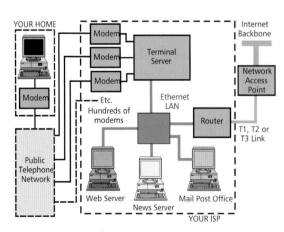

Figure 62.5 Typical connections to your ISP.

The modem is connected to one of the ISP's modems via the public telephone network. The connections might be via dial up connections, as shown in Figure 62.5, or other methods like **ISDN**, **ADSL** or a **leased line**. At the ISP end the terminal server multiplexes your signal onto the ISP's LAN.

The web server verifies you have permission to log on, and also undertakes any accounting necessary. There is a news server and post office, which handles the mailboxes of all the ISP's customers.

Any request for a web site not cached by the ISP is sent via the router into the internet backbone via the ISP's **NAP** or **Network Access Point**. Large ISPs will have very fast links into the internet. For example, T3 is typically 44.736 Mbit/sec.

There are only a limited number of modems (and telephone lines) that an ISP has. When all of these modems have been used up you will get a message saying that the line is busy.

As ISPs get busier, larger numbers of modem banks have to be provided for a reasonable service. The bandwidth to the internet backbone might need upgrading if the number of customers becomes very large. Also, when the internet itself becomes clogged, the response from your ISP, irrespective of the speed of connection, will get slower.

Self-test questions

1 Outline a typical scenario in which a star network topology would be ideal.
2 Why has the Ethernet bus topology been largely overtaken by the use of hubs?
3 Explain what peer-to-peer networking means. What equipment would be needed to set up peer-to-peer networking in your home?
4 What is the difference between a LAN and a WAN?
5 What is an VAN? Give an example.
6 Explain what is meant by EDI.
7 You are going to set up a simple ISP service for a limited number of people. Outline the equipment that you would need to provide Web, Usenet and e-mail facilities.
8 Compare and contrast ISDN and ADSL as a means of connecting to the internet. In what circumstances would each be ideal?
9 What device is usually placed at the end of a bus network?
10 Explain what is meant by a collision on an Ethernet network.
11 How might two different ADSL lines be used to give high bandwidth in both directions?
12 A high-bandwidth link is working very slowly. Assuming no technical fault, why might this be a fact of life?
13 How is your e-mail likely to be processed by your ISP?
14 What is a VPN?
15 What advantages does a VPN have to offer?
16 Outline the security considerations when building a VPN.
17 What is a terminal server?
18 What is a network access point?

In this unit you have learned about:

- Network topologies like star, ring, bus and tree
- Peer-to-peer and server-based networking
- Value Added Networks
- EDI
- On-line service providers (ISPs)

63 Connecting to the internet

In this section you will learn about:

- Dial up connections
- ISDN, ADSL and cable modems
- Leased lines
- Satellite connections

Dial up connections

A **dial up connection** is the conventional connection from home, via the public telephone system, as shown on the left-hand side of the diagram in unit 62, Figure 62.5. You are not restricted to internet connections. If you have two computers running a recent version of Windows, then you could set up your own **peer-to-peer networking** via your **modems**, **telephone system** and **dial-up networking**. Dial-up networking would allow you to access a company **intranet** site via a **virtual private network** and is ideal for the new breed of **road warriors** (sales people on the move who need office connectivity).

Example

A dial up connection is to be established between two computers in different places. Outline the equipment needed to do this. What software has to be set up using this dedicated connection? (You are not to make use of an ISP for this connection.)

Solution

Both computers will need a MODEM, a terminal adaptor, or some other suitable link. As far as the computer is concerned, the ideas are virtually identical to connection to an ISP. All you have to do is supply your colleague's phone number as shown in Figure 63.1

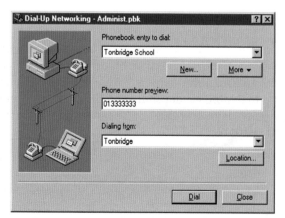

The phone book entry can be any name that you wish, but preferably reflect the place to which you are connecting. Your colleague must now set up his or her computer to respond appropriately when their modem answers your call. This will involve being presented with a log-on screen, into which you may type your user ID and password

Figure 63.1 Setting up the dial-up networking.

The act of logging on via a dial-up connection is no different from logging on via a network. The system can be set up to give access to the drives that you would see via an LAN. The only noticeable difference is the speed of the connection, which could be quite slow compared with networked connections.

ISDN lines

This is a *faster* connection called an **integrated services digital network**. Unlike a conventional analogue connection, which needs a **modem** to convert the **digital signals** from the computer into an **analogue form**, an **ISDN** connection is **digital**. Telecom companies usually provide an ISDN line, and the bandwidth of the line is 64 Kbit/sec. It is a **full-duplex line**, which carries either voice (the normal phone) or data. It is thus ideal for computer communication for use in the home, where the consumer may wish to use the same line for a telephone conversation. **ISDN2**, which is quite popular, is, in effect, **two 64K ISDN lines**. This has the advantage that one line can be used for computer communication while the other line is simultaneously being used for voice. Alternatively you can use both lines for computer data and get an effective bandwidth of **128 Kbit/sec**. The number of ISDN lines may be increased above 3. ISDN32 would, therefore, be 32 ISDN lines. This is typical of the internet connection that might be established in an educational organisation like a school or college. **ISDN32** would give you a bandwidth of 16×128 Kbit/sec (for ISDN2), which is about **2 Mbit/sec**. However, **leased lines** and **ADSL** (see below) may be more cost effective.

> *You must keep up to date with the latest technologies available to connect to the net. You can do this by surfing the net, looking at TV, reading magazines or looking at the press.*

Cable modems

Many homes have **cable TV**, and internet connection via this particular method is becoming popular. There are various methods, but it is often possible to receive computer data and TV at the same time, by assigning a **TV channel** to **computer data**.

The advantage of the **cable modem** provided by the TV company is that *you do not have to use dial up connections* – you are on-line 24 hours a day, 7 days a week (called **24/7**) and the connection is instant. Expect between 500–1000 Kbit/sec, but also expect to share bandwidth your neighbours! In practice this means a considerable drop in performance. Sometimes cable companies will remotely program modems to limit the speed with which data can be accessed!

There are also one-way cable modems, where the data from the ISP comes in at a very fast rate, but the data from the computer is transmitted by the conventional telephone system. Obviously this is less satisfactory than the cable modems described above. As a different channel is assigned to the computer data, you can watch cable TV at the same time as using your computer to surf the net.

ADSL

ADSL stands for **asynchronous digital subscriber line**. It is obviously a digital system, and the asynchronous part means that the data you can receive is at a different rate to the data you can transmit. Usually the **send data rate** is anything between 16 and 64 Kbit/sec, and the **receive data rate** can be anything up to 6 Mbit/sec depending on the cable used and the distance from the telephone exchange. BT launched the ADSL service for consumers in June 2000, but not all exchanges were ready.

More information on the internet can be found in chapter 4 of NUCSAL.

The **asynchronous nature** of the **full-duplex communication** is quite favourable for normal web surfing, where information transmitted by the client is usually trivial in comparison to the data received. It would obviously be useless if you were intending to send as much information as you receive. I would not recommend that you host a web site by this method. Fortunately, ASDL is absolutely ideal for home and office use, and will probably become the norm in the not-too-distant future but DSL will be with us soon.

Example

A department in a school has asked your advice on the merits of ISDN compared to ADSL. They already have a 128 K ISDN line serving 25 machines on a network, and too often it is painfully slow. They need to know if switching to an ADSL line will

give better performance. Outline the pros and cons of each case, explaining why fast connections may actually be quite slow on occasions, and what might be happening in practice in the classroom to slow down this, or indeed any other, connection.

Solution

A 128 K ISDN line would normally be very quick for a single user under optimum conditions. If the site they are trying to use is very busy, then any fast link would be slow, because access to this particular site would be dictated by the response of the server hosting it. It also depends on how many people might be sharing bandwidth at the exchange end. It is possible to have a fast connection, only to be slowed down by the exchange not able to cope.

A 128 K ISDN line shared between 25 users may well be satisfactory under some conditions, but the response for many users could be slowed down if an individual on the network is doing a large file download. For example, loading Service Pack 5 for NT4 requires a file of about 25 Mbytes! Even at 128 Kbits/sec, this would take, on average, 1600 seconds, or 26 minutes, assuming that this student hogged all the available bandwidth. If one or two selfish students do this frequently, then the response may be slow.

Assuming that the line is used only to surf the net, i.e. not to host your own site or send thousands of e-mail messages, an ADSL line should give much better performance because of the increased bandwidth from the ISP to the school. Even with the significant increase in bandwidth offered by the ADSL line, you may have to share the bandwidth to get onto the internet backbone, and this is something that you will need to discuss with your local telecom provider and your ISP.

To sum up, the ADSL should give a significant increase in performance unless the local telephone exchange to which you are connected cannot cope. In this case you may need to consider a leased line, as described in the next section. However, this might be too expensive compared with ADSL.

Leased lines

Table 63.1

Typical transmission rate of leased lines		
Line	Multiples	Transmission rate (Bit/sec)
T1	24 × 64K	1.536 Mbits/sec
T2	4 × T1	6.312 Mbits/sec
T3	28 × T1	44.736 Mbits/sec
T4	6 × T3	274.176 Mbits/sec

A **leased line connection** is a permanent connection to your ISP. The speed of this type of connection varies enormously, but you obviously have no phone bills to pay. A leased line is also known as a **dedicated line**, and these typify the sort of connection used by large schools, universities and commercial organisations. Table 63.1 shows typical connection speeds of different leased lines at the time of writing. The second column gives the multiples of 64 Kbit/sec. Thus a T1 line is 24 × 64 Kbit/sec = 1536 Kbit/sec.

Leased lines are quite expensive, but would speed up internet access. They are for large institutions that can afford the tens of thousands of pounds a year such bandwidths would cost.

Satellite connections

If you have access to Sky Digital, programs like dot.TV keep you up to date with the latest developments.

Surfing the net via a **satellite TV** or having a real satellite internet connection is an attractive proposition. You have no provision for sending data to the satellite, and therefore have to rely on the normal **telephone system** to route your requests to the ISP. A good example of a simple system is the **Sky Digital Open TV connection**. If you wish to surf the net using your PC, then you need a proper internet connection via a satellite cable company who provides this sort of service. Typical speeds available from satellite systems (receive only) are up to 2 Mbits/sec.

Example

You are to connect a computer to the internet via an ISP who uses the telephone system for the uplink (i.e. you to the ISP) and a satellite system for the downlink (i.e. the ISP to you). What equipment is needed to set this up? Suggest advantages over a conventional modem-based link.

Solution

You will need a conventional modem and telephone line set up as though you were using a standard ISP. To receive data from the satellite you will need an appropriate satellite dish, and a special interface between the satellite dish and your computer. The advantage of this system is that the bandwidth of the received information is considerably higher than that which could be expected from a conventional modem.

As new technologies such as ADSL come on stream, and if the number of internet users continues to grow at its present pace, the demands on the bandwidth of the **internet backbones** and **file servers** will be enormous. Fortunately the telephone infrastructure is being upgraded, and digital connectivity is now largely completed in the UK. Cable and satellite companies are providing extra bandwidth too, and companies like CISCO are striving to keep the communication-nodes up to speed.

There is always a constant struggle between the available bandwidth, and the facilities, which people expect from the net. There are now hundreds of radio stations and some TV stations broadcasting over the net, and even people with low-bandwidth links expect these services to work efficiently! As soon as the bandwidth is raised, the technology and software moves on, and video phones, free telephone calls anywhere in the world, live pop concerts on the net and a whole host of other activities will ensure that the bandwidth needs will be increased still further.

Self-test questions

1 What is meant by a dial-up connection?
2 How does an ISDN line differ from a conventional modem connection?
3 What is a typical speed for an ISDN2 line? What can be done to increase this speed even further?
4 What is the difference between a cable modem and a conventional modem?
5 What are the advantages and disadvantages of surfing the net via satellite?
6 What is a current limitation of surfing the web using a conventional TV?
7 ADSL is likely to become one of the standard ways of connecting to the net. What makes this method of connection ideal for home surfers?
8 A business has its own VPN. State, with reasons, whether you would advise them to set this up with ADSL or ISDN.
9 A large university has a T4 link to the internet. Why might it choose this method of connection?

In this unit you have learned about:

- Dial-up connections, ISDN, ADSL and cable modems
- Leased line connections
- Satellite connections

64 Embedded systems and data logging

In this section you will learn about:

- Embedded systems
- Control systems
- Sensors and transducers
- Scientific applications
- Data logging
- Forecasting the weather
- Simulators

Embedded systems

Embedded systems involve one or more **microprocessors** *embedded* into a system for a specific purpose. They are not the same as a general purpose PC, but are likely to be found in **washing machines, cameras, DVD players** and other consumer equipment. They are also used in the military to **guide missiles**, in the computer **arcade gaming** industry, in **manufacturing industry** to control robots, and in houses to undertake **domestic control functions**. Embedded systems follow instructions given them by programs. They do *not* usually have an operating system, because they are very specific in what they do.

Much electronics is being replaced by **embedded systems**, because it is cheaper to manufacture, and new ideas are possible. With a TCP/IP enabled oven, you could remotely delay cooking if stuck in a traffic jam. The possibilities are great. It is one reason why the communications industry is booming.

Example

Describe four of the functions that an embedded microprocessor system may perform in a digital camera.

Solution

(1) Controlling the amount of light that reaches the chip makes sure the exposure is correct. In automatic mode the camera ensures that light reaching the sensitive chip is optimum by using this **automatic exposure feature**.
(2) The **digital zoom** can be controlled by the embedded system. This could work by selecting a small part of the picture and making it appear large to the user.
(3) The **duration of the flash** may be controlled by the embedded system, and thus night time photography can be correctly exposed.
(4) The camera needs to be synchronised with the computer when **downloading the pictures** that have been taken into your main computer system. The embedded system would be able to talk to the computer via the fire wire, USB or other serial interface, and manage the communication protocols.

Common sense is needed in abundance to answer questions on embedded systems. It is usually possible to work out something along the right lines, even if you have never used the device. For example, try listing four functions of an in-car navigation system using GPS (the satellite Global Positioning System). Try to do this before looking at the next question.

Example

Describe four of the functions that an embedded microprocessor system may perform in an in-car navigation system.

Visit our portal to find information on embedded system technology.

Try to be familiar with common electronic gadgets such as PDAs, digital cameras, video recorders and DVD players etc. It may help you to answer questions on embedded systems.

Solution

(1) A **real-time map** is displayed on the screen. It is the function of the embedded microprocessor system to update the display.
(2) **Audio instructions**, via a computer voice, could be used to give directions.
(3) The destination address could be input into the system, either by **voice input** or **keyboard**. It is the job of the embedded system to interpret these commands and take action.
(4) The embedded system can work out things like **ETA** given the current and likely speeds that the journey will involve.

Answers to the last two questions are not unique. They are not right or wrong, but would get appropriate marks in an exam. We could have concentrated on traffic information when dealing with GPS navigation, or used automatic dating on the camera.

Control systems

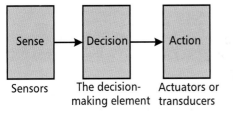

Sensors   The decision-making element   Actuators or transducers

Figure 64.1 Three control-system elements.

Most embedded systems considered so far have one thing in common. They take **real-time readings** via **sensors**, and use the data to feedback information to the decision-making element, which takes appropriate action and activates the mechanisms. This **feedback** is of fundamental importance; without it no intelligent control would be possible.

Robots, like Sony's AIBO dog, for example, give a huge insight into the way that embedded system technology might be used in the future.

There are three essential elements to a **feedback control system** as shown in Figure 64.1.

A camera could sense the amount of light via a **light sensor**, decide on the exposure for the film (controlled by the software **embedded** into the microprocessor's memory), and then activate the flash (the light **transducer**) for the appropriate amount of time.

Example

Explain how feedback might be used in a missile-guidance system controlled by an embedded microprocessor.

Solution

There are many different missile systems (heat seeking, anti-radar, cruise missile etc.). Assume a laser-guided missile, which navigates via tracking a laser beam held on the target.

Sensors inside the missile pick up feedback from the laser beam during flight. If the missile is veering off course then corrections are made until the missile is headed straight towards the beam. The process of monitoring the beam and supplying small course corrections to the thrusters continues until the missile explodes or is aborted.

Sensors and transducers

A variety of **sensors** and **transducers** exist, enabling control systems to be used in all **domestic, industrial, military** and **scientific** applications. A range of sensors includes, **light, heat, sound, pressure, voltage, current, resistance, radiation** and **pH** to name but a few. A range of **activators** or transducers includes **motors, solenoids, light bulbs** and **loud speakers**.

A **sensor** can be regarded as a device, which converts a quantity (like sound, heat and light etc.) into electrical energy. A **transducer** converts electrical energy back into other forms of energy (like sound, heat and light).

Control systems play a major part in embedded systems, as most embedded systems of any complexity make use of feedback. This is often referred to as a feedback loop, because information from sensors is used to make decisions, which would alter the actions taken by the transducers. In this way a nuclear power station could be controlled via a variety of embedded systems and computers.

Scientific applications

The range of scientific applications is vast, and varies from data logging, via mapping the human genome to forecasting the weather. Data logging is a particularly important scientific use of a computer, and you should be familiar with common techniques.

Data logging

Sensors like those described in the last section are used to monitor the progress of scientific experiments. If you wanted to monitor heat in a chemical reaction over time, then a heat sensor placed in the solution might do the trick. The advantages of data logging over conventional data recording are obvious, and can be listed as follows:

- The data recorder does not get bored and miss readings.
- Errors are less likely if data is recorded automatically.
- The rate at which data can be captured is much faster. For example, thousands of data readings may be taken each second.
- The length of time over which readings can be taken could be much longer. For example, one reading can be taken every half hour for a period of five years.

Data logging equipment may be connected, via an appropriate interface, to a microcomputer, where the data can be captured and recorded in some suitable format. The data may be analysed by a spreadsheet, stored in a database, and summaries automatically generated by linking to a word processor.

Scientific and engineering applications of computers are covered in chapter 7 of NUCSAL.

Example

Suggest how it is possible to monitor river pollution over a period of several years. Include a list of sensors, and explain the main components needed.

Solution

The pollutants being detected would determine the sensors: a pH meter to measure the acidity of the water, a flow meter to measure the rate of flow, a water-level meter to measure the height of the river and a thermometer to measure the temperature of the water are a good start.

Sensors should be placed at salient positions in the river, and linked into a data-logging system or a computer system with an appropriate interface. The computer or data-logging equipment would normally be housed on the bank of the river, and set up to automatically monitor the data at appropriate intervals.

At set times, the data would need to be collected by downloading it into a file for further analysis. If the data logging equipment had a radio or internet link, then data could be transferred automatically to the science labs where further analysis could be performed.

Portable self-contained data-logging devices may be used in the field. These usually have small LCD screens to enable the embedded microprocessor system to confirm that the data has been captured correctly. At some later date the data may then be downloaded into a PC via the internet or via a serial port.

Forecasting the weather

There are many centres of excellence around the world like the National Hurricane Prediction Centre or the Met Office to name but two. These centres have one or more

supercomputers performing an enormous number of calculations to produce a variety of forecasts for **TV**, **radio**, **industry**, and the **military**. They are also used for general research into global conditions like El Nino.

Complex mathematical models process the information gathered from **satellite** and **ground monitoring stations** globally. Some weather stations automatically send data back via radio or internet communications, and others are operated manually, requiring readings to be sent in to organisations.

Simulators

These range in complexity from the small simulators used to test driving skills, via the theme park rides of the sort found in Disneyland to sophisticated pilot training used by the aviation industry. Simulators usually integrate **embedded** and **mechanical systems** and are usually controlled by one or more **computer systems**.

At the heart of these simulators is a small environment (pod) into which users are placed. This is usually mounted on hydraulic jacks enabling the pod to experience controlled rapid motion in all directions. Users will observe very large screens through a window in the pod. The projected images, together with the synchronised motion of the pod and the sound effects give very convincing experiences, which make the users feel as if they are fully immersed in a real environment. Large screens and projection systems, often identical to those used in Imax cinemas, project high quality coloured imagery, the movement of which is synchronised to the hydraulic systems which are also controlled by the computer.

The most sophisticated of these simulators are those used for pilot training. Here the characteristics of individual aircraft like the Jumbo Jet or Concorde, for example, are programmed into the system so that the response of the system to pilot input is identical to that which would be experienced in the real aircraft.

A bank of computers, under the control of the flight-training instructor, provides a variety of scenarios into which the pilots may be put. Trying to land the aircraft in very bad weather or with an engine fire is typical of the sort of thing that a pilot is required to do every six months to keep his or her licence. Even though the cost of these simulators can run into tens of millions of pounds, this is the only sensible way to give pilots experience of life and death scenarios, which hopefully will never occur during their careers.

Self-test questions

1 What is an embedded system?
2 Why is real-time processing important for embedded systems?
3 What are transducers and sensors?
4 Name five different sensors, indicating a typical situation in which they might be used.
5 Name five different output transducers, indicating a typical situation in which they might be used.
6 Explain what is meant by data logging.
7 Outline the sensors that might be needed for monitoring the pollution in a river.
8 What three elements are typical in a control system?
9 Why is feedback important in a control system?

In this unit you have learned about:

- What is meant by an embedded system
- Computer control systems
- Sensors and transducers
- Scientific applications like data logging, forecasting the weather and computer simulations

65 Further ethical issues and legislation

In this section you will learn about:

- Social and economic issues of computer applications
- Ethical issues
- Artificial intelligence and expert systems
- Legal implications
- The Data Protection Act
- The Computer Misuse Act
- European legislation

Legislation, such as the Data Protection Act, the Computer Misuse Act and current European directives provide for easy examination questions. Do not throw away these marks by not bothering to learn the main points.

Social and economic issues

Modern computers are **all-pervasive**. Few areas are left untouched by **ICT**. You should be able to comment on issues, ranging from **social** and **economic** to **legal** and **ethical**.

The web and ICT in general are **socially divisive**. Most of the population of the world is denied access to ICT because they have no access to computers. In the developed world, the population is being split into those who can benefit because they have computers at home, and those who cannot.

Example

Suggest ways in which computer access to ICT and the web can be improved for less well off members of society.

Solution

Internet access can be placed in libraries, shopping centres and other suitable publicly accessible places. This enables access to the net for nothing. The government is proposing a scheme whereby reconditioned computers can be rented for a small amount of money each week, thus enabling more of the population to have an internet-ready computer in their home. However, even the cost of local calls may be prohibitive in some cases, and the poorer families may not have a phone line.

Schools and colleges now have access to the net, although in common with the machines placed in public libraries and shopping centres, the queues may be long. It also takes a long time to learn the skills, and thus people gain from the convenience of having a PC or internet access via Web TV at home.

The **economics** of the introduction of ICT are far reaching. **Less people are needed** in industry and commerce, and people left working need a **high degree of skill**. Companies cannot ignore the introduction of new technology because it usually results in **higher productivity** and **lower costs**.

During the early part of the 21st century there is a **serious shortage of skilled ICT professionals**, and this has led to an increase in labour costs, where companies, able to give a significant increase in salary, often poach key personnel.

We are currently going through the experimental stage regarding **e-commerce**. New things are being tried out on the web to see if the public respond. **E-mail** is a good example, where most people with a computer at home now have an e-mail address. Few companies these days are without a **web site**, whether or not they actually need one!

Example

Electronic banking is starting to take off. Outline why this is so, and the social consequences of going down this path.

Solution

Electronic banking is cheaper as no branches and fewer staff are needed. Banks are able to offer competitive rates to savers, unlikely to be matched by banks with branch networks.

Internet banking enables accounts to be managed from anywhere in the world. You can pay bills, look at your statement and balance, set up standing orders or order cheque books from anywhere, at any time 24 hours a day, 7 days a week, including holidays. This level of service is obviously unprecedented in the history of banking, and is cheaper to operate.

The problem here is that the internet is socially divisive. You are allowing the better off with access to computers to have convenient banking, and are denying this service to those who do not have access. As the branch network shrinks, many small villages no longer have banking facilities, and the elderly, technologically illiterate and the poor suffer the consequences.

Addiction to computers

This is a growing social phenomenon, usually among people **addicted** to **computer games** or **surfing the net**. The advent of very cheap, and often free internet access means that people can now surf the net 24 hours a day for next to nothing. The **chat lines, on-line gambling, Usenet user groups** and **shopping** on the net are examples of areas where people can use the net so often it is to the detriment of other parts of their lives. It is the case that schooling suffers because of this, and some people have little control over their ability to keep off the internet once they become hooked. **Computer games** are just as addictive; especially games like *Quake* and adventure games like *Baldor's Gate*, for example. Most computer science students probably know people who play these games into the early hours each morning, only to find that they do not function well the next day. This is also a problem in most universities.

Ethical issues

The use of computers, and the web in particular, breaks down **national boundaries**, and provides a high degree of **freedom of speech** for individuals, no matter where they are. For most people this is an advantage, but some people use the internet to try to corrupt others. Sites that incite racial hatred or promote Nazi propaganda are good examples of misusing these rights.

Although the subjects mentioned above are at one extreme, issues like abortion or euthanasia also divide members of society. It is difficult to suggest whether sites like this ought to be banned, because it depends on your opinion. Issues that some would consider extreme, others do not, and it is therefore an ethical minefield. Some people favour censorship and some freedom of speech. Different governments have different reactions to varying degrees of pornography, soft drugs like cannabis, and material that might upset different ethnic or religious groups. You can review the computer policy documentation in unit 59 to remind you of the things that cause problems in this area.

Artifical intelligence and expert systems

AI ranges from attempts to enable machines to think to the use of **expert systems** to take over roles previously held by respected members of the community. In medical diagnostics it is possible for an expert system to diagnose illnesses more effectively and more

Keep up to date by looking at the main news programmes, and specialist technology programmes like those found on Sky Digital, for example.

quickly than a team of specialists. Computers can also act as tireless tutors for pupils – there few areas of human endeavour, including writing poetry and writing and playing music, where the computer is unlikely to intervene.

Legal implications

Computers always have the potential to be misused, but the introduction and widespread use of the internet has compounded this potential. The legal system finds it difficult to keep pace with changing technologies, but some **legal structures** have been put in place to protect individuals and companies.

The Data Protection Act of 1998

The **Data Protection Act** legislates to protect information about individuals held on a computer system. In a nutshell the Act provides for the following:

- The data should be processed fairly and lawfully.
- The data should not be used for any other purpose.
- The data shall be adequate and relevant.
- The data shall be accurate and kept up to date.
- The data shall not be kept for longer than necessary.
- The data shall be protected from unauthorised access.
- The data shall not be transferred outside the EEC unless the country concerned complies with the Act.
- The person about whom the data is stored must have given their consent.

In addition to the above, the user about whom the data has been stored has the right to examine the data and demand it to be changed if there are errors.

Example

Why is it necessary to have the Data Protection Act of 1998? Give an example of a right that a user has under this act, and how this legal right might be useful in practice.

Solution

Before the advent of the Data Protection Act people had no legal redress as to how information, stored about them in computer systems, is used. Before large-scale data processing and the internet, information held about individuals in filing cabinets in different locations was difficult to process and correlate. With computer systems this is trivially easy, and large dossiers could be built up on individuals and transferred to others. Financial institutions might refuse to grant funding based on incorrect information, stored on a computer by a credit reference agency. For a small fee, an individual now has a right to examine the information, and change it if it happens to be in error.

The Computer Misuse Act

Until this Act was passed, the only crime committed by hackers was that of stealing electricity from the company into which they might have hacked. This act makes it a crime to **illegally gain access** to information in computer systems to which you should have no access. The act also makes it illegal to deliberately **inject a virus** into a computer.

European legislation

There is now a surfeit of **European legislation** on **computers** and **e-commerce**. With electronic commerce taking off, there is a huge wealth of legislation needed to make sure that everything from the **protection of credit-card numbers** to the **privacy of the individual**

Many social implications regarding the use of computers are covered in chapter 9 of NUCSAL.

Visit our portal to find out about European ICT legislation.

using the Internet is covered. Some of the relevant issues covered by the part of the site dealing with law and e-commerce are as follows:

- Distance selling
- Electronic signatures
- Electronic contracts
- Internet management
- IPR (Intellectual Property Rights)
- IPR Copyright
- IPR Databases
- IPR Software
- IPR Semiconductors
- Privacy
- Taxation
- Legal documents

The main points covered include **security of information**, **intellectual property rights**, **privacy**, **taxation issues**, and **validation** of **authentication** (electronic signatures).

Example

Why is taxation becoming an important issue when using the web?

Solution

If you purchase goods in the UK then they are subject to VAT. If you purchase the same goods abroad via the net they are not. Tax revenue lost can therefore be enormous. Many parcels are intercepted by customs, and when collecting the parcel from the post office you must pay the VAT due, but millions each year are still lost to this form of trading.

Self-test questions

1 Why might it not be a good idea to introduce high-tech computer-based solutions into a third world country? Give arguments for and against this view.
2 What ethical issues would have to be argued if computers ever became intelligent?
3 Computers are addictive. Outline a typical scenario in which this could be true, saying what you would do about the problem.
4 Pupils learn more effectively using computers. Outline a case for keeping teachers.
5 Suggest three different areas in which expert systems may be employed, giving typical examples of each in your chosen areas of interest.
6 Suggest six different ways computers might be misused in the workplace.
7 What legislation is in operation to protect individuals from the misuse of data held about them on computers?
8 How might it be possible to collect tax from internet transactions?
9 List some modern European legislation regarding e-commerce.
10 Suggest three areas of ethical concern regarding computers.

In this unit you have learned about:

- Consequences of the use of computers like **Computer addiction**
- **Expert systems**
- Computer legislation like the **Data Protection Act** and **Computer Misuse Act**
- **European legislation**

66 A2 project work – getting started

In this section you will learn about:

- Getting started on your projects
- The mark schemes
- What sorts of projects are suitable
- Finding a client (third party)
- Brainstorming
- The formal interview
- Mapping of key skills

Photocopy the mark scheme for your board. Keep it with you while you undertake all the project work, and refer to it constantly.

Getting started

You have already experienced project work in your AS year, and know only too well how much work is involved. This is probably compounded by project work in other subjects, and key deadlines must obviously be met. This is a daunting task, and anything that you can do to help manage the equally tough second year of your course is therefore worth attempting.

Start during the summer holidays

It is strongly advised that computer science students get a project approved by their supervisor *before* the summer vacation. You can then do much of the groundwork, or even delve a significant way into the project. Time spent over the summer holiday researching the project, gathering information, and talking to clients is invaluable, and makes the project easier to do in the time that you have.

Gather information before June or July in the lower sixth and start in the summer holidays. You need a good deal of help from your teacher or lecturer during the summer term of the previous year. It only make matters worse if you do not seek advice from your teachers. Without this you may choose a project, which is inappropriate, and this would be worse than not starting at all. **Without being able to see your teachers until the final academic year, you would be unwise to go too far ahead with a project of your own choosing.**

The mark scheme

The most important piece of information that you can lay your hands on is the mark scheme – ignore this at your peril. Many students have produced wonderful projects, only to be awarded fewer marks because they have ignored sections of the mark scheme. Most boards have similar mark schemes for the main project. We will use the AQA mark scheme for the 2002 project as an example. It is split up into the sections shown in Table 66.1.

The A2 project for AQA is worth 20% of the total AS and A2 marks. This is a substantial number of marks for a piece of work over which you have absolute control. **The number of marks awarded for the project makes the difference between a 'grade A' and a 'grade C'** Although you should not go overboard, losing marks through lack of organisation, carelessness, lack of attention to the mark scheme or lack of time is unforgivable.

Table 66.1 A typical mark scheme

The AQA 2002 project marking structure	
Analysis	12
Design	12
Technical solution	12
System testing	6
System maintenance	6
User manual	6
Appraisal	3
Quality of communication	3
Total	60

What sort of projects are suitable?

This is the six million dollar question! Without going into too much detail, projects involving the design of a **relational database** (see unit 47), advanced use of **spreadsheets** (see unit 32), **web-site design** *with* **some programming element** or a **pure programming** exercise make ideal projects. Some of the projects at the author's school have involved the following:

- A relational database for a jeweller's shop (programmed using **Microsoft Access**)
- An electronic-reporting system for teachers for a school in Hong Kong (programmed using **Access** and **Excel**)
- An automatic report-generation and profiling system to produce ICT reports and profiles (programmed using **Access**)
- An electronic glossary for Computer Science (programmed using **PERL**)
- A microprocessor simulation and teaching aid (programmed using **Visual Basic**)
- A statistical analysis program for Post Office closures based on demographic data from a post-code database (programmed using **Visual Basic**)
- An advertising package for showing business clients the facilities that can be hired at Tonbridge School (programmed using **Power Point** with **VBA extensions**)

As you can see, the variety of projects is wide, but one thing that all projects have in common is that they all have a **client**.

Getting a third party (a client)

Most boards require that you find a third party. This is somebody for whom you can carry out the project. **Without a third party it is difficult, if not impossible, to get some of the marks awarded**.

It is important to choose your third party wisely. They will have to provide you with a considerable amount of **feedback** regarding your project, from an **initial acceptance letter**, though many stages of **questionnaires** and **interviews**, through **prototyping**, **testing** to **final evaluation** and **acceptance**. This is a lot of work for your client to do. Make sure that he or she willing to do this *before* undertaking any project work.

Never embark too far into a project without getting it approved by your teacher or lecturer first.

It is convenient if you can get a **teacher**, a **parent** or a **close relative** to be your client. It must be someone that you can see on a regular basis. Parents and relatives are a good source of ideas if they have a business.

Brainstorming

Before starting a project of any complexity you need to think about the possibilities in detail. One of the best ways of doing this is to **brainstorm** possible ideas. Assuming you know roughly what you are going to do, it is probably best to do this *before* you meet for the first **formal interview** with your **client**. A brainstorm will show thoughts about the project in detail. It does not matter if some of your ideas will not be used, others might produce fruit and impress your client.

Student Activity

Think up at least three or four different possible ideas for a project. Brainstorm each of your ideas to see how it might progress. For each idea write down who would be your client for the project.

Solution

*A brainstorm is simply a set of ideas that enter your head. They do not have to be categorised into good or bad ideas – just write them down as fast as you possibly can. Then organise your thoughts into a **bubble diagram**.*

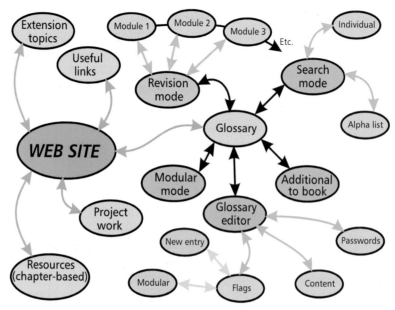

Figure 66.1 Brainstorming for a web site.

Suppose, for example, you had the job of brainstorming the web-site contents for the site that accompanies this revision guide and the *New Understanding Computer Science for Advanced Level* textbook. These ideas might be as shown in Figure 66.1

The main sections are outlined, together with important subsections. It does not matter if they will all be implemented; it is the initial ideas that are important. Only part of the brainstorming has been shown in Figure 66.1. It would take up too much space to show it all.

Take the glossary section, which has been shown in detail. There are many computer glossaries available on the internet – what makes this one different? As you can appreciate, it is a glossary specifically for students of 'A' level Computer Science and other similar courses. Therefore, all the terms are relevant to the study of computing at this level.

The glossary may be listed in a variety of different ways, and this is what makes it special. If you are studying for module one, for example, then we have provided a cut-down version of the glossary that is applicable to module one only. There is also a revision mode, which will list glossary entries at random, thus prompting students to think about possible answers. The glossary entries can then be uncovered at the touch of a button.

There will need to be an editor so that the author may edit individual glossary entries without having to FTP (see unit 55) a large part of the site. This editor must also be able to edit flags that indicate the module and board to which the entry belongs.

In addition to this there is a flag that indicates whether the glossary entry is actually in the glossary at the back of the main *New Understanding Computer Science* textbook. This will enable readers to print out a list of additional glossary items, so they may add these to their printed glossary. Although these items will be in the 5th edition of the book, the technology changes rapidly, and new entries will appear on this site at frequent intervals.

It is unlikely that a student would come up with all the detail shown in Figure 66.1, but it should give you an idea of how to proceed with your project before the start of the formal interviews with your client.

Extra work on projects is covered in chapter 33 of NUCSAL.

The formal interview

This is an **important stage of your project**. It determines the groundwork from which all of the project will grow. You need to make **copious notes** at this stage, to make sure that you and your client agree *exactly* what you will do. Your client will then need to write a **formal letter** outlining the project which you can include in your final-project write up. It is inevitable that your client will forget something important at this stage!

Don't promise the Earth!

One of the most important things for both you and your client to realise is that the project may never work properly. Do not forget that you are not undertaking a commission to design a commercial piece of software; you are undertaking an A-level project. If the product can be used at the end of the time then this is a bonus, but **your A-level work is** *the* **top priority**.

You must be realistic about the amount of time you have to do the project, and the website example described in the last section is a good case in point. Although the author's students are constructing parts of the site, only the glossary is being undertaken by one of the students for the purposes of their A2 project. This is because an unrealistic amount of work would be needed to implement the site in its entirety, and this is a long way beyond any sensible time limit imposed by the A2 project.

Before proceeding

Before committing yourself to the final project you must check with your teacher or lecturer that the work you are proposing is suitable for your particular course. You will need to check both the **quantity**, the **likely resources** that you have to implement the project, and the **suitability** in terms of *your ability* to carry out the necessary technical solution. As suggested at the beginning of this unit, if you can carry this out at the end of the first year of your course, you will be using the summer-holiday time productively.

Mapping of key skills

Undertaking a course in **Computer Science** gives you an added bonus in that you can pick up some useful **UCAS points** in the form of **Key Skills**. Your A2 project is an ideal vehicle for doing this, and should mop up most, if not all, of the skills awarded for the 'Information Technology' component at **levels 3 and 4**. With care it can also pick up many of the 'Communication' and 'Application of Number' skills too. Ask your teacher to give you all the necessary information that will enable you to do this.

Visit our portal for some exemplar 'A' level projects that have been done in the past.

To find out about Key Skills

In this unit you have learned about:

- How to get started on your **main project work**
- The importance of adhering to the **mark scheme**
- What projects are suitable
- How to find a **client**
- **Brainstorming**
- The **initial interview**
- How **key skills** may be mapped to this area

67 Further A2 project work

In this section you will learn about:

- Choosing the right project
- The analysis phase
- Background, problem ID and users
- The write up
- Possible solutions
- The design and testing

The AS units 32, 33 and 25, and the A2 units 47, 48 and 49 are useful reading before starting your A2 project work.

Make sure you have the technical capability to carry out a project to its conclusion before starting. Your teacher will be able to advise you of this.

Visit our portal where you can use the actual glossary on the web.

Have you chosen an appropriate project?

You should not proceed far with the analysis phase without deciding if your project is appropriate. If you have your teacher's approval then it should be fine. If you did not manage to get approval, and want to start thinking before the new academic year, an outline of features given for the AQA examining board is as follows:

- Is it a real situation that the candidate can investigate?
- Is there a user whose needs can be investigated and taken into account when designing the solution?
- Does it conform to the specification requirements, i.e. will the finished product be a tailored solution which allows interaction between the user and the computer system with input, storage and manipulation of data and output of results?
- Is it of Advanced Level standard?
- Is it within the capability of the candidate to complete in a reasonable time?
- Are the necessary facilities readily available to the candidate?
- Is it a subject the candidate has knowledge of/interest in?

Unless you can answer yes to all the above points you are advised to consider another project. **You should not proceed with your project beyond this point unless all the above criteria have been met.**

The analysis phase

Having decided on a project you now need to start on the **analysis** of the project. It is essential to look at the mark scheme, and the AQA scheme for the 2002 A2 project will be used as an example. The analysis section of the project consists of the following sections:

- Background/identification of problem
- Identification of prospective user(s)
- Identification of user needs and acceptable limitations (using appropriate methods – summarised as necessary)
- Realistic appraisal of the feasibility of potential solutions
- Justification of chosen solution
- Data source(s) and destination(s) and logical DfDs (existing system and proposed system) and E-R Model (where relevant)
- Objectives of the project.

We will continue with the electronic glossary as an example (unit 65). It would be impossible to cover *all* work necessary for this project here. The write up (carried out for the OCR board 2001 entry) can be found on the web site. Here we will concentrate on using this particular project as a vehicle to learn about tackling your project work.

Background, problem identification and users

The following information is typical of that which would be obtained from the first interview with your client.

Student Activity

For your project, briefly identify all bulleted points outlined in the previous analysis phase. Write them down to prove that you have a detailed understanding of the problem you are about to solve.

Solution

The sort of information appropriate to the electronic glossary project is as follows.

Given the dynamic nature of computer science, small parts of the existing glossary given in the back of the 'A' level textbook are inevitably out of date. There is a need for an up-to-date electronic version delivered via the Web.

Due to the nature of an electronic glossary, it is possible to structure it to the needs of the student. For example, it is possible to show separate views of the glossary for each modular component. This will help with revision for particular modules.

The electronic version of the glossary will enable the student to use revision mode to view random glossary entries and reveal answers.

A glossary editor needs to be developed to enable the manager to update individual glossary entries on line, without the need to ftp the entire glossary or individual pages.

The site will need to be attractive for the students, but must also have a quick response time and be functional. It must work on standard browsers, and users without 'appropriate plug ins' (like Macromedia Flash, for example), must be able to view and use the site satisfactorily.

The project is obviously feasible as there are many electronic glossaries in existence.

The programming aspects of the project to display the glossary in many different forms make it suitable for an A2 project. A sever-side database needs to be interrogated by a browser at the client end. The source of the data for the project is a text file containing the data in an appropriate form for the A-Level book.

The write up for the analysis

Another good piece of advice is to write up the project as you are going along. Also, keep a project diary, in which salient points about your design decisions have been entered. There is nothing worse than not remembering why 'this or that' decision was made several months ago. If you have a diary, and write up your project as you proceed, then important points will not be missed. Make sure that you start your project write up on a word processor. *Choose a suitable professional style for the write up, including headers, footers, footnotes and page numbers.*

Adhere to the mark scheme

A sample of projects is sent to the board for **moderation**. This ensures candidates have been treated fairly. Put yourself in the position of the moderator. He or she must find evidence of why your teacher has awarded marks. Always study the mark scheme, and *document places where you have shown evidence*, right down to the page numbers. Nothing is more frustrating than trying to find information in a badly laid out project. Consider the following examples of **good practice**.

- *Does your project require a user?*

Keep at least two backup copies of your project in different buildings. Perhaps keep one or two at home, one at school and one on a Zip disk in your pocket. Don't forget to keep them all up to date!

Where have you introduced your user, and where have you written down information about them, including the background of the company or institution for which the project is being done? List the page number where this evidence can be found.

- *Does your project require that you have input, output, and manipulation of data?*

Where have you said how you will input data? In what form are you going to store the data? What outputs are required? Where in your project have you outlined this? How is the data manipulated? Have you written down the page numbers where you have shown this?

The above **rigorous approach** to the project write up, together with a **professionally produced document** enables the teacher, and hence the moderator to find information quickly. Only the quality of the work is then in doubt. In the analysis section, for example, they will be marking along the following lines:

- *Little or no evidence of analysis*
- *Some analysis but limited in scope*
- *Evidence of a well-structured analysis*
- *Evidence of an extensive well-structured analysis.*

Keep the moderators happy. With many projects to mark, they appreciate a well-written project in which it is easy to find information.

Possible solutions

There is probably more than one way to solve your problem, and preferably you should think of several viable alternatives, making a list of why each may or may not be the best. Things to consider here are as follows:

(1) **Technical efficiency** (is this the best technical way to solve the problem?)

(2) **Resources** (Are the appropriate resources available – if not, you might have to use a less than optimum solution.)

(3) **The client's preferences** (Do special circumstances regarding the client place any restrictions on the solution?)

Presentation of diagrams

Many students are surprisingly reluctant to produce diagrams to illustrate their thinking. They would rather write a few hundred words than use an appropriate **system flowchart**, **ER diagram** or **hierarchical diagram** etc. This is usually a bad move, and *you will lose marks without diagrams in your analysis section*. Diagrams are even more important when you implement the design stage shown next.

The design of your project

The AQA 2002 mark scheme will be used as an example. In your project design they will expect most of the following:

- Overall system design
- Description of modular structure of system (not detailed algorithm design)
- Definition of data requirements, such as input and output data types and formats
- Identification of appropriate storage media and format
- Identification of suitable algorithms for data transformation (not detailed algorithm design)
- Identification and implementation of validation
- User interface design including input/output, forms and reports
- Sample of planned data capture and entry
- Sample of data validation, illustrating the operation of error messages
- Description of record structure or database structure
- Sample of planned valid output

Extra work on projects is covered in chapter 33 of NUCSAL.

Do not forget that most of the marks awarded for the project are for the written report seen by the moderator. It is vital that this document conforms to the mark scheme.

- File organisation and processing
- Database design including E-R model
- Description of measures planned for security and integrity of data.
- Description of measures planned for system security (access control)
- Overall test strategy

Students often fail to realise that *most of the marks are not awarded for implementing the system*, but for the **analysis**, **design**, **testing**, **maintenance** and **documentation**.

Some **important considerations** for different project types are as follows, all of which could be represented using a **hierarchical diagram**.

Designing a website? – Lay out the site with respect to the home page.

Writing a program? – Modularise the program into smaller self-contained sub-modules, outlining the function of each.

Designing a database? – Identify main parts like construction of the database, entering the data, validation and production of reports etc.

Working with a spreadsheet? – Identify the major parts of the model, how data is input, validation, and any special functions like macros or code that needs to be written.

Prototyping is an important part of the design of your project. Be in constant touch with your client to make sure that you get a **user interface** that is acceptable. When designing a program or a database, draw pictures of different ways of entering data (e.g. drop down menus, radio buttons etc.). Explain the advantages and disadvantages, and get the user to say which method he or she likes. Get the user to **approve the user interface** in a *written letter; this will make for few arguments later*!

Filling in the detail

You can now work in more detail, making sure that you use information from your project analysis section. For example, if you are designing a database, then start to think about the tables, the data types (like numeric, date or Boolean etc.), what length should each field be? Think in detail about the validation that is needed on each data item.

Visit our portal to see how a typical A Level project has been marked.

Make sure appropriate diagrams are shown at all possible stages. Students often ignore data capture. If data has to be put into your system (a requirement for meeting the specifications), then where does the data come from? If manual data must be entered, have you designed a form for this purpose? If not, have you shown the current manual methods? If, for example, you are writing a program to analyse student data, then show part of a teacher's register (with names blanked out), to show existing manual methods of recording.

Testing

Do not forget to include measures for **testing** the system, and design these *before* actually setting up the system. There is nothing worse than spending a long time debugging your system to end up with a perfectly working system, and only then to think about testing it. You will end up thinking that it does not need testing because it appears to work perfectly. It is unlikely that any project you develop will work perfectly first time, and it is easier to think up ways of testing the project before it is actually implemented.

In this unit you have learned about:

- How to make sure you have chosen the right project
- The analysis phase
- Background write up
- Identifying the problems and coming up with **possible solutions**
- Starting to consider testing

68 A2 project work – wrapping it up

In this section you will learn about:

- Implementing the solution
- Screen captures
- Code listings
- System testing
- System maintenance
- The user manual
- The appraisal
- Spelling, punctuation and grammar

The technical solution

At last you have reached the part of your project which is usually the most exciting – the part where you actually sit at the computer and implement it.

All too frequently students sit down at the computer before completing the analysis and design phases outlined in the last two units. There is nothing worse than trying to start your project without a thorough analysis and design with which to work. Most students who take this approach are unwise and may well fail, or at least find writing up the project work exceptionally difficult. Some students find it difficult to analyse and design a problem – they have no experience in taking this approach, and do not really know why one method might be better than any other until they have tried it out, by which time it might be too late!

The discovery-based approach revisited

Having read units 28 through 33, when the AS project exercises were carried out, you will know exactly what is meant by the discovery-based approach. Students will often not know enough about computer science to be able to make the sensible decisions required regarding which way they should implement parts of their project. Understandably they are unable to commit themselves one way or the other because they lack suitable experience of either method. However, by the second year of your course you are considerably more experienced compared to when you undertook the AS work. Nevertheless, the principles are the same, and can be summed up as follows.

(1) If you do not know which package is best for implementing a solution to a particular problem, try out a similar example using each of the packages, or ask somebody with more experience.

(2) If you do not know how to do something specific, try it out on the computer (e.g. validation using a spreadsheet).

(3) Use the help files and manuals to find out how to do specific things. The help files in systems like Visual Basic, for example, are extremely good, and you can often cut and paste examples of code, which may be used in your project. (Do not forget to acknowledge this.)

If possible look at projects that have been done in the past. There are a range of past projects at www.revisecomputing.com.

Point 3 above is particularly important. In the time that you have available you will not be able to reinvent the wheel. There is no point developing code to sort data into alphabetical

---

Make your project documentation look professional. You should have access to all the software needed to do this. Badly laid out final reports indicate lack of commitment and lack of time.

Use a CAD or art package to do the diagrams. However, do not scan in images when you can include originals, or re-write handwritten interview notes, which look quite good in the appendix of any project. It shows you have actually had the interviews.

order if it is already available, either in a book, or from a third party. If you have access to a piece of publicly available code that does the job you require – use it. *Do not forget that the actual implementation of the project does not make up the majority of the marks.*

Take lots of screen captures

You should take many screen captures of the project as you develop it. **This will provide major evidence that the project you have designed actually works.**

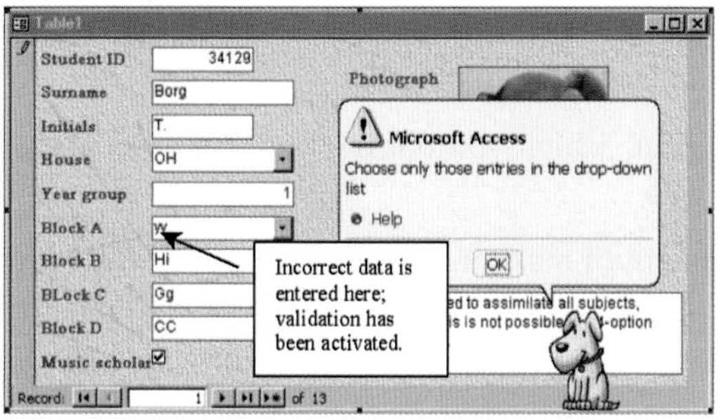

Figure 68.1 Annotate with callout boxes.

Screen captures provide ideal evidence that validation works (by taking a shot of a suitable error message), or for showing the results of queries and reports from a database. Try to add annotation to your screen captures to explain to the moderator the point you are making. The callout boxes in Microsoft Word, for example, look particularly good when used in conjunction with a screen capture. Figure 68.1 shows a typical example.

Code listing

If you are making use of your own code, either in a high-level language or by using languages that accompany spreadsheets and databases etc., you should put the code in an appendix if there are large quantities of it.

```
This example tests the size of the active form after a
change in screen resolution and adjusts the size of the form
if it exceeds the visible screen area. To run this example,
put a SysInfo control on a form. Paste this code into the
DisplayChanged event of the SysInfo control. Run the
example, then change the screen resolution.

Private Sub SysInfo1_DisplayChanged()
    If Screen.ActiveForm.Width > SysInfo1.WorkAreaWidth Then
        Screen.ActiveForm.Left = SysInfo1.WorkAreaLeft
        Screen.ActiveForm.Width = SysInfo1.WorkAreaWidth
    End If
    If Screen.ActiveForm.Height > SysInfo1.WorkAreaHeight
Then
        Screen.ActiveForm.Top = SysInfo1.WorkAreaTop
        Screen.ActiveForm.Height = SysInfo1.WorkAreaHeight
    End If
End Sub
```

Figure 68.2 Suitable code annotation.

Figure 68.2 is from the help files in Microsoft Visual Basic. It is a good example of **annotation**, similar in principle to what you need in your project. It illustrates the point that most of the comments should appear at the beginning of the **function** or **subroutine**. All your code should be well documented in this way, and placed in an appendix. The code should also relate to the **design module** that you have produced in the **design section**. Note the use of indentation to emphasise structures being used like **if-then-else-endif**.

It should be easy to identify a **module** from the **design section**, and to see the exact part the module plays in a particular section of your program, and to trace it through to the appropriate page in the appendix. It is worth **annotating** your **hierarchical diagrams** to show how the system integrates into your chosen solution.

System testing

The **modularisation** referred to at numerous points throughout the last few units will serve you well when it comes to testing your system. If you are designing a database, for example, then you should show that any validation actually works by using both valid and invalid data, and illustrate what happens when the data is correct (the value is accepted) and incorrect (the data is rejected with an appropriate error message). You should **justify your choice of test data**, and use **extreme ranges** of data if possible.

Do not forget that you already have a **test plan**, which you outlined during your **design section**! *Make sure that you use it!*

If you are feeling particularly brave then you could make use of **black box** and **white box testing** (see unit 51), but the latter is probably too time consuming considering the nature of most projects at this level.

Do not forget that there should be **screen captures supporting the test results**, and other screen captures showing the erroneous data.

Difficulty with testing some parts?

Some things are more difficult to test than others. For example, testing parts of a website which accept no input from the user. Here all you can do is test the links. Check that there are no orphans (i.e. all the links actually go somewhere), and check that they go to the right places. A tabular tick list approach is suggested here, where you can demonstrate to the moderator that you have checked the links.

There are some other useful web site testing strategies too. Find the **average time taken for the page to load**. Is it acceptable? If not, then find out why and remove the offending part of the page. You will often find that you have an unacceptably large graphic or a graphic in the wrong format.

Do not assume that your web site will work on all browsers – try it out with different browsers and different versions of browsers if possible. Things like **this can all be added to the testing section**. Carrying out these activities, along with the other more obvious testing like validation etc. convinces the moderator that you have made a good effort to check that the system works well.

System maintenance

As a good rule of thumb, the **technical documentation** that accompanies your project (i.e. virtually all your write up with the exception of the **user guide**) *should enable a competent programmer to modify your project* at a later date. If this cannot be done, then your project will effectively become useless over a period of time, and this is a senseless waste of the effort that you have put in.

If you have written up the analysis, design and implementation sections in the ways described earlier, then the system's maintenance document should be virtually complete! The **mark schemes** for the examination boards will award marks for the **detailed algorithms**, the **annotated code** and the **screen captures** which *illustrate how the project works*. The majority of this is present in the previous sections.

It is essential that a proper **contents list** be created for your project so that the examiner can find the relevant material when marking each section.

The user manual

This should be a **separate self-contained document**. Do not forget to include things like minimum system requirements in terms of **hardware, operating system** and any **other software** needed. Remember to include **instructions for setting up the system**, and **how to find appropriate help**. However, do not go overboard with this document. It is an important but small part of your system documentation, and you will not have the time to make it into something which helps the user in ways similar to the user manuals bundled with professional software. *Look at what your mark scheme requires and adhere to it.*

You must remember that your user manual should not be technical. It is intended for the **actual user** of the system, and not the person who designed the project.

You should tailor the system to the environment in which it is to be used. For example, if a user has to log onto your school or college network to get the system going, then an example of how to log onto your specific network should be included, together with appropriate screenshots showing the user how to log on.

The appraisal

You must **evaluate your project critically**, and make effective use of **client feedback**. You will get more marks for saying what could be improved than for saying that it is working perfectly. With the benefit of hindsight you should be able to **suggest ways in which the project could be improved**, and make suggestions concerning appropriate extensions to the project. Your **client** (third party) should also have a say in this **evaluation process**. He or she should be able to suggest possible extensions, and *a covering letter from your client suggesting how the project performs in practice is appropriate here.*

Spelling, punctuation and grammar

Finally, you should appreciate that marks are deducted for **bad spelling, punctuation** and other **grammatical errors**. It is unforgivable to print out a project report with a large number of errors that could have been detected easily with the use of a word processor. Students who hand in badly produced and presented projects are usually pushed for time, hastily typing out the report just hours before it is due to be handed in! Writing up the project as you go along will ensure that you will not be put in this predicament.

It is virtually impossible to have perfect documents, containing no spelling or grammatical errors. It is gross negligence, however, to submit documents containing a number of obvious errors that could easily have been picked up by a standard word processor.

In this unit you have learned about:

- How to implement your A2 project
- The importance of documentation that contains screen captures, code listings and system testing
- The user manual
- The appraisal
- The need for a high standard of spelling, punctuation and grammar in your report

Examination questions A2

1 In the context of object-oriented programming, what is meant by:
(a) an object (2 marks)
(b) inheritance (2 marks)
AQA specimen paper 5511 module 4

2 Figure 1 shows a binary tree.

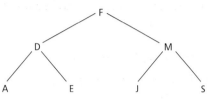

Figure 1

The letter at each node is printed as the tree is traversed. What will be printed when the traversal is:
(a) in-order (1 mark)
(b) pre-order (1 mark)
(c) post-order (1 mark)
AQA specimen paper 5511 module 4

3 Here a *recursively-defined* procedure B, which takes an integer as its single parameter, is defined. The operators DIV and MOD perform integer arithmetic. *x* DIV *y* calculates how many times *y* fits exactly into *x*. *x* MOD *y* calculates the remainder that results. For example, 7 DIV 3 = 2, 7 MOD 3 = 1.

```
PROCEDURE B(number)
IF (number = 0) OR (number = 1)
  THEN PRINT number
  ELSE
    B(number DIV 2)
    PRINT number MOD2
  ENDIF
END of B
```

(i) What is meant by recursively defined? (1 mark)
(ii) Explain why a stack is necessary to execute procedure B recursively. (1 mark)
(iii) Using a copy of the partially completed table shown below as an aid, dry run the procedure call B(43) showing clearly the values of the parameter and the PRINTed output for the six cells of B. (9 marks)

Call number	Parameter
1	43
2	21
3	10
4	
5	
6	

AQA specimen paper 5511 module 4

4 (a) Briefly explain the difference between a compiler and an interpreter in the translation of a high-level language program into executable form. (4 marks)
(b) Suggest in what circumstances it would be appropriate to use:
(i) a compiler rather than an interpreter (2 marks)
(ii) an interpreter rather than a compiler. (2 marks)
(c) Explain how a stack can be used to control calls to procedures. (4 marks)
OCR specimen paper 2509 module 4

5 The owner of a flower shop uses a relational database to store information about orders, and the types of flowers in stock.

(a) One entity is defined as CUSTOMERS. List four attributes which you identify as belonging to this entity. (4 marks)

(b) Another entity is defined as the orders placed by customers (CORDERS). Explain the relationship between the entities CUSTOMERS and CORDERS.
(4 marks)

(c) A third entity is flowers, defined as the types of flowers in stock. Draw an entity relationship diagram for the three entities in this database. (3 marks)

(d) Design the table in third normal form, called CUST, to hold the details of customers and explain why it is in third normal form. (2 marks)

(e) When a customer orders flowers, an order form has to be completed. The order form is shown in Figure 2.

Customer Order
Order Number: Date: / /
Customer Number:

Quantity	Flower ID

Figure 2

(i) Create a table, called ORDER, which contains all the attributes shown on the order form. Explain why this is not normalised.

(ii) Starting with the ORDER table, create a set of tables in third normal form.

(iii) Explain how the tables can be used to create a list of customers who bought roses on 23/12/99. (7 marks)
OCR specimen paper 2509 module 4

6 A reference book, containing about half a million words, has been stored in a text file with a view to publishing it in a CD-ROM based package. An index, listing up to five of the most important references to each main word, is to be provided as part of the package.

The following data structures have been considered for this index:

A: a one-dimensional array of fixed length records in alphabetical order with each record containing two fields:
Field One – a word;
Field Two – its page references.

B: a linked list of records with each record containing three fields:
Field One – a word;
Field Two – its page references;
Field Three – a link to the record containing the next word in alphabetical sequence.

C: a binary tree with each node in the tree consisting of a record containing four fields:
Field One – a word;
Field Two – its page references;
Field Three – a pointer to a sub-tree that contains only words that come before it;
Field Four – a pointer to a sub-tree that contains only words that come after it.

(a) Describe *four* advantages of data structure B in comparison with data structure A as the basis of the software. (8 marks)

(b) Describe in outline an algorithm for constructing data structure C. (6 marks)

(c) Describe *one* advantage and *one* disadvantage of data structure C in comparison with data structure B as the basis of the software. (4 marks)
Edexcel Specimen paper 6275/01 Module 5

Brief answers to these questions can be found at the back of this book. For full answers visit www.revisecomputing.com.

Answers

AS examination questions

1 (a) 122 (b) 0111/1010 = 7A (c) (i) 11110100
(c) (ii) −12 (Overflow has occurred)

2

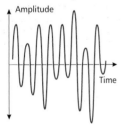

3 (a) *Hardware* – **Network Interface Card (NIC)** – to connect PCs to the network. A **hub** – box into which many computers can be plugged.

(b) *Software* – **File server software** to allow people to log onto the system and share common files. **NIC card drivers** – the software needed to interface the particular network card to the network operating system.

4 **Word Processor** – for the production of written comments for the main report. **Spreadsheet** – working out statistics like average and position in class. **Database** – for storing student names and form details for source of mail-merge data.

5 **Address Bus** – An address (one way only) is output from the processor, and used by the memory to decode the position at which the data is stored or retrieved. **Control bus** – (direction of flow depends on signal) e.g. a read/write signal to memory would be (one way only) from processor to memory. **Data bus** – (two way) used to carry data from/to the processor to/from memory or other devices.

6 (a) (i) An **analogue sound wave** (amplitude against time) is shown in the following diagram. Analogue data is continuously variable.

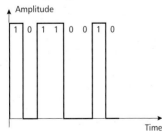

(ii) If the sound from (i) is digitised as thousands of 8-bit samples taken at different time intervals, each sample could be sent as a **digital** (1's and 0's) **signal**. One example could be as shown in the following diagram.

(b) (i) A conventional cassette tape machine.
(ii) A compact disc or CD.

(c) Samples of the analogue signal are taken at set time intervals and converted into discrete (digital) values.

7 (a) **Security** is keeping data safe from hackers; **integrity** is keeping data safe from being incorrect due either to human error or system failures.

(b) Method 1 – **Check digit** – See method of calculation in unit 18.

(c) **CRC check** – calculated from a polynomial as shown in unit 18.

8 **Program – data independence** means that you can easily change the database structure (via the database program) without having to alter the data in the database (i.e. you do not have to re-enter the data). **Data consistency** means that data, held in one part of the database, is consistent with data held in another part. If the same data is held twice, then misspelling of one of the entries would be a good example of this. **Control over redundancy** means that multiple entries are kept to a minimum. It is usual to design separate tables to get over this problem.

9 (a) **Nuclear Power Station** – important to get quick (real time) response, or a devastating accident might occur. **Greenhouse** – in general it would not matter if it takes an extra few minutes to operate various controls like opening the windows, for example.

(b) Bills are needed infrequently (e.g. once every three months) for a batch of customers, and all bill processing would be similar. Two characteristics and consequences are as follows: A **characteristic** (1) – The ability to run a large batch of jobs like utility billing. A **consequence** (1) of this is that you might tie up a large number of resources with this single task, thus preventing interrogation of bills, for example, taking place. **Characteristic** (2) of the operating system is the multi-programming aspect, allowing other programs, like interrogation of a particular bill to take place at the same time. A **consequence** (2) of this happening at the same time as the batch is that the response might be slow.

10 (a) **Prototyping** means setting up a 'mock up' for test purposes. Other parts of the system would usually be simulated, so that it appears to the user that they are using the real thing. Prototyping allows the users to give feedback, and to gain a better appreciation of the real system. Modifications can be made to the prototype and a new prototype produced.

(b) Some **advantages** of **prototyping** are:
(i) The users would be able to gain a feel for the new system and thus be able to give some positive feedback.
(ii) The developers would be able to see if the ergonomics of the system are appropriate.
(iii) Problems may be brought to light and solved before the real system is designed.
(iv) Etc.
Some **disadvantages** of **prototyping** are:
(i) You might get the opinions of too many people, all giving conflicting advice.
(ii) Prototyping often masks the considerable complexities regarding getting the real system working.
(iii) The users might expect the real system to work exactly like the prototype.
(iv) Etc.

(c) Organisation of the GUI interface, data validation and verification, ways of producing suitable outputs from the system etc.

11 (a) Two applications for serial processing could be the batch **production of utility bills** and the batch production of **wage slips** for a **payroll program**. Serial processing is appropriate in each case because a list of tasks (producing wage slips or electricity bills) has to be processed one after the other from beginning to end. All subtasks are virtually identical in nature.

(b) A file for the payroll might be accessed serially for the production of the wage slips but accessed directly for an *ad hoc* query regarding a particular employee.

12 (a) An **LAN**, or **Local Area Network** – connects computers together using a variety of topologies, but 100 Mbit/sec Ethernet is typical using hubs and switches. It enables the *sharing of resources* like printers and applications, for example. The LANs are under the control of a local institution like a college or business, and do not make use of the public telecommunications systems. They also involve other hardware like file servers, printer servers, hubs and routers etc.

(b) Typical ring and star network connections are shown in the following diagram.

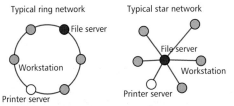

The location of the file server and printer server on the ring network is not important. However, on the star network the location of the file server is critical and as shown above.

(c) Sharing of common resources like printers, storage space and software/data on the file server. Communication links such as e-mail and video-conferencing etc.

(d) A **WAN** makes use of the public communications network; a **LAN** does not, and is entirely under the control of the local institution. Extra hardware a WAN would require could be a proxy server, modems and conventional phone lines, or ISDN or ADSL connections etc.

13 (a) A **stock-control system**. To keep account of the orders placed by customers, the suppliers of the goods, handling the stock, and dealing with related queries and requisitions.

(b) (i) Some important data items are as follows, followed by the source of the data:
Product code
Stock database/Customer order
Quantity
Customer order
Number in stock
Stock database

(ii) **Product code** – Bar code or manually entered from customer invoice. **Quantity** – manually entered from customer invoice or verbal order. **Number in stock** – calculated from stock database.

(iii) **Product code** – Quick to identify from product database – also less chance of data-integrity problems. **Quantity** – manual data entry is the only feasible way of entering this. **Number in stock** – generated automatically from database. This ensures that numbers are correct – human error is eliminated.

(c) One user interface is the rejected goods from the goods-inwards department. Drop down menus enable the operator to enter standard order numbers, supplies data and standard rejection reasons, thus entering the minimum of customised data.

A2 examination questions

1 An **object** is a variable in an object oriented programming language that encapsulates both *functions (i.e. routines)* and *data*. **Inheritance** means inheriting characteristics from the base class, from which it is derived, e.g. the class fiction could inherit many attributes from a base class of *books*. Extra attributes could then be added which best define fictional books.

2 (a) A, D, E, F, J, M, S (**in-order**)
(b) F, D, A, E, M, J, S (**pre-order**)
(c) A, E, D, J, S, M, F (**post-order**)

3 (i) A **recursively-defined procedure** is one that is able to call itself. It is usual to be able to call the procedure from within the procedure.

(ii) A **stack** is used as memory to keep track of the recursive calls and store data representing the values of variables at different depths of recursion.

(iii) (Student additions shown in **red**)

Call number	Parameter	Printed output
1	43	1
2	21	1
3	10	0
4	5	1
5	2	0
6	1	1

The printed output at each stage is shown above.

4 (a) A **compiler** converts all the source code into the object code in one go, and links to any library routines and macros etc. An **interpreter** will interpret (convert source code into machine code) just one line at a time. A compiler produces code that is quicker to execute and has no reference to the original source code. An **interpreter** must have the original source code on which to run.

(b) (i) When you do *not* want the users to have access to the source code, or speed is of the essence.

(ii) During development of a program it is more convenient for creating prototypes and debugging.

(c) A **stack** can be used as a temporary area of storage to store parameters representing values when the procedure is called. After servicing the procedure, the variables can be pulled off the stack to resume program execution from the point at which the call was made.

5 (a) **Customer ID, Name, [Address1, Address2, Town, County, Postcode etc.], On Mailing list etc.**

(b) A customer may place many orders, therefore the relationship is **one to many**.

(c)

(d) To put the **CUST** table in third normal form proceed as follows:

CUST (<u>Customer ID</u>, Name, [Address1, Address2, Town, County, Postcode], On Mailing list)

As the table stands there are no repeating values, therefore it is in 1NF. Looking at the 'three' attributes 'name', 'Address info' and 'telephone number', they are all functionally dependent (depend only upon) the primary key (Customer ID), therefore, it is also in 2NF. For third normal form there should be no dependencies existing between non-key elements. All non-key elements are independent; therefore it is also in 3NF.

(e) (i) ORDER(<u>Order Number</u>, Customer ID, Date, (*FlowerID*), (*Quantity*)) – Note the items in brackets show possible multiple entries. The table is not even in first normal form because of the possible repeating values of *FlowerID* and *Quantity*. Therefore, the table is obviously not normalised

(ii) To put into 1NF, repeating values (*FlowerID* and *Quantities*) need to be removed, this gives us two tables as follows:

Order number	Customer ID	Date	Flower ID	Quantity	Flower ID	Quantity
21678	223	11/12/99	37	36	12	8
21679	098	11/12/99	1	35		
21680	566	11/12/99	8	14	72	9

The tabular arrangement may help us to understand this a little better. The original table is as follows:

Order number	Customer ID	Date	Flower ID	Quantity
21678	223	11/12/99	37	8
21678	223	11/12/99	12	8
21679	098	11/12/99	1	35
21680	566	11/12/99	8	14
21680	566	11/12/99	72	9
Etc.				

The new table, in first normal form now becomes.

ORDER(<u>Order Number</u>, CustomerID, Date, FlowerID, Quantity)

This is now in 1NF as there are no repeating keys.

Note: we now have a fixed-length field for FlowerID and Quantity, in which we can have any number of entries. The original table, with (FlowerID) and (Quantity) had variable length fields because of the multiple entries. The second table (containing the fields which have been removed) is as follows:

FLOWERS(<u>Order Number</u>, FlowerID, Quantity)

Note: This too is now in INF, and the Order number shows the relational information. Looking at the above two tables, all attributes depend only upon the primary key. Therefore, the tables are also in 2NF.
Finally, all non-key elements are independent, so the tables are in 3NF too!

(iii) The description (roses) is associated with a unique FlowerID, which is then used to search the FLOWERS table, thus finding the Order Numbers corresponding to orders for Roses. The ORDERS table is then searched using Date to see if there is a match with 23/12/99. You can use the order number to find the CustomerID and hence the name and address of the customers who bought roses on 23/12/99.

6 (a) Four *advantages* of data structure B are as follows:
   (i) The array A has fixed length records, and some entries in data structure A might have to be truncated, B does not suffer from this limitation.
   (ii) Because list B is linked, it can be updated more easily without having to update the entire list (e.g. you would not have to re-sort).
   (iii) If the list in A fills up you will have to re-dimension the array, because it is a static data structure. With B, the only limitation is the amount of memory in the system.
   (iv) A sort routine would have to be run to get the original list A into alphabetical order. The linked list can be constructed on an *ad hoc* basis.

(b) The algorithm for creating a binary tree is as follows, assuming that the data in each node is stored as follows:

Word	Pages References	Left Pointer	Right Pointer

Create the first node data (root of the binary tree) using the first word in the list, setting up the left and right pointers to null.

The following method now needs to be repeated for each new word to be inserted.

Starting at the root node, compare the Word to be inserted with the Word resident in the node. If the Word to be inserted is < Word in the node then follow the left pointer else follow the right pointer, repeating the comparison process for each node until a null pointer is encountered.

When a null pointer is encountered, update the pointer from the previous node to point to this node, insert the Word and page references in the new node and set the new node pointers to null.

You must also consider the possibility of a duplicate word being entered. It depends whether this is considered to be a mistake, or whether an identical word can be used in a different context. For example, the word *layering* could be used for **network architecture** and **CAD packages**! The structure as it stands would not be able to cope with this. Identical multiple words with different meanings could have special entries like Layering(1) or Layering(2).

(c) An *advantage* of data structure C over data structure B is that it is very much quicker to search a binary tree than a linked list, especially if the data structure is large (500,000 words in this case). A disadvantage of data structure C over data structure B is that it is more complex to set up and maintain (e.g. insertion and deletion of nodes), and requires more storage for the data structure.

Self-test questions

These answers to the self-test questions have been kept **very brief indeed**. **Key terms** are **highlighted**. Examination answers would need to be expanded and written using the correct prose.

There are **suggested model answers** to the **examination questions** on our **web site**.

Unit 1

1 **ASCII** the **American Standard Code for Information Interchange** – an **8-bit encoding method**. Unicode is a **16 bit coding method** ideal for representing all languages.
2 (a) 100111 (b) 0011 1001 (c) 27
3 133
4 1001.001
5 **Group binary into 4s from RHS** and write **hex digits underneath each group of 4.**

6 Because it is not a number base.
7 11010
8 110
9 One with a **mantissa** and an **exponent**.
10 65,535
11 −29 = 11100011, −56 = 11001000
12 −16

Unit 2

1 **24 bits** giving us **16,777,216 colours.**
2 **Bit mapped** is based on **pixels**, Vector on **mathematical equations** using **vectors.**
3 **Musical Instrument Digital Interface** – computer control for musical instruments.
4 **MIDI** is **note control; computer-encoded sound** simulates the **analogue signals.**
5 **MP3 compression** allows music to be sent over the internet more quickly.

6   An **electronic circuit** for converting **analogue** to **digital** signals.
7   By taking **samples** at frequent intervals and storing each as a **digital value**.
8   One that is **continuously variable**.
9   **Red, Green Blue** used in **monitors**. It is **additive colour**, not **subtractive** like **CMYK** used in printers.
10 +2047 to −2048

Unit 3

1   (a)   Carries **data** put into or taken out of memory.
    (b)   Carries the **addresses** to be used by memory and other devices.
    (c)   Carries **control signals** like the read/write signal for memory.
2   The microprocessor type.
3   **Primary storage is RAM, secondary storage is disks, CD-ROMs** and tape etc.
4   **Arithmetic Logic Unit.** To work out the results of sums and logical operations like AND and OR.
5   **ROM – Read Only Memory** – holds BIOS etc. **RAM** holds temporary data like user programs.
6   **Binary digits** representing **instructions. Different codes** are used for each microprocessor.
7   **Very fast memory.** Used to store instructions needed quickly to speed up the system.
8   **Controls** the fetch-decode-execute cycle. Routes information from and to the correct place.
9   **Fetching** an instruction from memory, **decoding it** and **carrying out** the required operation.
10 **Instructions**, called a **program**, stored **one after the other** inside memory.

Unit 4

1   **Hardware** is the **equipment, software** is the **programs**.
2   **General purpose** – word processors, databases and spreadsheets. **Bespoke software** – school administration. **System software** – operating systems and related utilities.
3   **Systems software** is the **operating system and related software. Applications software** is applications like word processors, games, stock control etc.
4   The **Basic Input Output System** interfaces the hardware to the **OS. Loading the OS, checking hardware** and **looking at the user settings** in the CMOS RAM.
5   **Running a batch of commands, assigning many new users** on a network. **Applying security information** on many files.
6   **Renaming a file – running programs – finding a file.**
7   **High-level** is more **human oriented, low-level** is more **machine oriented.**
8   **Machine code** and **assembly language.**
9   **Fortran** – maths and science. **COBOL** – business. **Prolog** – AI applications. **C++** – system's programming.
10 Disk **formatter**, disk **defragmenter**, utility to restore your computer's OS.
11 **Compiler** – translates m/c code all at once. Less convenient but very quick. **Interpreter – translates** just one line at a time into **m/c code.** Good for development work.

Unit 5

1   Users get **instant feedback** regarding errors, and the process is less tedious and easier.
2   A language that supports **structures** such as **FOR-TO-NEXT** and **REPEAT UNTIL** etc. An example is **Visual Basic.**
3   Because the **compiled code** will run much **faster**, and **deny users access** to the original source code.
4   This is the only language that will run on the machine.
5   **Assignment** – giving a variable a value. **Variable** – something that can take on a range of values. **Declaration** – giving names to variables and constants and assigning memory to them. **Data type** – the computer can use the data in well-defined ways if a set data type is assigned.

Unit 6

1   A **function** may return one value only. A **procedure** is more versatile, and may return multiple values.
2   Depends on language used. (Area = πr^2)
3   **Case structure**
4   **By value** – original variable does not get altered (like a local variable). **By reference** – original variable gets altered (like a global variable).

Unit 7

1   String Reversal algorithm using Microsoft's Visual Basic

```
Private Sub Form_Load()

Target$ = InputBox("Please type in string to
be reversed") 'User types in string
    End_of_word = Len(Target$)
'Determine length of string
    For x = Len(Target$) To 1 Step -1
'Reverse string
        Final$ = Final$ + Mid(Target$, x, 1)
    Next x
    MsgBox (Final$)
'Output reverse string
End Sub
```

2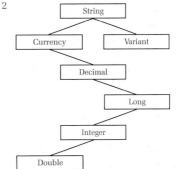

3   Example of a one-dimensional array could be daily sales figures in a shop for a week.
    e.g.   Week = (256, 278, 345, 298, 456, 877, 156) could correspond to
           (Mon, Tue, Wed, Thu, Fri, Sat, Sun)
Therefore Week(3) would be Wednesday's sales figures.
Example of a two-dimensional array could be daily sales figures in a shop for a 1-month period,

$$\text{e.g. } \mathbf{Jan} = \begin{pmatrix} 256 & 279 & 475 & 399 & 282 & 190 & 671 \\ 432 & 877 & 544 & 285 & 536 & 377 & 156 \\ 736 & 266 & 365 & 665 & 483 & 664 & 789 \\ 672 & 645 & 987 & 665 & 276 & 655 & 492 \\ 453 & 344 & 199 & * & * & * & * \end{pmatrix}$$

Could correspond to the sales figures for the dates of the month as follows:

$$\begin{pmatrix} 1st & 2nd & 3rd & 4th & 5th & 6th & 7th \\ 8th & 9th & 10th & 11th & 12th & 13th & 14th \\ 15th & 16th & 17th & 18th & 19th & 20th & 21st \\ 22nd & 23rd & 24th & 25th & 26th & 27th & 28th \\ 29th & 30th & 31st & * & * & * & * \end{pmatrix}$$

Therefore Jan(3, 2) could be the sales figures for January 16th.
A three dimensional array could be daily sales figures for a year, stacked up by having 12 monthly arrays like those shown above. Therefore, Year(1, 3, 2) might be January 16th sales figures.

4 The following uses Microsoft's Visual Basic
Method 1 – using code.

```
Private Sub Form_Load()

    Do While ((Dice1 <> 6) And (Dice2 <> 6))

  Print "You have rolled the following numbers"
        Dice1 = (Int(Rnd(1) * 6 + 1))
'Ensure integer number between 1 & 6 inclusive
        Dice2 = (Int(Rnd(1) * 6 + 1))
        Print Dice1, Dice2
'display current scores
    Loop
  Print "You have rolled two sixes - Well done"
'Loop ended - two sixes

End Sub
```

Method 2 – using a flowchart

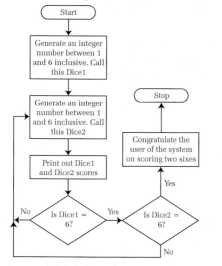

Unit 8

1 **Serial** – one bit a time. **Parallel** – several bits (usually 8, 16, 32 etc.) transmitted simultaneously. **Serial** – telecommunications. **Parallel** – the bus system inside a computer.
2 **Synchronous** is under the control of a **clock**, **asynchronous** is not synchronised.
3 By using **Quadrature Amplitude Modulation** (V90 modem) or similar techniques.
4 **Parity bits** are added as a check on the **integrity** of received data. **Parity** is good inside a computer, but more sophisticated methods like **CRCs** (unit 18) are better for **communications**.
5 New methods of modulation are being invented all the time. Different **protocols** are needed for each method that is in common use.

Unit 9

1 Data does not have to pass by other computers on its way to the server.
2 **Virtual Private Network**. The **hardware**, **software** and **security** needed to connect to an **LAN** via the **internet**.
3 The lines are used more efficiently as they are available to transmit any packet at any time.
4 **WAN** – uses the public service networks like the telephone system. An **LAN** is under the control of a local institution and does not make use of a public network.
5 **E-commerce** is business to business or individuals using computers over the **internet** to **trade**. **Encryption** is essential for security and peace of mind.
6 **Protocol** – a set of standard rules. **ftp**, **telnet** and **smtp**.
7 **Hackers** would be able to get into the system more easily.

Unit 10

1 **DOS** and **Unix**
2 **Batch** – doing different jobs, one after the other in a batch e.g. processing utility bills. **Real time** – responding to events in a time that is critical, e.g. the control of a power plant or an aircraft.
3 **Disks, memory** and **time**
4 By allocating **permissions**, which give users rights to do things like **read**, **change** or **delete** files.
5 More than one person can use the system at the 'same time'.
6 **Faster** for many applications, **more powerful** processing ability.
7 **Easier to maintain**, users can't **mess up the system** so that it does not work.
8 It is **happening so quickly** that it looks as if it is happening at the 'same time'. A **single processor** is not able to do more than one thing at any one time.
9 **Setting up tedious things** like **file permissions** and **assigning new users** on a large network is useful.

Unit 11

1 Without this people would be able to delete the work of other people.
2 Apply **permissions** for use, **deny access** to it or **audit** accesses in a log. This can prevent accidental viewing, deletion or misuse by individuals.
3 Write a **batch file**, which logs people off after a set time. The OS can run this file automatically. Warnings can be issued before letting them know this is going to happen.
4 Creating a **group** for each department to which the users may belong. Each group will have different **access rights** and **security permissions**.
5 Put an **audit** on the file (i.e. make a log of who is accessing it and what they do).
6 The **audit trail** will let the administrator know who did what and when.
7 Control of **aircraft** or a **nuclear power plant**.
8 Booking **airline tickets, monitoring pollution** in a river, **stock-control** systems.

Unit 12

1 Not yet – too many people trained in its use. Voice is suitable for specialist input, used by disabled people and those who cannot type very quickly.
2 **Touch pad, stylus** (pen), **finger**, and **plug-in keyboard**.
3 A plug-in **qwerty keyboard**.
4 Entering **pre-typed text**. Computerisation of existing typed material. **Utility billing** used on a **turnaround document**.
5 **Turnaround document**, for electricity meter reading and billing-questionnaires in computer readable format.
6 It needs to be **scanned** and then subjected to **OCR**.
7 **Pedals** – control of rudder. **Yokes** – control of flaps etc. **Levers** – control of throttle.
8 Using a PC and transferring data via a **network**.

Unit 13

1 **Video conferencing**, production of **multimedia material**, **automated security** systems.
2 **Medial diagnostics**, where a doctor's hands are free to monitor the patient. Systems where the **user is unable to type** – e.g. they might have some disability.
3 **MIDI** is used by musicians to input and process music. Data about music such as **pitch of note, duration of note** and **how hard the musical keys have been pressed** can be processed like this.
4 **Infra red** – can be used to see if a person is near. **Sound** – can be used to respond to voice. **Switches** – can be used to detect if the robot has bumped into things.
5 They **automate** part of the process of getting standard data into the computer with **few errors**.
6 By using **on-line data capture forms** linked to a **database** on the **file server**.
7 Suggestions for **School** are – name, address, age, sex, previous schools etc. Other data capture could be a photograph.

8 Suggestions for **University** are – same as school + qualifications, predicted grades, special interests etc.
9 Suggestions for **Music Shop** are – name, address, e-mail address, shopping habits like type of music preferred, type of format preferred (CD, DVD etc.).

Unit 14

1 **Architects**, and **engineers' drawings**.
2 **LCD** – Liquid Crystal Displays. **LEP** – Light Emitting Plastic displays.
3 To produce **fast graphics** in **high resolution**. A better card gives more impressive graphics. Some motherboards have on-board cards, but these usually do not give top performance.
4 **Ink jet** – slow compared to lasers, cheap to purchase, expensive to run. **Laser printers** – faster than ink jets, more expensive to purchase, cheapest to run.
5 A **reader** in which **microfiche** may be inserted to be read without the aid of a computer.
6 A **professional printer** for **high quality high volume work** used in publishing.
7 For the production of **till receipts** and **invoices** in some shops.
8 Between 10 and 50 at the time of writing.
9 Putting a **paper-thin screen** on the wall.
10 **Computer monitors**

Unit 15

1 **ROM** to store permanent programs like the BIOS, **RAM** to store temporary programs.
2 **Volatile** means data will be lost during a power failure. Use an **uninterruptible supply**.
3 **Disk caching** is using a disk as though it were RAM. The **effective RAM** is increased.
4 **Primary storage** is RAM – holding programs currently running on the computer. **Secondary storage** is disk – holding programs not needed by the computer at the present moment.
5 They **spin faster** and so data can be read from them more quickly. They are **mechanically more robust** and **sealed** which increases reliability.
6 Data takes **longer to load** – this slows down the computer system. **Defragment** the disk.
7 **Mirroring** helps to maintain a service in the event of a **crash**. Using **two disks** can **increase speed of access** as data is read from both at the same time.
8 **Modern software** is much more **massive** than software of a few years ago. Also **graphics** have **more colour** and **higher resolutions** etc. and **video** is now common, all **using more disk space**.
9 **Serial access** means all data before the item of interest must be read. **Direct access** means you can go straight to the item of interest.
10 2000 pupils at 100 Mbytes each would give 200 Gbytes. With application delivery, OS and expansion, allow 300 Gbytes. (The size depends on the allowance for each pupil.) Several disks would be joined together to get this size in practice.

Unit 16

1 Much **software** is not designed to work at these **high speeds** and thus 100× is unlikely to be achieved in practice.
2 **DVD** and the **internet**.
3 **Compact Disc Recordable**. Creating a **backup**, creating an **archive**, **distribution of software** you have written yourself.
4 **CDR** – can only write once to the disk. **MO drives** can be written to many times.
5 **Archive** – keeping **little used material** off line. **Backup** – **emergency copy** of data used in the event of a crash. Many CD-Roms required, therefore inconvenient compared to a large tape system.
6 **System files** etc. could be put onto a **smaller tape**. This enables important files to be recovered more quickly than on a single large tape. Data too might be able to be split up in this way.
7 Use a **RAID** system set up for **mirroring**.

Unit 17

1 A **record** is information about one entity within a file. An 'employee' or a 'book', for example. A **field** is a subsection of a record, like 'name' or 'age'. **Alphanumeric characters** make up the data in the **fields**.
2 **Item** description – 50 bytes (data type text). **Product description number** – 4 bytes (numeric integer long). **Price** – 4 bytes (data type currency). **Description** – 100 (data type text). **Page number** – 2 bytes (numeric integer short). **Total bytes/Record** = 50 + 4 + 4 + 100 + 2 = 160 bytes. Therefore, 1,600,000 bytes are needed. **Allow 2 Mbytes** with overheads and room for some expansion.
3 **Serial** – one record after the other with no regard to order. **Sequential** – records in a particular sequence.
4 **Tape** and **disk**.
5 Having an **index** pointing to **salient parts** of the file. Set up an index containing 26 entries A to Z. Search for Bradley by following the B index and **sequentially searching** the B's.
6 You can use **large ID numbers** for employees to generate a **smaller well-defined range** of addresses.

Unit 18

1 **Integrity** – keeping data safe from **computer error**. **Security** – keeping data safe from **hackers**.
2 **Check digit** – single digit produced by applying a **weighting algorithm**. **Check sum** – algorithm involving a batch of data, which is processed to produce a sum for error detection.
3 It is one of the **most reliable** and produces a **very small amount of extra data** for a lot of data being transmitted.
4 Use **passwords** and **encryption**.
5 **Weak encryption** – easily possible to decrypt using powerful computers. **Strong encryption** – virtually impossible to crack in a sensible time.

Unit 19

1 Each day the **transaction file** is used in combination with a **father file** to produce a new **son** file. The **old father file** then becomes a **grandfather**, giving **three generations** of backup.
2 The **data files** are usually backed up to another **disk** or **tape**. The **applications** can be re-**installed**, although a **disk image** is more useful to restore a system quickly as it contains **permissions** and **other customisation** such as drivers etc.
3 **Backup** – used to recover current data in the event of an emergency. **Archive** – little used data taken off line.
4 **Physical drive** – the actual drive in the machine. **Logical drive** – a partition created on a hard disk to present the user with an apparent physical drive.
5 **Fat clients** – disk image for systems. **Tape** or **disk** backup for data. **Thin clients** – only the file server needs backing up, no disks are held locally.

Unit 20

1 **Flat file** – a **single file** (table) database. **Relational database** – set of **tables** (files) **linked** by common fields.
2 A **table** relates to a **file**.
3 The **primary key** is a unique identifier for a particular table.
4 **Surname** – text. **Age** – Numeric. **Male or Female** – Boolean. A **picture** – graphic data type (depends on database – Access treats this as an object). A **telephone number** – text.

Unit 21

1 **Primary key** – identifies a table. **Foreign key** – a field in another table to which we are establishing a relationship by linking.
2 **Primary index** – the index created by the primary key. **Secondary index** – the index created by an alternate key. (Usually used for sorting into sub-sections.)
3 **Validation** – checking to see if data is sensible in the context being used. (a) age >= 65 (b) price >= min AND price <= max (Min and max chosen to reflect a particular business.)
4 **Data validation, drop-down menus**

Unit 22

1 A **set of criteria** a database uses to find particular sets of records.
2 Depends on houses, years and forms in your school.
3 **Export data** to a **spreadsheet** via **CSV**, and then perform the analysis of the data in the sheet.
4 A **programmer** using a **macro language** could work out some statistical functions, not available from within the database. Their code can then be called up and used by the database.

Unit 23

1 **Formatting text, spell checking, grammar checking, tables, print previews, rulers, templates, find** and **replace, mail merge** etc.
2 **Formulae in cells**, financial and **statistical functions, what if** scenarios, **sorting** data into order, **summing** columns, **number** and **text formatting, export of data** via **CSV, macro language, locking** parts of the sheet, **protecting cells,** viewing **formulae** instead of results etc.
3 Creation of **tables**, creation of **records**, creation of **fields, data types, validation, queries, reports, CSV export** and **import, ODBC, SQL language** etc.
4 By using **CSV**.
5 Any **alteration** in the spreadsheet data may be **reflected** by the **graph being redrawn** in the **word processor**.
6 **WP** – production of **text**. **DTP** – production of **complex layouts** including text and pictures.
7 By the addition of a **third party add on** like **graphing software**, for example.
8 WP – for the **automated production of documents**. Spreadsheet – for carrying out **functions not available from the standard list** of functions.
9 **Standard letters linked** to a **database** to produce many 'personalised' letters.
10 **Running the numbers** on a spreadsheet to see what happens if some of the variables are altered.

Unit 24

1 Draw **different shapes**, alter **styles of lines**, draw shapes to **exact dimensions**, join object to create others, use **libraries** of shapes, **render**, apply **filters, lighting conditions, export data** to CNC machines, transform **2D objects** into **3D** etc.
2 To help with **stock control** and **ordering of components** in a **CAD/CAM** environment.
3 A **wire frame image** is an image constructed of lines, which is used to model the artefact's physical appearance in the computer. A **rendered image** adds realism by adding texture to simulate real surfaces on the wire-frame models. **Wire frame** is useful for building and analysis, **rendered** is useful for aesthetic visualisation.
4 **Computer Aided Manufacture.** Using computers to help with the manufacturing process.
5 By linking the **design, manufacture** and **stock control systems** etc.
6 **Object-oriented package** – images are made up from mathematical equations. **Pixel-based package** – images are made up from tiny squares called pixels.
7 You can mix and match the best of each technique. For example, you can build a precise model (object-oriented) having a texture like marble (pixel-based).
8 Different **brushes, airbrush, crayons, pencils,** extensive **filters** such as **blurs, sharpen, soften,** extensive colour **control of printer,** large range of **library textures** and **fills,** tools like **droppers, rubbers** and **pens** etc.
9 See last example in this unit.
10 Goods may be ordered **just in time** because the entire production process is under the control of a computer. The computer automatically orders the goods just before they are needed in production.

Unit 25

1 A **study** to see if a project would be **possible** or would be **improved** by using computers.

2 **Interview, observation, questionnaire** (see unit for detailed examples).
3 A diagram showing the **movement of data** and the interaction of different people and processes. Movement of **goods through a factory,** movement of **data through an office** etc.
4 See Figure 25.3

Unit 26

1 Validation, **help,** appropriate **error messages, drop down menus,** use of colour etc.
2 **Technical competence** of users, **environment** in which it is used, **quick access to records** on many standard criteria etc.
3 **Manually testing** a program to see if it produces the expected data (see unit for detailed examples).
4 It helps **end user to visualise the system,** points out **potential mistakes** and **generates ideas.** The design of a new gaming interface.
5 It is virtually impossible to cover all scenarios. **White Box Testing** helps. (See unit 51)

Unit 27

1 **Surf the net.** Receive e-mail. Deal with **text messages.** For the text-message system make sure that the system is tested for all types of text message. Make sure that it does not hang if the message is zero bytes or very long. What is the maximum length of text message, etc.?
2 **Module testing** – tests a small self-contained part of a program. **Integration testing** – tests two or more modules **simultaneously.** Modules may not work in combination with each other.
3 (a) Very large numeric and other function keys operated by mouse or touch screen.
   (b) **Touch screen** or large **monitor.**
   (c) Touch screen could be used as it is easy to point a finger (don't have to rely on cursor positioning.)
4 See Table 27.4 – do similar table. (Define limits of system like number of decimal places etc.). Test to the **limits** of the **data types** you are using in the **programming language** in which the project is implemented.
5 Look at the **specification** then check to see if it is **fully implemented.** Make **subjective comments** about the **ease of use** and the **user interface** etc.
6 **Maintenance** is looking after the project post delivery to the customer. It is important to check that the system works after being put in the field. **Bug reports** need to be fixed by team of experts; help in the field may be needed.
7 A **loop through the program never encountered** before causes a bug to come to light. The **customer's needs may change** and new routines need to be written. The team should be armed with appropriate **technical manuals, user documentation, debugging tools** etc.

Units 28 to 33 inclusive are project-based

Unit 35

1 A **pointer** is a number that points to an item of interest such as other data. Pointers enable data to be **referenced without being moved.** In this way **queues** and **lists** can be set up very efficiently.
2 A **tree** is a **data structure** like a family tree, in which **nodes** represent **data** and **pointers.** Many real life scenarios may be modelled using a tree.
3 See Figure 35.6 for ideas on how this may be achieved.
4 See Figure 35.4.

Unit 36

1 They are used to manage **queues** and are particularly useful for **interrupt handling.**
2 See Figure 36.1.
3 **FIFO – First In First Out,** like a queue in a shop. **LIFO – Last In First Out,** as used with **interrupt handling.**
4 A **LIFO stack** is used. **Higher priority interrupts** get **preference.** If an interrupt is being serviced, and a higher priority one occurs, **contents of registers** are **stored on the stack** and **retrieved** when original **interrupt is reinstated,** after servicing the higher priority one.

5 See Figure 36.3.
6 **Forward** and **backward pointers** are set up in addition to the **start** and **stop pointers**.
7 **Static** – cannot be altered during running of program (e.g. a dimensioned array). **Dynamic** – can have size altered during the running of a program – e.g. a **file** stored on disk.
8 Stack – **LIFO** or **FIFO** structure. A **heap** is a temporary area of storage used for any purpose.

Unit 37

1 **Pre-order**, **post-order** and **in-order traversal**.
2 See Figure 37.2
3 (a) {D,B,A,C,E} (b) {A,B,C,D,E} (c) {A,C,B,E,D}
4 (a)

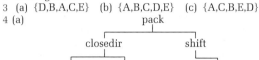

(b) bind, getc, stat (c) pack (d) closedir, chmod, getc, bind
5 Construct the **tree** using the '<' **and** '>' on the **list**. See Figure 37.2.
6 **Recursion** is a routine that may call itself (see unit 39). Use any of the **traversal mechanisms** for an example.

Unit 38

1 A list is examined, one entry after another, until the item of interest is found, or found not to be in the list.
2 An ordered binary tree is searched, beginning at the root. If the item of interest is not found, left or right pointers are followed (depending on whether the item of interest is before or after the data in the root). Recursion is then used to search the sub-trees to be followed by the pointers.
3 The list must already be arranged as an ordered binary tree.
4 On average, fewer comparisons are needed compared to a linear search.
5 If a linear search is used, for a 3 item list the average search time is $(1 + 2 + 3)/2 = 2$. For a 4 item list it is $(1 + 2 + 3 + 4 +)/2 = 2.5$. For an N item list the average is $(N + 1)/2$. Therefore, for a 100-item list it is $101/2 = 50.5$ comparisons. If a binary search is used, for a two element list the number of comparisons is 1, $(\log_2 2 = 1)$ for a 4 element list it is 2 $(\log_2 4 = 2)$, for an 8-element list it is 3 $(\log_2 8 = 3)$. For an N element list it is $(\log_2 N)$. For a 100-element list we would need a maximum of about $\log_2 100 \cong 33$ comparisons.
6 We start with the second element in the list, compare it with the first, and insert it into the right place if necessary. The third element is then considered, inserted into the right place and so on until the last element has been considered, in which case the list is sorted. The first pair of numbers in the list are compared and swapped if necessary. We move onto the next pair, then compare and swap if necessary. If any swaps were needed, then the whole process is repeated until no swaps are necessary in which case the list is in order.

Unit 39

1 **Recursion** is a routine that calls itself. It leads to efficient code because many recursive calls can be made, assuming that the **stack** does not **overflow**.
2 A **LIFO** stack. See example in unit 36.
3 There may be many levels of **directory**, each having many **sub-directories**. A **recursive call** could make sure that **all nested sub-directories** have **permissions** applied to them.
4 Result will be 5.

Unit 40

1 **Data structures** like **trees** and **stacks** are processed using many similar sub-ordinate operations. These are ideal for recursive calls, which mirror these techniques exactly.
2 An **ordered binary tree** is useful for printing out alphabetical listings etc.

3 **No**. The E and B boxes need interchanging to make it ordered.
4 5 and 6 See **algorithms** developed in this unit.

Unit 41

1 **Code, called up by name**, often used in **applications** like **word processors** and **spreadsheets** etc. where the user may **record a macro** by going through manual operations.
2 A system set up to **mimic a human expert**. It works by using a suitable **knowledge base**.
3 A **programming paradigm** using **objects, class, encapsulation, inheritance, polymorphism** and **containment**.
4 One **programmed** by making use of an **environment like Windows** (menus and icons etc.). It is an event driven programming environment.
5 (a) **VBA**, (b) **Prolog**
6 **C++** and **Java** *(not JavaScript)*
7 Only the **object** that **controls the data** may have **access to the data**.
8 The **occurrence** of something in **different forms** e.g. a routine may be altered to perform slightly different functions.
9 To **manage large projects more effectively**. Too much unnecessary interaction between modules of large programs is the reason for development of **OOP**.

Unit 42

1 **Java** is an **object-oriented programming language**. A **Java Applet** is an instance of a **Java class** designed to be run on the **web**.
2 **Programs** that respond to **mouse clicks** or **menu selections** etc.
3 A **declarative language** is a **paradigm** where **relationships are defined** and then **interrogated**. You do not have to make use of procedural elements here.
4 A **knowledge base** can be built up and interrogated more easily than when using a typical **3GL**.
5 A **structure** like a **FOR-TO-NEXT** or **REPEAT-UNTIL LOOP**, for example.
6 **Boolean, integer, floating point, string**.
7 The **syntax** used is very easy to understand, e.g. **COBOL**
8 **Computer Aided Software Engineering**. Getting systems to write the code from tightly controlled specifications.
9 **FORTRAN** – maths and science. **COBOL** – business data processing.

Unit 43

1 See example 1 in this unit.
2 A method by which the **processor may be interrupted** to pay attention to something.
3 See example in unit.
4 The **interrupt** currently being executed **is itself interrupted**, and **registers** are **saved on the stack** in the normal way. When serviced, the computer **pulls the information from the stack** and carries on servicing the first interrupt.
5 By using a **numerical system** whereby lower numbers, for example, have a **higher priority**.

Unit 44

1 A method of **generating an addressing range** in assembly **language programming**.
2 A **base register** can be used along with an **index register** to generate the **memory address** at which data may be found. This is useful for implementing **arrays** in a **low level language**.
3 **Software**, which helps with the **assembly language process**, including putting the program in memory, checking **syntax** and linking to **libraries**, for example.
4 **Assembler** – converts **assembly language** into **machine code**. **Compiler** converts a **high-level language** into **machine code**.

5 A **reference** to locate a memory location. You do not have to know the number of the memory location, which is tedious and does not allow for **relocatable code**.
6 **Routines written by others** to help build up your programs.
7 **Different instructions** may be **fetched, decoded** and **executed** at the same time using a **single processor**.
8 **Assembles the code, checks the syntax, links to libraries, loads macros**, helps **print out source** and **object code**, contains a **debugger** etc.

Unit 45

1 **Multiprogramming** – doing more than one thing at the same time or apparently the same time. **Multiprocessing** – more than one processor is able to do more than one thing **simultaneously**.
2 **Multi user** – system where more than one person can use it 'simultaneously'.
3 A **request** for **processor attention**.
4 To give **higher priority tasks** the importance needed.
5 By means of a **scheduler**.
6 **Fixed** – fixed size RAM only is available. **Variable** – **any size RAM** (within limits) is available.
7 **Disk space** pretending to be **RAM**.
8 **Data** being taken **out of RAM** to **disk** and **back again** very frequently.
9 **Code** that can be **used by more than one routine** 'simultaneously'.
10 Users can **modify** third party **dlls**.
11 An **area of memory or disk** set up for **temporary storage**.
12 See **I/O management** at end of unit.
13 To determine what process is carried out next.

Unit 46

1 **Physical, conceptual** and **user's views**.
2 **DDL** – used to **describe the data** (i.e. create the structures). **DML** used to **manipulate it** (i.e. search, edit etc.)
3 The **Database Administrator** – sets up and manages the **DBMS**.
4 **More powerful** as **detailed parameters** may be used and **accessed via other programming**.
5 **Run macros** to perform **custom operations. Automate** some processes.
6 Getting **data** into a form that **another application may understand. CSV format** may be used for exporting data to a **spreadsheet**, for example.
7 Hardware – **SQL fileserver, network** and **workstations** etc. Software **SQL database, local front end** on workstations (perhaps via Access, for example).
8 Use **record locking**.
9 Can use **different databases**. Do not have to upgrade old systems to access the data.

Unit 47

1 A set of **linked tables**.
2 They **minimise errors** and enable data to be **analysed efficiently**.
3 A **description of the database** to the **DBMS**.
4 To get a **visual indication** of the **relationships between entities**.
5 **One-to-one** or **one-to-many** etc.
6 A **file**. A table consists of **rows**, which map to **records in the file**, and **columns**, which map to the **fields in a file**.
7 Books(**ISBN**, Author, Title, Publisher ID, Price) – Books is the name of the table. ISBN is the **key field** (underlined). The other entries are **secondary fields**.
8 It is a **set of rules**, which, if followed, leads to an **efficient relational database design**.
9 **Attributes** in a **table** having **multiple values** must be removed so that the **rows** (records) in the table are **all the same length**.
10 **Entity** – An **object**, which is the subject of a table. **Table** – a file. **Rows and columns** of a table – correspond to records and fields respectively. **Primary key** – a unique identifier for a table.

Unit 48

1 It is **difficult to search for some items**, which might be contained in a multiple-value field.
2 Items may **not have to be repeated on data entry**. See Tables 48.1 and 48.2.
3 **Less data usually has to be entered**. See Tables 48.3 and 48.4.

Unit 49

1 To see if **current processes are efficient**, and to see if **methods**, suggested in the manual, are **actually those carried out in practice**.
2 It helps to **visualise** the data, and the **relationships between the data**. See Figure 49.4.
3 It is simply **a table of data about data**. It outlines the **data types** and **how each might be used**.
4 The **software** and **hardware** needed depends on how much **volume** needs to be processed in a given amount of time.

Unit 50

1 **Technical competence, stress under use, physical characteristics** such as disability.
2 To get an **overall view** of parts of a project, ready to be used by the **programmers**.
3 To get a feel for the **user interface** and get **feedback from the users**.
4 **Bright colours, large keys, sounds**, plenty of **visual stimulation** etc.
5 (a) **Large keys** on the screen. (b) **Braille keyboard**. (c) **Touch sensitive equipment**. (d) **Voice activation** may be possible.
6 Splitting up a project into **smaller, more manageable parts**.
7 To show how **top-down design methods** may be implemented.
8 They are **easy to use** by **novices**.
9 See Figure 50.2.

Unit 51

1 **Top down** – used to **modularise** the project. **Bottom up** – used to **prototype individual parts** of the project.
2 System treated as a **black box** with **inputs** and **outputs. Salient data** chosen to test **extremes** and **valid data**.
3 **Code split up into small sections. Flowgraphs** are drawn to identify individual paths through the code. **Black box testing** is applied to **each path**.
4 **Unit testing** tests individual modules. **Integration testing** tests two or more modules interacting as a system.
5 **Software** helps to carry out these **tedious tasks**.
6 See list at beginning of unit 25. (**Maintenance** should be carried out at the end.)

Unit 52

1 **Parallel running, phased implementation, direct implementation** and **pilot schemes**.
2 **The new one may go wrong**. If all subsystems depend on each other.
3 **Beta testing** means that users use a pre-release version of the software. Many **bugs** come to light because of the huge number of people involved and the **variety of systems being used**.
4 **Personal training** – most useful but expensive. **On-the-job training**. Uses a real system but could slow down the business. **CAL** – individuals may go at their own speed. Might not cover some of the things that could go wrong.
5 See **bulleted list** at the end of this unit.
6 **CD-ROMs, Internet** (HTML documents) and **Adobe Acrobat. Can be electronically searched**. Users need to be **computer literate** and have the **appropriate systems** on their computer.

Unit 53

1. See **user-manual list** in this unit. **Auto run files** can make installation easy on a PC.
2. **Video presentations, PowerPoint presentations, seminars, CAL** etc.
3. **Feedback** is from **customers in the field**. The people who have to code patches for the new system should use data received from the customers.
4. The **needs of the customer may change**.
5. An **audit** is taken to see how it is performing. Any changes necessary should be noted and implemented if possible.

Unit 54

1. A **4-byte number** that **identifies a computer** connected to the **internet**.
2. **Internet registry** is a **database**; an **internet registrar** is a **company** that allocates **domain names**.
3. An **internet address** that **identifies the owner** of the site like 'www.mickeymouse.com'.
4. The **internet** is the 'computers, connections and other hardware' and the **www** are the resources like **web pages**.
5. The **protocol**, used to connect **clients** and **servers** on the net.
6. **HyperText Transfer Protocol**. The S represents a secure connection.
7. **Hierarchically**
8. See Figure 54.6 for main sections. Products will be **CDs, Tapes, DVDs** etc. Split up **CDs** into **classical, rock, jazz, popular** etc.
9. A **server** that receives a **domain name** like **https://www.nwolb.co.uk** and turns it into **the IP address** like '**62.172.189.210**'
10. One of the **main servers** that hosts the **databases** containing **definitive information** about the **domain name structure** of the web.

Unit 55

1. **HTML** is **HyperText Markup Language**, the **base language** used to construct web pages.
2. A **link** to another part of the **page, site** or **internet**, which can be activated by **clicking** over it with a **mouse**.
3. Ability to change **colour, format, fonts, insert links, insert pictures** and **sounds** etc.
4. **WYSIWYG** means **What You See Is What You Get. WYSIWYG HTML editors** can be used in identical ways to modern **word processors**.
5. A **form**, which captures **user feedback** and passes information over to **programs** (e.g. a **database**) on the server.
6. Using a language like **PERL**, for example. (See unit 57).
7. **FTP** is **File Transfer Protocol** and is used for **transferring files via TCP/IP** on the web. It is the main way of **publishing** a web site to a **server**.
8. A **file server** that supports **FTP** enabling **uploading** or **downloading** of sites, for example.
9. **Telnet** is a **protocol**, which supports **remote access** to a computer over the **internet**. It enables **remote administration** of a computer via the **web**.
10. Without a suitable **structure**, using **relative path names**, and ensuring all **resources** are put in well-defined places it probably will not work properly.
11. Using **FTP software**.

Unit 56

1. A **conventional search engine** has its **own database**, a **Meta search engine** searches **other databases**.
2. Something like **Jaguar-automobile*-car*** – it depends on the syntax of the search engine
3. A **Uniform Resource Locater**. It is a **web address** locating a resource like a **particular html page**, like http://www.connectfree.co.uk/Online_Games/Half-Life/half-life.html, for example.
4. Use of the **https secure protocol**, use of **digital signatures** (see unit 57), **warnings on receipt of cookies, history folder** to view what has been happening etc.
5. They provide **information** about your **surfing habits**.
6. A **browser** ideally suited to **small screens** like those found on **mobiles** and **PDAs**.
7. Much of the functionality **cannot be implemented on such a small screen** and with a **limited number of peripherals** etc.

Unit 57

1. Use a **WAP phone** or a specially set up **TV** with **cable** or **satellite link**, for example.
2. A **Java class** (see unit 42) running on a **web browser**.
3. **Java Servlets, CGI** and **PERL** are ways of interacting with the server. Typical examples are **processing information** from **forms** displayed on the user's browser.
4. **Multipurpose Internet Mail Extensions** are a way of encoding data to be sent over parts of the net that make use of **ASCII** and **parity bits**.
5. A **digital signature** together with a **public encryption key** defines a **digital certificate**. It is one way of ensuring the **authenticity** of e-commerce transactions.
6. **Usenet** provides information about anything, it is **useful** while at the same time providing **a lot of controversial material**. It is not interactive.
7. **IRC** enables users to join discussion bulletin boards in **real time**.
8. A **server** that provides access to **Usenet newsgroups**.

Unit 58

1. An **agent** is a program to search for information.
2. **Specialist agents** are for **shopping** or other specialist areas. **General agents** are for **searching other search engines** and **correlating the results** on any topic.
3. **Buying on line** using a **secure transaction**, paying **by credit or debit card, getting e-mail confirmation** etc.
4. Advantages are **24-hour access** to virtually all day-to-day functions except cash deposit. The **branch network is likely to close** if too many people bank on line. You get **no personal service**.
5. A small company can make use of the services provided by **on-line retailing systems**.
6. A **VPN** is an **extension of an LAN** into the internet. Much **extra security** in the form of **firewalls** is required if **hackers** are to be **prevented from breaking into the system**. It makes use of the point to point tunelling protocol.

Unit 59

1. Access to any information, on-line shopping, e-mail communication, joining like-minded groups, making new friends.
2. Addiction, illegal activities, spamming, viruses, loss of personal interaction.
3. Using the net for **illegal activities, e-mail, stealing software, wasting time** on the net.
4. A **log** can be created on a **proxy server** to monitor each page visited. These log files would be very large indeed and **slow down the operation** of the system.
5. Organisations give their **private decryption key** to the **government**.
6. Your **public key**, used to **encrypt a message**, is available to **everybody**, but your **private key**, needed to **decrypt the message** is only available to you.
7. Lists of **banned words**, lists of **banned sites**.
8. The net is **too dynamic** for the lists to be completely up to date.

Unit 60

1. **Baseband** uses a single frequency and sends only one signal at a time. **Broadband** uses different carrier frequencies and can send more than one signal simultaneously.

2 Sending **many different signals** down a **single link**.
3 **Circuit switching** – A dedicated circuit is available for the duration of the 'call'. **Packet switching** – Message is split up into packets, each of which may travel to the destination via different routes. Other 'callers' may use the same lines for the duration of the your 'call'.
4 **Layers** are useful because they enable changes to be made (like **protocols** or **hardware** etc.) without affecting the other layers.
5 By the strategic placement of **switches** and **bridges** etc.
6 The **data** is assembled together with **headers** representing **different protocols**. **Layer 2** adds a **final footer**, and the entire **packet** is transmitted over the available **network link**.
7 A **switch** is **much more intelligent** and can be **programmed remotely**.

Unit 61

1 See Table 61.1
2 **10 Mbit/sec** – slow bus connection, not used on new systems. **100 Mbit/sec** – **fast Ethernet** is the most common; **hubs** are used to construct these networks. **Gbit Ethernet** is becoming common for backbone connection. **Fibre** is one method of setting up this very fast network.
3 It allows for **audio** and **video** signals to be sent more easily than other systems.
4 **Video on demand** and **videoconferencing**.
5 **Fibre optics** are not prone to interference and can take a higher bandwidth.
6 (a) A **single crossover cable**. (b) A **hub**.

Unit 62

1 For **maximum security** and **speed of access**.
2 It's **faster** and **more versatile**.
3 **Individual users** controlling resources each may have on a network. **Two computers** and a **crossover Ethernet lead** connecting the **network cards**.
4 LAN – **local area network** under the control of the user. WAN – **wide are network** making use of public telecommunication systems.
5 A **Value Added Network** – a network, which provides **many other facilities** other than simply forwarding messages. Most people use value added networks without realising it.
6 **Electronic Data Interchange**. Sending information electronically from one computer to another, like sending **examination results** to an exam board from a school, for example.
7 See Figure 62.5 – Simple system is identical, but **fewer modems, less powerful computers** and **slower backbone internet** connections are needed.
8 **ISDN** – fast connection depending on how many lines are used. **ADSL** more useful for home networking, but much more cost effective, and just as fast as many of the slower ISDN links but not in both directions.
9 A **terminator**
10 **Two computers** have tried to use the network **simultaneously**, and the signals have **collided**.
11 Use them **back-to-back**.
12 The **computer** being accessed might be **busy**.
13 It is sent to the **mail server** of the **recipient's ISP**.
14 A **Virtual Private Network** – connection to your **intranet** via the **web**.
15 All the **advantages** that you would gain from being **logged onto your LAN**.
16 You need a **firewall** to prevent **hacking**.
17 A **server** that deals with **many different internet connections** 'simultaneously'.
18 A **link** to the **internet backbone**.

Unit 63

1 A **connection**, via a **modem** and **telephone line**.
2 It is **completely digital** and **faster**.
3 **128 Kbit/sec**

4 A **cable modem** is a modem used by a **cable TV company**. You are probably **permanently connected** with no phone bills to pay.
5 **Faster downloads** compared to a conventional modem. However, you still need a **modem** and **telephone line** to **transmit information** to the ISP.
6 The **display of text on the TV** is limited compared to a computer monitor. Unless you have a **QWERTY keyboard** then it is tedious to operate the system. There are also **no peripherals** like printers available at the time of writing.
7 A **very fast connection** from the **ISP** to your **local machine**.
8 An **ISDN line** would be better because you have a **fast two-way speed**. However, two **back-to-back** lines are possible if **ADSL** is used.
9 Because **thousands of students and staff may want to access the net simultaneously**.

Unit 64

1 One or more **microprocessors** set up to perform a very specific **control task** such as controlling a **camera** or **video recorder**.
2 An **instant response** is usually needed to make **effective use of the feedback** to **control** the device.
3 A **transducer** converts electrical energy into a physical quantity such as rotary motion, sound or light. A **sensor** converts a physical quantity into an electrical signal.
4 **Light** – camera sensor; **sound** – burglar alarm; **pH** – pollution monitoring; **pressure** – scales for weight measurement; **heat** – fire alarm.
5 **Motor** – rotating a lock; **solenoid** – opening a valve; **light bulb** – indicator; **loudspeaker** – audio warning; **heater** – help to control temperature.
6 **Data logging** is the automatic collection of (usually scientific) data at set intervals over a period of time making use of a variety of sensors. The data is automatically put into computer readable format ready for analysis by suitable software.
7 **Sensors**, suitable for measuring the pollution in a river, might be 'pH', 'temperature', 'flow rate', 'radiation' etc. or any device that detects particular chemicals like ammonia, phosphates and nitrates, for example.
8 **Sensors, decision making** and **Actuators**
9 Without **feedback** you cannot actually **monitor** what is happening.

Unit 65

1 **For** – bring up to date quickly, not burdened with outdated high-tech systems, can compete with developed countries. **Against** – skills base may not be there, other infrastructure not established to support high-tech solutions.
2 How much **autonomy** is given to a machine? Is it a **life form**? It might be **possible to solve problems** that hum thought alone has not yet managed to do etc.
3 **Computer gaming** – if a parent, limit the playing time teacher or lecturer, point out future problems and talk about it or refer the student for professional help.
4 **Teachers** are able to **tailor a course to the exact needs** of the student. Some **students do not react well to machines**. The **human touch** is still needed in many cases.
5 **Medical system** – diagnosis of illness. **Oil exploration** – feed in geographical data to find oil deposits. **Car repairs** – lead a mechanic through a set of actions to repair a vehicle.
6 **Playing games, abusive e-mail**, looking at **pornography, stealing software, injecting a virus** or **spamming**.
7 The **Data Protection Act of 1998**.
8 Look at the **delivery address** and **add costs** onto the **transaction** at the time of purchase.
9 **Taxation, legal documentation, electronic signatures, privacy** etc.
10 **Religious issues** regarding material on the net. **Political structures** threatened by **freedom of speech** via the net. **Computers** replacing **manual** and **non-manual workers**.

Units 66 to 68 inclusive are project-based

Index